BRAIN-COMPUTER INTERFACE SYSTEMS – RECENT PROGRESS AND FUTURE PROSPECTS

Edited by **Reza Fazel-Rezai**

Brain-Computer Interface Systems – Recent Progress and Future Prospects
http://dx.doi.org/10.5772/50696
Edited by Reza Fazel-Rezai

Contributors

Montri Phothisonothai, Katsumi Watanabe, Taciana Rached, Angelo Perkusich, Tiago Falk, Kelly Paton, Tom Chau, Farhad Faradji, Farshad Faradji, Rabab Ward, Gary E. Birch, Shu Shigezumi, Hideyuki Hara, Hironao Namba, Yumi Dobashi, Chikako Serizawa, Atsushi Takemoto, Katsuki Nakamura, Takashi Matsumoto, Toshimasa Yamazaki, Christoph Hintermüller, Christoph Kapeller, Günter Edlinger, Christoph Guger, Heung-No Lee, SeungChan Lee, YoungHak Shin, SooGil Woo, Kiseon Kim, Reza Fazel-Rezai, Setare Amiri, Vahid Asadpour, Ahmed Rabbi, Andrea Kübler, Alexander Frolov, Lili Huang

Published by InTech

Janeza Trdine 9, 51000 Rijeka, Croatia

Publishing Process Manager Ana Pantar
Technical Editor InTech DTP team
Cover InTech Design team

Additional hard copies can be obtained from orders@intechopen.com

Brain-Computer Interface Systems – Recent Progress and Future Prospects, Edited by Reza Fazel-Rezai
p. cm.
ISBN 978-953-51-1134-4

For EU product safety concerns:
IN TECH d.o.o., Prolaz Marije Krucifikse Kozulić 3, 51000 Rijeka, Croatia,
info@intechopen.com or visit our website at intechopen.com.

Meet the editor

Dr. Fazel-Rezai received his BSc. and M.Sc. in Electrical Engineering and Biomedical Engineering in 1990 and 1993, respectively. He received his Ph.D. in Electrical Engineering from the University of Manitoba in Winnipeg, Canada in 1999. From 2000 to 2002, he worked in industry as a senior research scientist and research team manager. Then, he joined academia at Sharif University of Technology and later the University of Manitoba as Assistant Professor in 2002 and 2004, respectively. Currently, he is the Director of Biomedical Signal and Image Processing Laboratory at the Department of Electrical Engineering, University of North Dakota, USA. His research interests include biomedical engineering, biomedical signal and image processing, brain computer interface, seizure detection and prediction, neurofeedback, human performance evaluation, and health monitoring based on physiological systems.

Contents

Preface

Communication and the ability to interact with the environment are basic human needs. Millions of people worldwide suffer from severe physical disabilities so that they cannot even meet these basic needs. Although they may have no motor mobility, the sensory and cognitive functions of the physically disabled are usually intact. Brain-Computer Interface (BCI) systems allow communication based on a direct electronic interface which conveys messages and commands directly from the human brain to a computer. Majority of BCI systems rely on the electroencephalogram (EEG) signals to detect patterns of brain activity that reflect user intent, since EEG equipment is safe, portable, and requires relatively little preparation. BCI technology involves monitoring conscious brain electrical activity via EEG and detecting characteristics of EEG patterns via digital signal processing algorithms. It has the potential to enable the physically disabled to perform many activities, thus improving their quality of life and productivity, allowing them more independence and reducing social costs. The challenge with BCI, however, is to extract the relevant patterns from the EEG signals produced by the brain.

Recently, there has been a great progress in the development of novel paradigms for EEG signal recording, advanced methods for processing them, new applications for BCI systems, and complete software and hardware packages used for BCI applications. In this book a few recent advances and future prospects are discussed. In the first chapter, important issues concerning end-users including needs, gaps, paradigm designs, and BCI evaluations are discussed. Chapter 2 describes different approaches to interconnect a BCI system with one or more applications, and their advantages and disadvantages. In Chapters 3 to 9, different advanced signal processing methods and their applications in BCI systems are discussed. The methods include adaptive network fuzzy inference systems (Chapter 3), Bayesian sequential learning (Chapter 4), fractal features and neural networks (Chapter 5), autoregressive models of wavelet bases (Chapter 6), hidden Markov models (Chapter 7), equivalent current dipole source localization (Chapter 8), and independent component analysis (Chapter 9). Chapters 10 and 11 review hybrid approached and wireless techniques used in BCI systems, respectively. Finally, in the last two chapters, two applications of BCI systems in epilepsy treatment and emotion detections are discussed.

As the editor, I would like to thank all the authors for their contributions. Without these contributions it would not be possible to have a quality book and help expand the field of BCI systems, especially regarding their utilization in real-world applications.

Dr. Reza Fazel-Rezai
University of North Dakota
Grand Forks, ND, USA

Chapter 1

A User Centred Approach for Bringing BCI Controlled Applications to End-Users

Andrea Kübler, Elisa Holz, Tobias Kaufmann and Claudia Zickler

Additional information is available at the end of the chapter

http://dx.doi.org/10.5772/55802

1. Introduction

In the past 20 years research on BCI has been increasing almost exponentially. While a great deal of experimentation was dedicated to offline analysis for improving signal detection and translation, online studies with the target population are less common. Although BCIs are also developed for entertainment and thus potentially for healthy users, the main focus for BCI applications that are aiming at communication and control are people with severe motor impairment. There is a great need for translational studies that test BCI at home with the target population. Further, long-term studies with users in the field are required to improve reliability of BCI control. The user centred approach appears suitable to foster such studies.

In this chapter we will first define the needs and the gaps for bringing BCI to end-users and explain the model of BCI control which guides our interventions. Then we will describe the user-centered design and report first results of studies that adopted this approach for evaluating BCI applications. Those results led us to develop novel BCI components which we then tested with healthy and severely ill end-users. More specifically, we will introduce the optimized communication interface, the face speller, and remotely supervised BCI controlled brain painting with a locked-in patient in the field. We will end the chapter with summarizing the requirements for improvement and reasons for cautious optimism that the BCI community will be successful in providing end-users in need with reliable and independent BCI controlled applications.

1.1. The needs and the gaps

In 1973 J.J. Vidal posed the question whether "electrical brain signals" can "be put to work as carriers of information in man-computer communication or for the purpose of controlling such external apparatus as prosthetic devices…?" (p. 157 [1]). Already in those days Vidal answered the question with a clear *Yes* and time has proved him right. Since the early nineties, when only few articles on brain-computer interfacing were available, publication activity has increased almost exponentially [2]. We performed a coarse search in Pubmed and PsychInfo with the terms *BCI OR brain computer interface* for 2011 through Sept 12 and received 461 hits. Thus, we may expect at least 700 publications by the end of 2013 indicating unbowed research activity, and thus funding. However, the amount of studies including the major target population, namely severely motor impaired individuals were 39 only. Less than 10 percent of the papers published, which refer to BCI in one way or another, deal with motor impaired individuals, although many authors mention those as target of their research [3, 4]. This illustrates quite overwhelmingly the gap between prosperous and active research in BCI laboratories with healthy participants and the transfer of the gained knowledge to the main target population of BCI, namely patients with severe motor impairment.

We are thus, facing a *translational gap*, i.e. a lack of translational studies that investigate the problems and obstacles that emerge when BCIs are to be applied to severely ill patients in their home environment. Such studies would include a thorough quantitative and qualitative evaluation of BCI. We argue and will describe that a user-centered design may be suitable to bridge this gap.

Further, we are confronted with a *reliability gap*, i.e. intra- and inter-individual performance varies tremendously when controlling an application with a BCI in the short-term and even more so in the long-term use. Many studies exist that introduce one or the other more or less small improvement in accuracy, bit rate or error rate – the main outcome measures of performance in BCI research. However, only few of them deal with targeted end-users in the field, where multiple sources of artefacts exist including changes of the health status of the user, such as altered brain responses due to neuronal degeneration in the brain. Thus, the reliability gap can only be bridged with longitudinal studies that include end-users in the field. Such studies need to take into account the several aspects that may contribute to successful BCI control. An integration of these aspects leads to a neuro-bio-psychological, data analytical, and ergonomical model of BCI-control (Fig.1) [5], which will be defined in the next section.

2. A model of BCI control

A BCI acquires input from the human brain, mostly its electrical activity recorded with electroencephalography (EEG), which is filtered, classified and transferred to an output signal. This output signal relates to the brain response or pattern of the BCI users and conveys the respective intention of the user. Importantly, the user receives feedback of his or her action and thus, BCIs imply a closed-loop between the system and the user. The output signal can be used to control an application – ideally, one that meets the desire of the user. Four aspects can be identified that contribute to BCI control: (1) individual characteristics of the BCI user, (2) characteristics of the BCI, (3) type of feedback and instruction, and (4) the BCI-controlled application [5]. The individual characteristics of the user include psychological, physiological and neurobiological factors. For example, visuo-motor coordination and motivation have been identified to predict performance with BCI controlled by sensorimotor rhythms [6] and event-related potentials [7]. Better inhibitory control, i.e. ability to allocate attention and inhibit distracting stimuli, measured as heart rate variability was related to better ERP-BCI performance [8]. The amplitude of the SMR peak at rest and the P300 amplitude evoked in an auditory oddball paradigm were also related to performance with the respective BCI [9, 10]. Further, the location and quantity of neuronal loss due to accident or disease may deteriorate performance. Besides the hardware used, the software components, namely the classifier of the input signal further determines BCI control (for review [11]). Common spatial pattern technique and stepwise linear discriminant analyses proved to perform well in SMR- and ERP-BCIs [12, 13].

Little research is available on how the type of feedback and instruction provided in a BCI setting may influence performance. From early neurofeedback studies it is known that immediate feedback is superior to delayed feedback which held also true in a BCI context [14]. It may also be the case that a more ecologically valid feedback in a virtual environment outperforms traditional two-dimensional feedback on a computer screen [15-17]. A quite robust finding across BCI types is that visual feedback is superior to auditory feedback [18-20]. In the SMR based BCI instruction to imagine motor imagery kinaesthetically leads to increased performance as compared to visual motor imagery [21].

Finally, the complexity of the application influences performance. Usually simple spelling tasks are mastered more accurately and faster than environmental control or control of information technology, such as internet [22, 23].

As can be seen, the model offers multiple toeholds for improvement and user feedback. In the following sections we will introduce novel achievements for BCI that improve and facilitate BCI use and are based on feedback provided by end-users within the user-centred approach. Before we detail the novel approaches, the user-centred design and its application to BCI will be outlined.

3. The user centred design and its application to BCI

BCI development demands for close investigation of the end-users' needs and requirements and of the restrictions that come along with their diseases. The latter restrictions may range from small artefact contamination of the recorded brain signal up to loss of perception modalities, e.g. loss of ocular control as often the case with progression of neurodegenerative diseases. Furthermore, attention allocation may be limited and long lasting training sessions may be too demanding. BCIs are required to accommodate for such restrictions and to offer appropriate solutions, such as switching to auditory or tactile modalities when vision is impaired. Many of these restrictions are not evident when testing systems with healthy users. Furthermore, a system in daily use has to meet other requirements than a system developed for research purpose only, e.g. with regard to hardware setup, software handling and technical support. Bringing BCI technology to end-users' homes thus, inevitably requires involving them into this developmental processes.

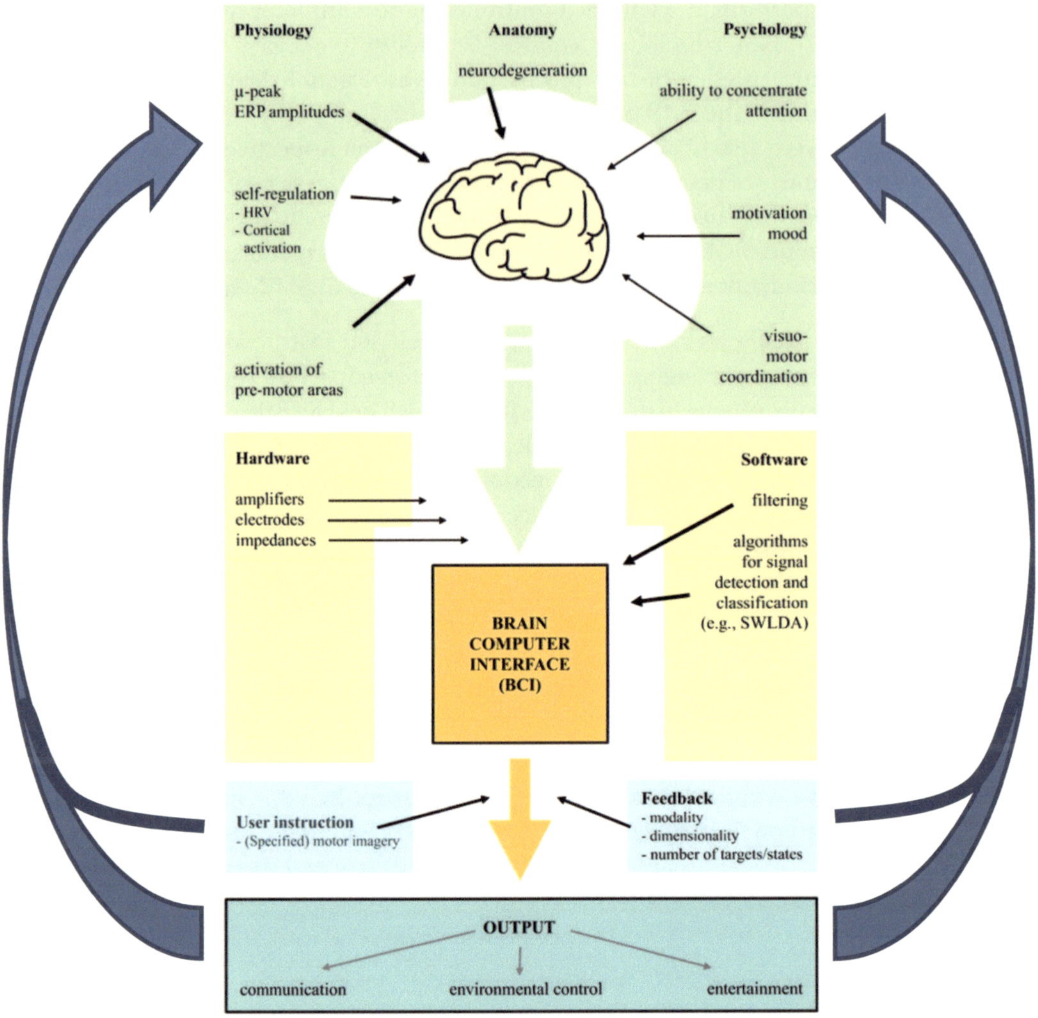

Figure 1. A model of BCI-control comprised of 4 aspects: individual characteristics, BCI characteristics, feedback and instruction, BCI-controlled application. Colours serve for distinction of categories only. Boldness of black arrows indicates possible strength of influence on BCI control [5].

More recently the potential user of a BCI came more into the focus of BCI development and user-centred approaches were adopted [22, 24, 25]. A user-centred approach implies early focus on users, tasks and environment; the active involvement of users; an appropriate allocation of function between user and system; the incorporation of user-derived feedback into system design; and an iterative process whereby a prototype is designed, tested and modified [26]. The user-centred approach was standardized with the International Organization for Standardization (ISO) 9241-210 (Ergonomics of human-system interaction - Part 210: Human-centred design for interactive systems). According to this approach three kinds of requirements have to be taken into account: (1) Business requirements: Here, typically, a specific number is set in terms of how many systems should be sold in a defined time frame. Although our face speller and brain painting (see below) have already been adopted by a company (http://www.intendix.com/) and are thus, available on the market, these products are not yet suitable for daily use in the field. (2) User requirements and functional specification: BCI requirements need to be specified from a user's point of view, including the functions required to support a user's tasks, the user-system and interfaces. Usability goals that must be achieved and the approach for system maintenance at the user's home need to be defined. (3) Technical requirements: It has to be specified how the system will achieve the required functions and what data structure must be available for internal processing for the approach to be successful. Technical constraints need to be defined, such as the maximum data communication speed over a network or the trade-off between good EEG measurement and comfort with regards to the EEG cap. On the basis of these requirements Zickler and colleagues asked experts in using assistive technology (AT), i.e. people with severe motor impairment, what they would consider the most important requirements for BCI [25]. Those requirements were functionality, independent use, and easiness of use (see section on "User-centred improvements of BCI controlled applications").

Two different approaches to BCI control were subject of evaluation following these standards: BCIs dependent on modulation of sensorimotor rhythms, referred to as SMR-BCI, and on detection of event-related potentials, referred to as ERP-BCI. To better understand the applications and their evaluation, we provide a condensed description of the SMR- and ERP-BCI as implemented for control of the specific applications described below.

3.1. SMR-BCI

BCIs can be established by detecting an active modulation of sensorimotor rhythms (SMR) over sensorimotor areas of the brain. In a resting state, these rhythms are highly synchronised in the alpha (10-12 Hz) and beta (12-30 Hz) bands. When moving or imagining a movement, these rhythms desynchronise, i.e. the power of these frequency bands can actively be modulated by the user. Thus, SMR modulation constitutes a signal for BCI control [27, 28]. Different classes of motor imagery can be selected depending on a user's individual brain signals and the degrees of freedom that are required for control of an application. In a typical SMR-BCI, users trigger control signals for two classes by either imagining movement of the right or the left hand. Feedback is provided during the imagery tasks to enhance participants' performance thereby reinforcing correct behaviour. As hand areas are largely separated in the sensorimotor cortex, the evoked patterns are usually well distinguishable. Importantly, it has been shown that people with amyotrophic lateral sclerosis can utilize such modulations of the SMR to operate a BCI [29]. One of the remaining issues, however, is that a large number of participants is not able to achieve sufficient SMR-BCI performance [7, 9, 30, 31]. BCI systems that do not rely on such active modulations of brain signals are available. The most frequently used system is described in the next section.

3.2. Event-related potential (P300) BCI

A typical BCI based on event-related potentials is the so called P300-Speller, providing muscle independent communication on a character-by-character basis [32]; for recent reviews: [33] and [34]. A character matrix is displayed on a computer screen and groups of characters (usually rows and columns in a matrix) are highlighted (flashed) in random order. Users focus their attention on the desired field of the matrix (the target) by counting the number of flashes whilst ignoring all other characters (non-targets). This pattern constitutes an oddball-paradigm as target flashes are rare (odd) as compared to the high amount of non-target flashes. For example, in a 6x6 matrix one row and one column contains the target character whereas 5 rows and 5 columns are to be ignored. Each stimulus triggers distinct event-related potentials among which the P300 usually is the most prominent. It is a positive deflection in the EEG which occurs roughly around 300 ms post stimulus. Its latency may strongly vary with paradigms and across individuals (for review [35]). Yet other ERPs are also elicited, therefore a time window of up to 1000 ms post stimulus (typically 800 ms) is recommended to investigate users' individual ERPs (i.e., negative and positive deflections at distinct latencies). The characteristic sequence of event-related potentials is identified for each row and each column. The row and column with the most prominent ERPs are selected and the respective letter appears on the screen. It has been shown that 72.8% of N=81 healthy BCI users were able to communicate with 100% accuracy by means of such an ERP-BCI and that less than 3% could not achieve any control [30]. Importantly, these results transfer to individuals with severe motor impairment, e.g. due to neurodegenerative disease, in that the speller can be utilized as a muscle independent tool for communication (e.g., [22, 36-39]; for review [40]). Since its first description in 1988, the P300-Speller has been used intensively, further investigated and modified in a plethora of research publications leading to new applications for communication and device control (for review, e.g. [34]).

4. Evaluation of BCI controlled applications

The ISO 9241-201 (2010) defines usability as the "extent to which a ... product ... can be used by specified users to achieve specified goals with effectiveness, efficiency and satisfaction in a specified context of use" (ISO 9241-201, 2010, p. 3). Effectiveness refers to how accurate and complete the users accomplish the task. Efficiency relates the invested costs, i.e. users' effort and time, to effectiveness. User satisfaction refers to the perceived comfort and acceptability while using the product. Context of use refers to users, tasks, equipment (hardware, software and materials) and the physical and social environments in which a product is used (ISO 9241-201, 2010, p. 2) [22].

To accommodate for these aspects when evaluating newly developed BCI driven applications, a set of measures has been compiled to assess *effectiveness*, *efficiency* and *satisfaction* [22]. Effectiveness refers to how accurately end-users can communicate with the BCI and is operationalized by the numbers of intended and thus, correct selections in relation to the total number of selections. This measure is also often referred to as accuracy. Efficiency comprises the amount of information transferred (bit rate), which expresses speed and accuracy with one value, and the workload experienced by the end-user. A measure to assess subjective workload is the NASA task load index (TLX) which quantifies the workload for each task and identifies its sources [41]. Workload is defined as physical, mental, and temporal demands, and performance, effort, and frustration. User satisfaction can be addressed with the Quebec User Evaluation of Satisfaction with assistive technology (QUEST 2.0) which is the only standardized satisfaction assessment tool that was designed specifically for AT-devices [42]. It explicitly allows for deleting inadequate and adding informative questions with respect to a specific AT so that BCI specific items could be integrated. Reliability, speed, learnability, and aesthetic design were added to accommodate for specific aspects of BCI and the resulting questionnaire was referred to as Extended-QUEST [22]. Possible ratings range from 1 to 5 with 5 indicating best possible satisfaction.

As another measure of device satisfaction the ATD PA Device Form was used. The Assistive Technology Device Predisposition Assessment (ATD PA) is a set of questionnaires based on the Matching Person and Technology Model (MPT) of Scherer (2007) [43]. It addresses characteristics of an AT-device and asks respondents to rate their predisposition for using the AT under consideration. The questionnaire rates the AT-person match and the expected support in using the device, in other words the expected technology benefit [44].

As a coarse measure for overall satisfaction with the device, a visual analogue scale (VAS) ranging from 0 to 10 (not at all – absolutely satisfied) was included in the evaluation procedure. An open interview allowed participants to state their opinion about the BCI and its application and recommendations for further development.

To date, with this instrumentation three studies were performed with severely impaired end-users [22, 45], which we will describe in the following subsections.

4.1. Extended communication

Zickler and colleagues investigated the first prototype in which BCI was integrated into a commercially available AT software [22]. Control of AT was realized by means of the ERP-BCI described above. Participants tested the text entry, emailing and internet surfing options (Fig 2). The oddball paradigm had to be implemented such that these applications provided by the standard software could be controlled. Instead of rows and columns flashing red dots were assigned to each possible selectable item. The red dots then flashed in random order. Participants were able to write a text, send an email and surf the internet for a specific website.

Selection accuracy (*effectiveness*) ranged between 70 and 100% correct responses and for all participants internet surfing was the most difficult task. Information transfer rate (*efficiency*) was between 4.5 and 8 bits per minute. Experienced workload (*efficiency*) was quite different among users. While one user rated workload on all dimensions between 9 and 12 (of 100 possible, with 100 being the maximum possible workload experienced), two participants were always between 34 and 46 indicating moderate workload for all tasks. In one user, who was confronted with BCI for the first time, workload decreased with every session from 49 to 15, which was encouraging as it demonstrated that workload can be decreased with practice.

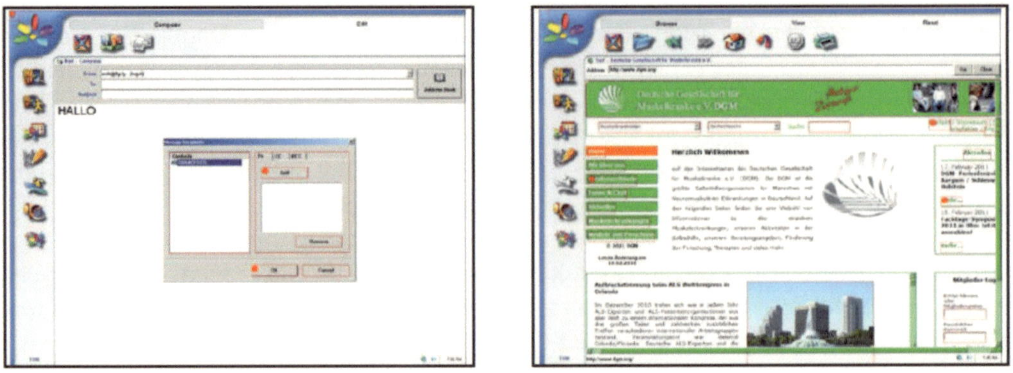

Figure 2. Emailing and internet surfing with the Qualilife software. Possible items to select are indicated with a red frame. The red dots appear randomly at every item which can be selected. Thus, the to-be-selected item again constitutes a rare target within frequently appearing irrelevant items, and hence, the oddball paradigm is realized (Figure 1 from [22] with permission).

Satisfaction was high for safety of the device and the professional services and low for adjustment. With regards to the BCI specific items, reliability and learnability were rated high while speed and aesthetic design were only moderate. Obstacles for use in daily life were (1) low speed, (2) time needed to set up the system, (3) handling of the complicated software and the (4) demanding strain that accompanies EEG recordings (washing hair, etc.). Overall satisfaction ranged from 4 to 9 indicating substantial variance and considerable room for improvement. In the interview participants stated that the greatest obstacle for use in daily life would be the EEG cap, there should be no cables, no gel and it should look less eye catching. Hardware should be within one device (instead of an amplifier, a laptop and a screen) and wheelchair control should be integrated. None of the participants could imagine using the BCI in daily life unless substantially improved.

The above described BCI controlled application already goes beyond simple verbal communication and may constitute a step toward inclusion via the world wide web. Some of our patients have been participating in BCI studies for a long time [46] and stated that they would also like to control other, more entertaining applications such as playing games or painting.

4.2. Brain painting

Together with an artist (Adi Hösle www.retrogradist.com) the letter matrix controlled by the ERP-BCI was transformed into a painting matrix which allowed the user to select shapes, size, colours, and contours and to move a brush on a virtual canvas (Fig 3). One participant stated "Everyone talks about freedom, but the worst oppression is to be locked into my own body. This art form allows me to break from the prison…". With his painting (see Fig 4) he wanted to illustrate that there is a light at the end of a tunnel.

http://dx.doi.org/10.5772/55802

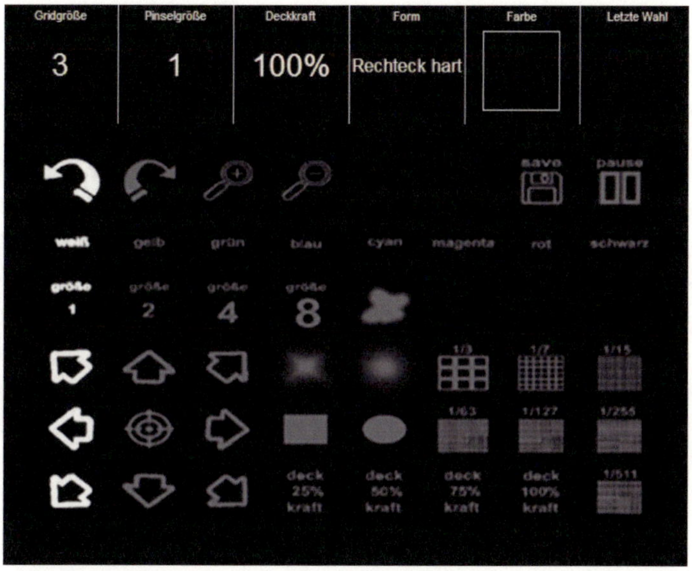

Figure 3. Brain Painting matrix. For painting an object and its shape, location and transparency have to be defined. Only after the selection of "color" the object is transferred to the "canvas". In the toolbox at the top of the screen the latest selections are shown (from left to right in this figure): grid size (3), brush size (1), transparency of color (100%), object shape (rectangle), color (black). In the last square of the toolbox the latest selection is shown, which in this example is "black".

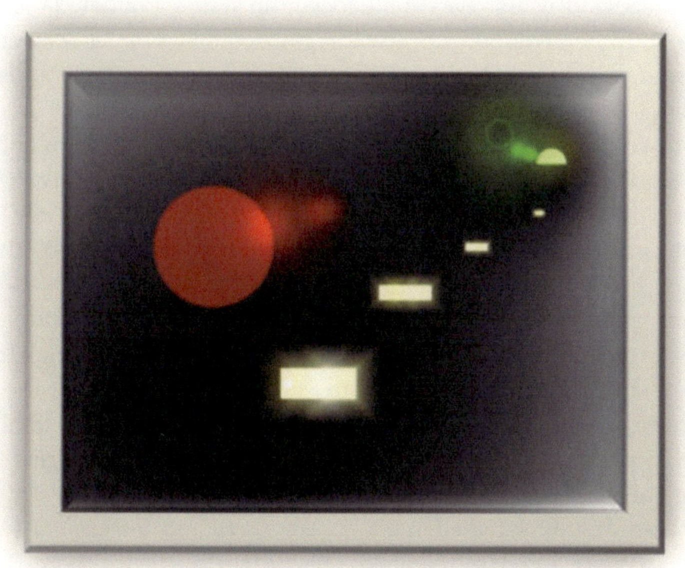

Figure 4. Painting "Who" by a brain painter with locked-in syndrome.

Four severely motor impaired potential end-users participated in the evaluation study which comprised seven daily sessions. In five of those sessions, participants could freely paint pictures of their choice. *Effectiveness* ranged between 80 and 90%, i.e. in 80 to 90% of the time participants selected the item they intended to. With an average around five bits per minute the information transfer rate (*efficiency*) was relatively low. This was due to an extended break between selection of items, to provide the user with sufficient time to think about what to select next ("creative pause"), and users explicitly appreciated this adaptation of the selection speed. Workload varied considerably between 20 and 50 and was sometimes due to disease related physical problems experienced by the users, and thus, independent of the specific BCI application. Like in the communication application described above, reliability and learnability were rated high (4.2 and 5.0) whereas users were not so satisfied with speed, adjustment and dimensions [44]. For two users the ATD PA Device Form indicated a good match between the system and the user (4.3 and 4.2 of 5 possible), but for the other two only 3.4 and 3.8 indicating that the match could be improved [44]. Overall satisfaction ranged between 5 and 8 also leaving room for improvement.

Taken together, users enjoyed painting and painted up to one picture per session. Three users would have liked to use Brain Painting in daily life once or twice a week. They reported high satisfaction with the learnability, ease of use, and reliability of the device. The EEG-cap and system operability clearly required improvement if the BCI application was to be used in daily life [44].

4.3. Gaming

Four severely disabled end-users - two in the locked-in state – evaluated the gaming application *Connect-Four (*http://en.wikipedia.org/wiki/Connect_Four) [45]. Connect-Four is a SMR-BCI based prototype, enabling end-users to select either a row or column and setting a coin by regulating their brain activity. In six BCI sessions end-users were trained to regulate their brain activity in copy-tasks (location of coins were pre-defined by the experimenter), which were followed by free mode game playing. *Effectiveness* in the copy-task was low to medium in three of four end-users, with accuracies varying between 47% and 73%, and only one end-user, in the locked-in state, achieved high BCI control with up to 80% accuracy. With an ITR ranging between 0.05 and 1.44 bits/min, *efficiency* was low. The end-users rated their subjective workload moderate (on average between 28 and 52 of 100), with mental and temporal demand contributing most to their workload (*efficiency*). Two end-users reported high frustration which first increased and then decreased again with sessions. Nevertheless, the BCI game was accepted well by the end-users. On average end-users were moderately to highly (3.8 for the total Quest score and 3.9 for the added BCI items total score; ratings ranging between 1 and 5 with 1 indicating "not satisfied at all" and 5 "very satisfied") satisfied with the BCI (*satisfaction*). End-users were highly satisfied with *weight, safety* and *learnability* (4.3, 4.5 and 4.8). *Reliability* and *speed* were rated moderately (3.5). Main obstacles were the EEG-cap and electrodes, time-consuming and complex adjustment, difficulty to handle BCI equipment and low *effectiveness*. Like in the other two BCI controlled applications, the evaluation by the end-users implied that there is need for improvement. It seems to be more challenging to implement

http://dx.doi.org/10.5772/55802

an SMR-BCI in activities of daily living of end-users as compared to an ERP-BCI controlled application [22, 47]. Two end-users (one of them locked-in), however, stated that they could imagine using Connect Four in their daily life. The other end-user in the locked-in state could imagine using the BCI in his daily life provided substantial improvement. The fact that both locked-in end-users were highly motivated throughout the BCI sessions and did not report any frustration, even when BCI control was low, implies the need and hope of these patients that BCI may provide better communication and control opportunities.

Taken together, such evaluation studies are first steps toward bridging the translational gap experienced in BCI research and development. Based on these evaluation results we state that to date ERP-BCIs are more effective and efficient for communication and interaction as compared to SMR-BCIs (Table 1). End-users indicated that the speed of the BCI controlled application was too low. Users would have liked to use the Brain Painting application several times a week, but none could imagine to use the BCI for emailing and internet surfing unless substantially improved. Somewhat surprisingly two end-users could imagine playing Connect Four in daily life despite low control. Table 1 summarizes the evaluation results for all applications.

Application	effectiveness	Efficiency	satisfaction	Use in daily life
Communication	🙂	😐	😐	🙁
Painting	🙂	🙂	😐	😐
Gaming	🙁	🙁	😐	😐

Table 1. Summarized evaluation results for the three applications. Clearly, all of them leave room for improvement. However, end-users would have liked to use the Painting and Gaming applications in their daily life.

5. User-centred improvements of BCI controlled applications

As outlined above, functionality, independent use, and easiness of use were rated by expert users of assistive technology (AT) as most important for BCI use in daily life. In the next sections we will describe how we addressed and improved these three aspects.

5.1. Functionality

In an effort to bridge the reliability gap and to address speed of the BCI, we changed the stimulation mode of the widely used P300 spelling matrix. In the commonly used ERP-BCI, characters are light flashed and attention to one of the characters will usually elicit a distinct P300 [32] and sometimes other ERP components such as N100 or N200 (e.g., [48-50]). One option to increase reliability of the system is to enhance signal to noise ratio of the recorded

ERPs. It is well known that familiar faces elicit characteristic ERPs, among which the N170 and N400f (f for faces, Figure 5) are very reliable ERPs. Thus, instead of flashing the letters of the matrix we overlaid row- and column-wise a famous face (the face of Albert Einstein or Ernesto Che Guevara, [51]). Figure 5 provides a screenshot from such modified BCI matrix and illustrates the grand average event-related potentials across N=20 healthy participants. Increasing the signal-to-noise ratio by eliciting more target specific ERPs, significantly boosted offline BCI performance. Importantly, these findings were replicated online in a group of possible end-user of BCI with severe motor impairment, e.g. users with amyotrophic lateral sclerosis or spinal muscular atrophy [38]. They benefited to such an extent that even some users who were unable to operate the traditional ERP-BCI, reached an online accuracy of 100% due to the face stimulation. As such it was possible to decrease the number of stimulation cycles without negatively affecting performance, i.e. bit rate was strongly increased. In six online runs, the number of stimulation cycles was decreased from 10 to 6, 3, 2 and 1 (i.e. single trial) stimulation sequences. Performance in N=9 users with neurodegenerative disease was significantly increased in all runs when exposed to the face speller as compared to the classic ERP-BCI. Furthermore, we compared their single trial performance to the online performance of N=16 healthy participants. As usual, performance was significantly worse in the classic ERP-BCI, however, no difference was found for the face speller. These results clearly underline how modifications to the system can diminish performance drops in end-user samples. Zhang and colleagues (2012) reported that inversion of faces may further increase the N170 component and thus, performance in the BCI task. Face motion, face emotion and face familiarity, however, did not affect BCI performance [38, 52]. We conclude that investigating stimulus material other than the classical character highlighting is a very promising direction for addressing speed and reliability of the system.

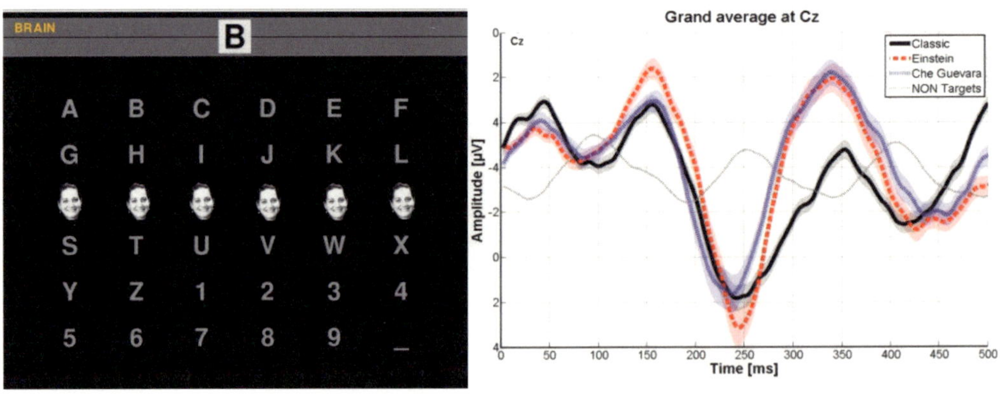

Figure 5. left: Instead of flashing letters in the rows and columns, rows and columns are overlaid with the face (Einstein is not shown due to copyright). Right: Averaged evoked potentials as response to targets and non-targets. In the face condition prominent N170 and N400f appear in addition to the P300. The ERP amplitude is depicted as a function of time [51].

5.2. Easiness of use

We developed a so-called optimized communication interface which allows for auto-calibration and word completion and is controlled with a user-friendly graphical interface [47]. After the subject is set up with the electrode cap and connected to the BCI by an expert, the calibration process for parameterizing the classifier can be started by pressing a single button on the screen. No familiarity with technical or scientific details of the BCI is required. Data from calibration is automatically analysed in the background, invisible to the user who only receives a feedback on successful or unsuccessful outcome of the calibration. In the latter case, calibration can be performed again with one click. Yet, if successfully calibrated, communication with the P300-BCI can be initiated with another button press. We tested if such a user-friendly BCI implementation can be handled independently by naïve users. All healthy subjects (N=19) handled the BCI software completely on their own and stated that the procedure was easy to understand and that they could explain it to a third person. A text completion option significantly decreased communication speed. We conclude that from a software perspective, a BCI system can easily be integrated into an automated application that allows caregivers, friends or relatives to control such complex systems without prior knowledge at the end-user's home or bedside.

5.3. Independent use

Finally, to bridge the reliability gap we implemented BCI controlled brain painting for long-term use at the home of a 72-years old locked-in patient diagnosed with amyotrophic lateral sclerosis (ALS) who used to be a painter [53]. The brain painting application, which was successfully tested and evaluated by healthy subjects [23], as well as patients ([44] and see above) was embedded into an easy-to-use interface enabling to use the application after a few steps only. Family was trained to set-up the 8-channel EEG-cap and amplifier and to control the brain painting interface. The brain painting software automatically saved the duration of painting time, number of runs, and the paintings, and transfered them to our lab for remote supervision. After every session, satisfaction was rated. In a separate window familiy and caregivers can comment on the session. In doing so, occurring problems can be noticed and remotely solved by our experts via remote internet access. Figure 6 shows the end-user in a brain painting session at her home.

After each session the end-user is asked to rate her satisfaction with the visual analogue scale (VAS) (Figure 7) and after approximately 10 sessions the workload and device satisfaction are assessed with the NASA TLX [41] and the Extended QUEST 2.0 [22, 42]. Her responses as well as her data can be observed by our experts remotely to allow for system modifications or other interventions if necessary (e.g. advise for recalibration of the system).

In more than 8 months the end-user has been painting in more than 86 BCI sessions with an average paiting duration of 66.2 minutes. Satisfaction with device strongly depended on functioning of the BCI (Figure 7). When implementing a remote-controlled BCI application problems of malfunctioning arise which are immediately visible in the satisfaction rating (e.g., sessions 9 and 17 in Figure 7). Three types of sources for her dissatisfaction could be identified: In most of the cases dissatisfaction was due to technical problems (software/hardware;

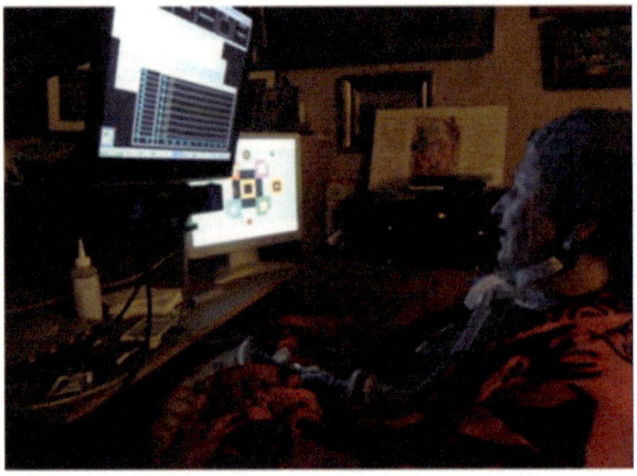

Figure 6. ALS patient at her home, after finishing her brain painting. While painting, the brain painting matrix appears on one screen while on an additional monitor, placed on the table in the background, she can follow the progress of her painting. The brain painting software is operated by the family or caregivers and requires few steps only for set up.

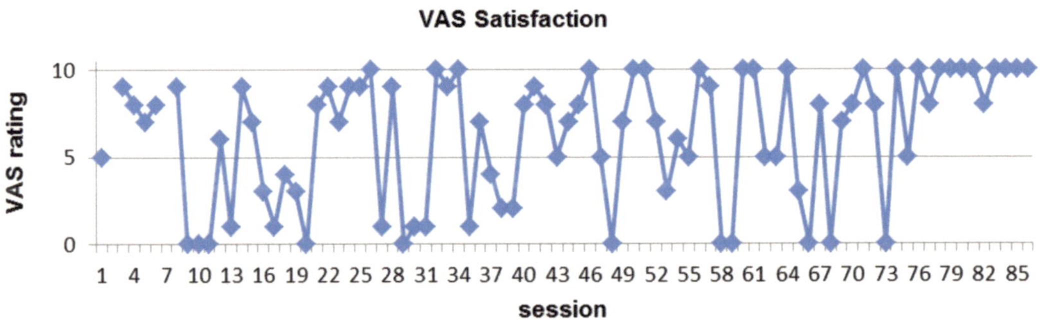

Figure 7. Ratings of satisfaction (VAS Satisfaction; VAS = visual analogue scale) after each of 86 sessions with the brain-painting application with 0 indicating „not satisfied at all" and 10 indicating "very satisfied". Satisfaction ratings vary strongly between very low satisfaction (rating between 0 and 3) and very high satisfaction (rating between 7 and 10). The low ratings in the first 20 sessions were always due to malfunction of the BCI which was still in the set-up state. Continuous remote access to these data allowed for in-time modifications to the system by our experts (Holz et al., in preparation).

especially in the first sessions after set-up of the BCI system at the end-user's home); second, due to problems from the end-user's side, e.g. low concentration or exhaustion or not being able to realize the desired painting; and third, due to bad control (e.g. due to false cap placement, insufficient electrode gel) or loss of control over time (e.g. due to electrode gel drying).

Also for this locked-in BCI end-user effectiveness, reliability and easiness of use were the most important aspects for device satisfaction. Additionally, she mentioned professional support, specifically during times in which the system was not running properly. With a mean VAS satisfaction score of 6.2, her overall satisfaction is moderate to high. However, there is high variability with lowest satisfaction when the system was not working (early sessions) and when the painting was not as she expected it to be (later sessions). Highest ratings indicate that the system worked properly and that she was satisfied with her painting. Despite initial problems with the BCI, her motivation to continue brain painting has remained high even after more than 80 sessions. The end-user is currently painting 2-3 times a week, but stated that she would like to paint every day, if she could do so. The limiting factor is the available time of the family setting up the BCI. But currently also caregivers and friends are willing to learn the set-up and control the application to enable her to paint more often. In conclusion, our results demonstrate that expert-independent BCI use by end-users in the field is possible and illustrate the important role of family and caregivers when transferring BCI technology from the research environment to the end-user's daily life. Figure 8 depicts some of her brain paintings.

Figure 8. Example Brain Paintings of the BCI -user with locked-in syndrome. All paintings were painted with the BCI in her daily life, independent of BCI expert's control, (with friendly permission from the brain painting artist).

6. Conclusions

Taken these results together, we can state that milestones were achieved in bringing BCIs to end-users. BCIs were combined with standard assistive technology, set up of the system including handling of software was facilitated tremendously and spelling speed was increased whilst maintaining high accuracy levels by altering the stimulation mode. In one exemplary end-user with severe motor impairment an application was installed at home such that family and caregivers can set up the system and maintenance and support is provided remotely. With innovative applications to be set-up at the end-users' home and long-term studies first steps have been undertaken to bridge the translational and reliability gaps encountered when bringing BCIs to end-users. The user-centred iterative process between developers and end-users proved successful and the results are powerful demonstrators that BCIs are well coming of age and can face the transfer out of the lab to the end-users' home.

Author details

Andrea Kübler[1*], Elisa Holz[1], Tobias Kaufmann[1] and Claudia Zickler[2]

*Address all correspondence to: andrea.kuebler@uni-wuerzburg.de, elisa.holz@uni-wuerzburg.de, tobias.kaufmann@uni-wuerzburg.de

1 Institute of Psychology, University of Würzburg, Würzburg, Germany

2 Institute of Medical Psychology and Behavioural Neurobiology, University of Tübingen, Tübingen, Germany

References

[1] Vidal, J. J. (1973). *Toward direct brain-computer communication.* Annu Rev Biophys Bioeng, 157-180.

[2] Wolpaw, J. R, & Wolpaw, E. Winter. (2012). *Brain-Computer Interfaces: Something new under the sun,* in *Brain-Computer Interfaces:Principles and Practice: Principles and Practice* J.R. Wolpaw and E. Winter Wolpaw, Editors. Oxford University Press: New York, USA, 3-12.

[3] Kübler, A, & Kotchoubey, B. (2007). *Brain-computer interfaces in the continuum of consciousness.* Curr Opin Neurol, 643-649.

[4] Kübler, A. *Brain-computer Interfacing- Science Fiction has come true.* Brain, in press.

[5] Kübler, A, et al. (2011). *A model of BCI control.* in *5th International Brain-Computer Interface Conference.* Austria: Graz University of Technology.

[6] Hammer, E. M, et al. (2012). *Psychological predictors of SMR-BCI performance.* Biol Psychol, 80-86.

[7] Kleih, S. C, et al. (2010). *Motivation modulates the 300 amplitude during brain-computer interface use.* Clin Neurophysiol, 1023-31.

[8] Kaufmann, T, et al. (2012). *Effects of resting heart rate variability on performance in the 300 brain-computer interface.* Int J Psychophysiol, 336-41.

[9] Blankertz, B, et al. (2010). *Neurophysiological predictor of SMR-based BCI performance.* Neuroimage, 1303-1309.

[10] Halder, S, et al. *Prediction of auditory and visual 300 brain-computer interface aptitude.* PlosOne, in press.

[11] Lotte, F, et al. (2007). *A review of classification algorithms for EEG-based brain-computer interfaces.* J Neural Eng, R1-R13.

[12] Blankertz, B, et al. (2006). *The BCI competition. III: Validating alternative approaches to actual BCI problems.* IEEE Trans Neural Syst Rehabil Eng, , 153-159.

[13] Krusienski, D. J, et al. (2006). *A comparison of classification techniques for the 300 Speller.* J Neural Eng, 299-305.

[14] Mcfarland, D. J, Mccane, L. M, & Wolpaw, J. R. (1998). *EEG-based communication and control: short-term role of feedback.* IEEE Trans Rehabil Eng, 7-11.

[15] Gruzelier, J, et al. (2010). *Acting performance and flow state enhanced with sensory-motor rhythm neurofeedback comparing ecologically valid immersive VR and training screen scenarios.* Neurosci Lett, 112-116.

[16] Ortner, R, et al. (2012). *A motor imagery based brain-computer interface for stroke rehabilitation.* Stud Health Technol Inform, 319-323.

[17] Wang, P. T, et al. (2012). *Self-paced brain-computer interface control of ambulation in a virtual reality environment.* J Neural Eng, 056016.

[18] Hinterberger, T, et al. (2004). *A multimodal brain-based feedback and communication system.* Exp Brain Res, 521-526.

[19] Nijboer, F, et al. (2008). *An auditory brain-computer interface (BCI).* J Neurosci Methods, 43-50.

[20] Furdea, A, et al. (2009). *An auditory oddball 300 spelling system for brain-computer interfaces.* Psychophysiology, 617-25.

[21] Neuper, C, et al. (2005). *Imagery of motor actions: differential effects of kinesthetic and visual-motor mode of imagery in single-trial EEG.* Brain Res Cogn Brain Res, 668-677.

[22] Zickler, C, et al. (2011). *A brain-computer interface as input channel for a standard assistive technology software.* Clin EEG Neurosci, 236-244.

[23] Münßinger J.I., et al.(2010). *Brain Painting: First Evaluation of a New Brain-Computer Interface Application with ALS-Patients and Healthy Volunteers.* Front Neurosci, 182.

[24] Millan, J. D, et al. (2010). *Combining Brain-Computer Interfaces and Assistive Technologies: State-of-the-Art and Challenges.* Front Neurosci

[25] Zickler, C, et al. (2009). *BCI applications for people with disabilities: defining user needs and user requirements*, in *Assistive Technology from Adapted Equipment to Inclusive Environments, AAATE. 25 Assistive Technology Research Series*, P.L.Emiliani, et al., Editors. IOS Press Amsterdam, 185-189.

[26] Maguire, M. C. (1998). *User-Centred Requirements Handbook WP5 D5.3 of the Telematics Applications Project TE- RESPECT: Requirements Engineering and Specification in Telematics.*

[27] Pfurtscheller, G, et al. (1997). *EEG-based discrimination between imagination of right and left hand movement.* Electroencephalogr Clin Neurophysiol, 642-651.

[28] Pfurtscheller, G, & Neuper, C. (1997). *Motor imagery activates primary sensorimotor area in humans.* Neurosci Lett, 65-68.

[29] Kübler, A, et al. (2005). *Patients with ALS can use sensorimotor rhythms to operate a brain-computer interface.* Neurology, 1775-1777.

[30] Guger, C, et al. (2009). *How many people are able to control a 300 brain-computer interface (BCI)?* Neurosci Lett, 94-8.

[31] Halder, S, et al. (2011). *Neural mechanisms of brain-computer interface control.* Neuroimage, 1779-1790.

[32] Farwell, L. A, & Donchin, E. (1988). *Talking off the top of your head: toward a mental prosthesis utilizing event-related brain potentials.* Electroencephalogr Clin Neurophysiol, 510-523.

[33] Sellers, E. W, Arbel, Y, & Donchin, E. (2012). *BCIs that use 300 Event-Related Potentials.,* in *Brain Computer Interfaces: Principles and Practice.,* J.R. Wolpaw and E. Winter Wolpaw, Editors. Oxford University Press.

[34] Kleih, S. C, et al. (2011). *Out of the frying pan into the fire--the 300 BCI faces real-world challenges.* Prog Brain Res, 27-46.

[35] Polich, J. (2007). *Updating P an integrative theory of 3a and P3b.* Clin Neurophysiol, 2128-48.

[36] Nijboer, F, et al. (2008). *A 300 brain-computer interface for people with amyotrophic lateral sclerosis.* Clin Neurophysiol, 1909-16.

[37] Sellers, E. W, Vaughan, T. M, & Wolpaw, J. R. (2010). *A Brain-computer interface for long-term independent home use.* Amyotroph Lateral Scler, 449-455.

[38] Kaufmann, T, et al. *Face stimuli effectively prevent brain-computer interface inefficiency in patients with neurodegenerative disease.* Clin Neurophysiol, in press.

[39] Hoffmann, U, et al. (2008). *An efficient 300 brain-computer interface for disabled subjects.* J Neurosci Methods, 115-25.

[40] Mak, J. N, et al. (2011). *Optimizing the 300brain-computer interface: current status, limitations and future directions.* J Neural Eng, 025003.

[41] Hart, S. G, & Staveland, L. E. (1988). *Development of NASA-TLX (Task Load Index): Results of experimental and theoretical research,* in *Human mental workload,* P.A. Hancock and N. Meshkati, Editors. North-Holland: Amsterdam, 139-183.

[42] Demers, L, Weiss-lambrou, R, & Ska, B. (2000). *Quebec user Evaluation of Satisfaction with assistive Technology. QUEST version 2.0. An outcome measure for assistive technology devices* Webster, New York: Institute for Matching Person and Technology.

[43] Scherer, M. J. (2007). *The Matching Person & Technology (MPT) Model Manual and Assessments, [CD-ROM]*. The Institute for Matching Person & Technology, Inc.: Webster, NY.

[44] Zickler, C, et al. *Brain Painting: usability testing according to the user-centered design in end users with severe disabilities.* Art Intell Med., under revision.

[45] Holz, E. M, et al. *BCI-controlled gaming: evaluation of usability by severely motor restricted end-users.* Art Intell Med, under revision.

[46] Kübler, A, & Birbaumer, N. (2008). *Brain-computer interfaces and communication in paralysis: extinction of goal directed thinking in completely paralysed patients?* Clin Neurophysiol, 2658-2666.

[47] Kaufmann, T, et al. (2012). *Spelling is Just a Click Away- A User-Centered Brain-Computer Interface Including Auto-Calibration and Predictive Text Entry.* Front Neurosci, 72.

[48] Allison, B. Z, & Pineda, J. A. (2003). *ERPs evoked by different matrix sizes: implications for a brain computer interface (BCI) system.* IEEE Trans Neural Syst Rehabil Eng, 110-113.

[49] Treder, M. S, & Blankertz, B. (2010). *C)overt attention and visual speller design in an ERP-based brain-computer interface.* Behav Brain Funct, 28.

[50] Kaufmann, T, Hammer, E. M, & Kübler, A. (2011). *ERPs contributing to classification in the 300 BCI.* in *5th International Brain-Computer Interface Conference*. Graz, Austria: University of Technology.

[51] Kaufmann, T, et al. (2011). *Flashing characters with famous faces improves ERP-based brain-computer interface performance.* J Neural Eng, 056016.

[52] Jin, J, et al. *The changing face of 300 BCIs: A comparison of stimulus changes in a P300 BCI involving faces, emotion, and movement.* PlosOne, in press.

[53] Holz, E.M., Botrel, L., & Kübler, A. (2013). Bridging Gaps: Long-Term Independent BCI Home-Use by a Locked-In End-User. Proceedings of the TOBI Workshop IV, Sion, Switzerland.

Chapter 2

BCI Integration: Application Interfaces

Christoph Hintermüller, Christoph Kapeller,
Günter Edlinger and Christoph Guger

Additional information is available at the end of the chapter

http://dx.doi.org/10.5772/55806

1. Introduction

Many disorders, like spinal cord injury, stroke or amyotrophic lateral sclerosis (ALS), can impair or even completely disable the usual communication channels a person needs to communicate and interact with his or her environment. In such severe cases, a brain-computer interface (BCI) might be the only remaining way to communicate [1]. In a BCI, the brain's electrical activity during predefined mental tasks is analyzed and translated into corresponding actions intended by the user. But even for less severe disabilities, a BCI can improve quality of life by allowing users to control a computer or specially prepared electronic devices, or to stay in contact with friends through social networks and games. P300 evoked potential [2, 3, 4] based BCIs can provide goal-oriented control as needed to operating spelling devices [5] or control computer games [6]. For navigating in space e.g. moving a computer mouse [7]), controlling the motion and movement of a robot or a wheelchair, steady state visual evoked potential (SSVEP) [8, 9, 10, 10] and motor imagination [12, 13] based BCI paradigms can be used.

All these applications require integrating the BCI with an external software application or device. This chapter will discuss different ways this integration can be achieved, such as transmitting the user's intention to the application for execution, updating the options available to the user, related actions and integrating visual BCI stimulation and feedback paradigms with the Graphical User Interface (GUI) of external applications. The current developments and efforts to standardize the application interfaces will be presented.

2. General structure of a BCI

A BCI system consists of several components (figure 1). The first is the biosignal acquisition system, which records the body's signals (like the EEG) used to extract the user's intentions and responses to the presented stimuli and feedback. It consists of a set of electrodes and a dedicated biosignal amplifier, which typically directly digitizes the signals and transmits them to the feature extraction system. The feature extraction processes the signals and analyzes them with respect to specific signals like P300, SSVEP or error potentials [14, 15, 16, 17].

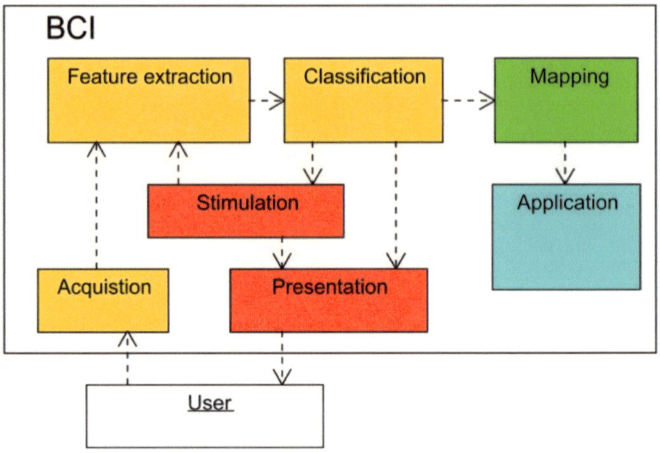

Figure 1. A BCI system consists of various components, which acquire, process and classify signals from the user's brain. Other components handle the presentation of dedicated stimuli and the feedback of the classification results. A dedicated mapping component converts them into commands and tasks to be executed by an attached or embedded application or service.

The classification determines the intention of the user based on the extracted features, which may reflect that the user does not intend to communicate at that time. The classification results are converted by a dedicated mapping component or appropriate methods into commands, actions and tasks to be executed by the attached applications such as a spelling device [2, 3, 4] or robot [10]. In order to enhance the user's response to the presented stimuli and to help assess the system's efficacy, a feedback related to the classification results is presented and the stimulation is adopted accordingly. Furthermore, the stimulation unit provides information about the presented stimuli using trigger signals and events, which are used to synchronously process the input signals and extract corresponding features.

3. Methods for integrating a BCI with an application

There exist three basic approaches to interconnect the BCI with a user application. The following sections, 3.1-3.3, discuss the different designs, their advantages and disadvantages. Each section will present some of the currently available BCI systems and frameworks that use that design. Section 3.4 compares the possibilities to establish standardized interfaces for interconnecting an application with the BCI system.

3.1. Direct integration

The most straight forward approach is to integrate the application within the BCI system. This approach, which is sketched in figure 1, allows developers to hardcode the symbols and feedback presented. In other words, the conversion of the classification results into application commands, tasks and actions, and the application itself, represent a static addendum to the BCI systems. This approach was used for the first proof of concept systems, and can still be found in simple spelling devices such as the P300 speller distributed by g.tec medical engineering along with the g.HIGHsys, a Highspeed Online Processing block set [18] for Matlab/Simulink™ (Mathworks, USA) and other BCI systems used for demonstration and educational purposes.

Modern BCI frameworks [19] such as OpenViBE [20], BCILAB [21] or xBCI [22] that are based on this design use a module based approach to allow application developers and designers to integrate their own application within the existing BCI framework.

The advantage of directly integrating the application within the BCI system is that it can be distributed and used as a compact, all-in-one component. Despite the need for appropriate acquisition and processing hardware, no additional interfaces or protocols are required.

The downside of this approach is that application developers and designers require some knowledge of the interpretation of the feature signals and classification results and how to convert them into appropriate commands, tasks and actions. Whenever an application must be added, updated, exchanged or removed, the presentation of stimuli and feedback has to be adjusted.

3.2. External executable component

The limitations of the tight integration approach can be reduced or eliminated by modeling the application as an individual executable that act as an external component of the BCI. As shown in figure 2, all other components like feature extraction, classification, stimulus and feedback presentation remain inside the core BCI system. This design is utilized by BCI systems which use the BCI2000 [23] or the TOBI platform [24], among other examples.

A well defined interface, such as the TiC output interface [25] used by the TOBI platform, allows applications to receive information based on the action that the user chooses to execute. If supported by the stimulus and presentation components, applications even may update and modify the choices available to the user through the BCI. Within TOBI, the TiD trigger interface [24] can be used by the application to initiate the processing of the change requests.

As a consequence, applications become independent from the BCI and may be connected and disconnected to and from the BCI any time. Both the BCI and the applications can, for example, be adapted to the user's needs independently without affecting each other. On the BCI side, this includes the selection of the acquired biosignals and features, improvements in the algorithms used to assess the user's intentions and the stimulation and feedback paradigms used. On the other hand, applications may dynamically adopt the available choices to some internal state or provide new commands and actions to the user without the need to modify any of the core BCI components.

As shown in figure 2, converting the feature classification results has to be done by the application. This basically requires that developers and designers of BCI enabled applications have some knowledge of how to interpret these results with respect to the services, actions and tasks offered by their applications. Propagating changes from the internal state of the application to the user is only possible if the BCI is able to reflect these changes by adopting the options presented to the user accordingly.

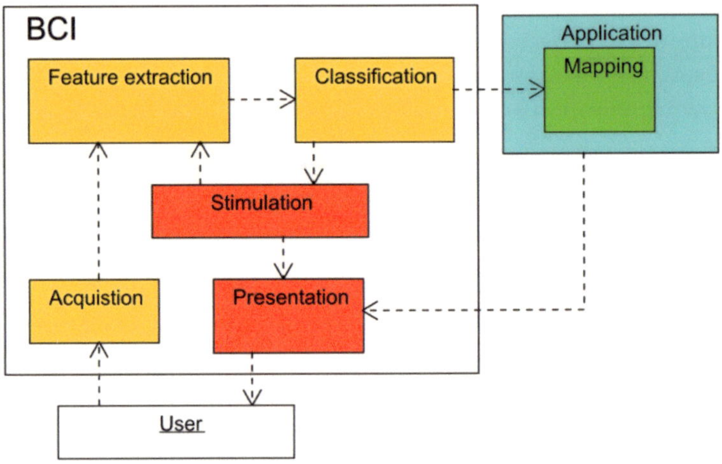

Figure 2. The application acts as additional, external executable component of the BCI system. It attaches to the different data and trigger interfaces to receive information about the user's intention and initiate the adoption of the stimulus and feedback presentation to its internal states.

3.3. Message based

The limitations of the approaches described in the previous sections, 3.1 and 3.2, can be overcome by integrating a dedicated interface module or component within the BCI system. The mapping component collects the classification results and converts them to corresponding application control messages and the connection interface component transmits each of them to the application, where they are interpreted and the requested services, actions or tasks are executed.

Depending on the capabilities of the core components of the BCI and the interface component, the application may request an update of the presented stimuli and feedback based on the application's internal state. Figure 3 shows the bidirectional case, where the application can acknowledge the reception of the transmitted messages and send update requests to the BCI whenever its internal state changes. The interface component of the connected BCI system decodes the corresponding messages and initiates the required changes and updates of the stimulus and feedback presentation. Hence, the paradigms and input modalities the BCI uses do not matter.

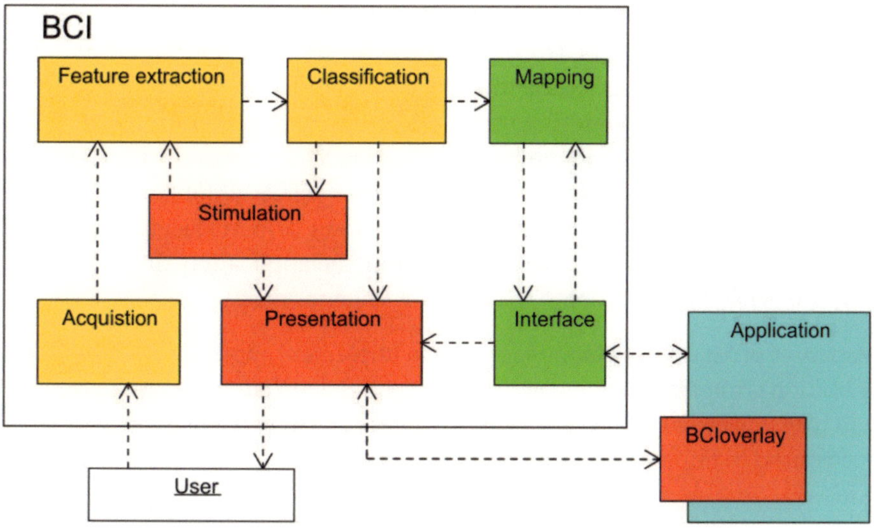

Figure 3. The BCI and the application are loosely coupled through dedicated interface components. An optional BCI overlay module allows embedding the presentation of the BCI stimulation and feedback remotely within the applications when requested by the application.

The message based approach provides a loose coupling between the BCI system and the attached applications. It is used, for example, by the intendiX™ system (g.tec medical engineering GmbH, Austria), which is further described in section 4. Structural and technical changes applied to the BCI system, such as modifications of the signal acquisition, feature extraction, classification, stimulus or feedback presentation, have no impact on the attached application. Improvements and modifications of the services, actions and tasks offered by the applications do not require any technical or algorithmic changes to any part of the BCI system. The dedicated interface component, in combination with a well defined, message based and standardized protocol, enables applications to provide new features to the user any time, without modifying any of the BCI components.

In contrast to the approaches described in the previous sections, 3.1 and 3.2, a dedicated mapping component enclosed within the BCI (figure 3) interprets the classification results and converts them to their corresponding application control message. This encapsulation enables developers with little or no expertise in biosignal processing, analysis, classification and interpreting results to develop applications controllable by a BCI.

The resulting decoupling of the application from the BCI can be taken one step further by transparently embedding it within the user interface of any application. This is achieved by overlaying the BCI stimuli and feedback on top of the application's standard user interfaces. This may be achieved using an overlay module as described in section 4.3.

3.4. Connection design

The previous sections, 3.1-3.3, described the different ways to integrate the BCI within an application. Independent of these different approaches, the dedicated communication and control interface between the BCI and the application can be implemented using two distinct methods. Platforms like TOBI, BCI2000 or the unidirectional extendiX clients described in section 4.1 and in [26] provide dedicated application programming interface (API) libraries that handle all the connection and data transfer related issues. An application, as shown in figure 4a, calls the API functions to retrieve information about the user's intention and initiate the update of the presented stimuli and feedback. All the details about the underlying protocol and connection are hidden by the library. This allows administering modifications and extensions to the protocol any time, without affecting the application, unless the interfaces of the API functions need to be adopted to reflect the changes made.

A large variety of programming languages exist to implement applications and the API library. If the application is implemented using a different language than the API, a so called language wrapper library is necessary. Such a wrapper provides access to the BCI client API from within the language used to implement the application.

User data, selections and information about the internal state of the application are stored in dedicated data structures and fields. Hence, it is likely that these differ from ones used by the API library to receive instructions from and to collect update requests to be sent to the BCI. As a consequence, an application has to convert all data to and from its internal data structures before and after calling a BCI client API function. Depending on the intended usage and the related requirements concerning responsiveness, user experience and usage of computational resources, this may cause additional, probably undesired effects from the application.

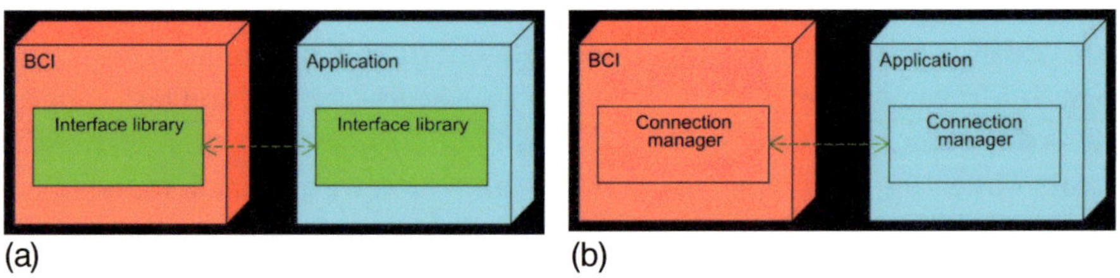

Figure 4. The interconnection of the BCI and the application can either be encapsulated within a dedicated library a) or be based on a dedicated protocol b).

Figure 4b shows a different way to establish a connection between the BCI system and an application. It is based on a well defined and standardized protocol only. Both the BCI and the application utilize their own, dedicated connection manager to handle the typically network based connection, process all received requests and generate all outgoing messages based on their current state. The connection manager interprets the incoming messages, extracts relevant data and information and converts them directly into the data structures and representations used by the application or the BCI respectively.

Changes to the application's internal state are directly converted into appropriate messages requesting changes and updates to the stimuli, the feedback presented to the user and the conversion of classification results to be returned to the application. Thus, it does not matter which programming language is used to implement the application. Instead of an API library wrapper, a dedicated connection manager has to be developed. This requires that the communication protocol uses a well defined and properly described handshake and communication procedures to avoid unnecessary workarounds, which might prevent the application from being used with BCI systems supporting a different version of the protocol.

4. Intendix™

The previous section discussed 3 different approaches to interconnect the BCI with user applications, services and devices. This section presents the intendiX™ system [26], which is used by the applications and projects presented in section 5.

The intendiX BCI system was designed to be operated by caregivers or the patient's family at home. It consists of active EEG electrodes to avoid skin abrasion, a portable biosignal amplifier and a laptop or netbook running the software under Windows (see figure 5a). The electrodes are integrated into the cap to allow a fast and easy montage of the equipment so it can be mounted quickly and easily. The software lets users view the raw EEG to inspect data quality, but automatically informs the inexperienced user if the data quality on a specific channel is good or bad.

(a) (b)

Figure 5. The user who is wearing the EEG cap equipped with active electrodes can run the intendiX system on a laptop a). By default, the intendiX presents a matrix of 50 characters using a layout comparable to a computer keyboard b).

This control can be realized by extracting the P300 evoked potential from the EEG data in real-time. The characters of the English alphabet, Arabic numbers and icons were arranged in a matrix on a computer screen (see figure 5b). Then the characters are highlighted in a random order while the user concentrates on the specific character he/she wants to spell. The BCI system is first trained on the P300 response of several characters with multiple flashes per character to adapt to the specific person.

During this training, 5-10 training characters are typically designated for the user to copy. The EEG data is used to calculate the user specific weight vector, which is stored for later usage. Then the software automatically switches into the spelling mode and the user can spell as many characters as desired. The system was tested with 100 subjects who had to spell the word LUCAS after 5 minutes of training. 72 % were able to spell it correctly without any mistake [4].

The speed and accuracy of the classification can be optimized by choosing the appropriate number of flashes manually. A statistical approach could also automatically determine the optimal number of flashes for a desired accuracy threshold. This latter approach could also determine whether the user is paying attention to the BCI system. The statistical approach could have a major advantage: no characters are selected if the user is not looking at the matrix or does not want to use the speller.

The intendiX™ user can perform different actions after spelling: (i) copy the spelled text into an editor; (ii) copy the text into an email; (iii) send the text via text-to-speech facilities to the loud speakers; (iv) print the text or (v) send the text via UDP to another computer by selecting a dedicated icon. The intendiX™ system offers two distinct ways to manage this interaction with external software and control various applications [26], described below.

4.1. extendiX

The first is the unidirectional extendiX protocol. It is accessible through the dedicated closed source extendiX library encapsulating the extendiX protocol.

For simple control applications, the extendiX batch file starter client allows users to start dedicated batch scripts whenever it receives information about the symbols selected by the user. This approach is suitable for all applications, services and devices that offer dedicated command-line interfaces for controlling their state and executing specific actions.

The intendix™ Painting [26] program, a small painting program comparable to Microsoft Windows Paint, allows users to create paintings and other images, as well as store, load and print them.

4.2. intendiX ACTOR protocol

For complex control tasks, the intendiX™ Application ConTrol and Online Reconfiguration (ACTOR) Protocol is provided. Compared to extendiX, it offers a bidirectional User Datagram Protocol (UDP) message based connection between the BCI and the application. A short summary of the standardized intendiX ACTOR protocol can be found in [27] and its detailed description is available from [26]. No dedicated API library is available. All applications have to implement their own dedicated connection manager, which handles all intendiX ACTOR based communication.

The Interface Unit handles the UDP connections to all simultaneously attached applications, services and devices and converts the classification results to the corresponding UDP message string. This dedicated connection manager processes all connect, disconnect requests and status updates received, prepares the next set of stimuli and feedback modalities to be presented to the user and instructs the corresponding components to adjust their outputs accordingly.

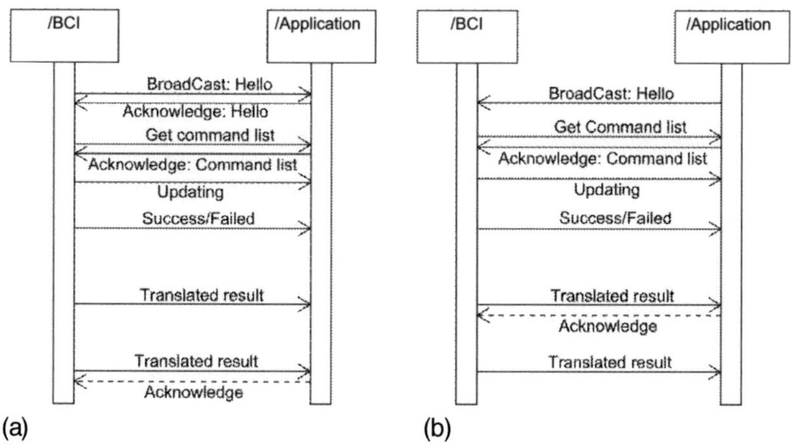

Figure 6. a) Handshake procedure used on startup by the BCI to identify all active applications and clients. b) Handshake procedure initiated by a starting application or client to register with a running BCI system.

The intendiX ACTOR protocol uses eXtensible Markup Language (XML) formatted message strings to exchange information between the BCI and the attached system. Whenever the BCI system is started, it broadcasts a dedicated hello message to identify the available and active applications, as shown in figure 6a. Each client responds by sending an appropriate acknowledgement message. As soon as the BCI has received this message, it will request from the application the list of applications and services available from this client. The BCI will acknowledge the received list of commands, services and actions and report whether it was able to process it successfully.

A similar handshake procedure is used when a newly started application connects to the BCI system. The only difference is that the BCI acknowledges the hello broadcast sent by the application by requesting the list of available commands, as shown in figure 6b.

Attached clients will receive a control message whenever the user has selected a service, action or task (figure 7a). The content of this message is fully defined by the application, which can ask the BCI to change this message and the related symbols, sounds and sequences presented to the user during stimulation and feedback. In this case, configured along with the definition of a single BCI control element, the BCI will pause the presentation of any stimuli and feedback until the application acknowledges the reception and execution of the control message or requests an update of the BCI user interface.

A single UDP message sent to the BCI may contain several distinct requests that are processed as an atomic batch. The presentation of stimuli and feedback that was paused while sending the last control message is not restarted before the last message within this batch has been processed. Each single message within such a batch may request the change of one single stimulus or feedback element, or contain the content of a whole XML formatted configuration file that describes complex BCI screens and groups of stimuli. The latter is used by the IU to determine which stimuli and feedback modalities should be presented to the user. The detailed description of the configuration file format used is available, along with the definitions of the intendiX ACTOR protocol from [26].

Whenever the BCI receives an update request, it will return an acknowledge message indicating that it is trying to process and execute the update request. After the update is finished, a message indicating whether the request was executed successfully or failed is returned.

Whenever an application, service or device is terminated, it sends a good bye message to the BCI, which acknowledges this message sending a simple bye message. As shown in figure 7b, the same message is used by the BCI to inform connected clients that it will terminate operation.

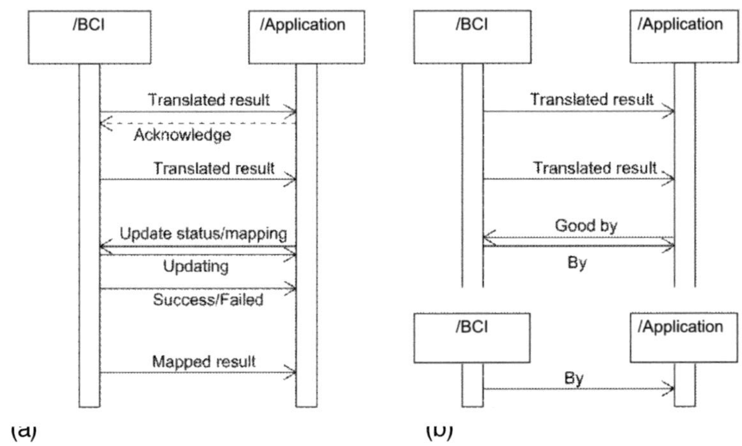

Figure 7. a) Sequences used by the BCI and application to transfer translated results and request updates. b) Sequences used by the application to disconnect from the BCI and by the BCI to dismiss applications on shutdown.

4.3. intendiX SOCI

For applications, especially virtual reality (VR) applications and remote control of robots, it is desirable to enhance the standard user interface by directly embedding the BCI stimuli (figure 8). The intendiX platform can be configured to remotely display its stimuli and feedback using the intendiX Screen Overlay Control Interface (SOCI) module [26]. The intendiX SOCI system implements a runtime loadable library based on OpenGL [28]. It is implemented as a dynamic linked library (DLL) for Microsoft Windows and as a shared object for LINUX, and can be used by OpenGL based host applications to embed targets for visual stimulation within the displayed scene. The host applications could be virtual reality environments or real-world videos acquired with a camera. Figure 8 presents an example of how to use the intendiX SOCI module to simultaneously control the camera direction and select amongst different actions and objects.

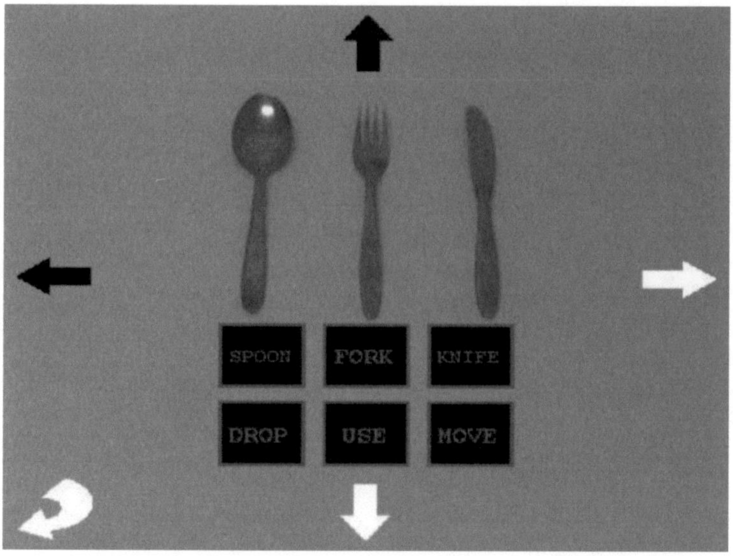

Figure 8. Example of how to use the intendiX SOCI module. Different BCI controls flash together within a running video application. In this example, the user uses the five outer controls to control the direction of the camera and the inner six controls to handle utensils like spoon, fork and knife.

The intendiX SOCI library is able to generate frequency (f-VEP) or code based (c-VEP) SSVEP stimuli, and supports single symbol and row column based P300 stimulation paradigms. It is initialized and fully controlled by the BCI system using a dedicated UDP based network connection. The application only needs to provide information on the network interface and port to be used when connecting to the BCI system and the screen refresh rate, which reliably can be achieved by the user display system. All other parameters are defined by the BCI system during startup and initialization phase. The intendiX SOCI module provides a standardized API, which allows the application to handle the stimulation and feedback devices attached to the user system appropriately.

Figure 9 shows the call sequence that the application must use to augment its own interface with the BCI controls. This sequence has to be repeated for each display, stimulation and feedback device that the BCI user wishes to use. The init function activates the BCI support for the selected device.

Every time before it calls the draw function, the application has to ensure that the openGL environment is initialized properly to display the BCI controls on top of any other graphical element. This is indicated in figure 9 by the call to the "set transformation" pseudo openGL function. After the swap buffer command from openGL has been called, the application has to call the displayed function to indicate that the stimuli have been updated.

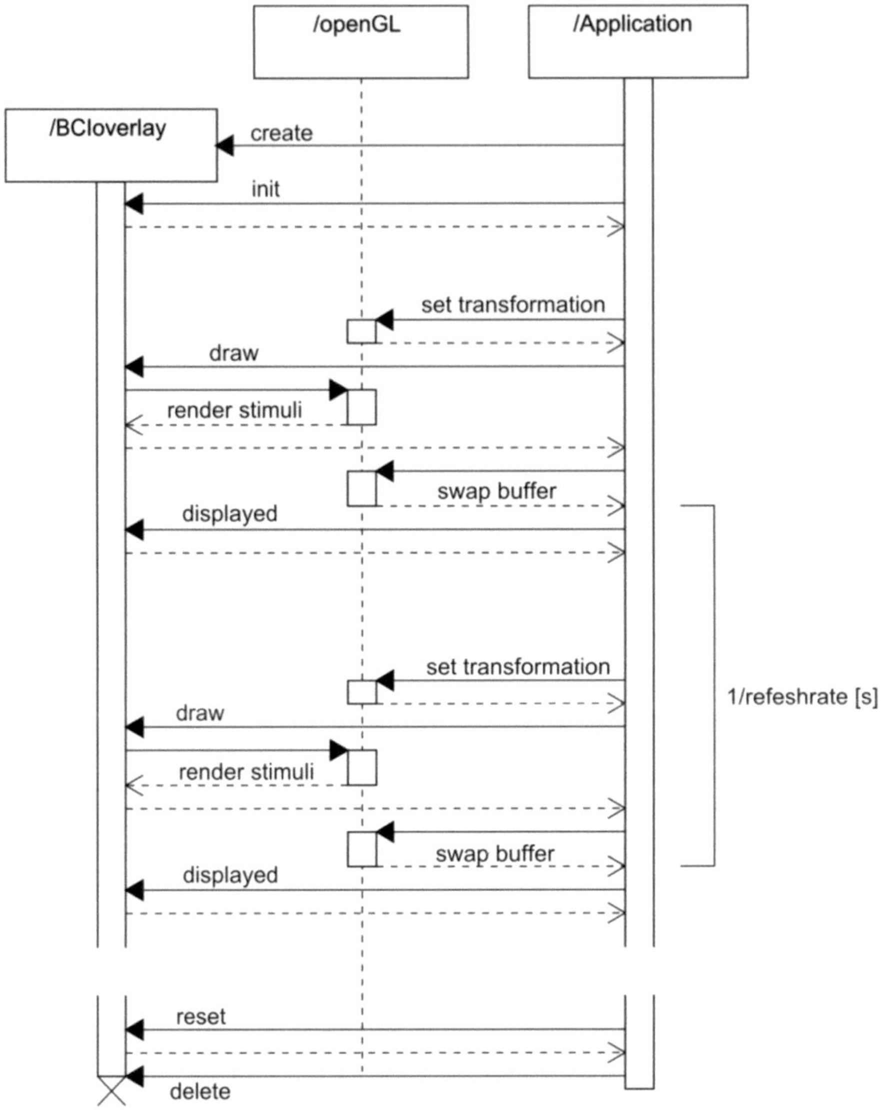

Figure 9. The order in which the init, draw, displayed and reset functions of the intendiX SOCI module have to be called by the application. The draw and displayed functions are called for every screen refresh cycle, which has a duration of 16.6 ms for a standard 60 Hz LCD flat screen.

When the application terminates, it disconnects the displays from the BCI by calling the reset function for each screen previously attached to the BCI through the init function. As indicated in figure 9, the application has to ensure that the interval between two consecutive calls to the displayed API function strictly corresponds to the screen refresh rate proposed by the application during initialization.

http://dx.doi.org/10.5772/55806

5. Applications

In section 3, the different concepts used to interconnect BCI systems and user applications were discussed. The application interfaces provided by the intendiX™ system were briefly presented in section 4. This section will list some projects and applications that utilize the intendiX ACTOR protocol and the indendiX SOCI API library to control virtual and robotic avatars and ambient assistance systems (sections 5.1, 5.2 and 5.3). Section 5.4 will present some examples in which the BCI was used to control cooperative multi player games such as World of Warcarft by Blizzard Entertainment [29] and social network platforms like Twitter (Twitter, Inc., USA). All of these applications either use the P300 matrix or a SSVEP paradigm with frequency coded stimuli.

5.1. VERE

The VERE project [30] is concerned with embodiment of people in surrogate bodies so that they have the illusion that the surrogate body is their own body – and that they can move and control it as if it were their own. There are two types of embodiment considered. The first type is robotic embodiment (figure 10a), where the person is embodied in a remote physical robotic device and control it through a brain-computer interface. For example, a patient confined to a wheelchair or bed, who is unable to physically move, may nevertheless re-enter the world actively and physically through such remote embodiment. The second type of embodiment (figure 10b) is virtual, where participants enter into a virtual reality with a virtual body representation. The basic and practical goal of this type of embodiment is to explore its use in the context of rehabilitation settings.

The VERE project uses the intendiX ACTOR protocol (section 4.2) to access the BCI output from within the eXtreme Virtual Reality (XVR) environment (VRMedia S.r.l., Pisa, Italy) to control both the virtual and robotic avatars. The BCI is part of the intention recognition and inference component of the embodiment station, which is developed through the VERE project.

The intention recognition and inference unit takes inputs from fMRI, EEG and other physiological sensors to create a control signal together with access to a knowledge base, taking into account body movements and facial movements. This output is used to control the virtual representation of the avatar in XVR and to control the robotic avatar. The user gets feedback showing the scene and the BCI control via either the HMD or a display and the tactile and auditory stimuli provided by the so called embodiment station. Thereby the intendiX SOCI module is used to embed the BCI stimuli and feedback modalities within video streams recorded by the robot (figure 10c, e) and the virtual environment of the user's avatar.

The user is situated inside the embodiment station, which provides different stimuli and feedback modalities such as visual, auditory and tactile. Figure 10d shows the setup for inducing the illusion of hand movement by mechanically stimulating the flexor and extensor muscles of the hand.

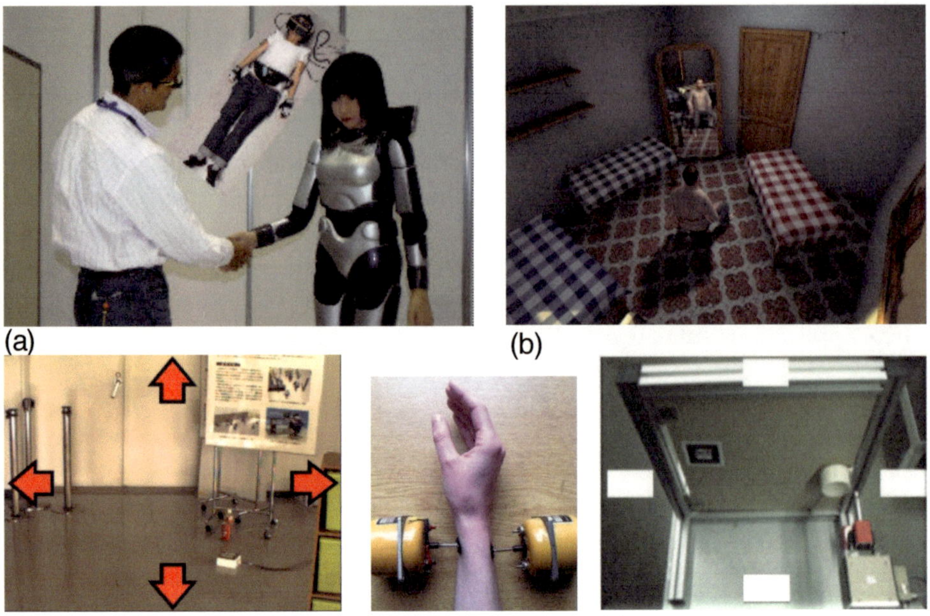

(c) (d) (e)

Images courtesy of VERE, Event lab Universitat de Barcelona, Centere National de la Recherche Scientifique France, Perco laboratory Scuola Superiore Sant' Anna Pisa and Institute of Automatic control Engineering at the Technical University Munich, 2012.

Figure 10. VERE project aims at dissolving the boundary between the human body and surrogate representations in physical reality (a) and immersive virtual reality (b).One of the key aspects is to develop a brain body computer interface enabling the user to control the movement of his robotic avatar robot (c), open doors (e) and to provide him with visual (c, e) and tactile feedback on the body movements executed by the avatar (d).

Depending on the selected stimuli, the BCI system offers distinct levels of control. These levels range from high level commands, tasks and actions such as turning on the TV or grasping a can to moving the robot within its environment (figure 10c) or teaching the robot new high level tasks such as opening a door (figure 10e). The message based intendiX ACTOR protocol can switch smoothly between the different control levels and control paradigms.

5.2. ALIAS

The Ambient Assisted Living (AAL) research programme supports projects that develop technology to compensate for the drawbacks of the aging society by applying modern information and communication technologies (ICTs). The Adaptable Ambient LIving ASsistant (ALIAS) project [31] is one the projects funded by AAL. It aims to improve the communication of elderly people, thus ensuring a safe and long independent life in their own homes. A mobile robot platform without manipulation capabilities serves as a communication platform for improving the social inclusion of the user by offering a wide range of services, such as web applications for basic communication, multimedia and event search and games.

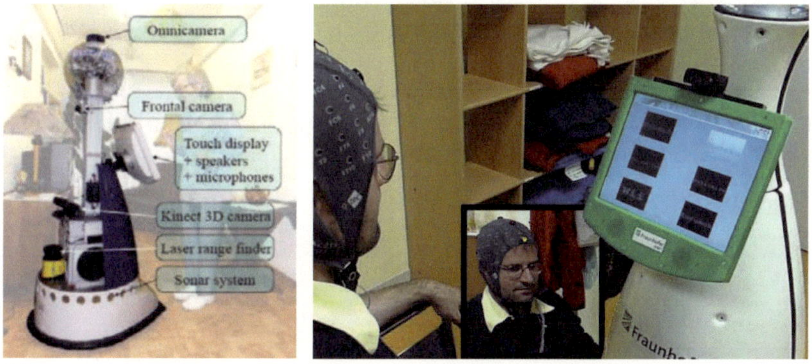

(a) (b)

Figure 11. The ALIAS robot utilizes several different sensors to perceive the user's input and intentions (a). In addition, it supports BCI systems through the intendiX ACTOR protocol and by embedding visual stimuli and feedback modalities using the intendiX SOCI module (b).

The ALIAS robot is equipped with sensing devices including cameras, microphones for speech input and a touch-screen (figure 11a) to perceive the user's input. The robot utilizes different modalities such as audio output, a graphical user interface (GUI) and proactive and autonomous navigation to interact with the user.

A so called dialog manager ensures that the dialog system can be controlled in a reasonable way. It is the central decision making unit for the behavior of the ALIAS robot and its interactions with the human user. It manages the interplay between input and output modalities of the ALIAS robot, communicates with all involved modules of ALIAS and controls them.

Besides the touch-screen, which is used to display the GUI and two independent automatic speech recognition (ASR) systems, a keyword spotter and a continuous context search also operate in parallel. The ALIAS dialog systems support the intendiX ACTOR protocol for receiving input from BCI systems and updating the presented stimuli and feedback online, based on the active state of the robot.

The intendiX SOCI module is used to embed the BCI stimuli within the GUI (figure 11b), aligned to their corresponding buttons. This tight integration of the BCI enables users to easily utilize the ALIAS platform during recovery, such as recover from stroke. The BCI interface of ALIAS allows them to navigate through the different menus, start programs, chat with friends using Skype, call and dismiss the robot or issue an emergency call.

5.3. BrainAble

The BrainAble project [32] conceives, researches, designs, implements and validates an ICT-based Human Computer Interface (HCI). Such an interface is composed of Brain Neural Computer Interface (BNCI) sensors combined with affective computing and virtual environments to restore and augment the two main shortcomings of people with disabilities. It entails inner and outer components. The inner component aims at providing functional independence for daily life activities and autonomy based on accessible and interoperable home automation.

The outer component provides social inclusion through advanced and adapted social network services. The latter component is expected to dramatically improve the user's quality of life.

Within the BrainAble project, the core structures of the intendiX ACTOR protocol were designed, developed and extended. The ACTOR protocol is used to interconnect the BNCI system with the user's living environment. This includes elements such as lighting, shades, heating, ventilation, audio, video services such as radio or TV, intercoms and many more.

It further provides access to social network and online communication services, thereby augmenting the user's social inclusion. The user has access to all of these devices, services and social interaction tools and is able to control them through the BCI system.

5.4. Games and social media

The intendiX ACTOR protocol, in connection with the intendiX SOCI API, can also be used to control games such as World of War craft (WoW) [29] and social media like Twitter (Twitter Inc. USA) or Second Life (Linden Lab, USA).

World of Warcraft is a common Massively Multiplayer Online Role-Playing Game (MMORPG) in which the player controls an avatar in a virtual environment. The BCI system uses an SSVEP paradigm to control an avatar in WoW [29]. For basic movements, selecting objects or firing weapons, four control icons as shown in figure 12 are required. The bottom three icons are used to move the avatar forward and turn left or right. The fourth icon, the action icon, is located top left. It used to perform actions like grasping objects or attacking other opponents. Stimulation is done on the same 60 Hz LCD-display that also renders the game itself.

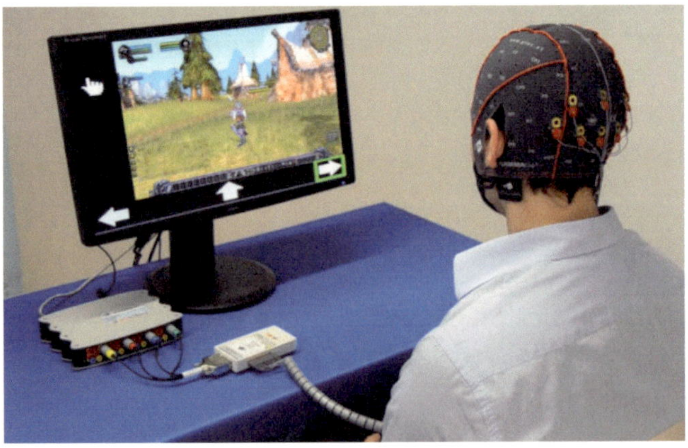

Courtesy of g.tec medical engineering GmbH, 2012

Figure 12. The intendiX SOCI module is used in combination with the intendiX ACTOR protocol to control the movements and actions of an avatar within the World of Warcraft multiplayer online game from Blizzard Entertainment, Inc.

Twitter (Twitter Inc.) is a social network that enables the user to send and read messages. The messages are limited to 140 characters and are displayed in the author's profile page. Messages can be sent via the Twitter website or via smart phones or SMS (Short Message Service). Twitter provides also an application programming interface to send and receive SMS.

Figure 13a shows a UML diagram of the actions required to use e.g. the Twitter service. The intendiX ACTOR protocol is used to interconnect the Twitter interface with the BCI. This system uses a standard P300 spelling matrix (figure 13b), which was extended with commands required for Twitter. The two top rows contain symbols representing corresponding Twitter services, and the remaining characters are used for spelling.

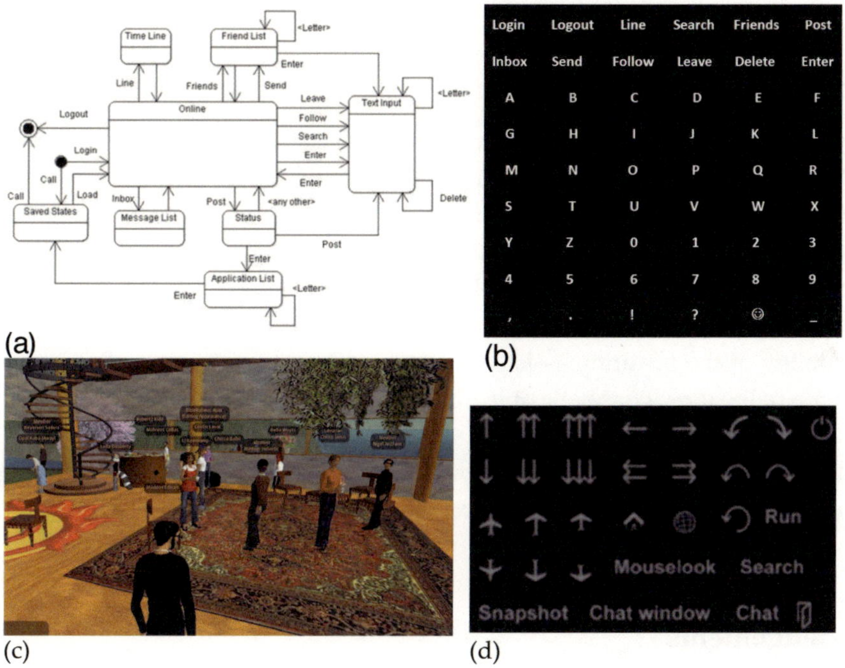

Figure 13. UML diagram of Twitter (a). A P300 BCI with a Twitter interface mask (b). Screenshot of a Second Life environment (c). The Second Life interface main mask for moving the avatar, climbing, running, flying, teleporting home, displaying a map, showing the search mask, taking snapshots, chatting with other members and managing the second life session (d).

Second Life is a free 3D online virtual world that can be accessed through the "Second Life Viewer", which is free client software. A dedicated user account is necessary to participate in Second Life. One of the main activities in Second Life is socializing with other so-called residents. Each resident represents a person in the real world. Furthermore, it is possible to perform different actions like holding business meetings, taking pictures or making movies, attending courses, etc. Communication takes place via text chats, voice chats and gestures. Hence, handicapped people could also participate in Second Life just like any other user if an appropriate interface is available.

To control Second Life, three different interface masks were developed. Figure 13c displays a screenshot of a Second Life scene. The main mask (figure 13d) offers 31 different choices. The masks for control like 'chatting' provided 55 control elements and the one for 'searching' 40 selections. Each of the icons represents an actual command to be executed within Second Life. Whenever a certain icon is selected, Second Life is notified to execute this individual action. Thereby, a dedicated keyboard event generator is used to convert messages based on the intendiX ACTOR protocol into appropriate key strokes. Further details on the BCI integration with Twitter and Second Life, including the results achieved by healthy subjects, are discussed in [33].

6. Conclusion

Current research projects aim to establish BCI systems as assistive technologies for disabled people, thereby helping them interact with their living environment and facilitating social interaction. These efforts rely on properly interfacing the BCI with supporting systems, devices, services and tools. For example, this interface could embody the user in an avatar or robot, as done within VERE, or in a robotic assistant, as implemented within ALIAS. The design and implementation of the interfaces between the BCI and the application do have an impact on the flexibility of the resulting assistive system or device and thus on the autonomy and independence of the user. Highly flexible interfaces like intendiX ACTOR and intendiX SOCI make it possible to adapt the BCI to the user's needs while providing a standardized interface for using the BCI as control and interaction device with a large and constantly growing number of applications, assistive services and devices.

Acknowledgements

This work was supported in part by the European Union FP7 Integrated Project VERE, grant agreement no. 257695 and BrainAble by the European Community's, Seventh Framework Programme FP7/2007-2013, grant agreement n° 247447. The authors gratefully acknowledge the support of the ALIAS project funded by the by the German BMBF, the French ANR and the Austrian BMVIT within the AAL-2009-2 strategic objective of the Ambient Assisted Living (AAL) Joint Programme.

Author details

Christoph Hintermüller, Christoph Kapeller, Günter Edlinger and Christoph Guger

g.tec Mmedical Eengineering GmbH/ Guger Technologies OG, Austria

References

[1] Wolpaw, J. R, Birbaumer, N, Mcfarland, D. J, Pfurtscheller, G, & Vaughan, T. M. Brain-computer interfaces for communication and control," Clin. Neurophysiol., June (2002)., 113(6), 767-791.

[2] Krusienski, D. J, Sellers, E. W, Mcfarland, D. J, Vaughan, T. M, & Wolpaw, J. R. Toward enhanced P300 speller performance," J. Neurosci. Methods, January (2008)., 167(1), 15-21.

[3] Ortner, R, Bruckner, M, Prückl, R, Grünbacher, E, Costa, U, Opisso, E, Medina, J, & Guger, C. Accuracy of a Speller for People with Motor Impairments," Proceedings of the IEEE Symposium Series on Computational Intelligence (2011). in press., 300.

[4] Guger, C, Krausz, G, Allison, B. Z, & Edlinger, G. (2012). A comparison of dry and gel-based electrodes for BCIs. Frontiers in Neuroscience, 6:60., 300.

[5] Farwell, L. A, & Donchin, E. Talking off the top of your head: toward a mental prosthesis utilizing event-related brain potentials," Electroencephalogr. Clin. Neurophysiol., December (1988)., 70(6), 510-523.

[6] Finke, A, Lenhardt, A, & Ritter, H. The MindGame: A P300-based brain-computer interface game," Neural Networks, November (2009)., 22(9), 1329-1333.

[7] Citi, L, Poli, R, Cinel, C, & Sepulveda, F. P300-Based BCI Mouse With Genetically-Optimized Analogue Control," IEEE Trans. Neural Syst. Rehabil. Eng., February (2008)., 16(1), 51-61.

[8] Friman, O, Volosyak, I, & Graser, A. Multiple channel detection of steady-state visual evoked potentials for brain-computer interfaces. IEEE Trans Biomed Eng., 54(4): 742-750, (2007).

[9] Wang, Y, Gao, X, Hong, B, Jia, C, & Gao, S. Brain-Computer Interfaces Based on Visual Evoked Potentials. IEEE Eng Med Biol Mag. (2008). Sep-Oct;, 27(5), 64-71.

[10] Faller, J, Müller-putz, G. R, Schmalstieg, D, & Pfurtscheller, G. An Application Framework for Controlling an Avatar in a Desktop-Based Virtual Environment via a Software SSVEP Brain-Computer Interface. Teleoperators and Virtual Environments-Presence, (2010)., 19(1), 25-34.

[11] Kapeller, C, Hintermüller, C, Abu-alqumsam, M, Schau, T, Gro, B, Windhager, V, Putz, R, Prückl, A, & Peer, C. Guger, SSVEP based Brain-Computer Interface combined with video for robotic control, IEEE Transactions on Computational Intelligence and AI in Games (2012).

[12] Guger, C, Ramoser, H, & Pfurtscheller, G. (2000). Real-time EEG analysis with Suject-Specific spatial patterns for a Brain-Computer Interface (BCI). *IEEE Transactions on Rehabilitation Engineering*, , 8-4, 447-456.

[13] Blankertz, B, Tomioka, R, Lemm, S, Kawanabe, M, & Müller, K. R. Optimizing spatial filters for robust EEG, *IEEE Signal Processing Magazine*, 25(1) ((2008).

[14] Schalk, G, Wolpaw, J, Mcfarland, D, & Pfurtscheller, G. EEG-based communication: Presence of an error potential," *Clin. Neurophysiol.*, (2000). , 111, 2138-2144.

[15] Parra, L, Spence, C, Gerson, A, & Sajda, P. Response error correction-A demonstration of improved human-machine performance using real-time EEG monitoring," *IEEE Trans. Neural Syst. Rehabil. Eng.*, Jun. (2003). , 11(2), 173-177.

[16] Blankertz, B, Dornhege, G, Schäfer, C, Krepki, R, Kohlmorgen, J, Müller, K. -R, Kunzmann, V, Losch, F, & Curio, G. Boosting bit rates and error detection for the classification of fast-paced motor commands based on single-trial EEG analysis," *IEEE Trans. Neural Syst. Rehabil. Eng.*, Jun. (2003). , 11(2), 127-131.

[17] Ferrez, P, Del, J, & Millán, R. You are wrong!-Automatic detection of interaction errors from brain waves," in *Proc. 19th Int. Joint Conf. Artificial Intell.*, (2005).

[18] g.tec medical Engineering GmBH. (2012). "g.HIGHsys." Retrieved September 2012, from http://www.gtec.at/Products/Software/High-Speed-Online-Processing-under-Simulink-Specs-Features.

[19] Brunner, C, Andreoni, G, Bianchi, L, Blankertz, B, Breitweiser, C, Kanoh, S, Kothe, C, Lecuyer, A, Makeig, S, Mellinger, J, Perego, P, Renard, Y, Schalk, G, Susila, I. P, Venthur, B, & Müller-putz, G. (2013). BCI Software Platforms. In: Toward Practical BCIs: Bridging the Gap from Research to Real-World Applications, Allison, B.Z., Dunne, S., Leeb, R., Millan, J., and Nijholt, A. Springer-Verlag Berlin, , 303-331.

[20] French National Institute for Research in Computer Science and Control (INRIA)INRIA), Rennes, France, "OpenViBe", Retrieved September (2012). from http://openvibe.inria.fr

[21] Swartz Center for Computational NeuroscienceUniversity of California, CA, San Diego, USA, "BCILAB", Retrieved September (2012). from http://sccn.ucsd.edu/wiki/BCILAB

[22] Department of Electronics and Intelligent SystemsTohoku Institute of Technology, Sendai, Japan, "xBCI", Retrieved September (2012). from http://xbci.sourceforge.net

[23] Wadsworth CenterNew York State Department of Health, Albany, NY, USA, "BCI2000", Retrieved September (2012). from http://www.bci2000.org

[24] TOBI Tools for Brain-Computer Interaction projectTOBI", Retrieved September (2012). from http://www.tobi-project.org

[25] Realtime bio-signal standardsTobi iC Definition, implementation and scenarios", Retrieved August (2012). from http://www.bcistandards.org/softwarestandards/tic

[26] g.tec medical engineering GmbH, "intendiX", Retrieved September 2012, from http://www.intendix.com/ and http://www.gtec.at/Products/Complete-Solutions/intendiX-Specs-Features

[27] Putz, V, Guger, C, Holzner, C, Torrellas, S, & Miralles, F. A Unified XML Based Description of the Contents of Brain-Computer Interfaces.," in Proc. 5th International Brain-Computer Interface Confernece 2011, (2011). pp. Pages.

[28] SGI(2012). OpenGL- The Industry's Foundation for High Performance Graphics." Retrieved July 2012, from http://www.opengl.org/

[29] Blizzard Entertainment Inc(2012). World of Warcraft." Retrieved July 2012, from http://us.battle.net/wow/en/.

[30] VERE Virtual Embodiment and Robotic Re-EmbodimentProject Website, Retrieved September (2012). from http://www.vereproject.eu/

[31] ALIASAdaptable Ambient Living Assistant, Project Website, Retrieved September (2012). from http://www.aal-alias.eu/

[32] BrainAbleProject Website, Retrieved September (2012). from http://www.brainable.org/en/Pages/Home.aspx

[33] Edlinger, G, & Guger, C. Social environments, mixed communication and goal-oriented control application using a Brain-Computer Interface", Prof. Human Computer Interface Conference, Orlando, (2011). in press.

Chapter 3

Adaptive Network Fuzzy Inference Systems for Classification in a Brain Computer Interface

Vahid Asadpour, Mohammmd Reza Ravanfar and
Reza Fazel-Rezai

Additional information is available at the end of the chapter

http://dx.doi.org/10.5772/55989

1. Introduction

Fuzzy theory provides the basis for Fuzzy Inference Systems (FIS) which is a useful tool for classifications of data, static and dynamic process modeling and identification, decision making, classification, and control of processes. These characteristics could be used in different kinds of FIS and be applied to Brain Computer Interface (BCI) systems which are discussed in this chapter.

The first kind of FIS is designed based on the ability of fuzzy logic to model human perception. These FIS elaborates fuzzy rules originates from expert knowledge and they are called fuzzy expert system. Expert knowledge was also used prior to FIS to construct expert systems for simulation purposes. These expert systems were based on Boolean algebra and were not well defined to adapt to regressive intrinsic of underlying process phenomena. Despite that, fuzzy logic allows the rules to be gradually introduced into expert simulators due to input in a knowledge based manner. It also depicts the limitations of human knowledge, particularly the ambiguities in formalizing interactions in complex processes. This type of FIS offers high semantic degree and good generalization ability. Unfortunately, the complexity of large systems may lead to high ambiguities and insufficient accuracies which lead to poor performances [1].

Another class of modeling tools is based on adaptive knowledge based learning from data. This category includes supervised learning and outputs of observations when the training data is provided. A numerical performance index can be defined in such simulators which are usually based on the mean square error. Neural networks have become very popular and efficient in this field. Their main characteristic is the numerical accuracy while they also provide a qualitative black box behavior. The first self-learning FIS was proposed by Sugeno that provided a way to design the second kind of FIS [2]. In this case, even if the fuzzy rules are expressed in the form of expert rules, a loss of semantic occurs because of direct generation of weights from data. These types of simulators are usually named Adaptive Network Fuzzy Inference System (ANFIS).

There are methods for constructing fuzzy structures by using rule-based inference. These methods extract the rules directly from data and can be considered as rule generation approaches. Generation of the rules includes preliminary rule generation and rule adaptation according to input and output data. Automatic rule generation methods were applied to simple systems with limited number of variables. These simple systems do not need to optimize the rule base. It is different for complex systems. The number of generated rules becomes enormous and the description of rules becomes more complex due to the number of variables. The simulator will be easier to interpret if it is defined by the most influential variables. Also, the system behavior will be more comprehensive when the number of rules becomes smaller. Therefore, variable selection and rule reduction are two important subcategories of the rule generation process which is called structure optimization. A FIS has many more parameters that can also be optimized including membership functions and rule conclusions. A thorough study in these fields and their respective advantages and considerations are provided in the following sections.

In this chapter, several feature extraction and classification methods which could be applied to BCI systems are discussed.

2. Feature extraction

In the following sections, the features which are used to compose feature vectors are discussed. These features provide various views of EEG signal which can be used in ANFIS classification system.

2.1. Energy ratio features

EEG features in a BCI system can be obtained by the frequency analysis of the observed data sequence. For example, in steady state visual evoked potential (SSVEP) BCIs, the frequencies of the light oscillation should be detected. The frequency domain analysis gives a clear picture of changes. Because of frequency changes during BCI, energy ratios between different EEG sub-bands can be computed for each channel during BCI. It is shown that there would be BCI related changes in the EEG according to the brain activities and electrode locations ([3], [4] and [5]). For instance, to discover the brain rhythms during BCI, alpha (8-13 Hz), beta (13-35 Hz), delta (0-4 Hz), and theta (4-8 Hz) band energy ratios of spectrogram SPEC(t, f) at time t and frequency f may be calculated as shown in equations (1) to (4) [6]. They show the total energy of each defined spectral band relative to total signal energy:

$$\alpha = \frac{\int_{8}^{13} SPEC(t,\ f)df}{\int_{0}^{35} SPEC(t,\ f)df} \tag{1}$$

$$\beta = \frac{\int_{13}^{35} SPEC(t,\ f)df}{\int_{0}^{35} SPEC(t,\ f)df} \tag{2}$$

$$\delta = \frac{\int_{0}^{4} SPEC(t,\ f)df}{\int_{0}^{35} SPEC(t,\ f)df} \tag{3}$$

$$\theta = \frac{\int_{4}^{8} SPEC(t,\ f)df}{\int_{0}^{35} SPEC(t,\ f)df} \tag{4}$$

2.2. Approximate entropy

Approximate entropy is a recently formulated family of parameters and statistics quantifying regularity (orderliness) in serial data [4]. It has been used mainly in the analysis of heart rate variability [7, 8], endocrine hormone release pulsatility [9], estimating regularity in epileptic seizure time series data [10] and estimating the depth of anesthesia [2]. Approximate entropy assigns a non-negative number to a time series, with larger values corresponding to more complexity or irregularity in the data. EEG signal represents regular and uniform pattern during synchronized cooperative function of cortical cells. This pattern results to low entropy values. In contrast, concentric functions and higher levels of brain activity lead to high values of entropy. Shannon entropy H is defined as:

$$H = -\sum_{i=1}^{N} P_i \log_2 P_i \tag{5}$$

in which P_i is the average probability that amplitude of i th frequency band of brain rhythm be greater than r times standard deviation and N is the total number of frequency bands. H is 0 for a single frequency and 1 for uniform frequency distribution over total spectrum. Because of the non-linear characteristics of EEG signals, approximate entropy can be used as a powerful tool in the study of the EEG activity. In principle, the accuracy and confidence of the entropy estimate improve as the number of matches of length r and $m+1$ increases. Although m and r are critical in determining the outcome of approximate entropy, no guidelines exist for optimizing their values. $m=3$ and $r=0.25$ could be selected based on an investigation on original data sequence. Therefore, one dimensions of feature vector could be provided.

2.3. Fractal dimension

Fractal dimension emphasizes the geometric property of basin of attraction. These dimension show geometrical property of attractors and is also computed very fast [15]. Our goal was to associate each 5-second segment data as a trial to its corresponding class. To do this, features were extracted from each 1 second segment with 50% overlap, and sequence of 9 extracted features were considered as the feature vector of a 5-second segment, which was to be modeled and classified. In Higuchi's algorithm, k new time series are constructed from the signal $x(1),\ x(2),\ x(3),\ \ldots,\ x(N)$ under study is [3]:

$$x_m^k = \left\{x(m),\ x(m+k),\ x(m+2k),\ \ldots,\ x\left(m+\left[\frac{N-m}{k}\right]k\right)\right\} \tag{6}$$

in which $m=1,\ 2,\ \ldots,\ k$ and k indicate the initial time value, and the discrete time interval between points, respectively. For each of the k time series x_m^k the length $L_m(k)$ is computed by:

$$L_m(k) = \frac{\sum_i |x(m+ik) - x(m+(i-1)k)|(N-1)}{\left[\frac{N-m}{k}\right]k} \tag{7}$$

in which N is the total length of the signal x. An average length is computed as the mean of the k lengths $L_m(k)$ (for $m=1,\ 2,\ \ldots,\ k$). This procedure is repeated for each k ranging from 1 to k_{max}, obtaining an average length for each k. In the curve of $ln(L(k))$ versus $ln(1/k)$, the slope of the best fitted line to this curve is the estimate of the fractal dimension.

2.4. Lyapunov exponent

Lyapunov exponents are a quantitative measure for distinguishing among the various types of orbits based upon their sensitive dependence on the initial conditions, and are used to determine the stability of any steady-state behavior, including chaotic solutions [4]. The reason why chaotic systems show aperiodic dynamics is that phase space trajectories that have nearly identical initial states will separate from each other at an exponentially increasing rate captured by the so called Lyapunov exponent. The Lyapunov exponents can be estimated from the observed time series [5]. This approach is described as follows: consider two (usually the nearest) neighboring points in phase space at time 0 and at time t, distances of the points in the i*th* direction being $\|\delta X_i(0)\|$ and $\|\delta X_i(t)\|$, respectively. The Lyapunov exponent is then defined by the average growth rate λ i of the initial distance [6]

$$\frac{\|\delta X_i(t)\|}{\|\delta X_i(0)\|} = 2^{\lambda_i}(t \to \infty) \tag{8}$$

or

$$\lambda_i = \lim_{t\to\infty} \frac{1}{t} \log_2 \frac{\|\delta X_i(t)\|}{\|\delta X_i(0)\|}. \tag{9}$$

Generally, Lyapunov exponents can be extracted from observed signals in two different ways [7]. The first method is based on the idea of following the time evolution of nearby points in the state space [17]. This method provides an estimation of the largest Lyapunov exponent only. The second method is based on the estimation of local Jacobi matrices and is capable of estimating all the Lyapunov exponents [18]. Vectors of all the Lyapunov exponents for particular systems are often called their Lyapunov spectra. This method was used for Lyapunov vector extraction in this section. An optimized size of 7 is considered for the vector which led to the best mean classification rate on the support vector machine (SVM) classifier.

2.5. Kalman feature extractor

The algorithm to be discussed in this section is based on the Kalman estimation, which is well known in statistical estimation and control theory ([8], [9], and [10]) but perhaps not so in parameter estimation. Therefore, the next paragraphs explain its function in the special context. Kalman filter is essentially a set of mathematical expressions that provides a predictor-modifier estimator. This estimator minimizes the error covariance and therefore is an optimum estimator if appropriate initial condition is selected. The condition for optimum estimation is rarely satisfied however the estimator performs well in sub-optimum situations. Kalman estimator is used for adaptive estimation of dynamic parameters of EEG. The estimator reduces the error variance adaptively and after a period of time a unique estimation is achieved [11].

A Kalman filter computes the response $x \in \mathrm{R}^n$ for the system which is defined by linear differential equation:

$$x_k = Ax_{k-1} + Bu_k + w_{k-1} \tag{10}$$

in which x is the system state, A and B are the state and input matrices, u is input and w is the process error. $z \in \mathrm{R}^m$ is the measured value and is defined as:

$$z_k = H x_k + v_k \tag{11}$$

in which H is the output matrix and v is the measurement error.

The estimate and process errors are considered independent additive white Gaussian noises. In practice these are time varying processes which are considered stationary for simplicity.

If there is not input or process noise the matrix $A_{n\times n}$ relates the state of the system at last stage to current stage. A is practically a time varying matrix but it is considered constant in computations. $B_{n\times 1}$ relates the control input u to the state x. $H_{m\times n}$ relates the state x to the measurements z_k. H is also time varying but is considered constant in computations.

Consider the system

$$x_{k+1} = (A + \Delta A_k)x_k + Bw_k \tag{12}$$

$$y_k = (C + \Delta C_k)x_k + v_k \tag{13}$$

in which $x_k \in \mathrm{R}^n$ is state space, $w_k \in \mathrm{R}^q$ is process noise, $y_k \in \mathrm{R}^m$ is measurements and $v_k \in \mathrm{R}^m$ is measurement noise. Furthermore ΔA_k and ΔC_k represent the variations of parameters. They could be considered as

$$\begin{bmatrix} \Delta A_k \\ \Delta C_k \end{bmatrix} = \begin{bmatrix} H_1 \\ H_2 \end{bmatrix} F_k E \tag{14}$$

in which $F_k \in \mathrm{R}^{i \times j}$ is a real time invariant matrix that satisfies the condition

$$F_k^T F_k \leq I, \ \ k \geq 0 \,] \tag{15}$$

and H_1, H_2 and E are real matrices that define how A and C elements are affected due to F_k variations. These matrices are estimated using a separate recursive least square estimation [12].

The state-space representation of a linear system is much more flexible and useful than the transfer function form because it includes both time-dependent and time-independent systems and also encompasses stochastic and deterministic systems. Furthermore, it is possible to evaluate precisely concepts of observability and controllability, which are useful in determining whether the desired unknown parameters of a system can be estimated from the given observations for instance.

A modification is performed on state estimation algorithm in this section to overcame the lake of deterministic and stationary input w_k. The algorithm is based on observations rather than inputs. The algorithm estimates the state vector given observations up to sample k. The algorithm will fail if the desired unknown states cannot be found from the observations gathered, therefore the observability of the system states must first be verified. This is performed by determining the rank of the observability matrix in the observation interval $n_1 \leq n \leq n_2$, defined as [13]

$$O = \sum_{i=n_1}^{n_2} \left[\left| \prod_{k=0}^{i-1} A_k^T \right| H_i^T H_i \left| \prod_{k=0}^{i-1} A_k^T \right|^T \right] \tag{16}$$

If O is rank-deficient, then it is not possible to obtain unique estimates of $\{x_{n_1}, \ \ldots, \ x_{n_2}\}$. A time-invariant system, in which H and A are not time-varying, O can be on a much simpler form, but in the nonlinear parameter estimator described here, this simplification is not available. Assuming the system model observable, the state-space parameter estimation problem may be stated as follows. Given observations $\{y_0, \ \ldots, \ y_n\}$ and the state-space model (2) and (3), find the optimal estimate of x_n, denoted $\hat{x}_{n|n}$.

If the noise vectors w_k and v_k assumed to be independent individually and mutually and uncorrelated with correlation matrices

$$E\left[w_i w_j^T\right] = Q_i \delta_{ij} \tag{17}$$

$$E\left[v_i v_j^T\right] = R_i \delta_{ij}] \tag{18}$$

$$E\left[w_i v_j^T\right] = 0 \tag{19}$$

Where δ_{ij} is the two dimensional delta function, then the Kalman filter provides the MMSE estimate of x_k as

$$\hat{x}_{n|n} = arg \min_{\hat{x}_n} E\left\{\| x_n - \hat{x}_n \|^2 | n\right\} \tag{20}$$

The recursive Riccati equations are used to estimate the parameters [14]. The algorithm for kalman feature extraction is as follows [15]:

1. Initial estimates for $\hat{x}_k^+$ and P_{k-1}^+

2. Project the state ahead:

$\hat{x}_k^- = A_k \hat{x}_{k-1}^+$

3. Project the error covariance ahead:

$P_k^- = A_k P_{k-1}^+ A_k^T + w_k$

4. Compute the Kalman gain:

$K_k = P_k^- A_k^T \left(A_k P_k^- A_k^T + R_k\right)^{-1}$

5. Update feature vector estimate $\hat{x}_k^+$ with measurement y_k:

$\hat{x}_k^+ = \hat{x}_k^- + K_k\left(y_k - A_k \hat{x}_k^-\right)$

6. Update the error covariance:

$P_k^+ = (I - K_k A_k) P_k^-$

Kalman feature extractor uses the estimates of dynamics system state equation, with the new information contained in y_k fed back into the system through the Kalman gain. The block diagram description of the Kalman filter is given in Figure 1. A very important feature of the Kalman filter is that the error covariance does not depend on the observations. Hence $P_{k|k-1}$ can be pre-computed and the accuracy of the filter assessed before the observations are made. In particular, we may investigate the asymptotic behaviour of the filter by analyzing the discrete time Riccati equation.

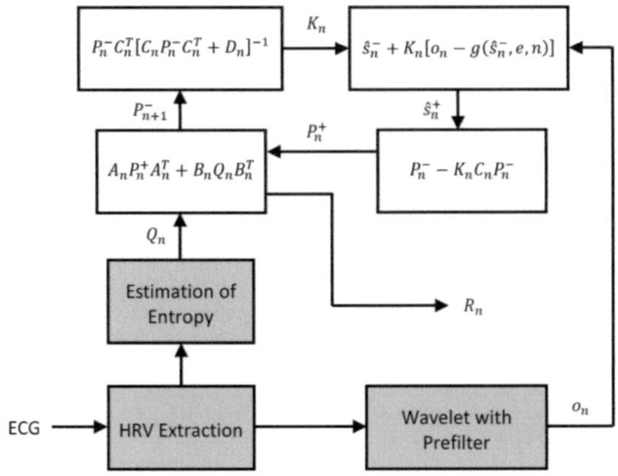

Figure 1. Block diagram of Kalman feature extractor [15].

3. Classification

The support vector machine (SVM) method has been used extensively for classification of EEG signals [16]. It is shown that EEG signal has separable intrinsic vectors which could be used in SVM classifier. SVM classifiers use discriminant hyper-planes for classification. The selected hyper-planes are those that maximize the margin of classification edges. The distance from the nearest training points usually measured based on a non-linear kernel to map the problem to a linear solvation space [17]. A Radial Basis Function (RBF) kernel based SVM is proposed here that Lagrangian optimization is performed using an adjustable ANFIS algorithm. It will be shown that due to conceptual nature of BCI for patients this proposed method leads to adjustable soft decision classification.

3.1. Classification using nonlinear SVM with RBF kernel

Training the SVM is a quadratic optimization problem in which the hyperplane is defined as [18]:

$$y_i(w\Phi(x_i,\ y_j)+b)\geq 1-\xi_i,\ \ \xi_i\geq 0,\ \ i=1,\ \ldots,\ l,\ \ j=1,\ \ldots,\ m \tag{21}$$

in which x_i is input vector, b is bias, w is adapted weights, ξ_i is class separation, $\Phi(x_i, y_j)$ is the mapping kernel, l is the number of training vectors, j is the number of output vectors, and y_i is desired output vector. The weight parameters should be achieved so that the margin between the hyperplane and the nearest point to be maximized. The only free parameter, C, in SVMs controlled the trade-off between the maximization of margin and the amount of misclassifications. Optimization of equation (9) yields to optimum w which is the answer of problem. It could be done using Lagrange multipliers defined as [11]:

$$L\ (w,\ b,\ \alpha,\ \mu)=\frac{1}{2}\|w\|^2+C\sum_{i=1}^{l}\xi_i-\sum_{i=1}^{l}\sum_{j=1}^{m}\alpha_i\alpha_j(y_j(w\Phi(x_i,\ y_j)+b-1+\xi_i))-\sum_{i=1}^{l}\mu_i\xi_i \tag{22}$$

in which $C > \alpha_i$, $\alpha_j \geq 0$ *and* $\mu_i \geq 0$ *for* $i = 1, \ \ldots, \ l$ *and* $j = 1, \ \ldots, \ m$ and C is the upper bond for Lagrange coefficient. The coefficient C is a representation of error penalty so that higher values yield to bigger penalties. Karush-Kuhn-Tucher conditions lead to optimization of Lagrange multipliers [19]:

$$\frac{\partial L}{\partial W_v} = W_v - \sum_i \alpha_i y_i x_{iv} = 0 \tag{23}$$

$$\frac{\partial L}{\partial b} = - \sum_i \alpha_i y_i = 0 \tag{24}$$

$$\frac{\partial L}{\partial \xi_i} = C - \alpha - \mu_i \tag{25}$$

subject to

$$\mu_i(w\Phi(x_i, \ y_j) + b - 1 + \xi_i) \geq 0, \ \ \xi_i \geq 0, \ \ \alpha_i \geq 0 \tag{26}$$

and,

$$\alpha_i(y_i(w\Phi(x_i, \ y_j) + b - 1 + \xi_i)) = 0. \tag{27}$$

Usually nonlinear kernels provide classification hyper-planes that cannot be achieved by linear weighting [20]. Using appropriate kernels, SVM offered an efficient tool for flexible classification with a highly nonlinear decision boundary. RBF kernel was used in this section which is defined as:

$$\Phi(x, \ y) = exp\left(\frac{-\| x - y \|^2}{2\sigma^2} \right) \tag{28}$$

in which σ is the standard deviation. The proposed feature extraction method is depicted in Figure 2. The outputs are fed to the adjustable ANFIS described in next section. Two parameters had to be selected beforehand: the trade-off parameter C and the kernel standard deviation σ. They could be optimized for an optimal generalization performance in the traditional way, by using an independent test set or n-fold cross-validation. It has been suggested that the parameters could be chosen by optimizing the upper bound of the generalization error solely based on training data [26]. The fraction of support vectors, i.e., the quotient between the number of support vectors and all training samples, gave an upper bound on the leave-one-out error estimate because the resulting decision function changed only when support vectors were omitted. Therefore, a low fraction of support vectors could be used as a criterion for the parameter selection.

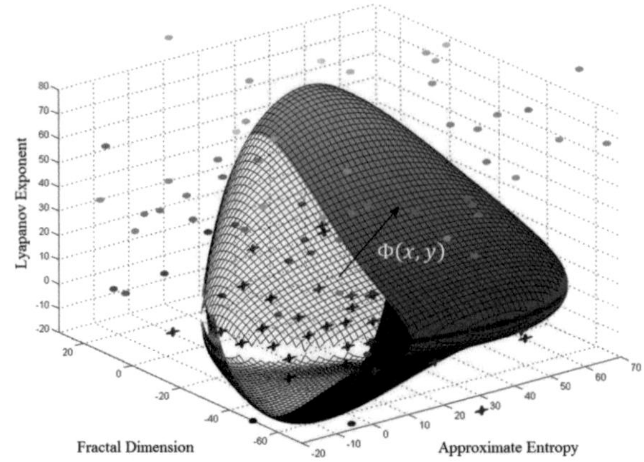

Figure 2. An example of feature vector for radial basis function kernel [15].

3.2. Adjustable ANFIS optimization

An ANFIS system could be used with Sugeno fuzzy model for fine adjustment of SVM classification kernels. Such framework makes the ANFIS modeling more systematic and less reliant on expert knowledge and therefore facilitates learning and adjustment. The ANFIS structure is shown in Figure 3. In the first layer, all the nodes are adaptive nodes. The outputs of layer 1 are the fuzzy membership grade of the inputs, which are given by [21]:

$$O_i^1=\mu_{A_i}(x),\ i=1,\ 2 \text{ and } O_i^1=\mu_{B_{i-2}}(x),\ i=3,\ 4 \tag{29}$$

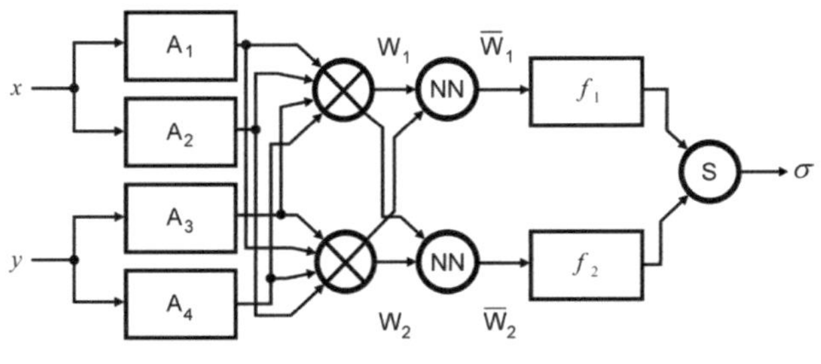

Figure 3. An example of feature vector for radial basis function kernel.

O_i^1 is the i th output of layer 1, $\mu_{A_i}(x)$ and $\mu_{B_{i-2}}(x)$ are type A and type B arbitrary fuzzy membership functions of nodes i and i - 2, respectively. In the second and third layer, the nodes are fixed nodes. They are labeled M and N respectively, indicating they perform as a simple multiplier. The outputs of these layers can be represented as:

$$O_i^2=w_i=\mu_{A_i}(x)\mu_{B_i}(x),\ i=1,\ \ldots,4 \tag{30}$$

$$O_i^3 = \bar{w}_i = \frac{w_i}{w_i + w_{i+1}} i = 1, \quad \ldots, 4 \tag{31}$$

which are the so-called normalized firing strengths. In the fourth layer, the nodes are adaptive nodes. The output of each node in this layer is simply the product of the normalized firing strength and a first order polynomial for the first order Sugeno model. The outputs of this layer are given by:

$$O_i^4 = \bar{w}_i f_i = \bar{w}_i (p_i x + q_i y + r_i) i = 1, \quad \ldots, 4 \tag{32}$$

in which f_i is the firing rate, p_i is the x scale, q_i is the y scale, and r_i is the bias for i th node. In the fifth layer, there is only one single fixed node that performs the summation of all incoming signals:

$$O_i^5 = \sum_{i=1}^{2} \bar{w}_i f_i = \sum_{i=1}^{2} \frac{w_i f_i}{w_i + w_{i+1}} \tag{33}$$

It can be observed that there are two adaptive layers in this ANFIS architecture, namely the first layer and the fourth layer. In the first layer, there are three modifiable parameters $\{a_i, \ b_i, \ c_i\}$, which are related to the input membership functions. These parameters are the so-called premise parameters. In the fourth layer, there are also three modifiable parameters $\{p_i, \ q_i, \ r_i\}$, pertaining to the first order polynomial. These parameters are so-called consequent parameters.

The task of the learning algorithm for this architecture is to tune all the above mentioned modifiable parameters to make the ANFIS output match the training data. When the premise parameters of the membership function are fixed, the output of the ANFIS model can be written as:

$$\sigma = (\bar{w}_1 x) p_1 + (\bar{w}_1 x) q_1 + (\bar{w}_1 x) r_1 + (\bar{w}_2 x) p_2 + (\bar{w}_2 y) q_2 + (\bar{w}_2) r_2. \tag{34}$$

This is a linear combination of the modifiable consequent parameters $p_1, \ q_1, \ r_1, \ p_2, \ q_2$ and r_2. When the premise parameters are fixed the least squares method is used easily to identify the optimal values of these parameters after adjustment of ANFIS weights using SVM. When the premise parameters are not fixed, the search space becomes larger and the convergence of the training becomes slower.

A hybrid algorithm combining the least squares method and the gradient descent method was adopted to identify the optimal values of these parameters [22]. The hybrid algorithm is composed of a forward pass and a backward pass. The least squares method (forward pass) was used to optimize the consequent parameters with the premise parameters fixed. Once the optimal consequent parameters are found, the backward pass starts immediately. The gradient descent method (backward pass) was used to adjust optimally the premise parameters corresponding to the fuzzy sets in the input domain. The output of the ANFIS was calculated by employing the consequent parameters found in the forward pass. The output error was used to adapt the premise parameters by means of a standard back propagation algorithm. It has been shown that this hybrid algorithm is highly efficient in training the ANFIS [21].

A classification method base on ANFIS adapted SVM proposed in this section. It showed that non-linear features improve classification rate as an effective component. Through the feature space constructed using approximate entropy and fractal dimension in addition to conventional spectral features, different stages of EEG signals can be recognized from each other expressly. The successful implementations of ANFIS-SVM for EEG signal classification was reported in this context. The results confirmed that this method provides better performance in datasets with lower dimension. This performance achieved for RBF kernel of SVM modified by ANFIS. This section can be a strong base for improved methods in the field of BCI cognition and analysis for therapeutic applications.

3.3. Recursive least square

In this method a third order AR model is used that directly estimates EEG parameters without using any intrinsic model. Such linear methods could be used to estimate nonlinear systems in piece wise linear manner. $\varphi^T(t-1) = -[X(t-1) \quad X(t-2) \quad X(t-3)]^T$ is input matrix in which $X(t)$ is input at time t and $\hat{\theta}(t) = -[b_1 \quad b_2 \quad b_3]^T$ is the model parameters. Iterative least square parameter modification is computed by following equations [23].

$$\hat{\theta}(t) = \hat{\theta}(t-1) + \left(\varphi^T(t)\varphi(t)\right)^{-1}\varphi(t-1)\xi(t) \tag{35}$$

$$\xi(t) = X(t) - \varphi^T(t-1)\hat{\theta}(t-1) \tag{36}$$

Use of parametric model provides a time variant estimate of state equations of system at the working point. It is in accordance to the highly variable nature of EEG signals. In fact the modeling of nonlinear and time variant signal using a feature vector with limited dimensions provides a filtering on data. The abstract characteristics of signal would be extracted that leads to lower variance compared to the frequency feature extraction methods. Dimension of feature vector is a critical point to avoid over learning for high values of features or lake of convergence due to small size of feature vector.

3.4. Coupled hidden Markov models

Use of multimodal approaches provides improvement in robustness of classification under disturbances. This could extend the margin of security for BCI systems. Integration of two sets of features namely set a and set b could be done by various methods. Several integration models have been proposed in the literature that can be divided into early integration (EI) and late integration (LI). In the EI model, information is integrated in the feature space to form a feature vector combined of both features. Classification is based on this composite feature vector. The model is based on assumption of conditional dependence between different modes and therefore is more general than the LI model. In the LI model, the modules are pre-classified independently of each other. The final classification is based on the fusion of both modules by evaluating their joint occurrence. This method is based on assumption of conditional independency of both data streams. It is generally accepted that the auditory system performs partial identification in independent channels, whereas, BCI classification seems to be based on early integration which assumes conditional dependence between both modules [24]. This theory is based on LI method and models pseudo-synchronization between modules to account some temporal dependency between them. It is a compromise of EI and LI schemes. The bimodal signal is considered as an observation vector consists of two sets of features. Optimum classifier which is based on Bayesian decision theory could be obtained using the maximum *a posteriori* probability function [25]:

$$\lambda_0 = \max_{\lambda} P(\lambda \mid (O^a, O^b)) = P((O^a, O^b) \mid \lambda) P(\lambda) / P(O^a, O^b) \tag{37}$$

$$\lambda = (A, B, \pi) \tag{38}$$

Where A is state transition matrix, B is observation probability matrix, π is initial condition probability matrix, O represents the sequence of feature vectors. In this context the superscript a, denotes the first stream parameters and superscript b denotes the second stream parameters.

The parameters are nonlinear which could be seen in equations 3 and 4. The system identification is based on linear ARMA model that means the parameters are computed well only around the operating point of the system. The operating point of system is time-varying and therefore the parameters vary with time. Therefore, the feature vector parameters are computed at each frame during train and test of HMM.

Training of the above mentioned multistream model could be done by synchronous and asynchronous methods. In this section the multistream approach is based on pseudo-synchronous coupled hidden Markov model. As it will be shown, it is an interesting option for multimodal continuous speech identification because of, 1) synchronous multimodal continuous speech identification, 2) consideration of asynchrony between streams. Some resynchronization points are defined at the beginning and end of BCI segments including phonemes or words.

Some resynchronization points are defined at the beginning and end of BCI segments including phonemes or words. Combination of the independent likelihoods is done by multiplying the segment likelihoods from the two streams, thus assuming conditional independence of the streams according to:

$$P((O^a, O^b) \mid \lambda) = P(O^a \mid \lambda^a)^w P(O^b \mid \lambda^b)^{(1-w)} \tag{39}$$

The weighting factor $w 0 \leq w \leq 1$ represents the reliability of the two modalities. It generally depends on the performance obtained by each modality and on the presence of noise and disturbance. Here, we estimate the optimal weighting factor on the development set which is subject to the same noise as the test set. The method used for final experiments however was to automatically estimate the SNR from the test data and to adjust the weighting factor accordingly. It can be observed empirically that the optimal weight is related almost linearly to the SNR ratio.

BCI with dynamic parameters was studied in this section. The algorithm adopted is based on pseudo-synchronous hidden Markov chains to model the asynchrony between events. The proposed combination of ARMA model and Kalman filtering for feature extraction resulted to the best identification rates compared to usual methods. Complimentary effect of video information and dynamic parameters on BCI was studied. Effectiveness of the proposed identification system was more beneficial in low signal to noise ratios which reveals the robustness of the algorithm adopted in this study. Owing to high rate of information, the voice of speakers has significant effect on the identification rate; however, it reduces rapidly due to environmental noise. It was also shown that a specific combination weight of voice and video information provides optimum identification rate which is dependent on the signal to noise ratio and provides low dependency on the environmental noise. The phonetic content of spoken phrases was evaluated and the phonemes were sorted based on their influence on BCI rate. Identification rate of proposed model based system was compared to other parameter extraction methods including Kalman filtering, neural network, ANFIS system and auto regressive moving average. The combination of proposed model with Kalman filter led to the best identification performance. Combination of feature vectors content has a great roll on identification rate, Therefore, more efficient methods rather than pseudo-synchronized hidden Markov chain could be used for better achievements. Application of feature extraction methods like sample entropy, fractal dimension and nonlinear model based approaches have shown appropriate performance in BCI processing and could result to better identification rates in this area. Lip shape extraction is a critical point in this identification method and more robust algorithms provide accurate and precise results.

4. Conclusions

Some promising methods for feature extraction and classification of EEG signal are described in this chapter. The aim of these methods is to overcome the ambiguities encountering BCI applications.

A feature extraction algorithm based on the Kalman estimation discussed. This estimator minimizes the error covariance and therefore is an optimum estimator if appropriate initial condition is selected. Kalman estimator is used for adaptive estimation of dynamic parameters of EEG. The estimator reduces the error variance adaptively and after a period of time a unique estimation is achieved.

The SVM has been used extensively for classification of EEG signals. It is shown that EEG signal has separable intrinsic vectors which could be used in SVM classifier. SVM classifiers use discriminant hyper-planes for classification. The selected hyper-planes are those that maximize the margin of classification edges. The distance from the nearest training points usually measured based on a non-linear kernel to map the problem to a linear solvation space. A RBF kernel based SVM is proposed here that Lagrangian optimization is performed using an adjustable ANFIS algorithm. It will be shown that this method leads to adjustable soft decision classification.

The combination of proposed model with Kalman filter can lead to the best identification performance. Combination of different feature sets has a great roll on classification rate, Therefore, more efficient methods rather than pseudo-synchronized hidden Markov chain could be used for better achievements. Application of feature extraction methods like sample entropy, fractal dimension and nonlinear model based approaches have shown appropriate performance and could result to better identification rates in this area.

Through the feature space constructed using approximate entropy and fractal dimension in addition to conventional spectral features, different stages of EEG signals can be recognized from each other expressly. These methods provide better performance in datasets with lower dimension. The RBF kernel of SVM modified by ANFIS can be a strong base for improved methods in the field of BCI cognition and analysis for therapeutic applications.

Author details

Vahid Asadpour, Mohammd Reza Ravanfar and Reza Fazel-Rezai

University of North Dakota, USA

References

[1] Guillaume, S. Designing Fuzzy Inference Systems from Data: An Interpretability-Oriented Review. IEEE Transactions on Fuzzy Systems (2001). , 9(3), 426-443.

[2] Guler, I D. Adaptive neuro-fuzzy inference system for classification of EEG signals using wavelet coefficients. Neuroscience Methods (2005). , 148-113.

[3] Anier, A, Lipping, T, Mel, S, & Hovilehto, S. Higuchi fractal dimension and spectral entropy as measures of depth of sedation in intensive care unit. Annual International Conference of the IEEE Engineering in Medicine and Biology Society (2004). , 526-529.

[4] Sandeep, P N, Shiau, D, Principe, J C, Iasemidis, L D, Pardalos, P M, Norman, W M, Carney, P R, Kelly, K M, & Sackellares, J C. An investigation of EEG dynamics in an animal model of temporal lobe epilepsy using the maximum Lyapunov exponent. Experimental Neurology (2010). , 216(1), 115-121.

[5] Derya, E. Recurrent neural networks employing Lyapunov exponents for analysis of ECG signals. Expert Systems with Applications (2010)., 37(2), 1192-1199.

[6] Derya, E. Lyapunov exponents/probabilistic neural networks for analysis of EEG signals 2010. Expert Systems with Applications (2010)., 37(2), 985-992.

[7] Lia, J, Chena, Y, Zhangb, W, & Tiana, Y. Computation of Lyapunov values for two planar polynomial differential systems. Applied Mathematics and Computation (2008)., 204(1), 240-248.

[8] Mendel, J. M. Lessons in Estimation Theory for Signal Processing, Communications, and Control. Englewood Cliffs; (1995).

[9] Franklin, G. F, Powell, J. D, & Chapterman, M. L. Digital Control of Dynamic Systems. Addison-Wesely; (1990).

[10] Choi, J, Lima, A. C, & Haykin, S. Kalman Filter-Trained Recurrent Neural Equalizers for Time-Varying Channels. IEEE Transaction on Communications (2005). , 53(3), 472-480.

[11] Brown, R. G. Hwang PYC. Introduction to Random Signals and Applied Kalman Filtering. Wiley; (1992).

[12] Bishop, G, & Welch, G. An Introduction to the Kalman Filter. University of North Carolina at Chapel Hill, Lesson Course; (2001).

[13] Verdu, S. Minimum probability for error for synchronous Gaussian multiple-access channels. IEEE Transactions on Information Theory (1986)., 32-85.

[14] Grewal, M. S, & Andrews, A. P. Kalman Filtering: Theory and Practice. Prentice Hall; (1993).

[15] Vatankhah, M, & Asadpour, V. Reza Fazel-Rezai, "Perceptual Pain Classification using ANFIS adapted RBF Kernel Support Vector Machine for Therapeutic Usage", Applied Soft Computing, (2013).

[16] Derya, E. Least squares support vector machine employing model-based methods coefficients for analysis of EEG signals. Expert Systems with Applications; (2009).

[17] Cheng, C, Tutwiler, R. L, & Slobounov, S. Automatic Classification of Athletes With Residual Functional Deficits Following Concussion by Means of EEG Signal Using Support Vector Machine. IEEE Transactions on Neural Systems and Rehabilitation Engineering (2008)., 16(4), 327-335.

[18] Taylor, J. S, & Cristianini, N. Support Vector Machines and other kernel-based learning methods. Cambridge University Press; (2000).

[19] Vahdani, B, Iranmanesh, S. H, Mousavi, S. M, & Abdollahzade, M. A locally linear neuro-fuzzy model for supplier selection in cosmetics industry. Applied Mathematical Modeling (2012)., 36(10), 4714-4727.

[20] Cristianini, N, & Shawe-taylor, J. Support Vector and Kernel Machines. Cambridge University Press; (2001).

[21] Jang, J. S. ANFIS: Adaptive-network-based fuzzy inference system. IEEE Transactions on System Man Cybernetic (1993).

[22] Zhan-li, S, & Kin-fan, A. Tsan-Ming Choi. Neuro-Fuzzy Inference System Through Integration of Fuzzy Logic and Extreme Learning Machines. IEEE Transactions on Systems, Man, and Cybernetics (2007). , 37(5), 1321-1331.

[23] Ljung, L, & Soderstorm, T. Theory and Practice of Recursive Identification. MIT Press; (1983).

[24] Fletcher, H. Speech and Hearing in Communication. Krieger; (1953).

[25] Doud, H. Y, & Gururajan, A. Bin He A. Cortical Imaging of Event-Related (de)Synchronization During Online Control of Brain-Computer Interface Using Minimum-Norm Estimates in Frequency Domain. IEEE Transactions on Neural Systems and Rehabilitation Engineering (2008). , 16(5), 425-43.

Chapter 4

Bayesian Sequential Learning for EEG-Based BCI Classification Problems

S. Shigezumi, H. Hara, H. Namba, C. Serizawa,
Y. Dobashi, A. Takemoto, K. Nakamura and
T. Matsumoto

Additional information is available at the end of the chapter

http://dx.doi.org/10.5772/56146

1. Introduction

Non-invasive Brain-Computer Interfaces (BCIs) have been an active research area where several different methods have been developed. They include Electroencephalography (EEG), Near-infrared Spectroscopy (NIRS), functional-MRI (fMRI) among others [1]. Of those BCIs, EEG is one of the most studied methods. This is mainly due to its fine temporal resolution, ease of use, and relatively low set-up cost. Each BCI method naturally has its own advantages and disadvantages. EEG is no exception.

One of the main disadvantages of an EEG-based BCI is its susceptibility to noise, which motivates development of a variety of machine learning algorithms for decoding EEG signals, and there have been significant advancements in the area [2].

One way of categorizing machine-learning algorithms for BCI is **batch** mode and **sequential (online)** mode. In the batch mode learning, the collectively acquired EEG data from a subject is divided into two subsets: training data and test data. The former is used for training the machine-learning algorithm, whereas the latter is used to evaluate the algorithm's capability to predict the subject's intention [2]-[4]. There are several facets in batch mode learning which call for improvements:

1. First, it is non-trivial to decide how much data should be used for training and how much data should be left for testing. It should also be noted that the number of necessary training data may depend on each subject.

2. Second, with the batch mode learning, by definition, one cannot perform sequential evaluations of predictive performance as time evolves.

3. Third, the batch mode learning presumes that the data is stationary, i.e., the subject's physical condition and/or the environment around the subject does not change over the period of the experiment.

In contrast, the sequential learning algorithm considered in this study starts learning with the very first single trial datum and proceeds with the learning each time a single trial datum arrives within a Bayesian framework.

This paper proposes a Bayesian sequential learning algorithm for steady-state visual evoked potential (SSVEP) classification problems in a principled manner. In particular, the paper performs the following:

a. Evaluation of the *sequential posterior distribution* of unknown parameters each time a trial is performed.

b. Computation of the *sequential predictive distribution* of the class label at each trial based on the posterior distribution obtained above.

c. *Automatic hyperparameter learning,* where hyperparameter in this study corresponds to the search region volume in the unknown parameter space.

d. Sequential evaluation of the error between the true label and the predicted label.

e. Sequential evaluation of *marginal likelihood* which quantifies the reliability of the prediction at each trial.

f. Experiments are performed on a four class problem in addition to two class problem, where the extension from the latter to the former is nontrivial.

g. Formulate the problem using nonlinear model to capture potential nonlinearities which can be easily extended to more difficult problems.

2. Related work

There are three ingredients in this study: (i) SSVEP, (ii) Sequential (Online) learning, and (iii) Sequential Monte Carlo implementations. The descriptions that follow will be given in terms of these keywords. For the batch mode learning, we cite the survey paper reported in [2] instead of citing individual papers.

Allison et al. [5] performed a demographic study of several different BCI methods and showed that an SSVEP-based BCI spelling system was competitive for different age groups, as well as different gender groups, with little experience, under noisy environments. It is also reported that most subjects stated that they did not consider the flickering stimuli annoying and would use or recommend such a BCI system. In [6], and also in [7], an SSVEP-based orthosis control system with an LED light source is proposed. The flickering frequencies were 6 Hz, 7 Hz, 8

Hz, and 13 Hz in the former, and 8 Hz and 13 Hz in the latter. Classification was performed using the second- and third-order higher harmonics in addition to the fundamental frequency component. In [8], an SSVEP-based speller is proposed. After Principal Component Analysis (PCA), the probability of each frequency component is estimated using a particular information matrix. The speller introduces a selection based on a decision tree and an undo command for correcting eventual errors. In [9], EEG signals are represented in the spatial-spectral-temporal domain by a wavelet transform. It also uses a multi-linear discriminative subspace by employing general tensor discriminant analysis (GTDA). The classification is conducted by support vector machine (SVM). Reference [10] proposes a biphasic stimulation technique to solve the issue of phase drifts in SSVEP in phase-tagged systems. The Kalman filter is used in [11] to decode neural activity and estimate the desired movement kinematics, where the filter gain is approximated by its steady-state form, which is computed offline before real-time decoding commences. Canonical correlation analysis (CCA) is used in [12] to analyze the frequency components of SSVEP, where the correlations between the target oscillation waveforms, as well as their higher order harmonics, and those of the acquired SSVEP waveforms are calculated. It is demonstrated that the scheme performed better than a fast Fourier transform-based spectrum estimation method. CCA is used in an online manner by updating the parameters each time data arrives. An online learning scheme called Stochastic Meta Descent (SMD), which is a generalization of the gradient descent algorithm, is proposed in [13]. The paper also discusses various aspects of errors incurred in online learning algorithms.

The Subject Specific Classification Model is discussed in [14], where model Gaussian parameters are updated online after an initial learning of the Subject Independent Classification Model from a pool of subjects. The data was taken from P300, which is one component of EEG.

Martinez et al. [4] propose an SSVEP-based online BCI system with visual neurofeedback. The algorithm is different from the one proposed in this paper. There is a report on Bayesian sequential learning for EEG signals [6], where the Sequential Monte Carlo is used for implementation. In addition to the task differences between [6] and this study, there are several algorithmic distinctions between the two. First, the basis function used in the former is linear with respect to the associated parameters, whereas the latter uses a basis function in which parameters appear in a nonlinear manner. Second, the parameter that controls the size of the parameter search region is fixed in the former, whereas it is learned automatically in the latter. These two differences, at least within our experience, are important for achieving better performance.

In addition, no extension for multi-class classification problems was performed in the former, whereas both algorithmic extension and a learning experiment by using multi-class real EEG data are performed in the latter. Our proposed algorithm is based on part of earlier work [16] of the authors' research group for a different application. Preliminary results on a two-class classification problem were reported by the present group in [17]. The current paper gives a full account of the results by expanding several parts of that conference paper. First, a four-class classification problem was formulated and tested experimentally. Second, the algorithm was further improved by incorporating an Effective Sample Size and Rao-Blackwellisation. Third, more detailed discussions are added.

3. Subjects and data acquisition

Of Event Related Potentials used in BCI, the target quantities considered in this study are SSVEPs, which are natural responses to visual stimulation at specific frequencies. These frequency components and their higher-order harmonics can be observed in the occipital region [4]. It is known that SSVEPs are often useful in research because of the reasonable signal-to-noise ratio and relative immunity to artifacts [5].

In an attempt to perform two-class and four-class classification problems, we gathered two sets of SSVEP data. The settings that we describe below for the two experiments are the same except for the number of stimuli and their frequencies. EEG data were recorded by a Polymate (Nihon Koden, Tokyo) with six active electrodes (O1, OZ, O2, O9, IZ, O10) according to the international 10-10 system and referenced to the left earlobe with a digitization rate of 500 Hz. Even though the highest flickering frequency was 10 Hz, we considered second and third order harmonics in one of the experiments reported below. Our original intention was to examine the harmonics higher than three even though they were not reported in this paper. In order to have a wide margin for the Nyquist frequency we chose 500 Hz. Five volunteers (aged 21-23 years) participated in the present study. All subjects were healthy, with no past history of psychiatric or neurological disorders.

Written informed consent was obtained from each subject on forms approved by the ethical committee of Waseda University.

Each subject was seated in a comfortable chair 60 cm in front of the monitor in an electrically shielded and dimmed room. The flow of task events is shown in Figure 1. The stimulus for the two-class problem is illustrated in Figure 2, whereas that of the four-class problem is illustrated in Figure 3.

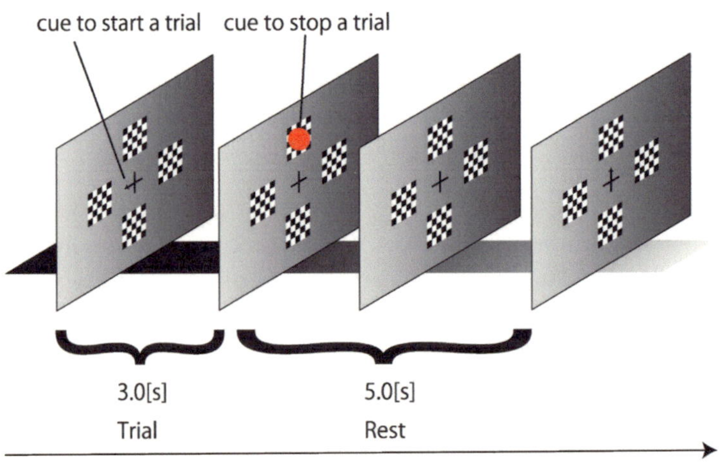

Figure 1. Task flow for the four-class classification problem

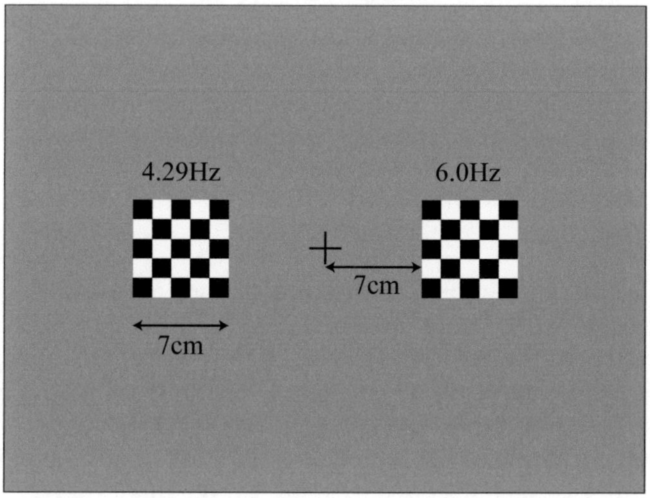

Figure 2. Monitor display for the two class classification problem

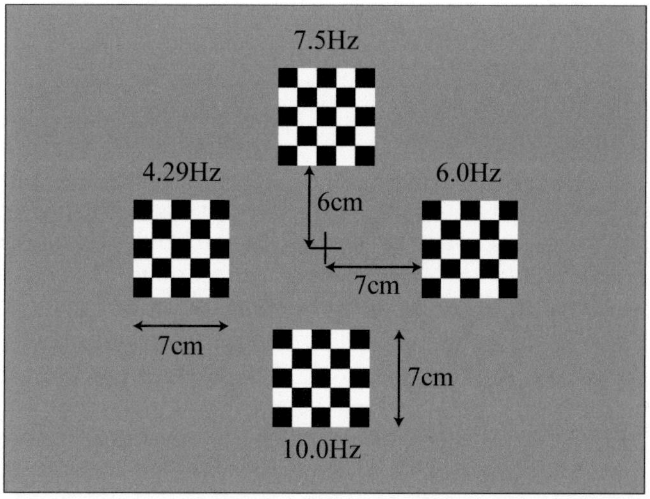

Figure 3. Monitor display of the four-class classification problem

In the two-class problem, two flickering checkerboard stimuli (left and right) were presented on the monitor, whereas in the four-class problem, four flickering checkerboard stimuli (left, right, top, and bottom) were presented. In addition, a fixation cross was placed at the center, which the subject was usually asked to fixate at.

In the two-class problem, the left stimulus was a checkerboard flickering with frequency of 4.29 Hz, whereas the right stimulus flickered at frequency of 6.00 Hz. In the four-class problem, there were additional stimuli, one at the top with frequency of 7.50 Hz, and one at the bottom with frequency of 10.0 Hz. There were three reasons for selecting these particular frequencies. First, it is known that SSVEPs are discernible in approximately the 4.0 Hz - 50 Hz band [18][19]. Second, higher harmonics of a particular frequency component should not overlap with the fundamental frequency component. Such overlap could give rise to a problem when one considers multi-class classification problem where multiple frequencies are involved as is described in section **6**. Third, since the monitor refresh rate is 60 Hz, choice of the flickering frequencies were restricted by 60/positive integer. We chose 60/14=4.2857.... which we approximated by 4. 29.

The subject usually fixated at a central fixation cross. When an arrow replaced the cross, the subject should move his or her eyes to the checkerboard indicated by the arrow for 3.0 s, after which a red circle is shown so that the subject would know when to rest for 5.0 s. This sequence was one trial, and trials were repeated twenty times, constituting one session. The direction of the arrow was selected at random. Each subject completed 600 trials, or 30 sessions. The measurements were performed with a Polymate AP1124, a multi-purpose portable bio-amplifier recording device, manufactured by TEAC Corporation, Tokyo, Japan. The device is equipped with 24 channels with a maximum sampling frequency of 1 kHz. In addition to electroencephalograms (EEGs), eyeball movement and other external signals can be measured. The dimensions are W90 mm x H 44 mm x D 158 mm, the weight is 300 g, and the device is powered by battery.

4. Algorithm

This section gives a description of the proposed sequential learning algorithm. It consists of several aspects: (i) the basis function to fit the data, (ii) the likelihood function, (iii) sequential parameter learning, and (iv) sequential hyperparameter learning. The actual predictive values are given by the predictive distribution of the target class labels, which will be described in **4.3**. In order to improve the learning capabilities, Rao-Blackwellisation will also be described. We begin with a two-class classification problem followed by a multi-class classification problem. A schematic diagram of the proposed algorithm is given in Figure 4.

4.1. Two-class classification problem

Let $x_k \in R^d$ be the feature vector at the k-th trial, where d represents the dimension of x_k which, in our paper, is the DFT spectrum of a single trial EEG. Let $y_k \in \{0,1\}$ be the binary class label of each trial, where 0 corresponds to the right flickering image and 1 corresponds to the left flickering image. Our purpose here is to learn parameters associated with the basis function, to be defined shortly, and predict the subject's intention given SSVEP data, each time datum arrives.

4.1.1. Basis function and classifier

Consider the parameterized family of nonlinear basis functions $f(\bullet)$ defined by:

http://dx.doi.org/10.5772/56146

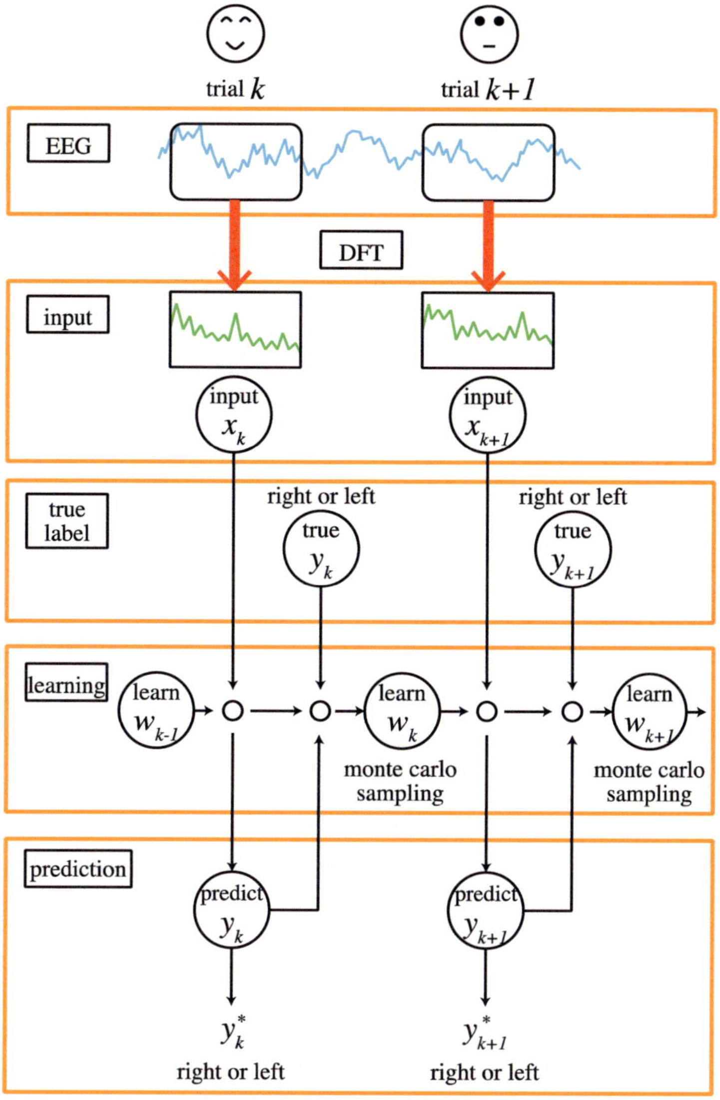

Figure 4. Schematic diagram of the proposed algorithm

$$f(x_k;\omega_k)=\sum_{j=1}^{h} v_{k,j}\sigma\left(\sum_{i=1}^{d} u_{k,ij}x_{k,i}+u_{k,0j}\right)+v_{k,0}, \tag{1}$$

where $u_k := (u_{k,0}, \cdots, u_{k,d})^T \in R^{h(d+1)}$, $u_{k,i} := (u_{k,i1}, \cdots, u_{k,ih})^T \in R^h$, $v_k := (v_{k,0}, \cdots, v_{k,h})^T \in R^{h+1}$, $\omega_k = (u_k, v_k)$.

The function $\sigma(\bullet)$ is a sigmoidal function defined by $\sigma(a)=\frac{1}{1+\exp(-a)}$, where h represents the number of hidden units.

Other popular basis functions often work as well. It should be noted that this basis function is nonlinear with respect to u_k as well as x_k, which enables capturing of potential nonlinearities involved.

In order to associate the quantity defined by (1) with the class label, consider:

$$P(y_k \mid x_k, \omega_k) := Be(y_k; \Phi(f(x_k; \omega_k))), \tag{2}$$

whereΦ is a function which monotonically maps the real numbers onto [0,1]. Several choices of Φ are possible. One is:

$$\Phi(u) := \frac{1}{1 + \exp(-u)}, \tag{3}$$

while another is:

$$\Phi(u) := \frac{1}{\sqrt{2\pi}} \int_{-\infty}^{u} \exp(-a^2/2) da. \tag{4}$$

We tested both functions and found them to work equally well for our SSVEP learning. In what follows, we will report our results with (4) by introducing a latent variable z_k and considering

$$P(y_k \mid x_k, \omega_k) = \int P(y_k, z_k \mid x_k, \omega_k) dz_k, \tag{5}$$

$$P(y_k, z_k \mid x_k, \omega_k) = P(y_k \mid z_k) P(z_k \mid x_k, \omega_k), \tag{6}$$

$$P(y_k \mid z_k) := Be(I(z_k \geq 0)), \tag{7}$$

$$P(z_k \mid x_k, \omega_k) := N(z_k; f(x_k; \omega_k), 1.0), \tag{8}$$

where $I(A)$ represents an indicator function defined as 1 when A is *true* and 0 when A is *false*.

4.1.2. Parameter search stochastic dynamics

In order to perform sequential learning, we perform a sequential stochastic search of the parameter ω_k each time trial data is acquired:

$$P(\omega_k \mid \omega_{k-1}, \gamma_k) := \frac{1}{Z_\omega(\gamma_k)} \exp\left(-\frac{\gamma_k \|\omega_k - \omega_{k-1}\|^2}{2}\right) \tag{9}$$

where Z_ω represents the normalization constant. This amounts to searching for a new value ω_k based on the previous value ω_{k-1}, but in a random walk manner. This is a first-order Markov process, so that the parameters of the distant past are naturally forgotten because of the noise,

http://dx.doi.org/10.5772/56146

whereas the parameters of the immediate past tend to be taken into account with higher weights. This stochastic parameter search is reflected in the posterior distributions (20) given sequential data. Since this transition probability is Gaussian, it involves γ_k, which is the reciprocal of the variance parameter. More specifically, if γ_k is small, the parameter search region for ω_k will be large, whereas if γ_k is large, the search region will be small.

4.1.3. *Automatic hyperparameter search stochastic dynamics*

Our experiences tell us that automatic adjustment of γ_k is often important in order to achieve better performance. γ_k is often called a hyperparameter since it controls the behavior of the target parameter ω_k. We perform the following automatic stochastic search of γ_k :

$$P(\gamma_k \mid \gamma_{k-1}) := \frac{1}{\sqrt{2\pi}\gamma_k\sigma_h}\exp\left(-\frac{(\log \gamma_k - \log \gamma_{k-1})^2}{2\sigma_h^{\ 2}}\right), \tag{10}$$

There are at least two reasons for this transition probability to be log-normal. One is that γ_k needs to be positive, and another is to cover a large range of values in the hyperparameter space. It should be noted that (10) is also a first-order Markov process, so that the hyperparameters of the immediate past are taken into account, whereas the hyperparameters of the distant past tend to be forgotten. In order to explain the importance of such hyperparameter learning, consider Figure 5. Letting $\theta_k := (\omega_k, \gamma_k)$ the blue region represents the likelihood function landscape in the θ-space, where the darker the blue color, the higher the likelihood function value. The white diamonds represent samples $\theta_{t-1}^{(i)} \sim P(\theta_{t-1} \mid x_{1:t-1}, y_{1:t-1})$, the yellow diamonds $\theta_t^{*(i)} \sim P(\theta_t^{(i)} \mid \theta_{t-1}, \gamma_t^{(i)})$, $\gamma_t^{(i)}$:*large*, and the light-green diamonds $\theta_t^{*(i)} \sim P(\theta_t^{(i)} \mid \theta_{t-1}, \gamma_t^{(i)})$, $\gamma_t^{(i)}$:*small*. Now suppose that the likelihood function landscape in the θ -space changed by a relatively large amount, as shown by the pink region, where the darker the color, the higher the likelihood. The yellow diamonds are scarce in the pink region, so that it is difficult to find θ samples that give rise to meaningful likelihood function values. This is due to the fact that $\gamma_t^{(i)}$ is large, so that the search region is restricted. If $\gamma_t^{(i)}$ is relatively small, on the other hand, then the green θ samples might capture at least a part of the pink region where the likelihood function values are meaningful. The proposed hyperparameter learning scheme automatically learns appropriate $\gamma_t^{(i)}$ values from the sequential data and lets the algorithm find reasonable θ samples.

4.1.4. *Rao-blackwellised SMC*

In this paper, we implemented not only the standard SMC but also Rao-Blackwellised SMC (RBSMC) for the purpose of performance improvement. Rao-Blackwellisation is a statistical variance reduction strategy for the Monte Carlo method [25], [26]. It is a combination of analytical integration (marginalization) and the Monte Carlo method. In order to explain this,

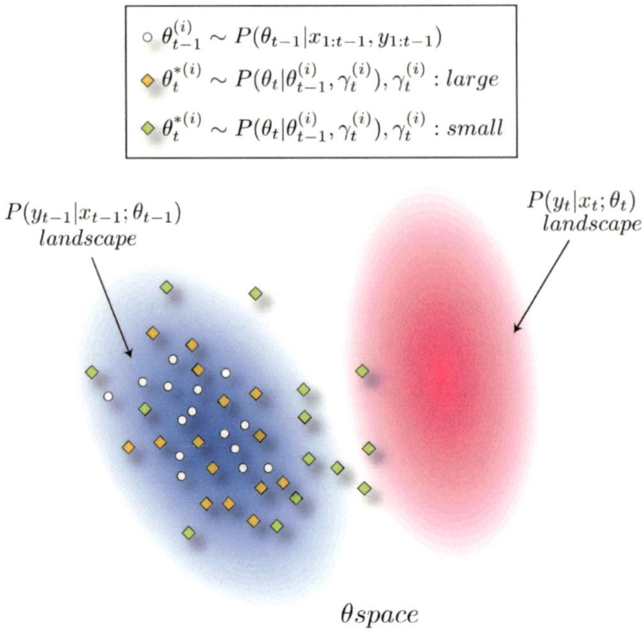

Figure 5. The proposed hyperparameter learning scheme automatically finds the appropriate region in the θ-space. The blue region indicates the likelihood function landscape at time t - 1, whereas the pink region indicates the likelihood function landscape at time t. The darker the color, the higher the likelihood function value. The white diamonds represent samples $\theta_{t-1}^{(i)} \sim P(\theta_{t-1} | x_{1:t-1}, y_{1:t-1})$, the yellow diamonds $\theta_t^{*(i)} \sim P(\theta_t^{(i)} \mid \theta_{t-1}, \gamma_t^{(i)})$, $\gamma_t^{(i)}$:*large*, and the light-green diamonds $\theta_t^{*(i)} \sim P(\theta_t^{(i)} \mid \theta_{t-1}, \gamma_t^{(i)})$, $\gamma_t^{(i)}$:*small*. The proposed scheme automatically learns appropriate γ values so that it can capture appropriate θ samples in relatively high-likelihood regions in the θ-space.

recall the parameters associated with the basis function (1), write $\omega_k := (u_k, v_k)$, and decompose the stochastic search dynamics (9) into two parts:

$$P(u_k \mid u_{k-1}, \gamma_k) := \frac{1}{Z_{u_k}(\gamma_k)} \exp\left(-\frac{\gamma_k \| u_k - u_{k-1} \|^2}{2}\right), \tag{11}$$

$$P(v_k \mid v_{k-1}, \delta_k) := \frac{1}{Z_{v_k}(\delta_k)} \exp\left(-\frac{\delta_k \| v_k - v_{k-1} \|^2}{2}\right), \tag{12}$$

where there are two hyperparameters γ_k and δ_k. The corresponding hyperparameter stochastic search dynamics will be given by:

$$P(\gamma_k \mid \gamma_{k-1}) := \frac{1}{\sqrt{2\pi}\gamma_k \sigma_h} \exp\left(-\frac{(\log \gamma_k - \log \gamma_{k-1})^2}{2\sigma_h^{\ 2}}\right), \tag{13}$$

$$P(\delta_k \mid \delta_{k-1}) := \frac{1}{\sqrt{2\pi}\delta_k \sigma_h} \exp\left(-\frac{(\log \delta_k - \log \delta_{k-1})^2}{2\sigma_h^{\ 2}}\right). \tag{14}$$

Since the basis function is linear with respect to v_k, the Rao-Blackwellisation can be conducted with the data augmentation of Z_k [26], where the likelihood function $P(y_k \mid x_k, \omega_k)$ is to be integrated out with respect to v_k, which, in turn, gives rise to smaller variances. A specific implementation of this particular Rao-Blackwellisation will be given in subsection **5.2.**

4.2. Multi-class classification problem

This section attempts to generalize the results of the previous section to multi-class problems. Although we will restrict ourselves to a four-class problem, the method can, in principle, be applied to cases with more than four classes.

Let $x_k \in R^d$ be the feature vector at the k-th trial, which is the power spectrum obtained through DFT over the trial period, where d stands for the dimension of x_k. Let $y_k \in \{1,2, 3,4\}$ denote the class labels at each trial, where left corresponds to label 1, right to label 2, top to label 3, and bottom to label 4. Our goal is to learn the parameters associated with the basis function described below in an attempt to predict the subject's intention.

4.2.1. Basis function

Consider the basis function $f_q(\bullet)$ defined by (15), which is nonlinear with respect to not only x_k but also the parameter vector ω_k. There are Q outputs associated with the basis function, where Q is the number of class labels, which is four in this paper. We have:

$$f_q(x_k;\omega_k)=\sum_{j=1}^{h} v_{k,jq}\sigma\left(\sum_{i=1}^{d} u_{k,ij}x_{k,i}+u_{k,0j}\right)+v_{k,0q}, \tag{15}$$

where $u_k := (u_{k,0}, \cdots, u_{k,d})^T \in R^{h(d+1)}$, $u_{k,i} := (u_{k,i1}, \cdots, u_{k,ih})^T \in R^h$, $v_k := (v_{k,0}, \cdots, v_{k,h})^T \in R^{Q(h+1)}$, $\omega_k = (u_k, v_k)$.

4.2.2. Multinomial logistic model

This paper assumes the Multinomial Logistic Model for the target problems, where it is assumed that the error $_{k,q}$ in each term follows an independently identically distributed logistic distribution. By introducing a latent variable $z_{k,q}$, we write:

$$z_{k,q} := f_q(x_k;\omega_k) + C_{k,q} + _{k,q}, \tag{16}$$

$$C_{k,q} := -\log\sum_{i\neq q}^{Q}\exp(f_i(x_k;\omega_k)), \tag{17}$$

where $C_{k,q}$ represents the score of the term controlled by the outputs of the other class labels. It follows from (15) that the probability of y_k belonging to class q is described by:

$$P(y_k = q \mid z_{k,q}) = \frac{\exp(f_q(x_k; \omega_k))}{\sum_{i=1}^{Q} \exp(f_i(x_k; \omega_k))} = \sigma(f_q(x_k; \omega_k) + C_{k,q}), \tag{18}$$

The predicted label y_{pred} is the label q_{max} that has the maximum value of $P(y_k = q \mid z_{k,q})$. Using (18), the likelihood function is described by:

$$P(y_k \mid x_k, \omega_k) := \prod_{q=1}^{Q} P(y_k = q \mid z_{k,q})^{I(y_k = q)} (1 - P(y_k = q \mid z_{k,q}))^{I(y_k \neq q)}, \tag{19}$$

The function $I(\bullet)$ is again an indicator described in **4.1**. The generalization to the multi-class problem (18)-(20) appears straightforward; however, our experience tells us that the multi-class problems are much more difficult than the equations look. Experimental results are reported in **6.4**.

4.2.3. Parameter/hyperparameter search stochastic dynamics

We use the same standard Sequential Monte Carlo (SMC) used in **4.1**.

4.3. Bayesian Sequential Learning

Letting $\theta_k := (\omega_k, \gamma_k, \delta_k)$, $x_{1:k} := (x_1, \cdots, x_k)$, $y_{1:k} := (y_1, \cdots, y_k)$, one can derive its sequential posterior distribution at trial k:

$$P(\theta_k \mid x_{1:k}, y_{1:k}) = \frac{P(y_k \mid x_k, \theta_k) P(\theta_k \mid x_{1:k-1}, y_{1:k-1})}{\int P(y_k \mid x_k, \theta_k) P(\theta_k \mid x_{1:k-1}, y_{1:k-1}) d\theta_k}, \tag{20}$$

The second factor in the numerator is the predictive probability for parameter θ_k, which is given by:

$$P(\theta_k \mid x_{1:k-1}, y_{1:k-1}) = \int P(\theta_k \mid \theta_{k-1}) P(\theta_{k-1} \mid x_{1:k-1}, y_{1:k-1}) d\theta_{k-1}, \tag{21}$$

$$P(\theta_k \mid \theta_{k-1}) = P(\omega_k \mid \omega_{k-1}, \gamma_k) P(\gamma_k \mid \gamma_{k-1}). \tag{22}$$

At the $k+1$-st trial, let the EEG data x_{k+1} be given. Then the prediction at the trial amounts to computing the predictive probability for label $P(y_{k+1})$:

$$P(y_{k+1} \mid x_{1:k+1}, y_{1:k}) = \int P(y_{k+1} \mid x_{k+1}, \theta_{k+1}) \, P(\theta_{k+1} \mid x_{1:k}, y_{1:k}) d\theta_{k+1}. \tag{23}$$

5. Implementation

The Sequential Monte Carlo (SMC) is a powerful means of evaluating the posterior or predictive probabilities of Bayesian nonlinear or non-Gaussian models in a sequential manner. This study uses the SMC to evaluate equations (20) and (23) in an attempt to evaluate the SER. The SMC first attempts to approximate the posterior distribution by an empirical distribution (delta mass) weighted by normalized importance weights (importance sampling). In order to avoid depletion of samples, caused by an increase in the variance of the weights, the SMC replaces the weighted empirical distribution by unweighted delta masses (resampling).

There are several different methods of determining when resampling should be done. We tried two of them. One method is to resample every step, and another is to perform resampling only when the Effective Sample Size (EES [22]-[24]) becomes smaller than a threshold value:

$$ESS = \frac{1}{\sum_{i=1}^{n}\left(\tilde{\Omega}_k^{(i)}\right)^2}, \tag{24}$$

where n is the number of samples, i is the index of a sample, and $\tilde{\Omega}_k$ is the normalized importance weight defined by $\tilde{\Omega}_k^{(i)}$.

The threshold value of ESS is often set at $N/2$ ([23],[24]), which we adopted.

Implementation of Standard SMC

(a) Importance Sampling step

(i) For $i = 1, ..., n$, draw samples of $\boldsymbol{\theta}_k^*$ from the proposal density Q:

$$\left\{\boldsymbol{\theta}_k^{*(i)}\right\}_{i=1}^{n} \sim Q(\boldsymbol{\theta}_k^*|\boldsymbol{x}_{1:k}, y_{1:k}).$$

(ii) For $i = 1, ..., n$, compute the importance weight $\Omega_k^{(i)}$:

$$\begin{aligned}\Omega_k^{(i)} &\propto \tilde{\Omega}_{k-1}^{(i)} \frac{P(y_k|\boldsymbol{x}_k, \boldsymbol{w}_k^{(i)})P(\boldsymbol{\theta}_k^{*(i)}|\boldsymbol{x}_{1:k-1}, y_{1:k-1})}{Q(\boldsymbol{\theta}_k^{*(i)}|\boldsymbol{x}_{1:k}, y_{1:k})}, \\ &= \tilde{\Omega}_{k-1}^{(i)} P(y_k|\boldsymbol{x}_k, \boldsymbol{w}_k^{(i)}).\end{aligned}$$

(iii) For $i = 1, ..., n$, compute the normalized importance weight $\tilde{\Omega}_k^{(i)}$:

$$\tilde{\Omega}_k^{(i)} = \frac{\Omega_k^{(i)}}{\sum_{j=1}^{n}\Omega_k^{(j)}},$$

where $\sum_{j=1}^{n}\tilde{\Omega}_k^{(j)} = 1$.

(iv) Calculate the ESS using (24).

$$\begin{cases}\text{if} \quad ESS < \left(\frac{n}{2}\right) & \text{go to (v)} \\ \text{else} & \text{k=k+1 and go to (i)}\end{cases}$$

(b) Resampling step

(v) Resample $\left\{\boldsymbol{\theta}_k^{*(i)}\right\}_{i=1}^{n}$ with probability $\{\tilde{\Omega}_k^{(i)}\}_{i=1}^{n}$, and then set all the normalized importance weights $\frac{1}{n}$.

Figure 6. Implementation of standard SMC.

5.1. Standard SMC

Figure 6 gives an overview of the standard SMC, where $\theta_k^* := (\omega_k, \gamma_k)$ and $Q(\bullet)$ denote the proposal distribution, which in this paper is set as $P(\theta_k^* \mid x_{1:k-1}, y_{1:k-1})$. This choice is due to its simplicity of implementation. Figure 6 demonstrates the case where resampling is done with the ESS. If resampling is performed every step, then the ESS step is simply ignored.

5.2. Rao-blackwellised SMC

In the Rao-Blackwellised SMC implementation, the marginal likelihood $P(y_k \mid z_{1:k}, u_{1:k})$ is used instead of the likelihood function $P(y_k \mid x_k, \omega_k)$, where $\Theta_k := (\omega_k, \gamma_k, \delta_k)$. This implementation is described in Figure 7.

Implementation of Rao-Blackwellised SMC

(a) Importance sampling step

(i) For $i = 1, ..., n$, draw samples of $\boldsymbol{\Theta}_k$ from the proposal density Q:

$$\left\{\boldsymbol{\Theta}_k^{(i)}\right\}_{i=1}^{n} \sim Q(\boldsymbol{\Theta}_k | \boldsymbol{x}_{1:k}, y_{1:k}).$$

(ii) For $i = 1, ..., n$, compute the importance weight $\Omega_k^{(i)}$:

$$\begin{aligned} \Omega_k^{(i)} &\propto \tilde{\Omega}_{k-1}^{(i)} \frac{P(y_k | z_{1:k}^{(i)}, \boldsymbol{u}_{1:k}^{(i)}) P(\boldsymbol{\Theta}_k^{(i)} | \boldsymbol{x}_{1:k-1}, y_{1:k-1})}{Q(\boldsymbol{\Theta}_k^{(i)} | \boldsymbol{x}_{1:k}, y_{1:k})}, \\ &= \tilde{\Omega}_{k-1}^{(i)} P(y_k | z_{1:k}^{(i)}, \boldsymbol{u}_{1:k}^{(i)}). \end{aligned}$$

(iii) For $i = 1, ..., n$, compute the normalized importance weight $\tilde{\Omega}_k^{(i)}$:

$$\tilde{\Omega}_k^{(i)} = \frac{\Omega_k^{(i)}}{\sum_{j=1}^{n} \Omega_k^{(j)}},$$

where $\sum_{j=1}^{n} \tilde{\Omega}_k^{(j)} = 1$.

(iv) For $i = 1, ..., n$, update $\boldsymbol{X}_k^{(i)}$ by using $(y_k^{(i)}, \boldsymbol{X}_{k-1}^{(i)})$. For details regarding the updating, see the Appendix, where $\boldsymbol{X}_k = (\boldsymbol{V}_{k|k}, \boldsymbol{v}_{k|k})$.

(v) Calculate the ESS using (24).

$$\begin{cases} \text{if} \quad ESS < \left(\frac{n}{2}\right) & \text{go to (vi)} \\ \text{else} & \text{k=k+1 and go to (i)} \end{cases}$$

(b) Resampling step

(vi) Resample $\left\{\boldsymbol{\Theta}_k^{(i)}, \boldsymbol{X}_k^{(i)}\right\}_{i=1}^{n}$ with probability $\{\tilde{\Omega}_k^{(i)}\}_{i=1}^{n}$, and then set all the normalized importance weights $\frac{1}{n}$.

Figure 7. Implementation of Rao-Blackwellised SMC.

Here, the marginal likelihood $P(y_k \mid z_{1:k}, u_{1:k})$ can be written as:

$$P(y_k \mid z_{1:k}, u_{1:k}) = \Phi\left(\frac{z_{k|k-1}}{\sqrt{S_k}}\right)^{y_k}\left(1 - \Phi\left(\frac{z_{k|k-1}}{\sqrt{S_k}}\right)\right)^{1-y_k} \tag{25}$$

http://dx.doi.org/10.5772/56146

Details of updating $z_{k|k-1}$ and S_k are given in the Appendix.

6. Results

This section reports the results of learning experiments using the algorithms proposed in the previous sections.

6.1. Observation data

As explained in **3**, the six channels (*O1, OZ, O2, O9, IZ, O10*) located in the occipital eye field were used for our classification problems. Data were taken in 600 trials from each of five subjects (*A, B, C, D, E*). One trial lasted for 3.0 seconds. Data in the first 0.0-1.0 s was deleted in order to eliminate the effect of eyeball movements on the EEG. The raw data were filtered by 50.0 Hz notch filter. After Hanning windowing, DFT was performed by *MAT-LAB_R2008a* to obtain the feature vector x consisting of the power spectrum.

Figure.8 demonstrates the power spectrum of subject D taken from one trial when a stimulus was presented at 6.0 Hz. The particular frequency component is relatively clear. Figure.9 is from another trial of the same subject, where the target frequency component is not clearly discernible.

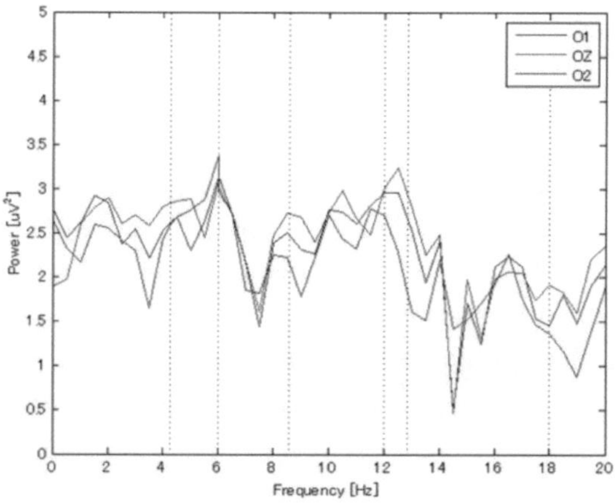

Figure 8. Frequency spectrum of Subject D. The target frequency of 6.0 Hz is reasonably discernible.

The vertical lines in the two figures indicate (from the left) 4.29Hz, 6.0Hz, 8.58(4.29 × 2) Hz, 12.0(6.0 × 2) Hz, 12.87(4.29 × 3) Hz and 18.0(6.0 × 3) Hz, respectively. It should be noted that even with SSVEP, the observed frequency components are not always identifiable by inspection. It should also be noted that SSVEP can contain higher harmonics of the target frequency [4] and that the classification accuracy may be improved by taking into account higher harmonics [4]. In order to examine the effectiveness of the higher order harmonics for our

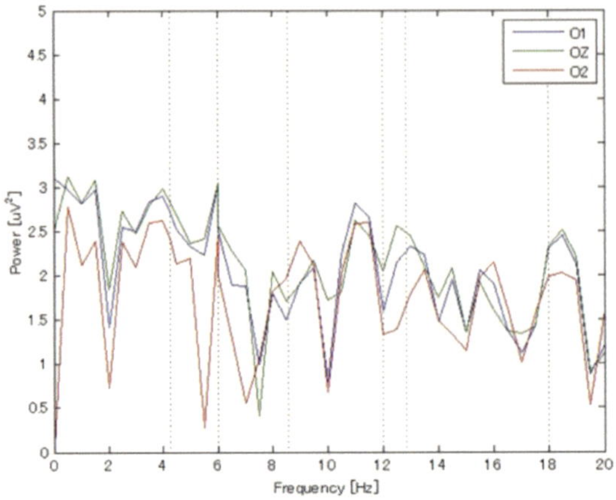

Figure 9. Frequency spectrum of the same subject at in Figure.8. The target frequency component is difficult to observe.

classification problem, this section considers the following three settings: (i) the fundamental frequency only, (ii) the second order harmonics, in addition to the fundamental frequency, and (iii) second and third order harmonics, in addition to the fundamental frequency. Since the number of channels is 6, the dimensions of our feature vectors are (i) 12, (ii) 24, and (iii) 36, respectively.

It should be noted that while more frequency components give more information, the number of parameters to be learned increases, so that learning becomes more difficult.

6.2. Experimental settings

This study examines several different versions of Sequential Monte Carlo for implementing the target sequential learning, as displayed in Table 1, where standard SMC means no hyperparameter learning and resampling is performed at every step. The abbreviated notation will be used throughout the rest of the paper. Various experimental settings are summarized in Table 2, where n denotes the number of samples; γ_0 and δ_0, the initial conditions for hyperparameters γ and δ ; σ_h, the hyper-hyperparameter; and h, the number of perceptron hidden units.

6.3. Performance evaluation criteria

We will propose three performance evaluation criteria. One is Sequential Error Rates (SER_k) defined by

$$SER_k := \frac{1}{M} \sum_{k'=k-M+1}^{k} I\left(y_{k'} \neq y_{k',pred}\right), \tag{26}$$

Abbreviation	Algorithm
SMC	Standard SMC
HP+SMC	SMC with hyperparameter auto-adjustment
SMCESS	SMC by calculating ESS
HP+SMCESS	SMCESS with hyperparameter auto-adjustment
RBSMC	Rao-Blackwellised SMC
HP+RBSMC	RBSMC with hyperparameter auto-adjustment
RBSMCESS	RBSMC by calculating ESS
HP+RBSMCESS	RBSMCESS with hyperparameter auto-adjustment
SMCmulti	Standard SMC for multi-class classification
HP+SMCmulti	SMCmulti with hyperparameter auto-adjustmen

Table 1. Algorithm names and their abbreviations

Algorithm	n	γ_0	δ_0	σ_h	h
SMC	1000	100.0	-	-	10
HP+SMC	1000	100.0	-	0.01	10
SMCESS	1000	100.0	-	-	10
HP+SMCESS	1000	100.0	-	0.01	10
RBSMC	1000	100.0	100.0	-	10
HP+RBSMC	1000	100.0	100.0	0.01	10
RBSMCESS	1000	100.0	100.0	-	10
HP+RBSMCESS	1000	100.0	100.0	0.01	10
SMCmulti	1000	100.0	-	-	10
HP+SMCmulti	1000	100.0	-	0.02	10

Table 2. Experimental Settings. n denotes the number of samples; γ_0 and δ_0, the initial conditions for hyperparameters γ and δ ; σ_h , the hyper-hyperparameter; and h , the number of perceptron hidden units.

where $y_k(y_{k'})$ is the true class, and $y_{k,pred}(y_{k',pred})$ is the predicted class defined by (23). Notation $I(\bullet)$ stands for an indicator described in **4**. This is the moving average of the prediction error over a window of size M. We will also compute Cumulative Error (CE)

$$CE := \sum_{k=1}^{K} I(y_k \neq y_{k,pred}), \tag{27}$$

in order to make performance comparisons with the existing methods. Another quantity we will be evaluating is the sequential marginal likelihood:

$$P(y_k \mid x_{1:k}, y_{1:k-1}) = \int P(y_k \mid x_k, \theta_k)\, P(\theta_k \mid x_{1:k-1}, y_{1:k-1}) d\theta_k \tag{28}$$

which is the marginalization of the likelihood with respect to the current predictive distribution. This quantifies the reliability of the prediction y_k with respect to $(x_{1:k}, y_{1:k-1})$. In order to explain a *rationale* behind this, recall that given data y, the likelihood $P(y \mid z)$ can be interpreted as the degree of appropriateness of z in explaining y. This, in turn, can be interpreted as the appropriateness of y in terms of z.

6.4. Experimental results

6.4.1. Two-class classification problem

a. Sequential Error Rate

Figure 10 shows the Sequential Error Rate of subject D over one session consisting of 600 trials. The algorithm was implemented by Sequential Monte Carlo together with the proposed hyperparameter learning (HP+SMC). Table 3 summarizes the Sequential Error Rates of subjects A-E, which were averages over ten learning trials.

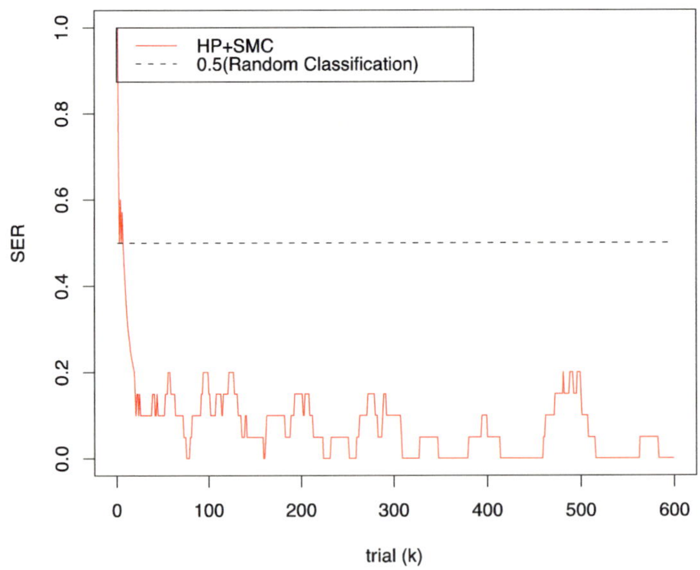

Figure 10. Sequential Error Rate of subject D with (HP+SMC), Sequential Monte Carlo together with the proposed hyperparameter learning. The dotted line at 1/2 corresponds to a random classification.

	A	B	C	D	E
minimum error rate	0.00	0.010	0.00	0.00	0.00
maximum error rate	0.75	0.75	0.71	0.75	0.80
average over 600 trials	0.16	0.26	0.19	0.077	0.13

Table 3. Sequential Error Rate of the subjects (M=20, HP+SMC)

b. Trajectory of hyperparameter

In Figure 11, the γ_t-trajectory (blue) is superimposed on the Sequential Error Rates (red) of Figure 10. The value of γ_t is the posterior mean. Note that there was a significant dip in γ_t around 380 and 480, due to the fact that the algorithm detected a sudden change in the data, so that it automatically widened the search region in the parameter space. Eventually, the algorithm re-started learning the parameters. This phenomenon was also discernible at around 475. The hyperparameter learning appeared functional.

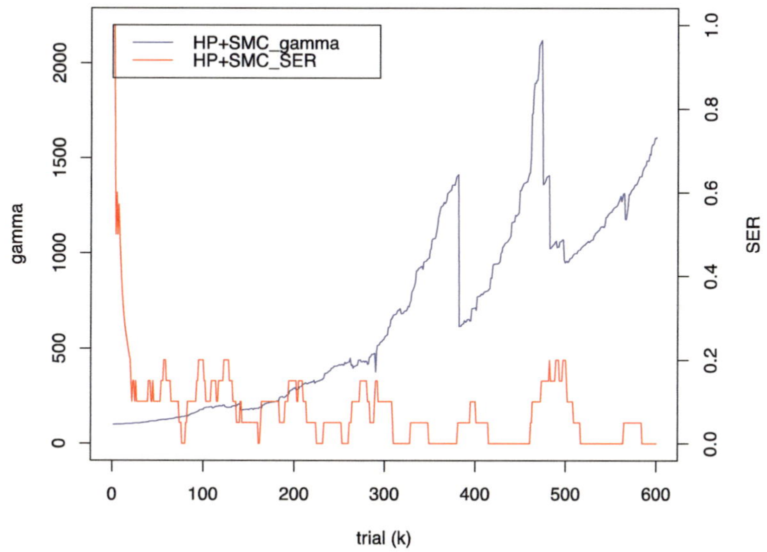

Figure 11. Trajectory of hyperparameter γ_k for Subject D with the SER in Fig.10 (HP+SMC) superimposed. The value of γ_k was its posterior mean

c. Sequential Marginal Likelihood (Reliability of the Predictions)

Figure 12 shows the negative log-Sequential Marginal Likelihood of subject D averaged over the window *M*=20 as was in Figure 10. Even though Figure 10 and Figure 12 are similar, the latter comes from the Bayesian concept where the latter appears slightly less abrupt. This particular quantity can be applied to the change detection problem as is done in [27].

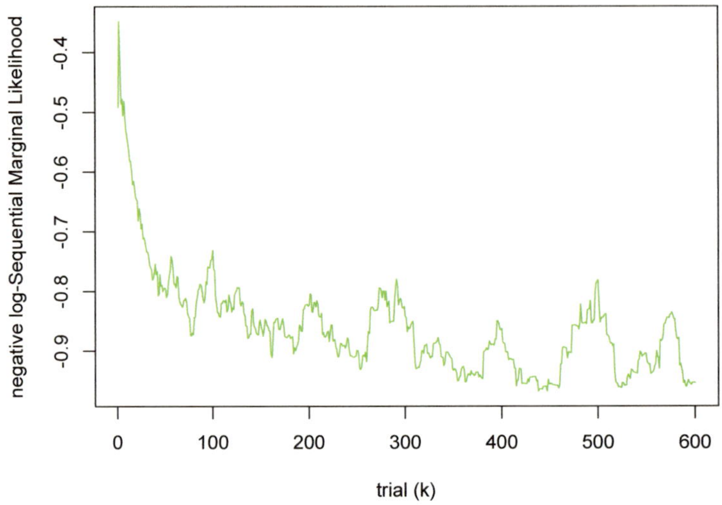

Figure 12. Negative log-Sequential Marginal Likelihood of subject D with moving average *M*=20.

d. Cumulative Error

Figure.13 shows the Cumulative Error of subject D with different algorithms, and Table.4 gives final Cumulative Errors of subjects A-E, that is, the Cumulative Errors at the last trial. These values were the averages over ten experiments.

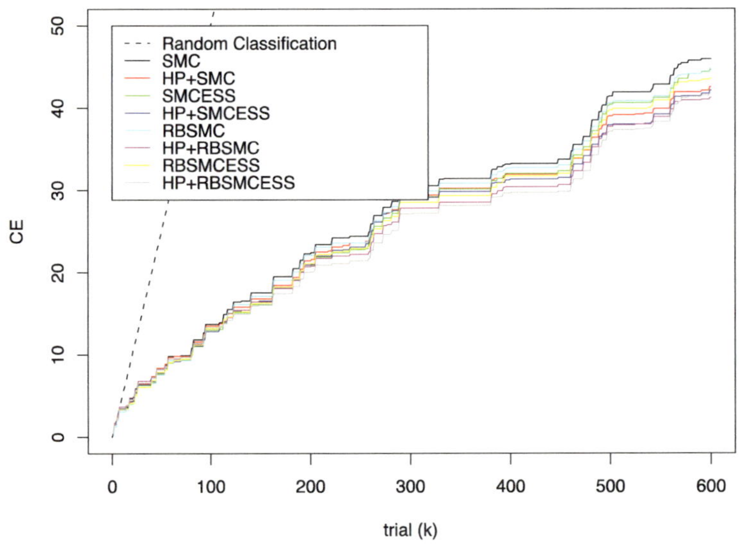

Figure 13. Cumulative Error (CE) of subject D. Different colors indicate different versions of the algorithms, as shown in Table. I.The dotted straight line at 1/2 corresponds to a random classification.

	A	B	C	D	E
SMC	95.50	159.2	109.3	45.90	80.10
HP+SMC	90.70	151.4	113.7	42.50	75.20
SMCESS	96.20	170.5	108.3	44.60	80.30
HP+SMCESS	92.10	155.9	110.0	42.10	71.70
RBSMC	91.90	155.8	109.1	44.80	75.20
HP+RBSMC	88.80	158.4	109.3	41.20	73.90
RBSMCESS	91.00	157.1	107.6	43.50	76.00
HP+RBSMCESS	89.40	154.6	106.3	41.70	72.70

Table 4. Final Cumulative Error

e. Effective Sample Size

Figure 14 shows the ESS trajectories (moving average over 20 trials) of subject D with several different methods.

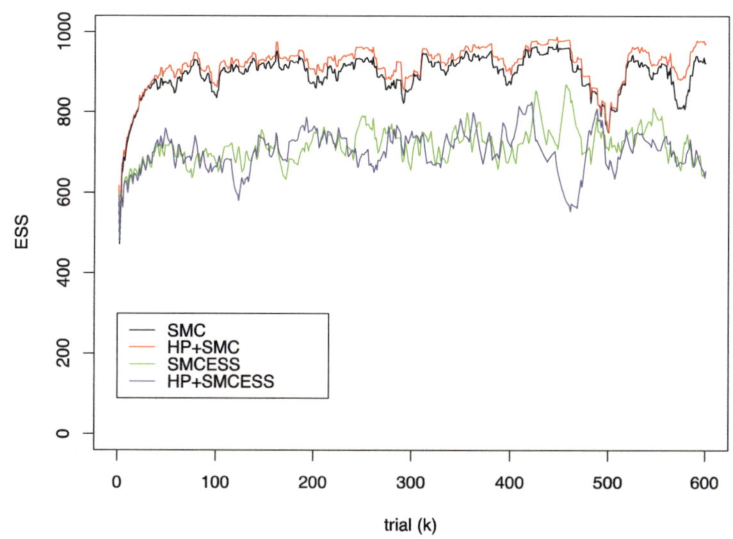

Figure 14. Trajectory of ESS of subject D.

f. Computation Time

Table 5 summarizes the computation time of the various methods averaged over ten experiments. The middle column shows the time per trial, whereas the right-most column shows the time needed for all trials. The par trial time does not contain the case where resampling is done with the ESS.

	1 step (S)	whole data (S)
SMC	0.120	72.0
HP+SMC	0.130	77.7
SMCESS	-	57.4
HP+SMCESS	-	63.9
RBSMC	0.320	192
HP+RBSMC	0.328	197
RBSMCESS	-	145
HP+RBSMCESS	-	121

Table 5. Computation time

g. Harmonic Frequency Components

Effects of the higher order harmonics were examined and are summarized in Table.6 for three cases: (i) fundamental frequency only, (ii) second-order higher harmonics in addition to the fundamental frequency, and (iii) second- and third-order higher harmonics in addition to the fundamental frequency. The numbers in the table indicate the final Cumulative Errors. The results were the averages over ten experiments.

	A	B	C	D	E
(i) fundamental	90.70	151.4	113.7	42.50	75.20
(ii) fundamental+2nd	98.20	141.1	46.50	37.60	92.80
(iii) fundamental+2nd+3rd	78.20	131.3	44.30	45.70	104.0

Table 6. Effect of Harmonics (Cumulative Error)

6.4.2. Multi-class classification problem

a. Sequential Error Rate: Figure 15 shows the Sequential Error Rates (moving average window size 20) of subject D for the the four-class problem with the HP+SMC algorithm, and Table 7 gives various values related to the Sequential Error Rates of subjects A-E averaged over 10 experiments.

	A	B	C	D	E
minimum error rate	0.23	0.39	0.25	0.15	0.58
maximum error rate	0.74	0.82	0.60	0.72	0.85
average over 600 trials	0.46	0.60	0.47	0.36	0.72

Table 7. Sequential Error Rate of the subjects (M=20, HP+SMCmulti)

http://dx.doi.org/10.5772/56146

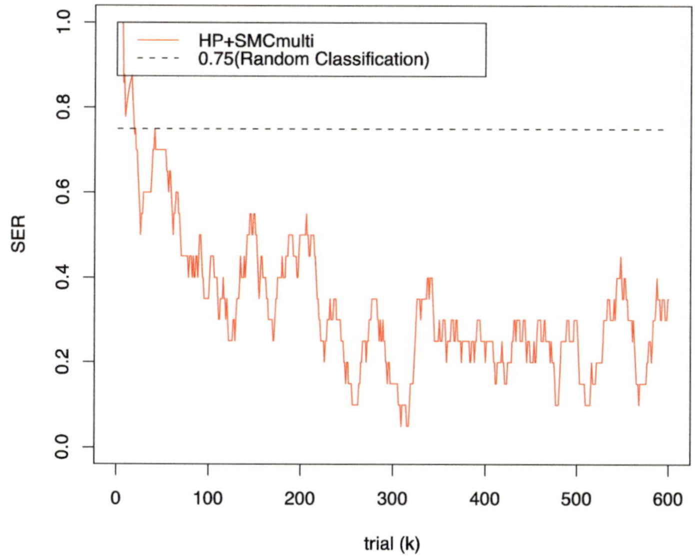

Figure 15. Sequential Error Rate of four-class classification for subject D, where the hyperparameter is learned together with SMC (HP+SMCmulti). The dotted line at 3/4 corresponds to random classification.

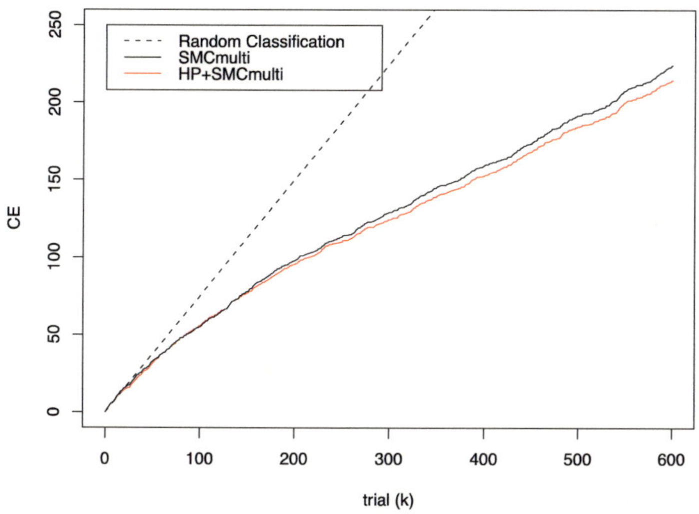

Figure 16. Cumulative Error of four-class classification for subject D with two different algorithms. One is the standard SMC without hyperparameter learning, and the other is with the proposed hyperparameter learning. The dotted straight line indicates a random classification.

b. Cumulative Error: Figure 16 shows Cumulative Errors of subject D for the four-class problem with two different algorithms. One is a standard SMC without hyperparameter learning (SMCmulti), and the other is the proposed SMC with hyperparameter learning

(HP+SMCmulti). The dotted line indicates a random classification. Table.8 summarizes the CEs for subjects A-E. These are the values averaged over ten experiments.

	A	B	C	D	E
SMC_{MULTI}	283.2	363.1	285.1	224.0	434.1
$HP + SMC_{MULTI}$	280.3	361.7	281.6	214.5	434.8

Table 8. Final Cumulative Error of four class classification

7. Discussion

7.1. Sequential error rate

We first observe that there are two errors involved in brain-computer interfaces in general, and in this study in particular. One is the error made by the brain (subject), and the other is the error made by the computer (algorithm), provided that the hardware behind the experiments is functional. Let us look at the Sequential Error Rate in Figure 10. It started decreasing immediately after the experiment began, and it had already dropped to about 0.1 at around the 20-th trial. At around the 80-th trial, the Sequential Error Rate became almost 0. One possible interpretation of this is that, if we can assume that the subject does not make an error during these 80 trials, then the SER trajectory represents the process of how the computer learns the classification problem. Recall that there are h(d+2)+1 parameters in (1), which in this case is 141. In addition, the hyperparameter γ needs to be learned. This means that the parameter/hyperparameter landscape is vague at the beginning in a high dimensional space, so that the computer searches for posterior samples in an attempt to find appropriate parameter values for better classification. It should be noted that the hyperparameter γ_t is relatively flat up to trial 80 but slightly increases. Since γ_t represents the reciprocal of the size of the parameter search region, this period can be interpreted as the computer's early effort to search for parameters by slightly narrowing down the parameter space search region.

At around trial 80, the SER dropped to almost zero, so that if the subject's EEG signals were consistent with the previous ones, the computer algorithm did not need to seek different samples in the parameter space. Therefore, the ups and downs after trial 80 could be interpreted as the fact that the subject's EEG signals became slightly inconsistent with the previous ones. During this period, the computer naturally needed to search for slightly different posterior samples, so that some errors were incurred.

This was followed by several ups and downs between 0.2 and almost 0 until approximately trial 310. The subject seemed to have obtained a reasonable amount of skill for the task, so that the subject achieved almost 0. The Sequential Error Rate in the trials between 310 and 330, as well as between 350 and 380, were almost zero. However, the subject's Sequential Error Rate again increased at around trial 380. A sharp dip was observed in the hyperparameter trajectory, as demonstrated in Figure 11. One possible interpretation of this is that by trial 380, the computer had found fairly good posterior samples for predictions so that the parameter search region was narrowed down; however, a sudden change was observed and the computer needed to quickly widen its stochastic parameter search region, which was indicated by the sudden drop of hyperparameter γ_t at around k=380. With this, the algorithm tried to learn parameter values different from the previous ones and eventually found better parameter values. The Sequential Error Rate again dropped to almost 0 at around trial 420, which lasted for approximately 40 trials. A similar phenomenon was discernible after around trial 480. It is important to notice that, in addition to the learning mechanism, a "forgetting" mechanism is naturally built in. Namely, 9 and 10 are first-order Markov stochastic dynamical systems, so that memories of the distant past are forgotten, whereas the more recent data are taken into account with higher weights. Note, however, that the Sequential Monte Carlo algorithm took into account several hundred parameter values instead of a single parameter value, which endowed the predictions with robustness.

A question might arise as to why was the drop in γ_t at around k=380 much more significant than, for instance, that at around k=270, where the SER increase was more significant at the latter than the former. Our interpretation is that at around k=270, γ_t is not too large, so that the parameter search region is still reasonably large, whereas at around k=380, the parameter search region was already sharp, and a more sudden change of the search region size was needed.

7.2. Sequential marginal likelihood

Since Sequential Marginal Likelihood can be interpreted as the reliability of each prediction of the subject, this quantity can also be used to evaluate subject's performance with probabilistic justification. Another potential application of this quantity is its use in change detection problem such that a significant change of this quantity would indicate occurrence of change in the subject's signal quality or/and environmental change. It should be noted that the sequential marginal likelihood is a well defined Bayesian quantity whereas such reliability index is not available in maximum likelihood method.

7.3. Rao-blackwellisation

Note that in Figure13, the best performance was achieved by HP+RBSMCESS, where the Rao-Blackwellisation and the Effective Sample Size were taken into account, in addition to the hyperparameter learning. The proposed scheme appeared functional.

Figure 13 shows the Cumulative Error of subject D, where the black dotted line shows the Cumulative Error corresponding to random classification. Since the Cumulative Error with the proposed algorithms grows slower than the random classification, the results appeared to indicate that the algorithms were functional. Figure 13 appears to indicate that the proposed γ_t-learning, as well as the Rao-Blackwellised SMC, was functional.

7.4. Effective sample size

From the trajectory of the Effective Sample Size (ESS), we observed that the ESS was generally large if resampling was performed at each step. This could be attributable to the fact that the purpose of resampling was to avoid degeneracy of samples, i.e., to bring in more diversity in the samples. Table 5 appears to indicate that the computation time with ESS was significantly reduced since it avoided sampling when ESS did not become smaller than a threshold value.

7.5. Higher-order harmonics

Taking the higher-order harmonics into account generally improved the prediction capabilities, except for subject E, as was seen in Table 6. One future research project could be to develop an algorithm to choose appropriate frequency components automatically. The number of frequency components is also related to the overfitting problem in machine learning, where the number of parameters is large compared with the number of data available, which sometimes results in performance degradation.

7.6. Multi-class classification problem

The extension of the two-class problem to the four-class classification problem discussed in Section 4.2 was nontrivial. One of the difficulties can be seen from the term $C_{k,q}$ in (17) - (19), where the values of equation (18) must be well-separated from each other for the four classes. The experimental results reported in subsection 6.4, however, appeared reasonable. The Cumulative Errors shown in Figure.16 appeared to indicate that the learning was functional.

8. Conclusion

This paper proposed Bayesian sequential learning algorithms for SSVEP sequential classification problems in a principled manner. Two experiments were conducted: one involving a two-class problem, and the other involving a four-class problem. The stimuli consisted of a flickering checkerboard at frequencies ranging from 4.29 to 10.0 Hz. The algorithms were implemented by the Sequential Monte Carlo. One of the points of the proposed algorithms was their hyperparameter learning, enabling it to automatically adjust to environmental changes, including changes in the subjects' physical conditions as well as their environments. Computation costs were also measured, which appeared to indicate that the algorithms could be implemented in real time. The proposed algorithms appeared functional. The proposed sequential algorithms are applicable to other brain signals besides EEG.

In the experiments performed in this study, the subjects were asked to look at the stimuli. A future research project is to examine sequential classification problems with covert selective attention [20], [21] where subjects are asked to pay attention to stimuli without eyeball movements. This project is in progress and will be reported in a future paper.

Appendix

Update Equations of $z_{k|k-1}$ and S_k

The update equations of $z_{k|k-1}$ and S_k can be summarized as follows:

$$v_{k|k-1} = v_{k-1|k-1}$$

$$V_{k|k-1} = V_{k-1|k-1} + \delta_k^{-1}$$

$$S_k = \Psi_k^T(x_k; u_k) V_{k|k-1} \Psi_k(x_k; u_k) + 1$$

$$z_{k|k-1} = \Psi_k^T(x_k; u_k) v_{k|k-1}$$

$$K_k = V_{k|k-1} \Psi_k(x_k; u_k) S_k^{-1}$$

$$v_{k|k} = v_{k|k-1} + K_k(z_k - z_{k|k-1})$$

$$V_{k|k} = V_{k|k-1} - K_k \Psi_k^T(x_k; u_k) V_{k|k-1}$$

Where $v_{k|k-1} := E[v_k \mid \Theta_{1:k-1}]$, $v_{k|k} := E[v_k \mid \Theta_{1:k}]$, $V_{k|k-1} := Cov[v_k \mid \Theta_{1:k-1}]$, $V_{k|k} := Cov[v_k \mid \Theta_{1:k}]$, $z_{k|k-1} = E[z_k \mid \Theta_{1:k-1}]$, and $S_k = Var[z_k \mid \Theta_{1:k-1}]$.

Acknowledgements

The authors thank A. Doucet for valuable comments.

Author details

S. Shigezumi[1], H. Hara[1], H. Namba[1], C. Serizawa[1], Y. Dobashi[1], A. Takemoto[2], K. Nakamura[2] and T. Matsumoto[1]

1 Department of Electrical Engineering and Bioscience, Waseda University, Tokyo, Japan

2 Primate Research Institute, Kyoto University, Aichi, Japan

References

[1] Niels Birbaumer ``Breaking the silence: Brain-computer interfaces (BCI) for communication and motor control*Psychophysiology*, (2006)., 43(6), 517-532.

[2] Bashashati, A, Fatourechi, M, Ward, R. K, & Birch, G. E. A survey of signal processing algorithms in brain-computer interfaces based on electrical brain signals," *J. Neural Eng.*, (2007). , 4(2), R32-R57.

[3] G. R. Mu¨ller-Putz, R. Scherer, C. Brauneis, and G. Pfurtscheller, ``Steady-state visual evoked potential (SSVEP)-based communication: impact of harmonic frequency components," *J. Neural Eng.*, vol. 2, pp. 123-130, 2005.

[4] Martinez, P, Bakardjian, H, & Cichocki, A. Fully Online Multicommand Brain-Computer Interface with Visual Neurofeedback Using SSVEP Paradigm," *Comput. Intell. Neurosci.*, , 2007, 1-9.

[5] B. Allison, T. Lu¨th, D. Valbuena, A. Teymourian, I. Volosyak, and A. Gra¨ser, ``BCI Demographics: How Many (and What Kinds of) People Can Use an SSVEP BCI?," *IEEE Trans. Neural Syst. Rehabil. Eng.*, vol. 18, no. 2, pp. 107-115, 2010.

[6] G. R. Mu¨ller-Putz and G. Pfurtscheller, ``Control of an Electrical Prosthesis With an SSVEP-Based BCI," *IEEE Trans. Biomed. Eng.*, vol. 55, no. 1, pp. 361-364, 2008.

[7] Ortner, R, Allison, B. Z, Korisek, G, Gaggl, H, & Pfurtscheller, G. An SSVEP BCI to Control a Hand Orthosis for Persons With Tetraplegia," *IEEE Trans. Neural Syst. Rehabil. Eng.*, (2011). , 19(1), 1-5.

[8] Cecotti, H, & Self-paced, A. and Calibration-Less SSVEP-Based Brain-Computer Interface Speller," *IEEE Trans. Neural Syst. Rehabil. Eng.*, (2010). , 18(2), 127-133.

[9] Li, J, Zhang, L, Tao, D, Sun, H, & Zhao, Q. A Prior Neurophysiologic Knowledge Free Tensor-Based Scheme for Single Trial EEG Classification," *IEEE Trans. Neural Syst. Rehabil. Eng.*, (2009). , 17(2), 107-115.

[10] Wu, H. Y, Lee, P. L, Chang, H. C, & Hsieh, J. C. Accounting for Phase Drifts in SSVEP-Based BCIs by Means of Biphasic Stimulation," *IEEE Trans. Biomed. Eng.*, (2011). , 58(5), 1394-1402.

[11] Malik, W. Q, Truccolo, W, Brown, E. N, & Hochberg, L. R. Efficient Decoding With Steady-State Kalman Filter in Neural Interface Systems," *IEEE Trans. Neural Syst. Rehabil. Eng.*, (2011). , 19(1), 25-34.

[12] Lin, Z, Zhang, C, Wu, W, & Gao, X. Frequency Recognition Based on Canonical Correlation Analysis for SSVEP-Based BCIs," *IEEE Trans. Biomed. Eng.*, (2007). , 54(6), 1172-1176.

[13] Buttfield, A, Ferrez, P. W, & Millan, J. R. Towards a Robust BCI: Error Potentials and Online Learning," *IEEE Trans. Neural Syst. Rehabil. Eng.*, (2006). , 14(2), 164-168.

[14] Lu, S, Guan, C, & Zhang, H. Unsupervised Brain Computer Interface Based on Intersubject Information and Online Adaptation," *IEEE Trans. Neural Syst. Rehabil. Eng.*, (2009). , 17(2), 135-145.

[15] Yoon, J. W, Roberts, S. J, Dyson, M, & Gan, J. Q. Adaptive classification for Brain Computer Interface systems using Sequential Monte Carlo sampling," *Neural Netw.*, (2009). , 22, 1286-1294.

[16] Sega, K, Nakada, Y, & Matsumoto, T. Online Bayesian Learning for Dynamical Classification Problem Using Natural Sequential Prior," in *Proc. IEEE MLSP'08*, (2008). , 392-397.

[17] Hara, H, Takemoto, A, Dobashi, Y, Nakamura, K, & Matsumoto, T. Sequential Error Rate Evaluation of SSVEP Classification Problem with Bayesian Sequential Learning," The 10th IEEE International Conference on Information Technology and Applications in Biomedicine, Nov.(2010). Corfu, Greece., 2-5.

[18] Regan, D. Human Brain Electrophysiology: Evoked Potentials and Evoked Magnetic Fields in Science and Medicine," Elsevier, New York, (1989).

[19] Danhua ZhuJordi Bieger, Gary Garcia Molina, and Ronald M. Aarts, ``A Survey of Stimulation Methods Used in SSVEP-Based BCIs, " *Computational Intelligence and Neuroscience*, Article ID 702357, 12 , 2010, 2010.

[20] Kelly, S. P, Lalor, E. C, Finucane, C, Mcdarby, G, & Reilly, R. B. Visual spatial attention control in an independent brain-computer interface," *IEEE Trans. Biomed. Eng.*, (2005). , 52(9), 1588-1596.

[21] Allison, B, Mcfarland, D, Schalk, G, Zheng, S, Jackson, M, & Wolpaw, J. Towards an independent brain-computer interface using steady state visual evoked potentials," *Clin. Neurophysiol.*, (2008). , 119(2), 399-408.

[22] A. Doucet et. al, eds., ``Sequential Monte Carlo in Practice," Springer, 2001.

[23] Del, P, & Moral, A. Doucet, and A. Jasra, ``Sequential Monte Carlo samplers," *J. Roy. Stat. Soc. Ser. B*, (2006). , 68(3), 411.

[24] Sisson, S. A, Fan, Y, & Tanaka, M. M. Sequential Monte Carlo without likelihoods," *Proc. Natl Acad. Sci. USA* 104, 17601765, (2007).

[25] Casella, G, & Robert, C. P. Rao-Blackwellization of sampling schemes", *Biometrika*, (1996). , 83, 81-94.

[26] Andrieu, C, De Freitas, N, & Doucet, A. Rao-Blackwellised Particle Filtering via Data Augmentation", *Advances in Neural Information Processing Systems*, (2001).

[27] Matsumoto, T, & Yosui, K. Adaptation and Change Detection With a Sequential Monte Carlo Scheme ", *IEEE Trans. System, Man, and Cybernetics.*, (2007). , 37(3), 592-606.

Chapter 5

Optimal Fractal Feature and Neural Network: EEG Based BCI Applications

Montri Phothisonothai and Katsumi Watanabe

Additional information is available at the end of the chapter

http://dx.doi.org/10.5772/55801

1. Introduction

This chapter provides the theoretical principle of fractal dimension analysis applied for a brain-computer interface (BCI). Fractal geometry is a mathematical tool for dealing with complex systems. A method of estimating its dimension has been widely used to describe objects in space, since it has been found useful for the analysis of biological data. Moreover, fractal dimension (FD) is one of most popular fractal features. The term waveform applies to the shape of a wave, usually drawn as instantaneous values of a periodic quantity versus time. Any waveform is an infinite series of points. Aside of classical methods such as moment statistics and regression analysis, properties such as the Kolmogorov-Sinai entropy [1], the apparent entropy [2] and the FD [3] have been proposed to deal with the problem of pattern analysis of waveforms. The FD may convey information on spatial extent and self similarity and self affinity [4]. Unfortunately, although precise methods to determine the FD have already been proposed [5,6], their usefulness is severely limited since they are computer intensive and their evaluation is time consuming. Recently, the FD is relatively intensive to data scaling and shows a strong correlation with the human movement of EEG data [7-9]. The time series with fractal nature are to be describable by the functions of fractional Brownian motion (fBm), for which the FD can easily be set. Waveform FD values indicate the complexity of a pattern or the quantity of information embodied in a waveform pattern in terms of morphology, spectra, and variance. This chapter, we investigate most widely popular six algorithms to be feature patterns for a BCI in which algorithms are in time and frequency domain approaches. However, many methods in evaluating FDs have been developed. As the existing algorithms, they present different characteristics therefore the optimum condition respects to the requirements of BCI application should be seriously considered.

2. Experimental paradigm[1]

In this study, we tested 7-male and 3-female. Their ages were 21-32 years (mean age, 25.3 years; SD ±3.6), with 180 trials per subject (30 trails per task). At the beginning of each EEG recording session, the subjects were instructed to relax with their eyes open for 30 s. The EEG data from this period was used as the baseline for the tasks. The duration of one trial was 6 s throughout the experiment. Each trail in the experiment was divided into two periods, a relaxing period of 0-3 s and an imaging period of 3-6 s. When the subjects had their eyes open on a blank screen, they would be in a relaxed state of mind (relaxing period). In the imaging period, the subjects imagined with eyes open, as represented by arrows. This study focuses on the motor movement functions in the brain. Therefore, imagination of motors movements are used as the tasks throughout this experiment. To assist the subject imagine the task without difficulty, we provide the acting stimuli in accordance to the given tasks. Explicit indicators are also shown on a monitor for informing subject during the experiment, all selected tasks are listed in Table 1.

Task	Imagine	Indicator
Left-hand movement (LH-MI)	Opening and grasping left hand	
Right-hand movement (RH-MI)	Opening and grasping right hand	
Feet movement (FT-MI)	Up-down lifting	
Tongue movement (TG-MI)	Up-down movement	

Table 1. Selected tasks in this study

3. Fractal analysis and methods

In this chapter, most widely popular six algorithms in time and frequency domain analysis have been addressed; the box-counting method (BCM), Higuchi's method (HM), variance fractal method (VFD), detrended fluctuation analysis (DFA), power spectral density analysis (PSDA), and critical exponent method (CEM). To measure the fractality in short time intervals of time-sequential data from one end of the waveform to the other sequentially, the dynamical changes in the FDs with respect the time series based on the time-dependent fractal dimensions (TDFD) were observed. For the classification process, two new feature parameters on the basis of fractal dimension; Kullback–Leibler (K-L) divergence and the different expected values were presented. In experimental results, DFA was selected to evaluate fraction dimensions on the basis of TDFDs [11, 36]. The reason is that, we found that the DFA provides fast computation

1 By NLAB, under supervision of Prof.Masahiro Nakagawa, Department of Electrical Engieering, Nagaoka University of Technology, 1603-1 Kamitomioka, Nagaoka-shi 940-2188 Japan. E-mail: masanaka@vos.nagaokaut.ac.jp Http://pelican.nagaokaut.ac.jp/

time and also presents reasonable values in terms of accuracy and variability when comparison with each other.

3.1. Time series-based analysis

3.1.1. Box-Counting Method (BCM)

One of the most common methods for calculating the FD of a self-similar fractal is the box-counting method (BCM). The definition of BCM is a bounded set in the Euclidian n -space that it composes self-similar property [25], $N_r \propto (1/r)^D$ by covering a structure with boxes of radii, r, the FD can be determined by

$$D_{BCM} = \lim_{r \to 0} \frac{\log_2 (N_r)}{\log_2 (1/r)} \tag{1}$$

We then repeat this process with several different radii. To implement this algorithm, number of contained box, n_r, is computed from the difference between the maximum and minimum amplitudes of the data divide by the changed radius, as

$$n_r(i) = \left\lfloor \frac{\max(x_r) - \min(x_r)}{r(i)} \right\rfloor, \quad \text{for } \{r \in 2^k \mid k = 1, 2, \ldots, \log_2(L) - 1\} \tag{2}$$

$$N_r = \sum_i n_r(i) \tag{3}$$

where N_r is a total number of contained boxes, x_r represents the EEG time series with length L , $r(i)$ is a radius by changing a step of k within the i-th subdivision window, and integer-part function denoted by $\lfloor \bullet \rfloor$. To obtain the FD, least-square linear fitted line corresponds to the slope of the plot $\log_2 (N_r)$ versus $\log_2 (1/r)$ is applied.

3.1.2. Variance Fractal Dimension (VFD)

This method is determined by the Hurst exponent, H, whose calculation was divided from the properties of the fBm data. The basic idea of calculation is based on the power law relationship between the variance of the amplitude increments of the input time series, which was produced by a dynamic process over time. The main advantage of VFD was its support of the real-time computation [17]. We also selected the VFD for estimating the FD of EEG data. The amplitude increments of a datum over a time interval Δt adhere to the following power law relationship $\mathrm{Var}[x(t_2\text{-}t_1)] \propto |t_2\text{-}t_1|^{2H}$, the Hurst exponent can be calculated by using a log-log plot then given by

$$H = \lim_{\Delta t \to 0} \left(\frac{1}{2} \frac{\log_2 \left(\mathrm{Var}\left[(\Delta x)_{\Delta t} \right] \right)}{\log_2 (\Delta t)} \right) \tag{4}$$

The variance in each window per stage k can be calculated as follows

$$\mathrm{Var}[\Delta x_{\Delta t}] = \frac{1}{(N_k - 1)}\left[\sum_{j=1}^{N_k} (\Delta x)_{jk}^2 - \frac{1}{N_k}\left(\sum_{j=1}^{N_k} (\Delta x)_{jk}\right)^2\right] \tag{5}$$

$$(\Delta x)_{jk} = x(jn_k) - x((j-1)n_k), \quad \text{for } j = 1, 2, \ldots, N_k \tag{6}$$

The least-square linear fitted line corresponds to the slope of the plot $\log_2(n_k)$ and $\log_2(\mathrm{Var}[\Delta x]_k)$, the Hurst exponent is computed as $H = 0.5s$ where s is the obtained slope then the FD can be estimated as

$$D_{VFD} = 2 - H \tag{7}$$

The process of calculating the FD essentially involves segmenting the entire input time series data into numerous subsequence (or window). The values k represents the integer range chosen such that each window of size N_T contains a number $n_k = 2^k$ of smaller windows of size $N_k = \lfloor N_T / n_k \rfloor$.

3.1.3. Higuchi's Method (HM)

FD is another measure of data complexity, generally evaluated in phase space by means of correlation dimension. Higuchi proposed an algorithm for the estimation of FD directly in time domain without reconstructing the strange attractor [18]. The HM also gives reasonable estimate of the FD in the case of short time segment. The HM algorithm based on the given finite time series $y = \{y(1), y(2), \ldots, y(N)\}$, a new time series, y_m^k, are constructed by the following equation

$$y_m^k = \left\{y(m), \; y(m+k), \; y(m+2k), \; \ldots, \; y\left(m + \left\lfloor \frac{N-m}{k} \right\rfloor\right) \bullet k\right\} \text{ for } m = 1, 2, \ldots, k \tag{8}$$

where both m and k are integers and they indicate the initial time and the time interval, respectively. The length, $L_m(k)$, of each curves is computed as

$$L_m(k) = \frac{1}{k}\left\{\left(\sum_{i=1}^{\left\lfloor \frac{N-m}{k} \right\rfloor} | y(m+ik) - y(m+(i-1)k) |\right) \bullet \frac{N-1}{\left\lfloor \frac{N-m}{k} \right\rfloor \bullet k}\right\} \tag{9}$$

The length of curve for time interval k, $L_m(k)$ is computed as the average of the m curves. A relationship of this algorithm is $L_m(k) \propto k^{-D_{HM}}$ therefore we apply the least-squares fitting line of $\log_2(L(k))$ versus $\log_2(k)$, the negative slope of the obtained line is calculated giving the estimate of the FD, D_{HM}.

3.1.4. Detrended Fluctuation Analysis (DFA)

The idea of DFA was invented originally to investigate the long-range dependence in coding and noncoding DNA nucleotide sequence [19]. Due to simplicity in implementation, the DFA is now becoming the most important method in the field of fractal analysis [20]. Therefore the DFA method was also applied to FD estimation in this study.

$$X(k)=\sum_{i=1}^{k}\left[x(i)-\bar{x}\right] \quad (10)$$

This integrated series is divided into non-overlapping intervals of length n. In each interval, a least squares line is fit to the data (representing the trend in the interval). The series $X(k)$ is then locally detrended by subtracting the theoretical values $X_n(k)$ given by the regression. For a given interval length n, the characteristic size of fluctuation for this integrated and detrended series is calculated by

$$F(n)=\sqrt{\frac{1}{N}\sum_{i=1}^{N}[X(k)-X_n(k)]^2} \quad (11)$$

This computation is repeated over all possible interval lengths (in practice, the minimum length is around 10, and the maximum is a half-length of input data, giving two adjacent intervals). In this experiment, we use the power of 2 based length for input EEG data therefore in this case we can range $n=2^k$ for $k=4,5, \ldots, \log_2(L)-1$. A relationship is expected, as $F(n)\propto n^{\alpha}$ where $\alpha$is expressed as the slope of a double logarithmic plot $\log_2(F(n))$ versus $\log_2(n)$. As PSD, Then α can be converted into the Hurst exponent $H=\alpha-1$ and the estimated FD according as$D_{DFA}=3-\alpha$.

3.2. Frequency-based analysis

3.2.1. Power Spectral Density Analysis (PSDA)

This method is widely used for assessing the fractal properties of time series, the method based on frequency domain analysis, and also works on the basis of the 1/*f*-like power scaling which can be obtained by the fast Fourier transform (FFT) algorithm. It is called a power-law relationship of Mandelbrot and van Ness [25] can be expressed as follows

$$f(s)\propto\frac{1}{s^{-\beta}} \quad (12)$$

where s is the frequency, $f(s)$ is the correspondence power at a given frequency, and β is the scaling exponent which is estimated by calculating the negative slope of the linear fit relating $\log(f(s))$ to $\log(s)$. The PSDA was applied to raw EEG data to classify the EEG characteristics. This study used the enhanced version of PSDA that initially proposed by Fougère [26] and modified by Eke [27]. To improve the stability of spectral estimates, raw EEG data of each individual trial were first detrending by subtracted the mean of the data series from each value, and then each value is multiplied by a parabolic window is given as below

$$\psi(i)=1-\left(\frac{2i}{M+1}-1\right)^2, \qquad \text{for } i=1,2,\ \ldots,\ M \tag{13}$$

Finally the scaling exponent was estimated by the least-square fitting of log-log domain for the frequencies lower than 1/8 of the maximum sampling rate, i.e., less than 64 Hz in this study. The Hurst exponent can be determined as $H=(\beta-1)/2$ where $1<\beta<3$ and the estimated FD can be computed by the following equation

$$D_{PSDA}=2+\frac{(1-\beta)}{2} \tag{14}$$

3.2.2. Critical Exponent Method (CEM)

This method was initially proposed by Nakagawa [21]. The CEM has been applied in the physiological data analysis and featuring [22-24]. The PSD of observed fBm data, $P_H(\upsilon)$, in the frequency domain is determined as

$$P_H(\upsilon)\propto \upsilon^{2H+1}=\upsilon^{-\beta} \tag{15}$$

The moment, I_α, and the moment exponent, α, of the PSD is determined as

$$I_\alpha=\int_1^\Omega P_H(\upsilon)\upsilon^{\alpha}d\upsilon, \qquad (-\infty<\alpha<+\infty) \tag{16}$$

We will consider the frequency bands as finite value and substitute Eq. (15) to Eq. (16) thus the equation was given as

$$I_\alpha\propto\int_1^\Omega \nu^{\alpha-\beta}d\nu=\int_1^\Omega \nu^{A-1}d\nu=\frac{1}{A}(\Omega^A-1)=\frac{2}{A}\exp\left(\frac{uA}{2}\right)\sinh\left(\frac{uA}{2}\right) \tag{17}$$

where $A=\alpha-\beta+1$, $u=\log(\Omega)$, and Ω is the upper frequency variable which was normalized to the lower bound of the integration region as 1. Hence taking the logarithm of moment and the third order derivative can be written as

$$\frac{d^3\log I_\alpha}{d\alpha^3}=\frac{2}{8}u^3\operatorname{cosech}^3\left(\frac{uA}{2}\right)\cosh\left(\frac{uA}{2}\right)-\frac{1}{A^3} \tag{18}$$

We then determine the critical value $\alpha=\alpha_c$ which satisfies for Eq. (18) is equal to zero. Finally, the FD can be estimated by

$$D_{CEM} = 2 - \frac{\alpha_c}{2} \tag{19}$$

The PSDA and CEM used the FFT algorithm for transforming the EEG time series data into frequency components.

4. Performance assessment

Since high computation time and low variability are the requirement of the BCI system, the optimal algorithm for evaluating fractal dimension should be examined carefully. In this experiment, we selected two signals that fractal dimension value can be easily set for assessing. The usefulness of output results can be helped us know which algorithm is suited for applying it as the feature extractor.

4.1. Assessing with artificially generated signals

1. Fractional Brownian motion (fBm) signal[2]. General model of the fBm signal can be written as the following fractional differential equation [32]

$$\frac{d^{H+1/2} B_H(t)}{dt^{H+1/2}} \propto w(t) \tag{20}$$

The mathematical model for solving the fBm signal in Eq.(20) was proposed by Mandelbrot and Van Ness [25], which is defined by

$$B_H(t) = \frac{1}{\Gamma(H+1/2)} \left(\int_{-\infty}^{0} \left[(t-s)^{H-1/2} - (-s)^{H-1/2} \right] dB(s) + \int_0^t \left[(t-s)^{H-1/2} \right] dB(s) \right) \tag{21}$$

where $\Gamma(\bullet)$ is the Gamma function $\Gamma(a) = \int_0^{+\infty} x^{a-1} e^{-x} dx$ and H is the Hurst exponent where $0 < H < 1$. B is a stochastic process. To simulate the fBm signal, we can simply implement the above definition to discrete time series at n-th index by Riemann's type sums as follows:

$$B_H(n) = \frac{1}{\Gamma(h+1/2)} \left(\sum_{k=-b}^{0} \left[(n-k)^{H-\frac{1}{2}} - (-k)^{H-\frac{1}{2}} \right] G_1(k) + \sum_{k=0}^{n} \left[(n-k)^{H-\frac{1}{2}} \right] G_2(k) \right) \tag{22}$$

In case $H = 1/2$, Eq.(4.22) can be reduced, we then obtain

$$B_{1/2}(n) = \sum_{k=0}^{n} G(k) \tag{23}$$

---

2 fBm data were simulated by NLAB, Department of Electrical Engieering, Nagaoka University of Technology, 1603-1 Kamitomioka, Nagaoka-shi 940-2188 Japan.

For $n=1,2, \ldots, N$ and $b=\sqrt{N^3}$. G is a normal distribution space.

2. Synthetic (Syn) signal. This signal was produced using the deterministic Weierstrauss cosine function [28]. To simulate the Syn signal, we can simply implement the above definition to discrete time series at n-th index by [33]

$$W_h(n)=\sum_{i=0}^{M}\gamma^{-iH}\cos\left(2\pi\gamma^{i}n\right) \tag{24}$$

where $\gamma>1$, and we set $M=26$ and $\gamma=5$. The fractal dimension of this signal is given by $D=2-H$.

4.2. Conditions for assessing

A summary of the selected parameter values in this experiment is shown in Table 2. The selection of signal lengths that are powers of two was motivated by the requirements of frequency-based algorithms (PSDA and CEM). Output performances of each algorithm were shown in Fig. 1.

4.3. Results of performance assessing

In order to test the effect of signal lengths on H estimation and each algorithm was applied on the entire series. The estimated fractal dimension values are then averaged at the change of H. Before utilizing those of algorithms, we should regard as the following things:

1. *Computation time.* Short computation time is the requirement of the BCI applications. The fBm and Syn signals are performed to complete the entire series on a laptop 1.6 GHz Pentium with memory of 512 MB. Table 3 shows the results of the average computation time.

2. *Accuracy.* To compare with the theoretical FD value (true FD value), we used a mean-squared error (MSE) value, which can be defined by

$$E_D=\frac{1}{L}\sum_{i=1}^{L}(D_i-\hat{D}_i)^2 \tag{25}$$

where D is a theoretical FD value (true value), $\hat{D}$ is an estimated FD value at ith step of H, and L is a signal length. Results are shown in Tables 4 and 5.

1. *Variability (or robustness).* The standard deviation (SD) value is computed to indicate that that variability of algorithms. Results are shown in Tables 6 and 7.

Algorithm	Parameter	Value
BCM	Step size of radius	$k=1,2, \ldots, \log_2(p)-1$
VFD	Step size of window	$k=2,3, \ldots, \log_2(p)-1$

Algorithm	Parameter	Value
HM	Maximum interval length	$k_{max} = p - 3$
DFA	Step size of interval length	$k = 4,5, \ldots, \log_2(p) - 1$
PSDA	FFT point; Maximum frequency	$N_{FFT} = p; f_{max} = 64$Hz
CEM	FFT point; Step size of moment exponent	$N_{FFT} = p;\ \alpha_{\Delta} = 0.001$

Table 2. Selected parameters in the experiment.

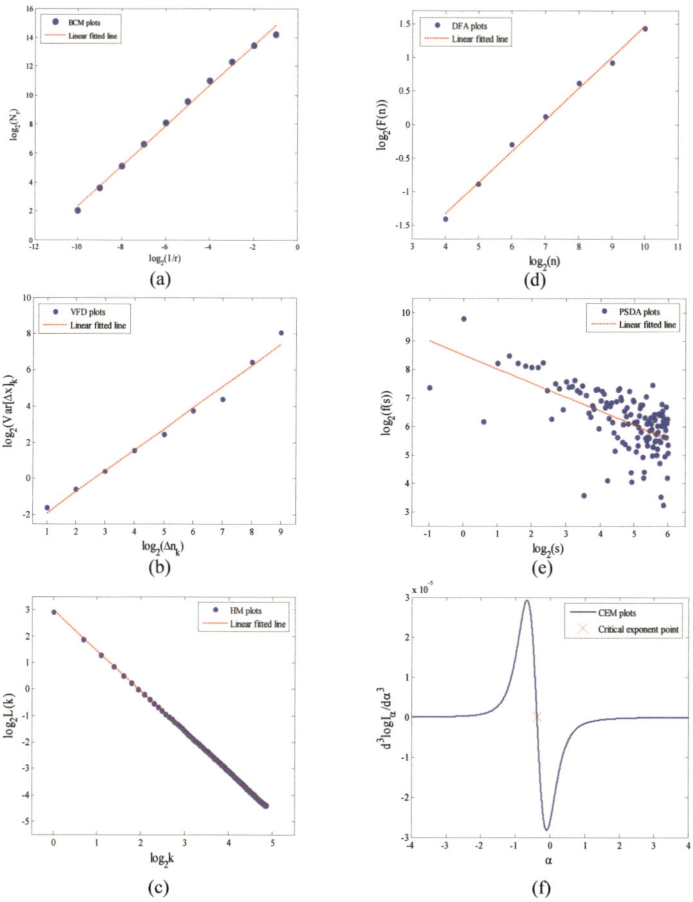

Figure 1. The results for fractal analysis, performed on a series of test EEG data. (a) BCM algorithm: a log-log plot of a total number of contained boxes versus radius. (b) VFD algorithm: a log-log plot of variance versus window length. (c) HM algorithm: a log-log plot of a curve's length versus interval length. (d) DFA algorithm: a log-log plot of a total length F(n) versus interval length. (e) PSDA algorithm: a log-log plot of power spectra versus frequency. (f) CEM algorithm: a log-log plot of moment function versus moment exponent value [16].

Signal length			t_{avr} **[ms]**			
BCM	VFD	HM	DFA	PSDA	CEM	
L = 2^7	2.60	**0.77**	14.90	10.05	2.07	140.40
L = 2^8	3.50	**1.10**	148.60	20.20	2.90	227.50
L = 2^9	6.80	**2.80**	385.20	40.20	4.90	1,767.80
L = 2^{10}	12.60	**4.30**	697.90	82.50	10.80	3,351.20
L = 2^{11}	26.00	**7.10**	1,400.70	168.80	20.30	6,538.50
L = 2^{12}	54.00	**12.40**	2,490.50	329.70	46.40	12,964.80
L = 2^{13}	114.90	**61.10**	4,160.70	895.10	137.80	25,318.10
L = 2^{14}	265.50	**164.70**	14,630.80	2,971.50	478.70	50,157.60
L = 2^{15}	676.10	**607.90**	47,082.50	11,210.20	1,882.30	101,809.70
Average	129.11	**95.79**	7,890.20	1,747.53	287.35	22,475.06

Table 3. Average computation time in millisecond (best value is marked in bold).

Signal length			**E_D(fBm signal)**			
BCM	VFD	HM	DFA	PSDA	CEM	
L = 2^7	0.091	0.018	**0.003**	0.004	0.027	0.039
L = 2^8	0.069	0.013	0.031	**0.002**	0.031	0.047
L = 2^9	0.054	0.008	0.033	**0.001**	0.096	0.040
L = 2^{10}	0.044	0.007	0.001	**0.001**	0.099	0.045
L = 2^{11}	0.038	0.005	0.019	**0.002**	0.102	0.042
L = 2^{12}	0.032	0.003	0.015	**0.001**	0.102	0.041
L = 2^{13}	0.023	**0.001**	**0.001**	0.004	0.101	0.046
L = 2^{14}	0.022	0.004	**0.001**	**0.001**	0.105	0.046
L = 2^{15}	0.019	0.007	0.002	**0.001**	0.103	0.053
Average	0.044	0.007	0.012	**0.002**	0.085	0.044

Table 4. MSE value performed with the fBm signal (best value is marked in bold).

Signal length			*SD***(fBm signal)**			
BCM	VFD	HM	DFA	PSDA	CEM	
L = 2^7	0.083	0.009	0.054	**0.003**	0.059	0.038
L = 2^8	0.067	0.023	0.004	**0.002**	0.048	0.048
L = 2^9	0.044	**0.002**	0.003	0.009	0.173	0.026

Signal length			***SD*(fBm signal)**			
$L = 2^{10}$	0.030	0.003	0.002	**< 0.001**	0.107	0.033
$L = 2^{11}$	0.020	0.057	0.003	**< 0.001**	0.098	0.041
$L = 2^{12}$	0.018	0.083	**0.002**	0.005	0.089	0.036
$L = 2^{13}$	0.026	0.105	**0.004**	0.022	0.027	0.044
$L = 2^{14}$	0.037	0.182	**0.004**	0.042	0.051	0.035
$L = 2^{15}$	0.049	0.183	**0.003**	0.065	0.029	0.029
Average	0.034	0.072	**0.009**	0.016	0.076	0.037

Table 5. MSE value performed with the Syn signal (best value is marked in bold).

Signal length			***SD*(fBm signal)**			
BCM	VFD	HM	DFA	PSDA	CEM	
$L = 2^{7}$	**0.056**	0.201	0.109	0.112	0.248	0.069
$L = 2^{8}$	**0.047**	0.150	0.089	0.095	0.154	0.056
$L = 2^{9}$	0.061	0.116	**0.040**	0.069	0.090	0.047
$L = 2^{10}$	0.034	0.088	**0.032**	0.049	0.056	0.042
$L = 2^{11}$	0.032	0.078	**0.019**	0.039	0.036	0.037
$L = 2^{12}$	0.023	0.079	**0.016**	0.036	0.028	0.031
$L = 2^{13}$	0.023	0.062	**0.014**	0.028	0.019	0.027
$L = 2^{14}$	0.018	0.054	**0.013**	0.024	0.014	0.026
$L = 2^{15}$	0.015	0.021	**0.011**	0.022	0.013	0.014
Average	**0.034**	0.094	0.038	0.053	0.073	0.039

Table 6. Deviation performed with the fBm signal (best value is marked in bold).

Signal length			***SD*(Syn signal)**			
BCM	VFD	HM	DFA	PSDA	CEM	
$L = 2^{7}$	**0.039**	0.151	0.056	0.085	0.278	0.036
$L = 2^{8}$	0.031	0.116	**0.026**	0.044	0.236	0.025
$L = 2^{9}$	0.023	0.074	**0.022**	0.043	0.141	0.046
$L = 2^{10}$	0.017	0.068	0.021	**0.016**	0.148	0.038
$L = 2^{11}$	0.018	0.070	0.019	**0.011**	0.165	0.030
$L = 2^{12}$	0.019	0.091	0.018	**0.010**	0.175	0.022
$L = 2^{13}$	0.022	0.063	0.017	**0.009**	0.127	0.020

Signal length			*SD*(Syn signal)			
$L=2^{14}$	0.019	0.049	0.015	**0.014**	0.121	0.017
$L=2^{15}$	**0.008**	0.011	0.009	0.012	0.119	0.012
Average	**0.022**	0.077	**0.022**	0.027	0.168	0.027

Table 7. Deviation performed with the Syn signal (best value is marked in bold).

4.4. Time-Dependent Fractal Dimensions (TDFD)

One of common measure of irregularity in fluctuations as time-sequential data may be the fractal dimension. Fractal dimensions estimate the degree of freedom of fluctuations in a signal. To measure the fractality in short time intervals of time-sequential data from one end of the waveform to the other sequentially, we may observe the dynamical changes in the fractal dimensions with respect the time series. These fractal dimensions, namely, the time-dependent fractal dimensions (TDFD) [22].

In this study, EEG signal was sampled at 512 Hz (or L =3,072 points) whose duration is 6 seconds. We set a window function is a rectangular type, window size = 512 points (1 s), moving window with intervals = 10 points (19.5 ms) because the temporal resolution of EEG is millisecond or even better [29]. The number of obtained points can compute from $N_{FD}=\lfloor (L - L_w)/\Delta t \rfloor + 1$ where L is a signal length, L_w is a window length ($L_w \leq L$), and Δt is an interval. Thus, we then obtained 257 points of fractal dimension. The time series-based algorithms of fractal dimension present more effective than frequency-based algorithms [16].

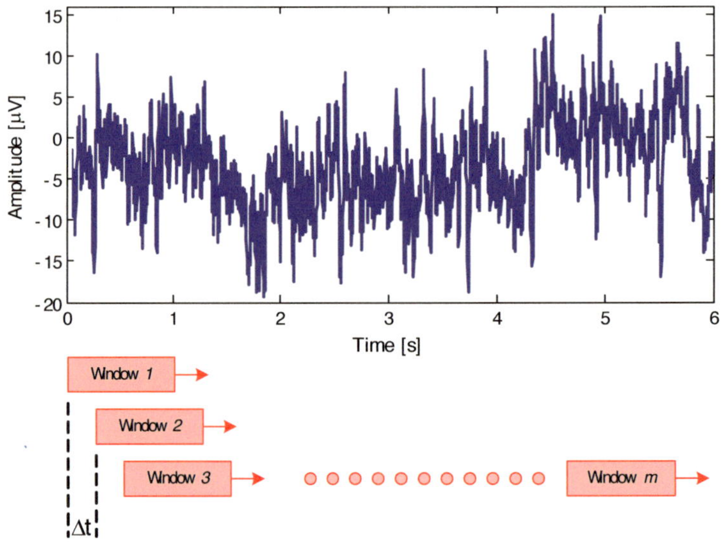

Figure 2. Computation process of TDFDs.

4.5. Evaluation of features by Kullback-Leibler divergence

In probability theory and information theory, the Kullback–Leibler divergence [34] (or called K-L divergence) is a measure of the difference between two probability distributions: from an actual probability distribution P to an arbitrary probability distribution Q.

$$D_{KL}\ (P \parallel Q)=\int_{-\infty}^{+\infty} p(x)\log \frac{p(x)}{q(x)}dx \tag{26}$$

For probability distributions P and Q of a discrete random variable is defined to be

$$D_{KL}\ (P \parallel Q)=\sum_i P(i)\log \frac{P(i)}{Q(i)} \tag{27}$$

Important properties of the K-L divergence are

1. The K–L divergence is always positive $D_{KL}\ (P \parallel Q)\geq 0$,
2. $D_{KL}\ (P \parallel Q)=0$ if and only if $P=Q$,
3. The K-L divergence is not symmetric $D_{KL}\ (P \parallel Q)\neq D_{KL}\ (Q \parallel P)$.

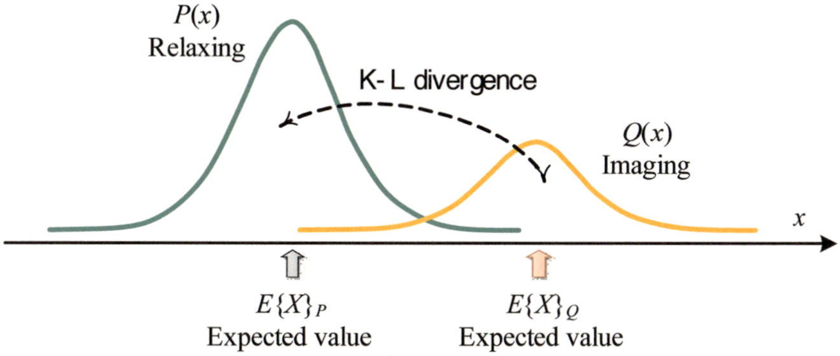

Figure 3. Feature extraction concepts on the basis of the K-L divergence.

The different expected values between imaging and relaxing periods are also proposed to use as the featuring parameter together with the K-L divergence. In general, if X is random variable defined on a probability space, then the different expected value of two random variables can be defined by

$$\Delta E\{X\}_{PQ}=\sum_i p_i x_i - \sum_j q_i x_j \tag{28}$$

In this study, we applied the K-L divergence and different expected values for finding the features between relaxing and imaging periods. According to Eq.(28), $P(i)$ is regarded as relaxing period, and $Q(i)$ is regarded as imaging period. The probability distributions can be approximated by normalizing histogram of the data. The output patterns of K-L divergences versus the different expected value are also shown in Fig. 4. These obtained results can be classified by the neural network. More explanations of this classification process are in chapter 5.

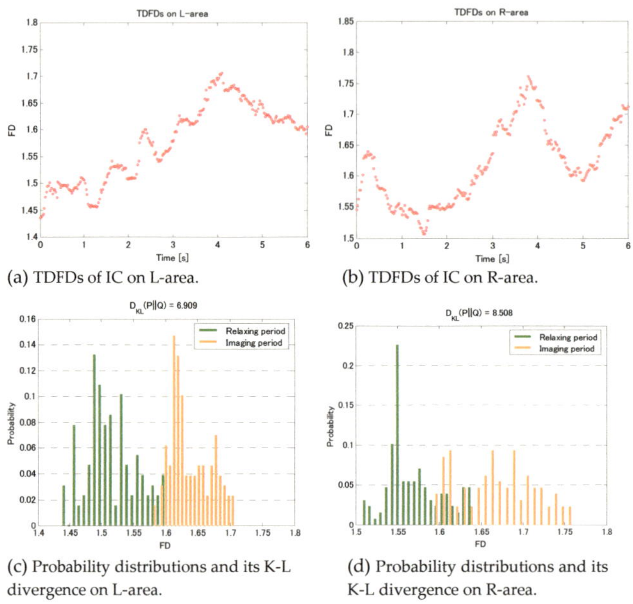

(a) TDFDs of IC on L-area.

(b) TDFDs of IC on R-area.

(c) Probability distributions and its K-L divergence on L-area.

(d) Probability distributions and its K-L divergence on R-area.

Figure 4. Left-hand movement imagination (LH-MI).

5. Neural network classifier

This study is concerned with the most common class of neural networks (NNs) called backpropagation algorithm. Backpropagation is an abbreviation for the backwards propagation of error. The learning process is processed based on the Levenberg–Marquardt (LM) backpropagation method [30] the Hessian matrix can be approximated as the following equation

$$\mathrm{H} \approx 2\mathbf{J}^T\mathbf{J} \tag{29}$$

and the gradient can be determined as

$$\nabla \mathrm{J} = 2J^{\,T}\mathbf{e} \tag{30}$$

where J is the Jacobian matrix that contains first derivatives of the network error with respect to weights and biases, and $\mathbf{e}$ is a vector of network errors.

$$J\left(w\right)=\begin{pmatrix}\frac{\partial e_1(w)}{\partial w_1} & \cdots & \frac{\partial e_1(w)}{\partial w_n}\\ \vdots & \ddots & \vdots\\ \frac{\partial e_N(w)}{\partial w_1} & \cdots & \frac{\partial e_N(w)}{\partial w_n}\end{pmatrix} \tag{31}$$

The LM algorithm can use for updating the vector of weights, **w**, by

$$\mathbf{w}_{n+1}=\mathbf{w}_n - \left(J^T J + \mu I\right)^{-1} J^T e \tag{32}$$

$$\Delta w= - \left(J^T J + \mu I\right)^{-1} J^T e \tag{33}$$

where I is an identity matrix, μ is a learning rate, and n is an iteration step. This algorithm is particularly well suited for training NN with MSE. Moreover, the LM algorithm has been shown to be much faster than backpropagation in a variety of applications [31].

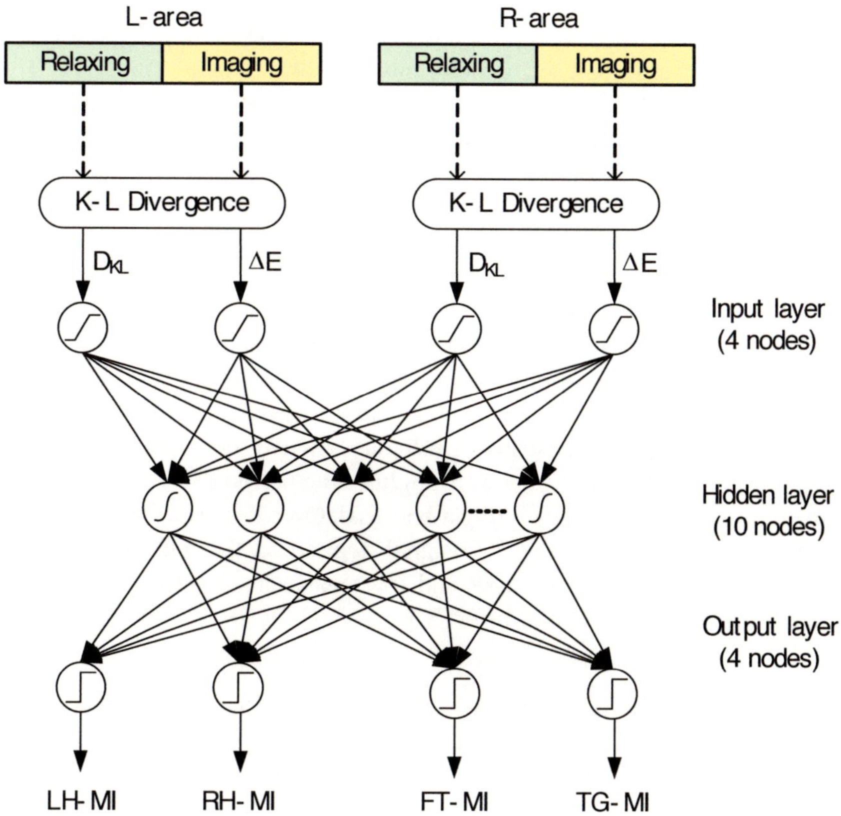

Figure 5. Classification diagram of the proposed method.

Task	Desired vector
LH-MI	$[1\ 0\ 0\ 0]^T$
RH-MI	$[0\ 1\ 0\ 0]^T$
FT-MI	$[0\ 0\ 1\ 0]^T$
TG-MI	$[0\ 0\ 0\ 1]^T$

Table 8. Desired vectors from the proposed network

5.1. Cross-validation procedure

Then, the featured parameters typically perform in terms of fractal properties. The NN was selected as classifier and it includes adaptive self-learning that was learnt to produce the correct classifications based on a set of training examples via cross validation process. A tenfold cross validation method was used to increase the reliability of the results [13]. For each experiment, we divided all the data into three sets, namely, the training set (50% of the entire data), cross validation set (20% of the entire data), and testing set (30% of the entire data). According to the tasks, a set of desired values for network training are shown in Table 8. The MSE rate is succeeded versus the iteration step is shown in Fig. 6. In Table 9, we compared the proposed method with the conventional feature, namely, band power estimation (BPE) [14]. The training process makes the network to define its decision boundaries. Figures 7 to 8 show a tight decision boundary after training the network.

6. Discussions

This chapter discusses the major contributions of this study, 12 electrode channels were used to measure EEG signal over the sensorimotor area of the cortex. The accuracy rates of motor imagery tasks are satisfactory. The error in this classification is due to the ambiguous data between the relaxing and imaging periods, particularly when the subjects have imagined the movements. However, in this experiment, throughout the period of recoding raw EEG signals without training and also without rejecting a bad trial. On contrary, they can be different for different individuals. This makes the EEG signal depend on the measured subject. Even if different persons perform the same tasks and the measurement was done under identical conditions the resulting signals could differ [35].

The proposed method provides 2880 features for each subject, whereas BPE method provides 21600 features. The current features obtained from the proposed method present an easy practicable and reliable method for training the classification algorithms. Nevertheless, the number of features from BPE method can be reduced by changing the number of electrodes. We used the NN to classify the features processed by BPE method. After learning the NN, learning curves and decision boundaries of BPE method is shown in Fig. 9. As the results,

http://dx.doi.org/10.5772/55801

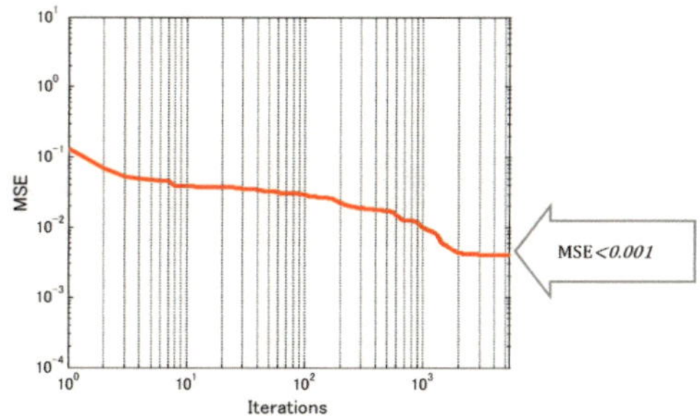

Figure 6. Log-log plot of learning curve.

Method		Accuracy [%]		
LH-MI	RH-MI	FT-MI	TG-MI	
BPE	77.6	79.5	76.4	77.3
Proposed	82.5	84.3	83.6	82.6

Table 9. A comparison result of average accuracy rates.

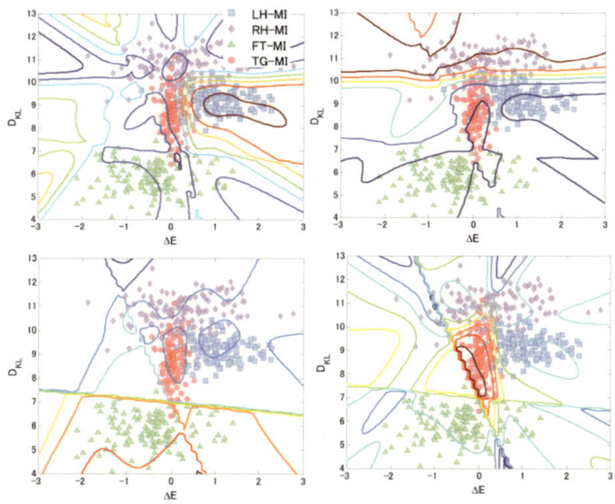

Figure 7. Decision boundary of the trained network.

output decision functions of classifying features based on BPE method does not perform well and cannot made clearly separation boundaries.

The six algorithms present specific properties in terms of capability and variability. Some algorithms appeared inapplicable for the EEG time series data in this study, such as PSDA and CEM algorithms, for example. The main reason was that two algorithms based on frequency analysis since estimating the Hurst exponent can be utilized by means of the FFT method where

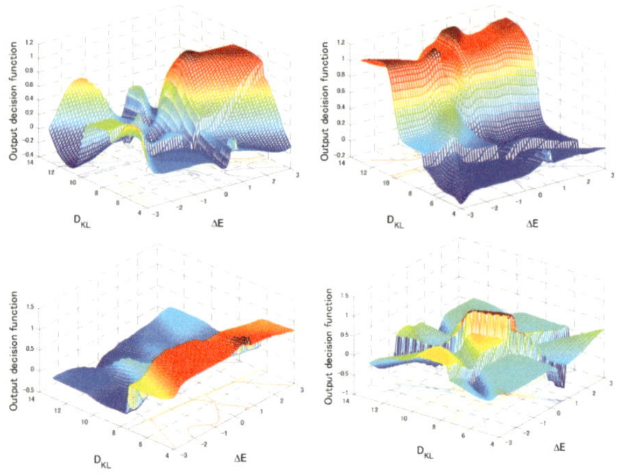

Figure 8. Corresponding 3-D surface of decision boundaries for each task.

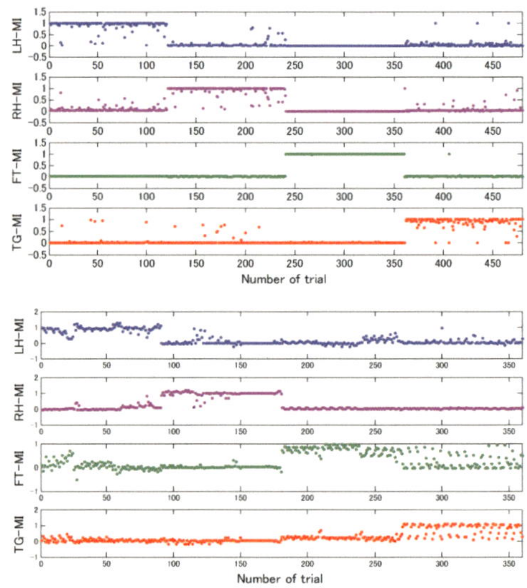

Figure 9. Updated weight values of the NN after learning; (Top panel) Proposed method, (Bottom panel) BPE Method.

the FFT can be substantially applicable in the long-time series data, and it easily declines when the EEG data has been analyzed in a short-time series. However, we can enhance the variability and avoid such drawbacks by increasing the sampling rate at the same period of experiment. In terms of variability, the HM algorithm presents the lowest average values of SD. The DFA provides the fast computation time and also presents reasonable values in terms of accuracy and variability when comparison with each other. Although, VDF gives extremely fast computation time but the VFD itself has the drawbacks in terms of accuracy and robustness. The VFD algorithm appropriates for real-time application, since its consumed computation time was less than 10 ms. Moreover, as proposed algorithms we suggest that the most

http://dx.doi.org/10.5772/55801

appropriate algorithm depends on an application purpose; for instance, the HM algorithm was suited for evaluating the FD of EEG data with high precision, whereas HM algorithm extremely consumed the processing time in comparison with the other algorithms. To show the performance of all algorithms, we then compared all estimated FDs with the theoretical value especially computed by short interval, i.e., 2^7, 2^8 and 2^9 points; these results were shown in Figs. 10 to 15.

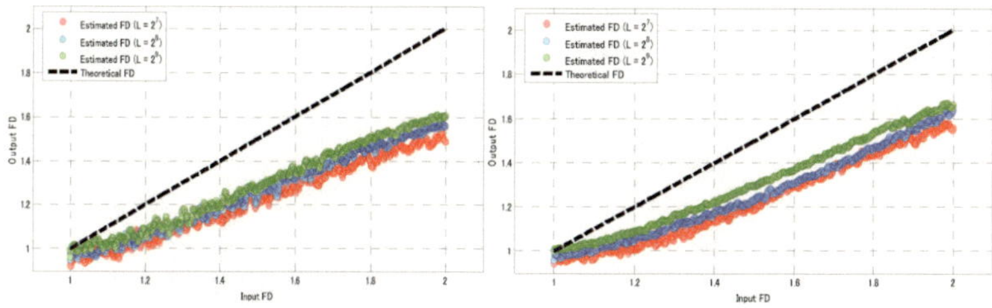

Figure 10. Fractal dimension evaluated by BCM. (Right) fBm signal; (left) Syn signal.

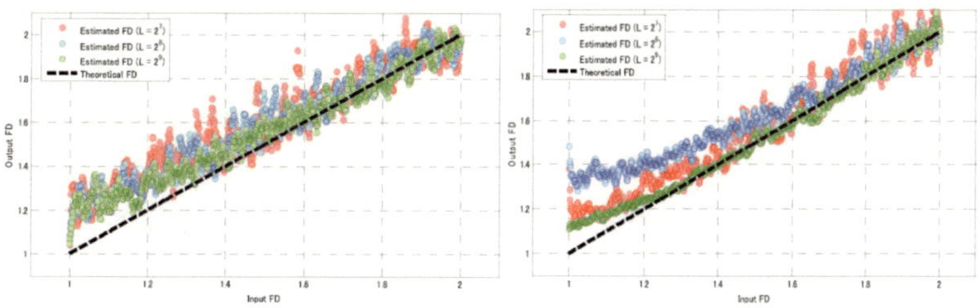

Figure 11. Fractal dimension evaluated by VFD. (Right) fBm signal; (left) Syn signal.

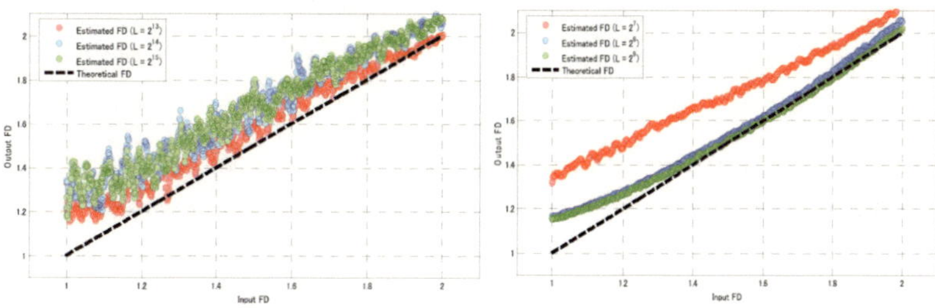

Figure 12. Fractal dimension evaluated by HM. (Right) fBm signal; (left) Syn signal.

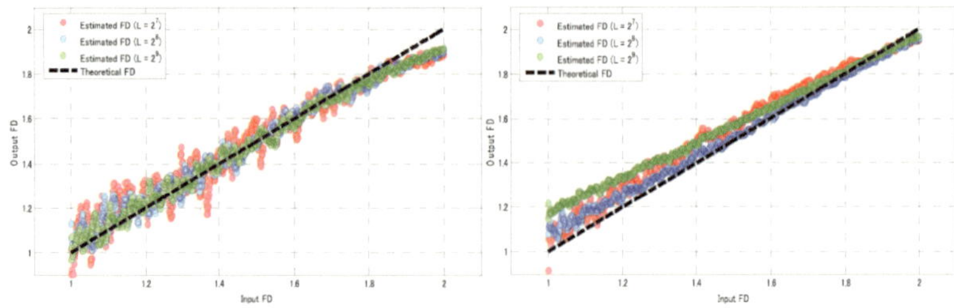

Figure 13. Fractal dimension evaluated by DFA. (Right) fBm signal; (left) Syn signal.

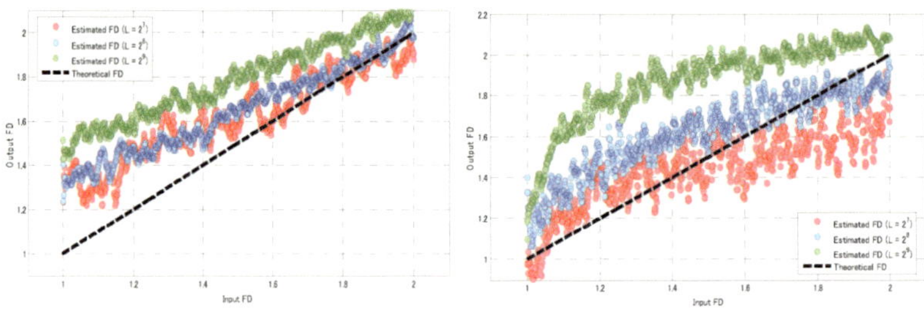

Figure 14. Fractal dimension evaluated by PSDA. (Right) fBm signal; (left) Syn signal.

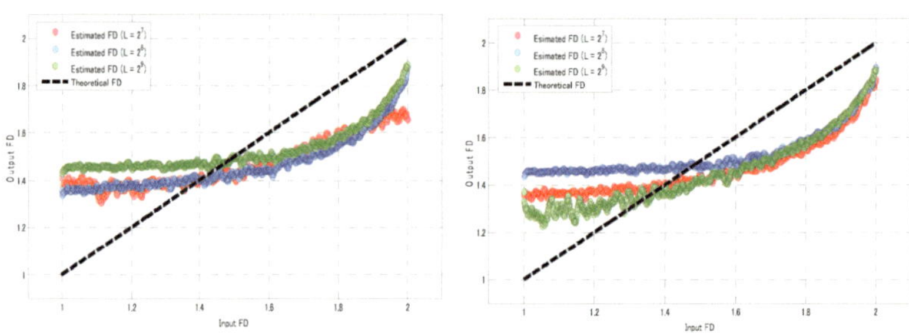

Figure 15. Fractal dimension evaluated by CEM. (Right) fBm signal; (left) Syn signal.

7. Conclusion

By selecting the best performance of fractal algorithm, we can obviously improve the rate of classification and can develop the novel methods in terms of fractal properties. Fractal features and the experimental framework can be applied not only binary-command BCIs, but also multi-command BCIs. The measurement of FD from EEG data can be capable not only in particular works, but also in publicity data. The FD characterizes the self-affine property of EEG data and has a direct relation to the different tasks.

Author details

Montri Phothisonothai and Katsumi Watanabe

Research Center for Advanced Science and Technology, The University of Tokyo, Japan Society for the Promotion of Science, Tokyo, Japan

References

[1] Grassberger, P, & Procaccia, I. Estimation of the Kolmogorov Entropy from a Chaotic Signal. Phys. Rev. A (1983). , 28, 2591-2593.

[2] Pincus, S. M, Gladstone, I. M, & Ehrenkranz, R. A. A Regularity Statistics for Medical Data Analysis. J. Clin. Monit. (1991). , 7, 335-345.

[3] Katz, M. J. Fractals and the Analysis of Waveforms. Comput. Biol. Med. (1998).

[4] Barnsley, M. F. Fractals Everywhere, Ch. II and III, Academic Press Professional; (1993).

[5] Grassberger, P, & Procaccia, I. Measuring Strangeness of Strange Attractors. Phys. Lett. D (1983). , 148, 63-68.

[6] Badii, R, & Politi, A. Statistical Description of Chaotic Attractors: The Dimension Function. J. Stat. Phys. (1985). , 40, 725-750.

[7] Boostani, R, & Moradi, M. H. A New Approach in the BCI Research based on Fractal Dimension as Feature and Adaboost as Classifier. J. Neural Eng. (2004). l., 1, 212-217.

[8] Popivanov, D, Jivkova, S, Stomonyakov, V, & Nicolova, G. Effect of Independence Component Analysis on Multifractality of EEG during Visual-Motor Task. Sig. Pro. (2005). , 85, 2112-23.

[9] Lutzenberger, W, Elbert, T, Birbaumer, N, Ray, W. J, & Schupp, H. The Scalp Distribution of the Fractal Dimension of the EEG and its Variation with Mental Tasks. Brain Topo. (1992). , 5, 27-34.

[10] Prei, l H, Lutzenberger, W, Pulvermüller, F, & Birbaumer, N. Fractal Dimensions of Short EEG Time Series in Humans. Neurosci. Lett. (1997). , 225, 77-80.

[11] Phothisonothai, M, & Nakagawa, M. EEG-based Classification of Motor Imagery Tasks using Fractal Dimension and Neural Network for Brain-Computer Interface. IEICE Trans. Inf. Syst. (2008). ED: 44-53., 91.

[12] Phothisonothai, M, & Nakagawa, M. EEG Signal Classification Method based on Fractal Features and Neural Network. The 30th IEEE EMBC (2008). , 3880-3883.

[13] Setiono, R. Feedforward Neural Network Construction using Cross Validation. Neural Comput. (2005)., 13, 2783-2786.

[14] Palaniappan, R. Utilizing Gamma Band to Improve Mental Task based Brain-Computer Interface Design. IEEE Trans. Neural Net. Rehabil. Eng. (2006)., 14, 299-303.

[15] Mandelbrot, B. B. The Fractal Geometry of Nature. W.H. Freeman, New York; (1983).

[16] Phothisonothai, M, & Nakagawa, M. Fractal-based EEG Data Analysis of Body Parts Movement Imagery Tasks. J Physiol Sci. (2007)., 57(4), 217-226.

[17] Kinsner, W. Batch and Real-time Computation of a Fractal Dimension based on Variance of a Time Series. Univ. Manitoba Canada. Tech. Report (1994). del, 94-6.

[18] Higuchi, T. Approach to an Irregular Time Series on the Basis of the Fractal Theory. Physica D (1988)., 31, 277-83.

[19] Peng, C. K, Mietus, J, Hausdorff, J. M, Havlin, S, Stanley, H. E, & Goldberger, A. L. Long Range Anticorrelations and Non-Gaussian Behavior of the Heartbeat. Phys. Rev. Lett. (1993)., 70, 1343-1346.

[20] Peng, C. K, Havlin, S, Stanley, H. E, & Goldberger, A. L. Quantification of Scaling Exponents and Crossover Phenomena in Nonstationary Heartbeat Time Series. Chaos (1995)., 5, 82-87.

[21] Nakagawa, M. A Critical Exponent Method to Evaluate Fractal Dimension of Self-affine Data. J. Phys. Soc. Jpn. (1993)., 62, 4233-4239.

[22] Sabanal, S, & Nakagawa, M. The Fractal Properties of Vocal Sound and their Application in the Speech Recognition Model. Chaos Soli. Frac. (1996)., 7, 1825-1843.

[23] Petry, A, Augusto, D, & Barone, C. Speaker Identification using Nonlinear Dynamical Features. Chaos Soli Frac. (2002)., 13, 221-231.

[24] Phothisonothai, M, & Nakagawa, M. EEG-based Fractal Analysis of Different Motor Imagery Tasks using Critical Exponent Method. Int. J. Bio. Life Sci. (2006). , 1(3), 175-180.

[25] Mandelbrot, B. B, & Van Ness, J. W. Fractional Brownian Motions, Fractional Noises and Applications. SIAM Rev. (1968)., 10, 422-437.

[26] Fougère, P. F. On the Accuracy of Spectrum Analysis of Red Noise Processes using Maximum Entropy and Periodogram Methods: Simulation Studies and Application to Geographical Data. J. Geograp. Res. (1985)., 95, 4355-4366.

[27] Eke, A, Hermann, P, Kocsis, L, & Kozak, L. R. Fractal Characterization of Complexity in Temporal Physiological Signals. Physio. Meas. (2002). R, 1-38.

[28] Tricot, C. Curves and Fractal Dimension. New York: Springer-Verlag;(1995).

[29] Koenig, T, Studer, D, Hubl, D, Melie, L, & Strik, W. K. Brain connectivity at different time-scales measured with EEG. Philos. Trans R. Soc. Lond. B Biol. Sci. (2005). , 360, 1015-1024.

[30] Marquardt, D. W. An Algorithm for Least-Squares Estimation of Non-linear Parameters. J. Soc. Indust. Appl. Math. (1963). , 11, 431-441.

[31] Principe, J. C, Euliano, N. R, & Lefebvre, W. C. Neural and Adaptive Systems: Fundamentals through Simulations. John Wiley & Sons; (2000).

[32] Nakagawa, M. Chaos and Fractals in Engineering. World Sciencetific; (1999).

[33] Esteller, R, Vachtsevanos, G, Echauz, J, & Litt, B. A Comparison of Waveform Fractal Dimension Algorithms. IEEE Trans. Circuits Syst. (2001). , 48, 177-183.

[34] Kullback, S, & Leibler, R. A. On Information and Sufficiency. Ann. Math. Statist. (1951). , 22, 79-86.

[35] Curran, E, & Stokes, M. Learning to Control Brain Activity: A Review of the Production and Control of EEG Components for Driving Brain-Computer Interface (BCI) Systems. Brain Cogn. (2003). , 51, 326-336.

[36] Phothisonothai, M, & Nakagawa, M. A Classification Method of Different Motor Imagery Tasks Based on Fractal Features for Brain-Machine Interface. J. Intre. Neurosci. (2009)., 8, 95-122.

Chapter 6

Using Autoregressive Models of Wavelet Bases in the Design of Mental Task-Based BCIs

Farshad Faradji, Farhad Faradji, Rabab K. Ward and Gary E. Birch

Additional information is available at the end of the chapter

http://dx.doi.org/10.5772/55803

1. Introduction

1.1. Wavelet packet analysis

A powerful tool for analyzing the characteristics of the signal in the frequency domain as well as in the time domain is wavelet analysis. To analyze the signal, it can be decomposed into some levels successively by wavelet transform. At each level, decomposition yields two types of components: the approximations component which is the low-frequency high-scale portion of the signal, and the details component which is the high-frequency low-scale portion. The resultant approximations component is decomposed repetitively after each level. This is usually referred to as wavelet decomposition. Fig. 1.a shows a signal decomposed into three levels by wavelet decomposition.

There is another approach for signal decomposition in which at each level, not only the approximations component but the details component is also decomposed. This is called wavelet packet analysis, and each of the components at different levels is referred to as a node or wavelet packet. Wavelet packet analysis is more flexible but more complicated than wavelet decomposition. Please see Fig. 1.b for more details. In this figure, the signal is decomposed into three levels using wavelet packet analysis.

Let us assume that the maximum frequency of the signal is f_m. At each level of decomposition, the approximations component has the lower half of the frequency spectrum of the signal decomposed, and the details component has the higher half of the signal's frequency spectrum. The frequency spectrums pertaining to different packets in three-level wavelet packet analysis is shown in Table 1.

		Frequency							
Signal		$0-f_m$							
Level	1	$0-0.5f_m$				$0.5f_m-f_m$			
	2	$0-0.25f_m$		$0.25f_m-0.5f_m$		$0.5f_m-0.75f_m$		$0.75f_m-f_m$	
	3	$0-0.125f_m$	$0.125f_m-0.25f_m$	$0.25f_m-0.375f_m$	$0.375f_m-0.5f_m$	$0.5f_m-0.625f_m$	$0.625f_m-0.75f_m$	$0.75f_m-0.875f_m$	$0.875f_m-f_m$

Table 1. Frequency Spectrums in Wavelet Packet Analysis

The packets produced by the wavelet packet analysis make an upside-down "tree", whose root is the initial signal and its branches are coming down. If we cut some branches of this tree (i.e., we exclude some packets from this tree), what remains is called a "sub-tree". The final nodes (terminal nodes or leaves) of each sub-tree are a "wavelet basis" for the initial signal. In other words, a wavelet basis is by definition a set of packets containing all non-overlapping frequency components of the initial signal. The packets of a basis can be selected from different levels. Each wavelet basis can serve as a representative for the initial signal in the wavelet domain. Here are some examples of the basis with respect to Fig. 1.b: $b_1 = \{A_1, D_2\}$, $b_2 = \{A_1, A_{21}, D_{22}\}$, $b_3 = \{A_{111}, D_{112}, D_{12}, D_2\}$, $b_4 = \{A_{11}, A_{121}, D_{122}, A_{211}, D_{212}, D_{22}\}$. It can be seen that wavelet decomposition is a special case of wavelet packet analysis (b_3).

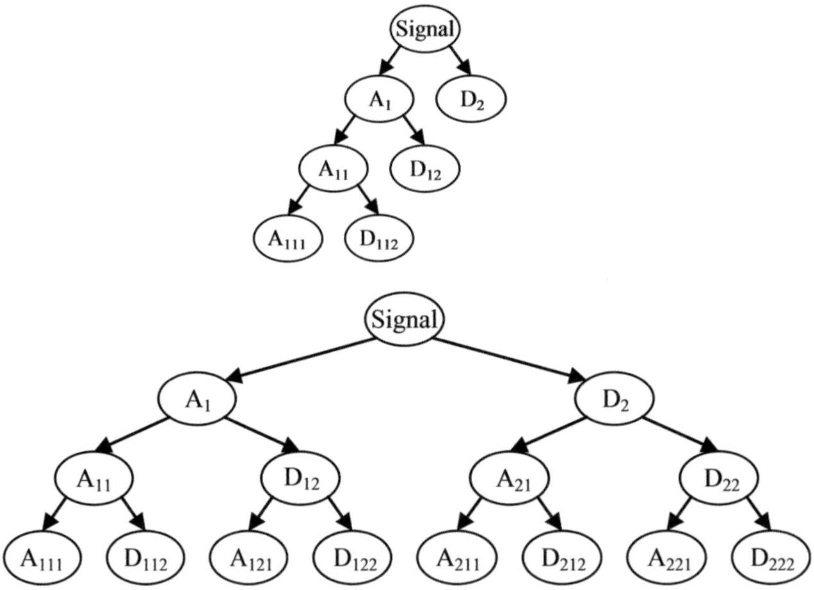

Figure 1. Decomposition of a signal: (a) wavelet decomposition, (b) wavelet packet analysis

The best sub-tree (or basis) is a sub-tree (or basis) which minimizes a specific cost function. Cost functions are usually defined based on an entropy function (e.g., Shannon's entropy function) [1]. One can also define his or her own cost function. To find the best sub-tree, the costs of all nodes in the main tree are measured. Then, in the direction from leaf to root and at each level, the cost of the node and its resultant child nodes are compared to each other. If the sum of the child nodes' costs is higher than or equal to the parent node's cost, the child nodes are cut off from the tree; otherwise, the child nodes remain in the tree, and the cost of the parent's node will be updated (replaced) with the sum of the child nodes' costs. This parent node is in turn one of the child nodes for the upper level. The same comparison (with updated costs) is done for the upper levels until the root level is reached. What remains at the end is the best sub-tree and its leaves are the best basis for the initial signal.

1.2. Brain–computer interfaces

Brain–Computer Interfaces (BCIs) providing an alternative channel for communication and intended to be used by motor-disabled individuals can be categorized into two main classes. Synchronized BCIs are the first and earliest class, in which the user is able to activate the system during pre-defined time periods only. The second class is referred to as asynchronous or self-paced BCIs. These systems are more useful, since the user can activate them whenever he or she wishes. At each time instant, a self-paced BCI is either in the intentional-control (IC) state or in the no-control (NC) state. IC is the active state, and NC is the inactive state (i.e., the state during which the output of the system is inactive).

The performance of a self-paced BCI is usually evaluated by two rates: the true positive rate (TPR) and the false positive rate (FPR). TPR is considered as the rate of correctly classifying intentional-control states, while FPR is defined as the rate of misclassifying no-control states.

A neurological phenomenon is a set of specific features or patterns in signals produced by the brain. They arise due to brain activities to which these phenomena are time-locked. Different types of neurological phenomena include the activity of neural cells (ANCs), P300, brain rhythms such as the Mu, Beta, and Gamma rhythms, movement-related potentials (MRPs), slow cortical potentials (SCPs), visual evoked potentials (VEPs), steady-state visual evoked potentials (SSVEPs), and mental tasks (MTs). For a review of the field of BCIs, please refer to [2]-[7].

The dataset of Keirn and Aunon [8] containing the EEG signals of five mental tasks is used in this paper, as it has been used in a variety of studies such as [9]-[55]. Although most of these studies can classify mental tasks to some extent, only a few of them care about false positives or confusion matrices and report them [32],[45]-[48]. The classification error is reported in studies [21],[31],[49] as well. The rates of correct classification are the only measure well paid attention to in the remaining studies. False positives are of great importance in BCI applications, they are hence fairly considered in this study.

1.3. Autoregressive modeling

The autoregressive (AR) model of an order K of a signal is defined as follows:

$$x[m]=\sum_{k=1}^{K}a_k x[m-k]+e[m] \tag{1}$$

where $x[m]$ is the one-dimensional signal at time instant m, and a_k represents the AR coefficients. It is assumed that the error signal, $e[m]$, is a stochastic process and is independent of previous values of the signal x. It is also postulated that $e[m]$ has a zero mean and a finite variance. The autoregressive coefficients, a_k, should be estimated from the finite samples of the signal $x[m]$.

The most popular method to find the AR coefficients is the Burg algorithm [56] which computes coefficients at successive orders in the forward direction as well as in the backward direction. This method is used in this paper to estimate the AR coefficients.

Figuring out the optimal AR model order is not straightforward, even though some techniques including the Reflection Coefficient [18], the Information Theoretic criterion or Akaike Information Criterion (AIC), the Autoregressive Transfer Function criterion, and the Final Prediction Error (FPE) criterion [57] have been introduced. If the order of the model is too low, the whole signal cannot be captured in the model. On the other hand, the more the order is, the more portion of the noise is captured. Since there is no guarantee that the above mentioned techniques work well in every application and since FPR is of great importance in our application, we do not use these techniques to find the optimal AR model order. Instead, to be on the safe side, we vary the order in a reasonably large range and select the best order based on the performance of the system evaluated via nested five-fold cross-validation.

1.4. Quadratic discriminant analysis

The Quadratic Discriminant Analysis (QDA) classifier [58] assumes the classes have normal distributions. For QDA method of classification, unlike the linear discriminant analysis, the covariance matrices of the classes can be different. For a two-class problem, the quadratic discriminant function by definition is as follows:

$$qdf(x) = -\frac{1}{2}x^T(\hat{\Sigma}_1^{-1} - \hat{\Sigma}_2^{-1})x + (\hat{\mu}_1^T\hat{\Sigma}_1^{-1} - \hat{\mu}_2^T\hat{\Sigma}_2^{-1})x - \frac{1}{2}\ln(\frac{|\hat{\Sigma}_1|}{|\hat{\Sigma}_2|}) - \frac{1}{2}(\hat{\mu}_1^T\hat{\Sigma}_1^{-1}\hat{\mu}_1 - \hat{\mu}_2^T\hat{\Sigma}_2^{-1}\hat{\mu}_2) - \ln(\frac{C_{21}}{C_{12}}\frac{\pi_2}{\pi_1}) \tag{2}$$

where x is the vector to be classified, $\hat{\mu}_1$, $\hat{\mu}_2$ are the estimated mean vectors of classes 1 and 2, $\hat{\Sigma}_1$, $\hat{\Sigma}_2$ are the estimated covariance matrices of class 1 and class 2, π_1, π_2 are the prior probabilities of the two classes, C_{12} is the cost of misclassifying a member of class 1 as class 2, and C_{21} is the cost due to misclassifying a member of class 2.

The decision rule for classification is:

$$x_0 \in \begin{cases} \omega_1 & if\, qdf(x_0) \geq 0 \\ \omega_2 & if\, qdf(x_0) < 0 \end{cases} \tag{3}$$

where ω_1, ω_2 represent class 1 and class 2, respectively.

http://dx.doi.org/10.5772/55803

In this paper, the same value for the cost of false negative C_{21} and false positive C_{12} is used. It is also assumed that the a-priori probabilities of the two classes are equal.

2. Methods

2.1. Data

As mentioned in the Section 1.2, we used the EEG data which has been collected previously by Keirn and Aunon [8]. The EEG signals of this dataset belong to seven subjects, each performing five different mental tasks. The mental tasks include baseline, mentally computing a nontrivial multiplication, composing a letter to a friend mentally, rotating a three-dimensional object mentally, and visualizing writing a sequence of numbers on a blackboard. The subjects did not vocalize or gesture in any way when their signals were being recorded. Each session of recording comprises five trials of each mental task; therefore, there are a total of twenty five trials in a session. Only one session was performed on a single day. The length of each trial is ten seconds. Two of the subjects (Subjects 2 and 7) completed only one session, while one of them (Subject 5) completed three sessions. In this study, we used the data of subjects who completed at least 10 trials. Since the signals of Subject 4 were missing some data, we did not use them. New numbers were assigned to the subjects whose signals have been used in this study (see Table 2). Table 2 also shows the number of trials completed by each subject.

Subject number								
	original study	1	2	3	4	5	6	7
	this study	1	–	2	–	3	4	–
Number of completed trials		10	5	10	10	15	10	5

Table 2. The Number of Completed Trials for Each Subject

EEG signals were recorded from six channels (electrodes) while the subjects were seated in a room which is sound-controlled and with dim lighting. The electrodes were placed at positions C3, C4, P3, P4, O1, and O2 (based on the International 10-20 System) on the scalp. The reference electrodes were two electrically linked mastoids, A1 and A2. Fig. 2 shows the electrodes' locations. During recordings, the impedances between each electrode and the reference electrodes were kept below 5 kΩ. The signals were sampled at 250 Hz with an A/D converter (twelve-bit Lab Master) and a bank of amplifiers (Grass 7P511, with the band-pass filters set at 0.1-100 Hz). The system was calibrated at the beginning of each session with a known voltage.

Two EOG electrodes were placed below and at the outside corner of the left eye for detecting ocular artifacts. Since in this study, we did not remove any segment of the EEG signals due to ocular artifacts, the signals of EOG electrodes were not used.

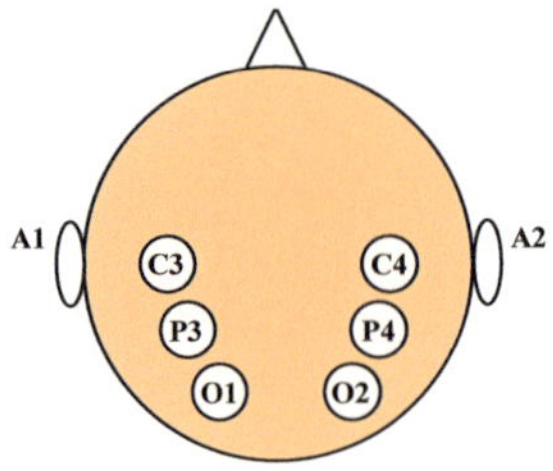

Figure 2. Electrodes positions based on International 10-20 System.

Even though this dataset has not been collected in a self-paced paradigm, we are using it as an introductory exploration. It is obvious that in a self-paced paradigm, brain activities do not change, but since the pacing information (the exact start and end time of the mental tasks) is not known, training the BCI system would be more complicated.

2.2. Procedure

2.2.1. The design of BCI systems

In this paper, we apply wavelet packet analysis to the design of a two-state self-paced mental task-based BCI. We develop and custom design five different BCIs for each subject based on the five mental tasks. In each BCI, one mental task is considered as the intentional-control task and the other four mental tasks are considered as the no-control tasks. Unlike the no-control tasks, the intentional-control task should activate the BCI system. Even though a BCI in which the baseline is the intentional-control task is practically useless, we consider it here for comparison purposes. We then determine the two most discriminatory mental tasks for each subject by comparing the performance of the five BCI systems of that subject. The overview of the proposed BCI system is illustrated in Fig. 3.

We customize the BCIs for every subject and mental task, since it has been proven that customized BCIs yield better results than general BCIs [59]-[60].

The EEG signals of four subjects are exploited. We use the first ten trials for Subject 3, and all ten trials for the other three subjects. The sampling rate is 250 Hz and each trial is 10 seconds long; therefore, there are 2500 samples in every trial of each mental task.

Each trial is divided into 45 256-sample overlapping segments. Each segment overlaps with the adjacent segment by 206 samples (about 80%). Hence, for each subject, the total number of segments for each mental task is 450. The segments with the length of more than 1 second are sufficiently long to get a good characteristic of the signal [61].

For each BCI, we have six different EEG channels. Each channel has its own feature vector and classifier. For each channel, the EEG segment is decomposed using wavelet packet analysis and the AR models of the resultant wavelet packets are estimated using the Burg algorithm. The AR coefficients of the packets belonging to a given wavelet basis are concatenated into a vector to form the channel's feature vector. The classifier of each channel is QDA. Each QDA

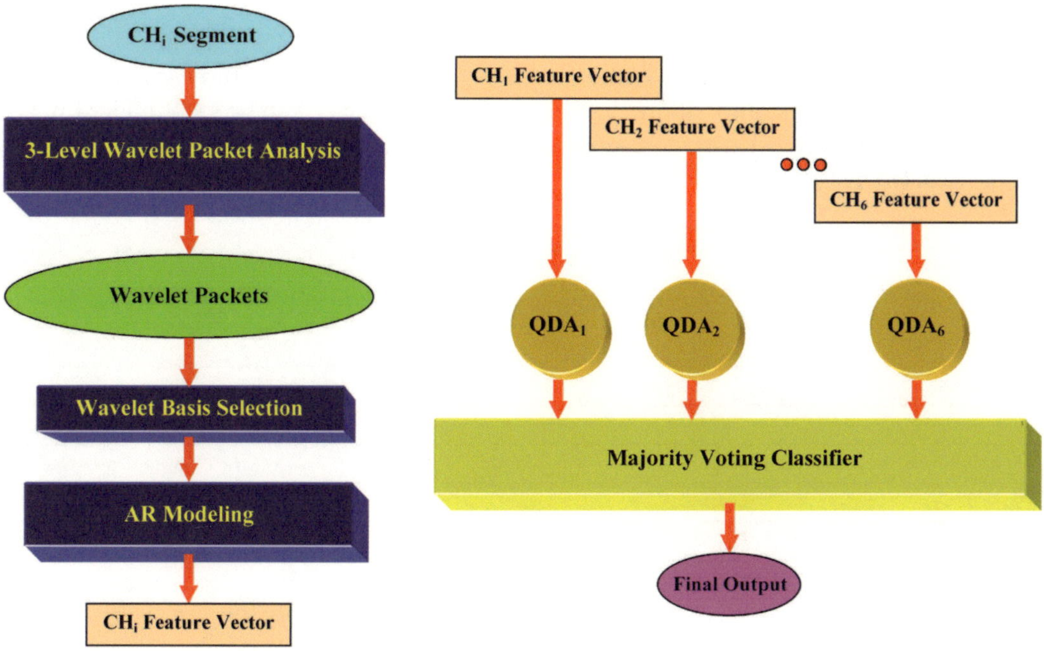

Figure 3. Overview of the proposed BCI system.

classifies the input EEG segment as an IC or NC segment. The task of the second-stage classifier which is a simple majority voting classifier is to determine whether the final output of the system is IC or NC.

2.2.2. Training, cross-validation, and testing

For each subject, the 5×450 segments pertaining to the five mental tasks are divided into a training set, a validation set, and a test set. The training set is used to train the system. The validation set is used to select the best wavelet, the best wavelet basis, and the best AR model order. The test set is used to evaluate the final performance of the system. The performance of a system evaluated based on a fixed split of data into training, validation and test sets is not accurate and robust, therefore, we perform nested five-fold (or 5×5) cross-validation. While the model selection is done during the inner cross-validation process, the system performance is estimated in the outer cross-validation.

The data are split into the five outer folds, for each of which 80% of the data is used for training and validation and 20% of the data is used for testing. The portion of data which is assigned for training and validation are further divided into five inner folds. For each inner fold, 80% of the data is used for training and the rest is used for validation. Hence, what we report as the cross-validation and testing results are the average over 25 and 5 different cases, respectively.

2.2.3. *Different wavelet bases*

Each of these segments is decomposed by wavelet packet analysis into three levels. In three-level wavelet packet decomposition, there exist 14 packets which can be seen in Fig. 1.b. We have 25 different wavelet bases representing the initial segment in the wavelet domain. These bases are listed in Table 3.

Basis	Packets							
1	A_1				D_2			
2	A_1				A_{21}	D_{22}		
3	A_1				A_{21}	A_{221}	D_{222}	
4	A_1				A_{211}	D_{212}	D_{22}	
5	A_1				A_{211}	D_{212}	A_{221}	D_{222}
6	A_{11}	D_{12}			D_2			
7	A_{11}	D_{12}			A_{21}	D_{22}		
8	A_{11}	D_{12}			A_{21}	A_{221}	D_{222}	
9	A_{11}	D_{12}			A_{211}	D_{212}	D_{22}	
10	A_{11}	D_{12}			A_{211}	D_{212}	A_{221}	D_{222}
11	A_{11}	A_{121}	D_{122}		D_2			
12	A_{11}	A_{121}	D_{122}		A_{21}	D_{22}		
13	A_{11}	A_{121}	D_{122}		A_{21}	A_{221}	D_{222}	
14	A_{11}	A_{121}	D_{122}		A_{211}	D_{212}	D_{22}	
15	A_{11}	A_{121}	D_{122}		A_{211}	D_{212}	A_{221}	D_{222}
16	A_{111}	D_{112}	D_{12}		D_2			
17	A_{111}	D_{112}	D_{12}		A_{21}	D_{22}		
18	A_{111}	D_{112}	D_{12}		A_{21}	A_{221}	D_{222}	
19	A_{111}	D_{112}	D_{12}		A_{211}	D_{212}	D_{22}	
20	A_{111}	D_{112}	D_{12}		A_{211}	D_{212}	A_{221}	D_{222}
21	A_{111}	D_{112}	A_{121}	D_{122}	D_2			
22	A_{111}	D_{112}	A_{121}	D_{122}	A_{21}	D_{22}		
23	A_{111}	D_{112}	A_{121}	D_{122}	A_{21}	A_{221}	D_{222}	
24	A_{111}	D_{112}	A_{121}	D_{122}	A_{211}	D_{212}	D_{22}	
25	A_{111}	D_{112}	A_{121}	D_{122}	A_{211}	D_{212}	A_{221}	D_{222}

Table 3. Different Wavelet Bases

2.2.4. *The relationship between the packet length and the AR order*

The length of a child packet is almost half of its parent packet's length. Since the initial decomposed segment is 256 samples long, the packets at levels 1, 2, and 3 contain approximately 128, 64, and 32 samples, respectively. When we estimate the packets' AR model, we

http://dx.doi.org/10.5772/55803

consider their lengths as a factor in selecting the appropriate AR order. In other words, we try to keep the same ratios between the orders of the packets at different levels. Therefore, if we set the AR order of a first-level packet as *K*, the AR orders for the packets at levels 2 and 3 would be close to *K*/2 and *K*/4, respectively. Table 4 provides the information on the sets of AR orders used for different levels of decomposition.

		AR Orders' Set												
		1	**2**	**3**	**4**	**5**	**6**	**7**	**8**	**9**	**10**	**11**	**12**	**13**
Level	**1**	12	13	14	15	16	17	18	19	20	21	22	23	24
	2	6	7	7	8	8	9	9	10	10	11	11	12	12
	3	3	4	4	4	4	5	5	5	5	6	6	6	6

Table 4. The Sets of AR Orders Used for Different Levels of Decomposition

2.2.5. *Different wavelets*

Wavelets from various families are used. For each subject and each mental task, the wavelet with the best performance during nested five-fold cross-validation is selected. The 36 wavelets tested are from the Haar, Daubechies, Biorthogonal, Coiflets, and Symlets families. We assign a number to each of the wavelets and list them in Table 5.

Number	Wavelet	Family	Number	Wavelet	Family	Number	Wavelet	Family
1	db1 (Haar)	Daubechies	11	bior1.3	Biorthogonal	25	coif1	Coiflets
2	db2		12	bior1.5		26	coif2	
3	db3		13	bior2.2		27	coif3	
4	db4		14	bior2.4		28	coif4	
5	db5		15	bior2.6		29	coif5	
6	db6		16	bior2.8		30	sym2	Symlets
7	db7		17	bior3.1		31	sym3	
8	db8		18	bior3.3		32	sym4	
9	db9		19	bior3.5		33	sym5	
10	db10		20	bior3.7		34	sym6	
			21	bior3.9		35	sym7	
			22	bior4.4		36	sym8	
			23	bior5.5				
			24	bior6.8				

Table 5. Wavelets Used from Different Families

2.2.6. The proposed method to find the best wavelet basis

As mentioned earlier in the Introduction section, to find the best wavelet basis, different cost functions, which are usually different types of entropy functions, have been proposed. Unfortunately, the methodology based on the cost function is not working here because of two main reasons. First of all, since we have a number of segments for training the system which are not fully stationary, different wavelet bases are chosen for different segments. Hence, we can not come up with a single basis. Secondly, if we suppose that we are able to find the best basis based on a defined cost function, there is no guarantee that the selected basis has the best performance for our system. Therefore, we propose a method to find the best wavelet basis which does not have the above problems. The idea is very simple. We select a basis as the best basis which shows the best performance during a cross-validation process. There are two measures for performance evaluation of our system, TPR and FPR. The ratio of TPR to FPR is calculated to compare the performance with different wavelet basis. This method is not only applicable to the BCI system but also to any system which is based on classification.

2.2.7. Selecting the best wavelet and the best wavelet basis

For each subject and each mental task, we run a nested five-fold cross-validation process with the first set of AR model orders in Table 4 (i.e., 12, 6, and 3 for levels 1, 2, and 3, respectively) in order to find the best wavelet and the best wavelet basis. For each of the 36 wavelets, we test all 25 possible wavelet bases. The best wavelet basis is firstly determined for every wavelet based on the ratio of TPR/FPR. Secondly, we compare the performance of the system with the best bases of different wavelets, and figure out the wavelet whose best basis yields the best system performance (in terms of the ratio of TPR to FPR). It is noteworthy that the results would be the same if we first find the best wavelet for each of the 25 wavelet bases and then select the basis with the best performance.

2.2.8. Optimizing the AR model order

Having selected the best wavelet and wavelet basis for the BCI of each subject and each mental task, we find the optimal AR order via another nested five-fold cross-validation process. To this end, we test different sets of AR orders (i.e., sets 2, 3, ..., 13 in Table 4) using the best wavelet and the best basis as previously determined, and select the set with the highest TPR/FPR ratio.

2.2.9. Testing the system

We test the system via the outer fold of nested five-fold cross-validation with the selected wavelet, the best wavelet basis, and the optimal AR order set for every BCI belonging to each subject and mental task. The results are given in the next section.

3. Results

The results of the cross-validation process (at AR order set 1 and the optimal AR order set) and the results of testing (at the optimal AR order set) are summarized in Table 6. This table

http://dx.doi.org/10.5772/55803

also shows the selected wavelet and the best wavelet basis for each BCI. The performance of a system which is based on three-level wavelet decomposition (instead of wavelet packet analysis) is furthermore given in Table 6 for comparison purposes.

		Baseline					Multiplication					Letter Composing					Rotation					Counting				
		AR Order Set	TPR		FPR		AR Order Set	TPR		FPR		AR Order Set	TPR		FPR		AR Order Set	TPR		FPR		AR Order Set	TPR		FPR	
			Mean	SD	Mean	SD		Mean	SD	Mean	SD		Mean	SD	Mean	SD		Mean	SD	Mean	SD		Mean	SD	Mean	SD
Subject 1	Validation	1	70.89	3.62	2.92	0.30	**1**	**71.17**	**1.06**	**3.18**	**0.37**	1	66.33	1.61	2.35	0.33	1	70.00	1.71	3.44	0.38	1	69.39	0.54	3.40	0.08
	Validation	13	65.61	2.16	0.08	0.14	**13**	**53.67**	**1.87**	**0.19**	**0.14**	13	57.78	0.92	0.28	0.07	13	61.44	0.69	0.21	0.08	13	63.06	1.40	0.21	0.16
	Testing	13	65.56	8.99	0.17	0.25	**13**	**52.67**	**6.55**	**0.28**	**0.20**	13	61.33	3.37	0.33	0.12	13	62.44	3.46	0.17	0.15	13	64.89	5.70	0.39	0.46
	Wavelet			13					**3**					25					18					3		
	Best Basis			1					**1**					1					1					1		
	Basis 16	13	47.56	3.96	0.22	0.36	**13**	**42.22**	**5.72**	**0.72**	**0.32**	13	44.89	5.07	0.61	0.36	13	41.56	5.42	0.61	0.36	13	49.11	5.74	0.44	0.25
Subject 2	Validation	1	59.50	1.14	4.25	0.29	1	60.39	2.32	4.90	0.19	1	79.72	1.11	7.90	0.26	1	64.72	2.99	6.82	0.37	**1**	**68.39**	**2.97**	**6.75**	**0.61**
	Validation	13	56.22	3.62	0.38	0.13	13	56.94	2.05	0.24	0.03	13	68.28	2.66	0.60	0.11	13	45.28	2.69	0.42	0.16	**13**	**63.39**	**1.57**	**0.50**	**0.12**
	Testing	13	60.89	4.26	0.44	0.50	13	56.44	5.85	0.17	0.25	13	68.22	5.75	0.39	0.32	13	46.67	5.09	0.67	0.75	**13**	**64.00**	**5.70**	**0.22**	**0.12**
	Wavelet			32					2					2					9					**2**		
	Best Basis			1					1					1					1					**1**		
	Basis 16	13	46.89	2.88	0.89	0.63	13	44.67	4.33	0.78	0.36	13	52.89	5.01	1.17	0.80	13	44.22	4.04	0.67	0.58	**13**	**46.89**	**4.40**	**1.11**	**0.56**
Subject 3	Validation	1	62.67	2.07	3.67	0.20	1	66.22	1.96	3.53	0.44	**1**	**66.56**	**2.82**	**2.51**	**0.15**	1	70.72	1.76	3.07	0.29	1	65.78	1.77	3.96	0.41
	Validation	13	60.72	0.65	0.19	0.12	13	59.89	1.48	0.11	0.08	**13**	**60.50**	**1.09**	**0.13**	**0.11**	13	52.39	2.31	0.14	0.06	13	61.94	1.62	0.03	0.09
	Testing	13	58.00	5.52	0.17	0.25	13	58.67	5.18	0.17	0.15	**13**	**60.00**	**3.24**	**0.00**	**0.00**	13	51.33	7.71	0.06	0.12	13	59.56	6.79	0.00	0.00
	Wavelet			11					34					**2**					5					2		
	Best Basis			1					1					**1**					1					1		
	Basis 16	13	37.78	6.89	0.72	0.37	13	45.33	2.65	0.22	0.12	**13**	**43.78**	**4.27**	**0.17**	**0.15**	13	48.22	5.86	0.11	0.15	13	39.11	4.26	0.50	0.30
Subject 4	Validation	1	73.67	4.36	3.89	0.22	1	79.00	1.61	3.35	0.20	**1**	**70.78**	**1.27**	**4.76**	**0.52**	1	86.89	1.64	4.14	0.47	1	70.83	1.08	3.04	0.26
	Validation	13	67.17	2.58	0.26	0.12	13	70.83	2.29	0.13	0.12	**13**	**62.06**	**3.11**	**0.10**	**0.20**	13	73.94	0.63	0.28	0.16	13	61.61	1.07	0.13	0.06
	Testing	13	68.89	3.24	0.28	0.39	13	69.78	2.41	0.17	0.15	**13**	**64.44**	**6.71**	**0.11**	**0.25**	13	75.78	3.08	0.33	0.30	13	63.56	9.04	0.06	0.12
	Wavelet			4					25					**19**					14					5		
	Best Basis			1					1					**1**					1					1		
	Basis 16	13	57.11	6.31	0.72	0.50	13	57.33	2.30	0.39	0.32	**13**	**48.00**	**3.08**	**0.50**	**0.46**	13	65.33	6.64	0.61	0.23	13	47.11	6.92	0.39	0.25

Table 6. Performance of BCIs for Different Subjects and Tasks during Cross-Validation and Testing

Table 6 is divided into 20 sections. Each section contains the information about the BCI belonging to a specific subject and mental task. The first line in every section shows the result of the first cross-validation process at AR order set 1. As mentioned before, this cross-validation is performed in order to select the best wavelet and the best wavelet basis for each BCI. The results include the mean and the standard deviation of the TPR and FPR values for the selected case (i.e., the best wavelet and basis). The best wavelet and the best basis are given on lines four and five of the table, respectively.

The optimal AR model order set is determined based on the results of the second cross-validation process done with the selected wavelet and basis. The results of the second cross-validation with the optimal AR order make the second lines of sections. It is noteworthy that the optimal AR order set for all BCIs is the last set which has the largest numbers.

The performance of the BCI systems with the best configuration (i.e., using the best wavelet, best basis, and optimal AR order set) are also given on the third line of each section. The last line of each section presents the performance of the BCI based on three-level wavelet decomposition as an example to be compared with the performance of the system based on the best basis. As previously discussed, three-level wavelet decomposition is one of the existing bases in three-level wavelet packet analysis (basis 16 according to Table 3).

The most discriminatory task for each subject is determined by comparing the performance of five BCIs pertaining to the subject. The most discriminatory mental task is in a section with solid black borders. For each subject, the second most discriminatory task is also chosen based on the results and shown in bold in the table.

Table 7 presents the average system performance of the BCIs for each subject (over tasks) and for each task (over subjects).

The preliminary results have been published in [62].

			TPR		FPR	
			Mean	SD	Mean	SD
Average over Tasks	Subject	1	61.38	5.61	0.27	0.24
		2	59.24	5.33	0.38	0.39
		3	57.51	5.69	0.08	0.10
		4	68.49	4.90	0.19	0.24
Average over Subjects	Task	Baseline	63.34	5.50	0.27	0.35
		Multiplication	59.39	5.00	0.20	0.19
		Letter Composing	63.50	4.77	0.21	0.17
		Rotation	59.06	4.84	0.31	0.33
		Counting	63.00	6.81	0.17	0.18
Total Average			**61.66**	**5.38**	**0.23**	**0.24**

Table 7. Average Performance of BCI Systems

4. Discussion

4.1. Best wavelet bases

As seen from Table 6, the best wavelet basis for all subjects and mental tasks is surprisingly the first basis which is made of the approximations and details components of the first level of wavelet decomposition. This implies that for the proposed BCIs, it is enough to decompose the signal into the first level, and further decomposition degrades the system performance.

4.2. Most discriminatory tasks

To determine the most discriminatory tasks for each subject, we consider the FPR values during testing and cross-validation at the optimal AR order set. We put the main weight on the FPR of testing since not only the portion of the dataset used for testing is larger than the portion used for cross-validation, but also the testing portion is completely separate from the portions exploited during training and cross-validation processes. The TPR values during testing and cross-validation are then considered if necessary to find out the most discriminatory tasks.

For Subject 1, the testing FPR for the baseline and the rotation tasks are the same and the lowest. The cross-validation FPR is lower for the baseline. Hence, the most discriminatory task must be the baseline. Since a BCI based on the baseline is activated when the subject wishes to relax and think of nothing, it is practically useless; therefore, we do not consider the baseline as the most discriminatory task. The rotation task is then selected as the most discriminatory task. The second most discriminatory task for Subject 1 is the multiplication.

For Subject 2, the most discriminatory task is the multiplication since it has the lowest testing and cross-validation FPRs. The counting is the second most discriminatory task for this subject.

For Subjects 3 and 4, the most and the second most discriminatory tasks are the counting and the letter composing, respectively. For Subject 3, the FPR values for these two tasks interestingly reach zero during testing.

4.3. Selected wavelets

Unlike the basis, the selected wavelets are not the same for all subjects and mental tasks. In eleven BCIs (out of the twenty BCIs designed for different subjects and tasks), a wavelet from the Daubechies family has been chosen as the best wavelet. Wavelet 'db2', the most selected wavelet, is the best wavelet for five BCIs. The BCIs for the most and the second most discriminatory tasks of Subjects 2 and 3 has the best performance with this wavelet among all other wavelets. In five BCIs, the Biorthogonal family is the best. Each of the Coiflets and Symlets families are also selected in two BCIs.

4.4. Average system performance

According to Table 7, the BCIs of Subject 3 have generally the best performance, with the average FPR of 0.08% and the average TPR of 57.51%. Moreover, the BCIs based on the counting task have the best performance overall. The average performance of BCIs based on the counting has FPR and TPR values of 0.17% and 63.00%.

4.5. Comparison of different wavelet bases

For each BCI, we consider and evaluate the system performance with different wavelet bases as further analysis. We then sort and rank the bases based on the ratio of TPR to FPR during testing. Considering the performance of each wavelet basis for different subjects and mental tasks, we count the number of cases that each basis ranks n-th among the other bases. The results are summarized in Table 8. The corresponding three-dimensional histograms are shown in Fig. 4. In this figure, the horizontal axes are related to different wavelet bases and their ranks. The vertical axis is showing the number of times that a basis has a specific rank amongst other bases. It can be seen from this bar diagram that as the basis number is increasing, the ranks of the basis is getting worse, i.e., the first basis has the highest ranks and the last basis has the worst rank. The results are almost along with the cross-validation results (with the first set of AR orders) and show that the first basis is the best basis for all BCIs except for three of them belonging to the multiplication task of Subject 1 and the rotation task of Subjects 2 and 3. For the multiplication task of Subject 1, the best basis is basis 2. The basis 6 ranks first for the rotation task of Subjects 2 and 3. The rank of the first basis for the multiplication task of Subject 1 and the rotation task of Subject 2 is two. The first basis is ranked third for the rotation task of Subject 3. In all other 17 BCIs, the first basis is the best.

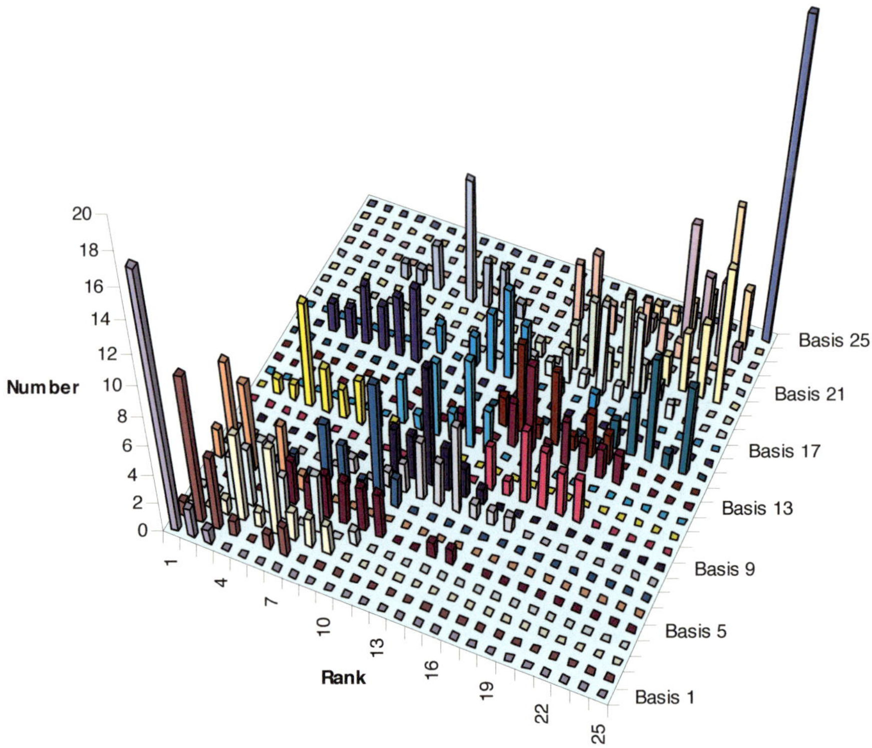

Figure 4. Comparison of different wavelet bases.

Number of Occurrence	Wavelet Basis																								
Rank	1	2	3	4	5	6	7	8	9	10	11	12	13	14	15	16	17	18	19	20	21	22	23	24	25
1	17	1				2																			
2	2	10				7					1														
3	1	5	1	3		6	1				1					2									
4		1	6	4							7					2									
5			1	5	1	4	1				3					4					1				
6		1	6	3	3	1					2					3					1				
7		2	2		2		4				3					4					3				
8			2	4	3		3	1			2					5									
9			2		3		1				1	3					2				8				
10				1	3		8	1	3			1									3				
11					3		2	2	3			5					2				3				
12								4	8			2	1				4				1				
13								3	3	1		6					6	1							
14					1			6	2			3		2			4	1	1						
15					1			1	1	3			3	6				1				4			
16								1		1			6	1			1	2	3			5			
17								1		5			1	5				1	5			2			
18										4			3	1			1	6	2			3			
19										3			2	3				1	6			3	1	1	
20										3			2	2	2			6	2			2		1	
21													2		4				1	2		1	8	2	
22															7			1		4			5	3	
23															1					5			5	9	
24															6					9			1	4	
25																									20

Table 8. Comparing Different Wavelet Bases during Testing at AR Order Set 13

5. Conclusion

In this paper, we presented a method to select the best wavelet basis in the design of a two-state self-paced mental task-based BCI. The use of the proposed methodology is not limited to the BCI systems and it can be also used in other applications. The previously introduced methods (based on cost functions) to find the best wavelet basis generally has two major drawbacks. First of all, they are not practical in classification problems where we have different training signal segments and each of them may result in a different basis. In this case, we cannot come up with a unique basis for all of the training signal segments; therefore, we are not able to finalize our design of the classification system. The second drawback is resulted by this fact that, supposing we can find a unique best wavelet basis for all training segments, there is no guarantee that this wavelet basis yields the best classification accuracy. Because of these two reasons, we decided to propose a method based on the classification accuracy to find the best basis. Since our BCI systems are evaluated by true positive and false positive rates, we used these two measures in the process of finding the best wavelet basis. It is worth noting that any other kind of classification accuracy measure can be potentially exploited in our proposed method to select the best basis.

We have tested our proposed method in the design of mental task-based BCIs. The output of the BCI should be activated when the subject performs a specific mental task. The aim is to minimize and maximize the false activation rate and the true activation rate, respectively.

The scalar autoregressive model coefficients of the components of the best wavelet basis were used as features. The classifiers studied were based on QDA and majority voting. We performed nested five-fold cross-validation two times to choose the best wavelet, the best wavelet basis, and the best autoregressive model orders. Results have shown that the most discriminatory tasks are different amongst the subjects confirming the findings of previous studies ([20], [30], [33], and [42]) based on the same dataset.

For each subject and each mental task, the best configuration (i.e., the best wavelet, the best wavelet basis, and the optimum AR order) is found during offline analysis of the data. During online analysis, the best configuration is used. Therefore, the system is applicable to real-time applications.

Author details

Farshad Faradji[1], Farhad Faradji[2,3*], Rabab K. Ward[3] and Gary E. Birch[3]

1 Qom University, Qom, Iran

2 Amirkabir University of Technology, Tehran, Iran

3 University of British Columbia, Vancouver, British Columbia, Canada

References

[1] R.R. Coifman and M.V. Wickerhauser, "Entropy-based algorithms for best basis selection," *IEEE Trans. on Inf. Theory*, vol. 38, no. 2, pp. 713–718, Mar. 1992.

[2] M.A. Nicolelis, "Brain-machine interfaces to restore motor function and probe neural circuits," *Nat. Rev. Neurosci.*, vol. 4, no. 5, pp. 417–422, 2003.

[3] S.G. Mason and G.E. Birch, "A general framework for brain-computer interface design," *IEEE Trans. Neural Syst. Rehabil. Eng.*, vol. 11, pp. 70–85, Mar. 2003.

[4] T.M. Vaughan, "Guest editorial brain-computer interface technology: A review of the second international meeting," *IEEE Trans. Neural Syst. Rehabil. Eng.*, vol. 11, no. 2, pp. 94–109, Jun. 2003.

[5] J.R. Wolpaw, "Brain-computer interfaces (BCIs) for communication and control: a mini-review," *Supplements to Clin. Neurophysiol.*, vol. 57, pp. 607–613, 2004.

[6] S.G. Mason, A. Bashashati, M. Fatourechi, K.F. Navarro, and G.E. Birch, "A comprehensive survey of brain interface technology designs," *Ann. Biomed. Eng.*, vol. 35, no. 2, pp. 137–169, Feb. 2007.

[7] A. Bashashati, M. Fatourechi, R.K. Ward, and G.E. Birch, "A survey of signal processing algorithms in brain-computer interfaces based on electrical brain signals," *J. Neural Eng.*, vol. 4, no. 2, pp. R35–57, Jun. 2007.

[8] Z.A. Keirn and J.I. Aunon, "A new mode of communication between man and his surroundings," *IEEE Trans. Biomed. Eng.*, vol. 37, no. 12, pp. 1209–1214, Dec. 1990.

[9] Z.A. Keirn and J.I. Aunon, "Man-machine communications through brain-wave processing," *IEEE Eng. Med. Biol.*, pp. 55–57, Mar. 1990.

[10] C.W. Anderson, E. Stolz, and S. Shamsunder, "Discriminating mental tasks using EEG represented by AR models," *In Proc. 17th IEEE EMBS*, pp. 875–876, 1995.

[11] C.W. Anderson, S.V. Devulapalli, and E.A. Stolz, "Determining mental state from EEG signals using neural networks," *Sci. Program.*, vol. 4, no. 3, pp. 171–183, 1995.

[12] C.W. Anderson and Z. Sijerčić, "Classification of EEG signals from four subjects during five mental tasks," *In Proc. Conf. Eng. App. Neural Net.*, pp. 407–414, Jun. 1996.

[13] C.W. Anderson, "Effects of variations in neural network topology and output averaging on the discrimination of mental tasks from spontaneous electroencephalogram," *J. Intell. Syst.*, vol. 7, pp. 165–190, 1997.

[14] C.W. Anderson, E.A. Stolz, and S. Shumsunder, "Multivariate autoregressive models for classification of spontaneous electroencephalographic signals during mental tasks," *IEEE Trans. Biomed. Eng.*, vol. 45, no.3, pp. 277–286, Mar. 1998.

[15] R. Palaniappan, P. Raveendran, S. Nishida, and N. Saiwaki, "Evolutionary Fuzzy ARTMAP for autoregressive model order selection and classification of EEG signals," *In Proc. IEEE Int. Conf. Syst. Man Cybern.*, pp. 3682–3686, Oct. 2000.

[16] R. Palaniappan, P. Raveendran, S. Nishida, and N. Saiwaki, "Fuzzy Artmap classification of mental tasks using segmented and overlapped EEG signals," *In Proc. IEEE Region 10 Conf.*, pp. II-388–II-391, Sep. 2000.

[17] R. Palaniappan and P. Raveendran, "A new mode of EEG based communication," *In Proc. IEEE Int. Joint Conf. Neural Net.*, vol. 4, pp. 2679–2682, Jul. 2001.

[18] R. Palaniappan, P. Raveendran, S. Nishida, and N. Saiwaki, "Autoregressive spectral analysis and model order selection criteria for EEG signals," *In Proc. IEEE Region 10 Conf.*, pp. II-126–II-129, Sep. 2000.

[19] M.I. Bhatti, A. Pervaiz, and M.H. Baig, "EEG signal decomposition and improved spectral analysis using wavelet transform," *In Proc. 23rd IEEE EMBS*, pp. 1862–1864, Oct. 2001.

[20] R. Palaniappan, R. Paramesran, S. Nishida, and N. Saiwaki, "A new brain-computer interface design using fuzzy ARTMAP," *IEEE Trans. Neural Syst. Rehabil. Eng.*, vol. 10, no. 3, pp. 140–148, Sep. 2002.

[21] V.A. Maiorescu, M. Serban, and A.M. Lazar, "Classification of EEG signals represented by AR models for cognitive tasks - a neural network based method," *In Proc. Int. Symp. Signals Circuits Syst.*, vol. 2, pp. 441–444, 2003.

[22] D. Garrett, D.A. Peterson, C.W. Anderson, and M.H. Thaut, "Comparison of linear, nonlinear, and feature selection methods for EEG signal classification," *IEEE Trans. Neural Syst. Rehabil. Eng.*, vol. 11, no. 2, pp. 141–144, Jun. 2003.

[23] D. Liu, Z. Jiang, W. Cong, and H. Feng, "Detect determinism of spontaneous EEG with a multi-channel reconstruction method," *In Proc. IEEE Int. Conf. Neural Net. Signal Process.*, pp. 708–711, Dec. 2003.

[24] X. Wu and X. Guo, "Mental EEG Analysis based on Independent Component Analysis," *In Proc. 3rd Int. Symp. Image Signal Process. Anal.*, pp. 327–331, Sep. 2003.

[25] D. Liu, Z. Jian, and H. Feng, "Separating the different components of spontaneous EEG by optimized ICA," *In Proc. IEEE Int. Conf. Neural Net. Signal Process.*, pp. 1334–1337, Dec. 2003.

[26] J.Z. Xue, H. Zhang, C.X. Zheng, and X.G. Yan, "Wavelet packet transform for feature extraction of EEG during mental tasks," *In Proc. 2nd Int. Conf. Machine Learn. Cybern.*, pp. 360–363, Nov. 2003.

[27] G.A. Barreto, R.A. Frota, and F.N.S. de Medeiros, "On the classification of mental tasks: A performance comparison of neural and statistical approaches," *In Proc. IEEE Workshop Machine Learn. Signal Process.*, pp. 529–538, 2004.

[28] M.S. Daud and J. Yunus, "Classification of mental tasks using de-noised EEG signals," *In Proc. 7th Int. Conf. Signal Process.*, pp. 2206–2209, 2004.

[29] K. Tavakolian, S. Rezaei, and S.K. Setarehdan, "Choosing optimal mental tasks for classification in brain computer interfaces," *In Proc. Int. Conf. Artificial Intell. and App.*, pp. 396-399, Feb. 2004.

[30] K. Tavakolian and S. Rezaei, "Classification of mental tasks using Gaussian mixture Bayesian network classifiers," *In Proc. IEEE Int. Workshop Biomed. Circuits Syst.*, pp. S3.6-9–S3.6-11, Dec. 2004.

[31] R. Rao and R. Derakhshani, "A comparison of EEG preprocessing methods using time delay neural networks," *In Proc. 2nd Int. IEEE EMBS Conf. Neural Eng.*, pp. 262–264, Mar. 2005.

[32] R. Palaniappan, "Identifying individuality using mental task based brain computer interface," *In Proc. 3rd Int. Conf. Intell. Sensing Infor. Process.*, pp. 239–242, Dec. 2005.

[33] R. Palaniappan, "Brain computer interface design using band powers extracted during mental tasks," *In Proc. 2nd Int. IEEE EMBS Conf. Neural Eng.*, pp. 321–324, Mar. 2005.

[34] N. Huan and R. Palaniappan, "Classification of mental tasks using fixed and adaptive autoregressive models of EEG signals," *In Proc. 2nd IEEE EMBS Conf. Neural Eng.*, pp. 633–636, Mar. 2005.

[35] R. Palaniappan and N. Huan, "Improving the performance of two-state mental task brain-computer interface design using linear discriminant classifier," *In Proc. EUROCON*, vol. 1, pp. 409–412, Nov. 2005.

[36] S. Rezaei, K. Tavakolian, and K. Naziripour, "Comparison of five different classifiers for classification of mental tasks," *In Proc. 27th IEEE EMBS*, pp. 6007–6010, Sep. 2005.

[37] Z. Jiang, Y. Ning, B. An, A. Li, and H. Feng, "Detecting mental EEG properties using detrended fluctuation analysis," *In Proc. 27th IEEE EMBS*, pp. 2017–2020, Sep. 2005.

[38] M.-C. Setban and D.-M. Dobrea, "Discrimination between cognitive tasks - a comparative study," *In Proc. Int. Symp.* Signals Circuits Syst., pp. 805–808, Jul. 2005.

[39] H. Liu, J. Wang, and C. Zheng, "Mental tasks classification and their EEG structures analysis by using the growing hierarchical self-organizing map," *In Proc. 1st Int. Conf. Neural Interface Control*, pp. 115–118, May 2005.

[40] C. Gope, N. Kehtarnavaz, and D. Nair, "Neural network classification of EEG signals using time-frequency representation," In Proc. IEEE Int. Joint Conf. Neural Net., vol. 4, pp. 2502–2507, Aug. 2005.

[41] H. Liu, J. Wang, C. Zheng, and P. He, "Study on the effect of different frequency bands of EEG signals on mental tasks classification," *In Proc. 27th IEEE EMBS*, pp. 5369–5372, Sep. 2005.

[42] R. Palaniappan, "Utilizing gamma band to improve mental task based brain-computer interface design," *IEEE Trans. Neural Syst. Rehabil. Eng.*, vol. 14, no. 3, pp. 299–303, Sep. 2006.

[43] G. Yan, X. Guo, R. Yan, and B. Yang, "Nonlinear quadratic phase coupling on EEG based on $1^{1/2}$-dimension spectrum," *In Proc. 3rd Int. Conf.* Advances Med. Signal Infor. Process., pp. 1–4, Jul. 2006.

[44] F. Abdollahi and A. Motie-Nasrabadi, "Combination of frequency bands in EEG for feature reduction in mental task classification," *In Proc. 28th IEEE EMBS*, pp. 1146–1149, Sep. 2006.

[45] K. Nakayama and K. Inagaki, "A brain computer interface based on neural network with efficient pre-processing," *In Proc. Int. Symp. Intell. Signal Process. Commun. Syst.*, pp. 673–676, Dec. 2006.

[46] C.W. Anderson, J.N. Knight, T. O'Connor, M.J. Kirby, and A. Sokolov, "Geometric subspace methods and time-delay embedding for EEG artifact removal and classification," *IEEE Trans. Neural Syst. Rehabil. Eng.*, vol. 14, no. 2, pp. 142–146, 2006.

[47] D.-M. Dobrea and M.-C. Dobrea, "An EEG (bio) technological system for assisting the disabled people," *In Proc. 5th IEEE Int. Conf. Comput. Cybern.*, pp. 191–196, Oct. 2007.

[48] D.-M. Dobrea, M.-C. Dobrea, and M. Costin, "An EEG coherence based method used for mental tasks classification," *In Proc. 5th IEEE Int. Conf. Comput. Cybern.*, pp. 185–190, Oct. 2007.

[49] K. Nakayama Y. Kaneda, and A. Hirano, "A brain computer interface based on FFT and multilayer neural network - feature extraction and generalization," *In Proc. Int. Symp. Intell. Signal Process. Commun. Syst.*, pp. 826–829, Nov. 2007.

[50] L. Zhiwei and S. Minfen, "Classification of mental task EEG signals using wavelet packet entropy and SVM," *In Proc. 8th Int. Conf. Elec. Measure. Instr.*, pp. 3-906–3-909, Aug. 2007.

[51] B.T. Skinner, H.T. Nguyen, and D.K. Liu, "Classification of EEG signals using a genetic-based machine learning classifier," *In Proc. 29th IEEE EMBS*, pp. 3120–3123, Aug. 2007.

[52] F. Abdollahi, S.K. Setarehdan, and A.M. Nasrabadi, "Locating information maximization time in EEG signals recorded during mental tasks," *In Proc. 5th Int. Symp. Image Signal Process. Anal.*, pp. 238–241, Sep. 2007.

[53] C.R. Hema, M.P. Paulraj, R. Nagarajan, S. Yaacob, and A.H. Adom, "Fuzzy based classification of EEG mental tasks for a brain machine interface," *In Proc. 3rd Int. Conf. Intell. Infor. Hiding Multimed. Signal Process.*, vol. 1, pp. 53–56, Nov. 2007.

[54] S.M. Hosni, M.E. Gadallah, S.F. Bahgat, and M.S. AbdelWahab, "Classification of EEG signals using different feature extraction techniques for mental-task BCI," *In Proc. Int. Conf.* Computer Eng. Syst., pp. 220–226, Nov. 2007.

[55] M.P. Paulraj, C.R. Hema, R. Nagarajan, S. Yaacob, and A.H. Adom, "EEG classification using radial basis PSO neural network for brain machine interfaces," *In Proc. 5th Student Conf. Research Develop.*, pp. 1–5, Dec. 2007.

[56] J.P. Burg, "A new analysis technique for time series data," NATO Adv. Study Inst. on Signal Processing with Emphasis on Underwater Acoustics, Enschede, The Netherlands, Aug. 1968, reprinted in *Modern Spectrum Analysis*, D.G. Childers, ed., IEEE Press, pp. 42–48, New York, 1978.

[57] P.J. Franaszczuk, K.J. Blinowska, and M. Kowalczyk, "The application of parametric multichannel spectral estimates in the study of electrical brain activity," *Biological Cybern.*, vol. 51, pp. 239–247, 1985.

[58] A.C. Atkinson, M. Riani, and A. Cerioli, *Exploring Multivariate Data with the Forward Search*, Springer Series in Statistics, XXI, 621 p., 2004, ch. 6.

[59] G. Blanchard and B. Blankertz, "BCI competition 2003-dataset IIa: Spatial patterns of self-controlled brain rhythm modulations," *IEEE Trans. Biomed. Eng.*, vol. 51, no. 6, pp. 1062–1066, Jun. 2004.

[60] A. Bashashati, M. Fatourechi, R.K. Ward, and G.E. Birch, "User customization of the feature generator of an asynchronous brain interface," *Ann. Biomed. Eng.*, vol. 34, no. 6, pp. 1051–1060, Jun. 2006.

[61] G.E. Birch, P.D. Lawrence, J.C. Lind, and R.D. Hare, "Application of prewhitening to AR spectral estimation of EEG," *IEEE Trans. Biomed. Eng.*, vol. 35, no. 8, pp. 640–645, Aug. 1988.

[62] F. Faradji, R.K. Ward, and G.E. Birch, "A simple approach to find the best wavelet basis in classification problems," *In Proc. 20th Int. Conf. Pattern Recog.*, pp. 641–644, Aug. 2010.

Chapter 7

Client-Centred Music Imagery Classification Based on Hidden Markov Models of Baseline Prefrontal Hemodynamic Responses

Tiago H. Falk, Kelly M. Paton and Tom Chau

Additional information is available at the end of the chapter

http://dx.doi.org/10.5772/55804

1. Introduction

A prevalent avenue in rehabilitation engineering is the development of new access technologies which enable individuals with severe and/or multiple disabilities to access or interact with their environment. Despite continued efforts to develop such technologies, many individuals still possess no means to communicate or control external devices [1]. Brain-computer interfaces (BCIs) have surfaced as promising access solutions for those with severe motor disabilities such as late-stage amyotrophic lateral sclerosis (ALS), brainstem stroke, or severe cerebral palsy [2]. Electroencephalography (EEG), a noninvasive method used in traditional BCI technologies, is safe and inexpensive, but long-term electrode fixation is difficult and the signal is inherently noisy [1, 3]. Other common noninvasive BCI technologies such as functional magnetic resonance imaging (fMRI), magnetoencephalography (MEG), and positron emission topography (PET) are theoretically feasible, but are expensive and technically demanding for online applications [3]. More recently, the possibility of using near infrared spectroscopy (NIRS) as a tool in this field has been investigated due to its affordability, portability, high temporal resolution (similar to that of fMRI), and higher signal-to-noise ratio than that of EEG due to the absence of artifacts [3–9].

Near-infrared spectroscopy is an analysis technique that operates by transmitting near-infrared (650 nm – 950 nm wavelengths) electromagnetic radiation through the skull and comparing the intensities of the returning and incident light. When functional mental activity occurs, metabolic demands cause an increase in the blood flow to pre-defined regions of the brain (e.g., motor cortex during motor imagery tasks [3]). The increase in blood flow causes changes to the regional concentrations of oxygenated and deoxygenated hemoglobin, hence altering the optical properties of the brain tissue [10, 11]. As a consequence, by measuring the intensity of the reflected light, NIRS technologies can be used to examine regional cortical activity with depths of up to 2 cm [10]. Previous research has shown that NIRS can be used to assess hemodynamic responses in the motor cortex using activities such as motor imagery [3, 7], as well as in the prefrontal cortex using higher cognitive tasks such as mental arithmetic [6, 11, 12], working memory [13, 14], and emotion induction [15, 16], both in silent (e.g., [17, 18]) and noisy environments [19].

A major drawback of measuring hemodynamic responses in the motor cortex is the interference of hair [8]. Additionally, for individuals who have congenital motor impairments or who are many years post-traumatic injury, motor imagery may be a difficult, or even impossible, task due to the absence of a somatosensory map of motor activities [20–22]. These problems can be avoided by using more intuitive tasks which activate the prefrontal cortex (PFC). In this study, we proposed to classify hemodynamic responses in the PFC resultant from an intuitive music imagery task. More specifically, we were interested in exploiting the emotional response that music imagery can have on an individual. We were motivated by previous studies which have shown that music can elicit [23] and enhance [24] intense emotional responses that activate brain regions believed to be associated with emotional behaviours, such as the PFC [25] and the orbitofrontal and frontopolar areas [26, 27]. More importantly, prefrontal hemodynamic responses due to subject-selected music imagery have been recently observed using fMRI [28]. An additional motivation for using the music imagery task was related to the simplicity of the cognitive task | relative to mental arithmetic, for example | which would allow younger children to use this classification system. Recent experiments have suggested that NIRS responses in the PFC resultant from music imagery are detectable and sufficiently different from those resultant from mental arithmetic tasks and baseline resting states [17, 18, 29].

The goal of this study was to investigate the potential of classifying rest and music imagery on the basis of non-invasively acquired NIRS signals. Automated detection of music imagery events could then be used to control a system-paced two-state BCI (e.g., a binary switch). To develop a music imagery classifier that is applicable to users with different characteristics (e.g., age, gender, disability) requires a significant BCI–user coordination effort [2]. For the task at hand, we have incorporated a client-centred paradigm where subject-specific physical and physiological factors such as movement, heartbeat, and respiration were taken into account during classifier development [10]. Additional motivations for pursuing a client-driven paradigm included *i)* dependency of the hemodynamic responses on the intensity and valence (i.e., happy or sad) of the emotions evoked [30], *ii)* the mode (major or minor) and tempo (fast or slow) of the imagined songs [31], and *iii)* the differences in age, race, gender, skull thickness and skull shapes which may lead to inter-subject variations in penetration depths of NIR light [7, 32]. In this paper, hidden Markov models (HMMs), which have been previously used for motor imagery classification [3, 33], were used to characterize the individuals' hemodynamic responses during rest (baseline). Client-centredness was achieved by optimizing HMM model parameters and classifier input parameters on a per-client basis.

2. Experimental methods

This section describes the experiment setup, execution, and data pre-processing.

2.1. Participants

Thirteen able-bodied adults (three male, mean age of 33.5 ± 12.8 years) were recruited from the University of Toronto and Bloorview Kids Rehab (Toronto). Exclusion criteria were metabolic, cardiovascular, respiratory, psychiatric, or drug- or alcohol-related conditions that could affect either the measurements or the participant's ability to follow the experimental protocol. Participants were required to have normal hearing. Ethical approval was obtained from the relevant institutions, and all participants provided informed signed consent.

2.2. Instrumentation

The hemodynamic response was recorded from each subject using the Imagent Function Brain Imaging System from ISS Inc. Two photomultiplier tube detectors were employed along with sixteen light sources — eight at 690 nm and eight at 830 nm. The sources delivered 110 MHz-modulated light to the forehead via 400 μm-diameter optical fibres, and the detectors received the returning light via 3 mm-diameter optical fibres. Light returned to the detectors was demodulated at a cross-correlation frequency (CCF) of 5 kHz. To avoid cross-signal contamination, the light sources were cyclically switched such that no two sources were on simultaneously. For one data collection cycle — defined as one complete sequence through all sixteen sources — each source remained on for eight periods of the CCF (i.e., 1.6 ms), separated by a two-period break (0.4 ms) to ensure no overlap. This resulted in an effective sampling rate of 31.25 Hz per full data collection cycle. For each cycle, the eight waveforms from each source-detector pair were averaged, and a fast Fourier transform (FFT) was applied to the result in order to obtain three output data components: AC (relative amplitude at the CCF), DC (relative amplitude at 0 Hz), and phase. In this study, only the AC and DC data were used.

The sixteen source fibres were grouped in pairs comprised of one source at each of the two wavelengths; this allowed a given location to be probed by both wavelengths simultaneously. Positioning four source pairs around one detector on each side of the participant's forehead allowed both the right and left prefrontal cortices to be probed, as shown in Figure 1(a). Emitters in position 3 on each side were located roughly at the left and right prefrontal cortices (FP1 and FP2 in the 10-20 system). The raw AC and DC signals obtained from each source can be represented as $x^{\lambda}_{p,i}(\gamma)$ where the subscript i indexes the source position ($i = 1, \ldots 4$), subscript p indicates the left or right side by L or R, and superscript λ indicates the wavelength (λ =690, 830 nm). The signal type (AC or DC) is indicated by the parameter γ.

On each side, the four source pairs were positioned 2.12 cm away from the detector (see Figure 1(a)). It has been shown (in the occipital region) that, although a larger source–detector distance (3.37 cm to 4.55 cm) gives a greater magnitude of response, the same features can be seen in a signal obtained at a distance of 2.25 cm [34]. While the chosen distance of 2.12 cm is slightly smaller, the region of interest is the prefrontal cortex, which previous NIRS studies have shown to have attenuation 1000 times smaller than the occipital region [34]. Such insight suggests hemodynamic responses should be observable with a source–detector separation of 2.12 cm. The promising results reported in 4, as well as the more recent results reported in [35], corroborate this assumption.

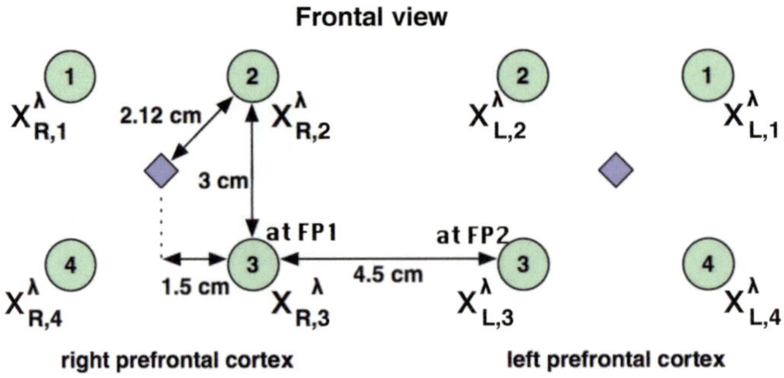

(a)

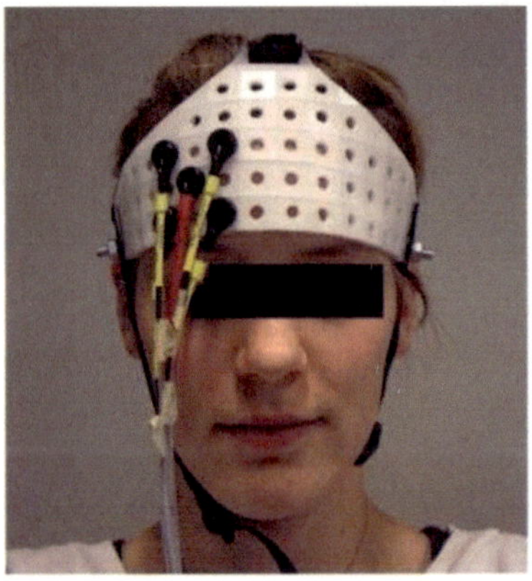

(b)

Figure 1. (a) Positioning of source pairs (circles) and detectors (diamonds). Each source pair represents one λ =690 nm source and one λ =830 nm source. The signal from each source is represented as $x^{\lambda}_{p,i}$, with $i = 1, \ldots 4$ and $p = L$ (left) or R (right). Source pairs at position 3 on each side are located, anatomically, at the prefrontal cortices FP1 and FP2. (b) Image of headband position on the forehead with only the right side detector and sources in place.

Sources and detectors were secured to the forehead with a specially designed headband constructed from 1.6 mm low density polyethylene, as shown in Figure 1(b). The area probed using this arrangement corresponds approximately to the frontopolar cortex, the superior portion of the orbitofrontal cortex, and the more medial sections of the dorsolateral prefrontal cortex. Subjects wore a blindfold and industrial earmuffs (AOSafety Professional Hearing Protector, noise rating of 30 dB) for the entire data collection duration in order to eliminate any visual and/or auditory distractions external to the experiment.

2.3. Protocol

NIRS signals were collected from each participant while they were outfitted with the headband, blindfold, and earmuffs and seated comfortably in front of a computer in a quiet room. Each subject performed four trials spread over two separate sessions (i.e., two trials were completed per session); each session lasted about 40 minutes, including the time for experiment preparation (e.g., headband placement) and NIRS sensor calibration. Each

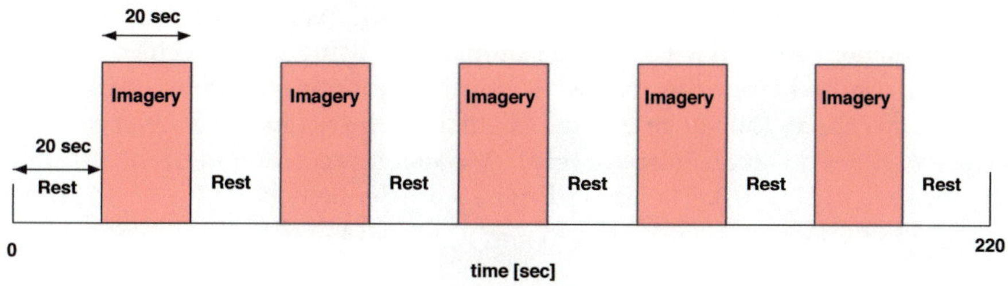

Figure 2. Stimulus pattern for the imagery trials. Imagery periods are shaded and rest intervals are not shaded.

session was performed on a separate day to ensure maximum concentration and focus and to reduce any effects of discomfort due to the headband. Participants were asked to remain as still as possible and to refrain from speaking during all experimental trials. Halfway through each session, the participant was given a short break to alleviate fatigue. While the blindfold and earmuffs were removed during the break, the NIRS sensors remained in place so as to preserve calibration and positioning.

Two of the trials consisted of the participant in a static state of rest with no music imagery (referred to as 'baseline' trials). Participants were instructed to clear their minds as much as possible, and to focus on their breathing for approximately two minutes. For the remaining two trials, participants were informed that they were required to sing *one* of their chosen songs vividly in their head when cued by the experimenter via a light tap in the shoulder (referred to as 'imagery' trials). Prior to each session, participants were asked to choose several songs of their own preference that were of the same emotional valence (i.e. happy or sad), which they felt elicited a strong emotional reaction. Participants were informed that the purpose of the music imagery task was to elicit an intense emotional reaction. As a consequence, they were instructed to switch to a new song once they began to feel emotionally habituated to the currently-used song.

Figure 2 shows the stimulus pattern used for the 220-second imagery trials. As can be seen, each imagery trial consisted of eleven 20-second intervals alternating between rest (six intervals) and music imagery (five intervals). An activation window of 20 seconds was chosen to take into account the task initiation delay, which we have found in previous experiments to be as long as 5 seconds, as well as the inherent physiological latency of the hemodynamic responses, which can be in the order of 5-10 seconds [3]. For similar reasons, twenty-second rest intervals were chosen. Such choice of stimulus pattern, however, can reinforce slow 3rd-order blood pressure waves and its subharmonics (circa 0.05-0.1 Hz); thus, a wavelet-based denoising algorithm was used, as described in 2.4.

2.4. Pre-processing

The raw signals (AC and DC) were filtered to mitigate physiological noise due, primarily, to cardiac signals (0.5–2 Hz), respiration (0.2–0.4 Hz) and the Mayer wave (approximately 0.1 Hz) [10], as well as the low-frequency artifacts (e.g., 3rd-order blood pressure waves) that may have been reinforced by the selected stimulus timing pattern. Since the frequencies of physiological noise and the desired hemodynamic response may vary slightly among participants, wavelet-based filters that would remove low-powered noise without relying on a specific cutoff frequency were used. Wavelet denoising has been shown to be effective for functional NIRS hemodynamics-driven signals [10], hence three wavelet filters were investigated which performed a 12-level decomposition using a Daubechies-12 wavelet. The filtered signals resulted from the reconstruction of the approximation wavelet coefficients and either the last three, four or five detail coefficients (henceforth referred to as 3-, 4-, and 5-detail wavelet filtered signals, respectively). A visual representation of the raw and filtered signals can be seen in Figure 3. The filtered signals are denoted as $x^{\lambda}_{p,i}(\gamma, d)$, with d indicating the 'detail' of the filtered signal ($d = 3, 4, 5$) and $\lambda, p, i,$ and γ as before.

2.5. Feature extraction

The estimated changes in the concentration of oxygenated hemoglobin ($\Delta[HbO_2]$) and deoxygenated hemoglobin ($\Delta[HHb]$) were also computed, using the modified Beer-Lambert law [3] as shown in Eq. 1 and Eq. 2:

$$\Delta[HbO_2] = \frac{(\varepsilon^{690nm}_{Hb} \cdot \frac{\Delta OD^{830nm}}{DPF^{830nm}}) - (\varepsilon^{830nm}_{Hb} \cdot \frac{\Delta OD^{690nm}}{DPF^{690nm}})}{r \cdot (\varepsilon^{690nm}_{Hb} \cdot \varepsilon^{830nm}_{HbO} - \varepsilon^{830nm}_{Hb} \cdot \varepsilon^{690nm}_{HbO})}, \tag{1}$$

$$\Delta[HHb] = \frac{(\varepsilon^{830nm}_{HbO} \cdot \frac{\Delta OD^{690nm}}{DPF^{690nm}}) - (\varepsilon^{690nm}_{HbO} \cdot \frac{\Delta OD^{830nm}}{DPF^{830nm}})}{r \cdot (\varepsilon^{690nm}_{Hb} \cdot \varepsilon^{830nm}_{HbO} - \varepsilon^{830nm}_{Hb} \cdot \varepsilon^{690nm}_{HbO})},$$

where

$$\Delta OD^{\lambda} = \log \frac{DC^{\lambda}_{0}}{DC^{\lambda}(t)}. \tag{2}$$

Parameter ΔOD^{λ} corresponds to the change in optical density of light at wavelength λ; DC^{λ}_{0} to the mean DC intensity; $DC^{\lambda}(t)$ to the DC intensity at time t; and r to the source-detector separation distance. Constant DPF^{λ} corresponds to the differential pathlength factor in the human adult head at wavelength λ, and $\varepsilon^{\lambda}_{Hb}$ and $\varepsilon^{\lambda}_{HbO}$ correspond to extinction coefficients for HHb and HbO_2 cromophores, respectively. Table 1 reports the constant values for each wavelength used in the experiments described herein. Concentration signals can be represented as $c^{h}_{p,i}(d)$, where the superscript h indexes oxygenated (HbO) or deoxygenated hemoglobin (Hb), and p=L, R, $i = 1, \ldots 4$, and d = 3,4,5 as before.

In addition to each individual channel, the mean left and right responses were also computed by averaging like-wavelength raw signals or like-chromophore concentration signals over the four measurement positions on each side, resulting in:

$$\bar{x}^{\lambda}_{p}(\gamma, d) = \frac{1}{4} \sum_{i=1}^{4} x^{\lambda}_{p,i}(\gamma, d), \tag{3}$$

$$\bar{c}^{h}_{p}(d) = \frac{1}{4} \sum_{i=1}^{4} c^{h}_{p,i}(d). \tag{4}$$

Wavelength	Variable	Value
690 nm	ε_{HbO}	0.3123 $mM^{-1}cm^{-1}$
	ε_{Hb}	2.1382 $mM^{-1}cm^{-1}$
	DPF	6.51 cm
830 nm	ε_{HbO}	1.0507 $mM^{-1}cm^{-1}$
	ε_{Hb}	0.7804 $mM^{-1}cm^{-1}$
	DPF	5.86 cm

Table 1. Differential pathlength factors (DPF) and extinction coefficients (ε) used in hemoglobin concentration calculations. Values are taken from [36] and [37].

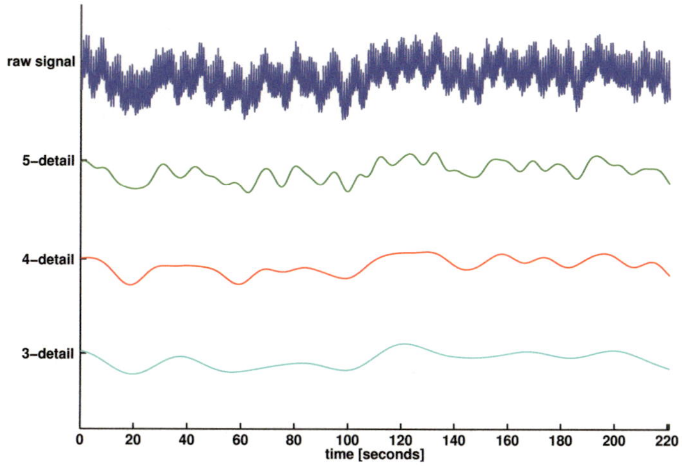

Figure 3. Comparison of raw DC data obtained during an imagery trial with its three different wavelet-filtered signals. From the top down, the signals are: raw, 5-, 4-, and 3-detail filtered.

3. Data analysis

This section discusses basic HMM theory and the application of HMMs to characterize baseline signals and detect music imagery events.

3.1. Hidden Markov models

A hidden Markov model is a statistical model which examines a Markov process wherein the observable outputs are dependent upon the unobservable states. Here, only a brief description of HMMs is given and the reader is referred to [38] for further details. An HMM representing the feature vector $\vec{u}$ (see 3.2.1) is completely characterized by the number of Q discrete states, a transition matrix $A = \{a_{ij}\}$ of transition probabilities between states i and j, an initial state distribution π and a state-dependent observation probability distribution $B = \{b_j(\vec{u})\}$ for state j. Commonly, Gaussian mixture models (GMM) are employed as observation probability distributions. A GMM is given by a weighted sum of M component densities,

$$P(\vec{u}) = \sum_{k=1}^{M} \alpha_k p_k(\vec{u}) \tag{5}$$

where $\alpha_k \geq 0$ are the mixture weights with $\sum_{k=1}^{M} \alpha_k = 1$, and $p_k(\vec{u})$ are N-dimensional Gaussian densities with mean $\vec{\mu}_k$ and covariance matrix Σ_k, given by:

$$p_k(\vec{u}) = \frac{1}{(2\pi)^{N/2}|\Sigma_k|^{1/2}} \exp\left(-\frac{1}{2}(\vec{u} - \vec{\mu}_k)^{\top}\Sigma_k^{-1}(\vec{u} - \vec{\mu}_k)\right). \tag{6}$$

A GMM with $M = 1$ indicates a conventional Gaussian density.

In this study, model parameters, such as state transition probabilities, initial state probabilities, and output distribution parameters, were computed using a recursive greedy-EM algorithm where model parameters and the number of Gaussian components were estimated simultaneously using a Bayesian information criterion to avoid overfitting [39]. Mean left and right concentration and raw features extracted from the imagery data were assessed against the baseline reference models via the log likelihood measure (see 3.2.1). Log likelihood values were computed using the so-called forward-backward procedure described in [38]. Normalization was performed based on the number of data points in the sampled signal under test. As mentioned previously, client-centredness was achieved by optimizing HMMs parameters for each individual participant. More details about HMM training and testing are described in 3.2.1 and 3.2.2, respectively. The publicly available HMM Toolbox for Matlab was used for the simulations [40].

3.2. Modeling process

3.2.1. Training stage

For each participant, HMMs were trained for different combinations of AC, DC, or concentration features using the signals obtained during the baseline trials. More specifically, the four-dimensional feature vectors included:

$$\vec{u}_{DC,d} = [\bar{x}_L^{690}(DC,d), \bar{x}_L^{830}(DC,d), \bar{x}_R^{690}(DC,d), \bar{x}_R^{830}(DC,d)], \tag{7}$$

$$\vec{u}_{AC,d} = [\bar{x}_L^{690}(AC,d), \bar{x}_L^{830}(AC,d), \bar{x}_R^{690}(AC,d), \bar{x}_R^{830}(AC,d)], \tag{8}$$

$$\vec{u}_{conc,d} = [\bar{c}_L^{Hb}(d), \bar{c}_L^{HbO}(d), \bar{c}_R^{Hb}(d), \bar{c}_R^{HbO}(d)], \tag{9}$$

where d indexes 3-, 4-, or 5-detail wavelet filters.

During hidden Markov model training, the number of parameters that need to be estimated depends on the number of HMM states Q, type of HMM (e.g., fully connected, left-right), number of Gaussian components M, data dimensionality K, and GMM covariance matrix type (i.e., diagonal or full). In this study, fully-connected HMMs and full covariance Gaussian components were used to explore correlations between NIRS signals measured from neighboring channels. Preliminary experiments with the recursive EM algorithm showed that the following HMM-GMM configurations were used most often:

- Q=4, M=1,
- Q=2, M=1,
- Q=2, M=2.

Such configurations were consistent with those reported in previous HMM-based BCI studies (e.g., [3, 33]). Participant-specific models were trained using the feature vectors $\vec{u}_{DC,d}$, $\vec{u}_{AC,d}$, and $\vec{u}_{conc,d}$, for all three types of filtered data (d = 3, 4, and 5) and all three combinations of HMM parameters listed above. This resulted in 27 (3 data types $\times$ 3 filters $\times$ 3 model parameter sets) different models for each of the thirteen participants, or 9 models per data type per participant.

3.2.2. *Testing stage*

For testing, consecutive, overlapping data samples from the imagery trials were scored against the per-subject baseline reference HMMs via the log likelihood measure. Sliding-window samples of various lengths (l = 1, 3, 5, 7, 10, and 15 seconds) were investigated with 0.5–second overlap and the log likelihood for a window was normalized by the length of the window. Window lengths of different sizes were investigated for two reasons. First, NIRS signal propagations have varied delay times ranging from 5–8 seconds [3]. Second, reaction times differ between subjects due to various external factors such as mental alertness, innate reflex reaction time, and familiarity with the procedure.

Higher log likelihood values suggest hemodynamic responses akin to those observed during the baseline trials (i.e., rest). Lower log likelihood values, in turn, indicate responses different from rest, i.e, music imagery events. Given this interpretation of the log likelihoods, a decrease in the log likelihood function was expected during imagery periods and either an increase or a constant value during the rest periods. The plot depicted in Figure 4 shows one subject's representative log likelihood temporal series clearly illustrating the expected increases and decreases during rest (un-shaded intervals) and imagery (shaded intervals), respectively.

3.3. Music imagery detection

Given the nature of the log likelihood functions, complex classifier training was not needed in order to detect music imagery events. Instead, changes from positive to negative slope in the log likelihood function were used for classification. In order to remove possible artifacts due to e.g., head movement, which may produce a momentary positive-to-negative slope change, music imagery events were only detected if a decrease in the log likelihood function persisted for at least five seconds after a slope change was detected.

An expected imagery event (true positive) was identified with the occurrence of an activation within the first thirteen seconds of a twenty-second imagery interval. This time period

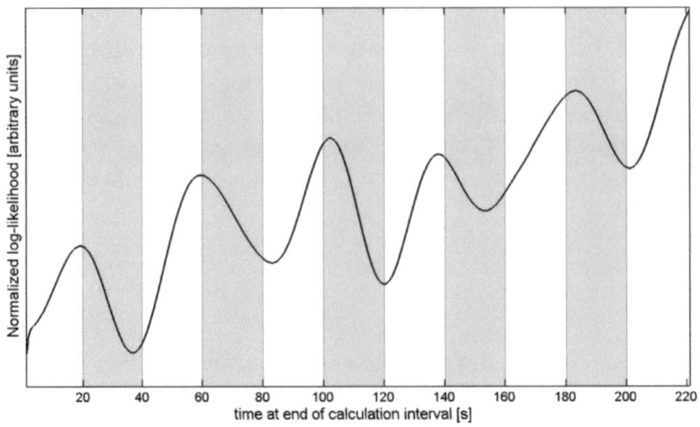

Figure 4. Normalized log likelihood function for a single subject, clearly showing the anticipated pattern for an imagery trial. Computed using $\vec{u}_{DC,3}$ data and tested against a 4-state 1-Gaussian HMM using l=3-second sliding windows. Imagery intervals are shaded. The X axis is time [sec] and the Y axis is normalized log likelihood [arbitrary units].

allowed for both the delay in the change of the hemodynamics-driven signal (up to eight seconds [3]) and the delay on the part of the subject to start music imagery once tapped on the shoulder, which, in turn, was found to be between 1–5 seconds in pilot experiments. If no activation occurred during this first portion of an imagery interval, the interval was deemed to be a false negative, or incorrectly classified as a rest interval. Intervals were also labeled false negatives if an activation occurred after thirteen seconds into the beginning of the imagery interval. A rest interval with no activations was considered a true negative, as was a rest interval with an activation within the first eight seconds after the previous imagery interval — this margin was motivated again by the delay in the NIRS signal, and the observed few seconds of delay in the participant's cessation of the music imagery [3, 10]. Rest intervals with an activation after the first eight seconds were deemed false positives or incorrectly classified as imagery intervals. The number of true/false positives (TP/FP) and true/false negatives (TN/FN) were computed and summed over the two imagery trials, for a total of 12 rest intervals and 10 imagery intervals, and were used to compute the performance metrics sensitivity and specificity, given by:

$$Sensitivity = \frac{TP}{TP + FN}, \tag{10}$$

$$Specificity = \frac{TN}{TN + FP}. \tag{11}$$

Sensitivity is a measure of how many actual activations were correctly identified, while the specificity indicates how many rest intervals were correctly identified as baseline.

4. Experimental results

In this section, calculated statistics and optimal parameters are reported.

Subject	DC					AC					Hemoglobin Concentration				
	Sens	Spec	Q–M	*d*	*l*	Sens	Spec	Q–M	*d*	*l*	Sens	Spec	Q–M	*d*	*l*
1	0.80	0.92	4–1	4	7	0.70	1.00	4–1	3	7	1.00	1.00	2–1	3	10
2	1.00	0.58	2–1	5	3	1.00	0.67	4–1	5	5	0.70	1.00	2–1	5	7
3	0.90	0.83	4–1	4	1	0.90	0.75	4–1	4	1	0.60	0.92	2–2	4	10
4	0.90	1.00	2–1	3	7	1.00	0.92	2–1	4	10	1.00	0.70	2–2	3	7
5	0.80	0.75	4–1	4	3	0.90	0.75	2–1	5	10	0.80	0.83	2–2	5	7
6	0.80	0.58	2–2	5	10	0.60	0.83	2–1	5	15	1.00	0.83	4–1	4	1
7	1.00	0.67	2–1	5	5	0.80	0.92	4–1	3	5	0.80	0.86	2–2	3	1
8	0.90	0.92	2–2	4	3	0.80	1.00	2–2	4	1	0.70	0.92	2–1	4	3
9	0.60	1.00	2–1	3	10	0.70	0.92	4–1	4	1	0.80	0.92	2–2	4	3
10	0.50	1.00	4–1	5	10	0.80	0.67	4–1	5	1	1.00	0.64	4–1	4	5
11	0.90	0.92	4–1	4	1	0.90	1.00	4–1	4	5	0.90	0.75	2–1	5	10
12	0.80	0.83	2–1	5	10	0.70	0.92	4–1	5	15	1.00	1.00	4–1	3	3
13	0.90	0.75	4–1	5	5	0.80	0.83	2–1	4	1	0.90	1.00	4–1	3	1
Mean	**0.83**	**0.83**	–	–	–	**0.82**	**0.86**	–	–	–	**0.86**	**0.87**	–	–	–
(SD)	**(0.14)**	**(0.15)**	–	–	–	**(0.12)**	**(0.12)**	–	–	–	**(0.14)**	**(0.12)**	–	–	–

Table 2. Optimal performance results for all three data types, by subject. Columns labeled 'Sens' and 'Spec' indicate sensitivity and specificity, respectively. The HMM parameters, namely, number of states and number of Gaussian mixtures, are shown by Q and M, respectively. Parameter *d* indicates the 'detail' of the filter and *l* the window size [seconds]. SD is standard deviation.

4.1. Quantitative results

Table 2 reports sensitivity (column labeled "sens" in the table) and specificity ("spec") for the HMM–filter–window combinations that resulted in the best per-user performance (defined as the highest average of sensitivity and specificity) out of the 27 possible combinations described in 3.2.1. The average over all participants is recorded in the last row, along with the standard deviation (SD). As can be seen, average sensitivities and specificities were all greater than 82%, and in many individual instances all imagery trials were correctly detected (100% sensitivity). These results are promising for the prefrontal cortical task of music imagery as they are comparable to previously reported results from a group of 3 subjects using motor imagery [8], but were obtained without having to compensate for the interference of hair. Additionally, as observed in the table, all three data types exhibited comparable average performances over all subjects. Although a slight improvement was observed with the hemoglobin concentration data, performance gains were not significant (p-values ≥ 0.38, t-test). This suggests that the additional computational effort required to calculate the concentrations may not be justified. Nonetheless, if computational power can be afforded, some subjects were shown to benefit greatly from using the concentration data (e.g., subjects 1 and 6).

4.2. Client-centred design

Table 2 further indicates the per-user and per-data type optimal HMM–filter–window combinations. The variation between parameters for all participants supports a client-centred design. For raw data (AC and DC), HMMs with observation probabilities represented by only one Gaussian ($M = 1$) were selected most often, whereas for all three data types, window sizes of $l \leq 10$ seconds were selected.

Subject	Window size l [seconds]											
	1		3		5		7		10		15	
	Sens	Spec	Sens	Spec	Sens	Spec	Sens	Spec	Sens	Spec	Sens	Spec
1	0.50	1.00	0.67	1.00	0.67	1.00	0.83	0.67	1.00	1.00	0.50	1.00
2	0.90	0.67	0.80	0.75	0.90	0.67	0.70	1.00	0.80	0.75	0.60	1.00
3	0.78	0.55	0.78	0.55	0.33	0.88	0.40	0.58	0.60	0.92	0.50	1.00
4	1.00	0.67	1.00	0.67	1.00	0.58	1.00	0.70	0.67	0.90	0.67	0.86
5	0.67	0.63	0.83	0.57	0.75	0.50	0.80	0.83	0.40	1.00	0.60	0.83
6	1.00	0.83	1.00	0.83	1.00	0.83	1.00	0.67	0.67	1.00	0.60	0.83
7	0.80	0.86	0.80	0.86	0.80	0.86	0.80	0.86	0.50	1.00	0.67	0.83
8	0.60	0.83	0.70	0.92	0.60	0.92	0.70	0.75	0.70	0.58	0.80	0.75
9	0.70	0.83	0.80	0.92	0.70	0.83	0.60	0.92	0.70	0.83	0.50	0.75
10	0.63	0.91	0.63	0.91	1.00	0.64	0.70	0.75	0.44	0.82	0.50	0.83
11	0.80	0.75	0.63	0.90	0.63	0.90	0.71	0.89	0.90	0.75	0.70	0.83
12	1.00	0.83	1.00	1.00	1.00	0.83	0.60	1.00	0.83	0.83	0.60	1.00
13	0.90	1.00	0.80	1.00	0.80	0.92	0.70	0.92	1.00	0.75	0.80	0.92
Mean	**0.79**	**0.80**	**0.80**	**0.84**	**0.78**	**0.80**	**0.73**	**0.81**	**0.71**	**0.86**	**0.62**	**0.88**
(SD)	**(0.16)**	**(0.14)**	**(0.13)**	**(0.16)**	**(0.20)**	**(0.15)**	**(0.16)**	**(0.13)**	**(0.19)**	**(0.13)**	**(0.11)**	**(0.10)**

Table 3. Time-dependent performance by subject for hemoglobin concentration data. Columns labeled 'Sens' and 'Spec' are sensitivity and specificity, respectively. SD is standard deviation.

Table 3 reports the effects of window size on system performance. For brevity, only the concentration data is included. As can be seen in the table, the best average performance occurred at a window size of 3 seconds, and sensitivity decreased as the window size increased. However, it is noted that the optimal window size varied between subjects. For example, subject 1 experienced the best performance at a window size of 10 seconds, while subject 12 displayed the best results for a 3-second window. This variability is likely due to one or more of the following factors: differences in reaction time, intensity of emotions evoked by the music imagery task, ability to concentrate on the imagery, probe location, and/or anatomical differences, all of which could have affected the propagation delay of the hemodynamic signal. This per-user effect of window size is taken into consideration via a client-centred approach.

5. Discussion

This section provides a comparison with previous work, discusses the use of music imagery for BCI control and the advantages of a client-centred approach, and considers the study's limitations.

5.1. Comparison to past work

The proposed mental activity classifier was exclusively based on statistical models of *baseline* temporal hemodynamic responses. This is a distinct advantage over other HMM-based classification systems (e.g., [3, 17, 33]) which require models to be trained on both mental states in order to perform classification. Such an approach requires the collected data to be separated for training and testing, hence limiting the amount of information available. The proposed method, in comparison, allows the use of all collected baseline data to train HMMs and all collected imagery data to serve as test data, thus reducing possible model overfitting artifacts.

The majority of past work has focused on converting light intensity signals into hemoglobin concentrations, with a few studies focusing on the AC or DC components directly (e.g., [6, 41]). Results observed here suggest that neither method is more discriminating than the other for the task of music imagery classification. As a consequence, the computationally-intense intensity-to-concentration conversion functions may be avoided, thus making it more conducive for future adaptation into a binary BCI.

5.2. Music imagery classification for BCI control

Music imagery classification may be used to control a binary BCI operating in a system-paced mode, akin to single-switch scanning found in conventional electronic augmentative and alternative communication systems. In system-paced mode, options would be highlighted sequentially at a fixed rate. The user would make a selection by performing music imagery, which in turn would be used to activate the BCI. As mentioned in 3.3, music imagery classification was performed once a sustained decrease in the log-likelihood function was observed for five consecutive seconds. This decision rule limits the information transfer rate (ITR) of the BCI to a maximum of 12 bits/min and the system scan rate (SR) to a minimum of 5 seconds. Such values are somewhat lower than those achieved with existing EEG-based BCIs which can be in the order of $ITR = 25$ bits/min and $SR = 2.4$ s [4]. However, it is emphasized that participants had no prior training in using the technology; user training may lead to improvements in system response times [2], thus allowing for a faster decision rule to be implemented.

5.3. Client-centred paradigm

In this study, a client-driven approach was used and HMM model parameters were optimized on a per-participant basis. The optimal number of HMM states Q and Gaussian components M varied between subjects and also between data types (i.e., AC, DC, and hemoglobin concentrations), suggesting that throughout the course of the trials participants did not transition directly from rest to an active mental state. The intermediate activity between rest and music imagery likely varied significantly between participants due to irregularities in level, temporal and spatial distribution of the activity within the task interval. Such irregularities could be present due to specific participant-specific factors such as mind wandering, mental alertness, innate reflex reaction time, familiarity with the procedure, and NIRS signal levels and spatial distributions caused by varying emotional intensities of user-selected songs [25]. It is also observed that for the majority of the participants, the temporal light intensity signals after the intensity-to-concentration mapping are smoother than their original counterparts. This smoothing behaviour is likely the reason that a lower number of states were required, in general, for hemoglobin concentration data relative to AC or DC data.

In order to customize the proposed NIRS-driven classifier for an individual user for BCI control, a short calibration session can be undertaken with known imagery and rest intervals

— much like the imagery trials of this experiment — in order to choose the optimal parameters for the data (data type, filter), the HMM (states, Gaussians) and the response time of the switch (window size). The optimization process can be hardcoded into a calibration program, and executed with minimal intervention by an outside party, thus likely will not pose a burden on the user. This would be akin to the training phase required by widely-used speech recognition engines.

5.4. Study limitations

Experimental conditions were restrictive in the sense that participants were required to remain quiet and immobile for the duration of the data recording sessions; all focus was placed on the given task. All auditory and visual distractions were suppressed as much as possible by the earmuffs and blindfold. If BCI technologies are to be used in everyday settings, however, movement artifacts [10], auditory and visual distractions [42], and mind-wandering still have to be detected and accounted for (e.g., as in [19]). Additionally, experimental sessions lasted less than one hour. For BCIs, however, systems may be used for multiple consecutive hours. As a consequence, the effects of fatigue on classifier performance also need to be quantified. However, multiple calibration sessions may be performed throughout the day such that the detrimental effects of fatigue on the harnessed signals can be incorporated directly into the reference baseline hidden Markov models. Lastly, further work must be done to investigate the feasibility of music imagery classification for individuals in the target population. The prospects are promising, however, as hemodynamic responses due to mental activity have been shown to be detectable by NIRS for individuals with ALS [6].

6. Conclusions

This study proposed a client-centred NIRS-driven system that uses HMM as a classification tool to differentiate between music imagery and baseline (rest). The classifier performance, reported both in terms of classifier sensitivity and specificity, averaged over thirteen subjects was greater than 82%, and in many cases exhibited successful detection of all imagery events (100% sensitivity). To allow for a client-centred design, three different wavelet filters (3-, 4-, and 5–detail), three HMM parameter sets (Q–M values of 4–1, 2–2, and 2–1), and six different sliding window sizes (1, 3, 5, 7, 10 and 15 seconds) were considered. The resultant wide range of optimal parameters suggests that parameters be selected for each individual via a short, simple calibration session wherein the user alternates between rest and music imagery in a predetermined pattern. Moreover, since concentration calculations require additional computational power, the comparable results obtained here between all data types suggest that NIRS raw data (AC, DC) should be considered in future studies as an alternative to hemoglobin concentrations. The promising performance of the system suggests that a user-centered NIRS-based BCI is a concept that deserves further feasibility studies, as does the use of HMM as a classifier of cognitive activity versus rest.

Acknowledgements

The authors would like to acknowledge the financial support from the WB Family Foundation and the Natural Sciences and Engineering Research Council of Canada, as well as Ka Lun Tam and Pierre Duez for their hardware/software support.

http://dx.doi.org/10.5772/55804

Author details

Tiago H. Falk[1,*], Kelly M. Paton[2] and Tom Chau[3]

* Address all correspondence to: tiago.falk@ieee.org

1 Institut National de la Recherche Scientifique (INRS-EMT), University of Quebec, Montreal, Canada
2 Institute of Applied Mathematics, University of British Columbia, British Columbia, Canada
3 Bloorview Research Institute, University of Toronto, Toronto, Canada

References

[1] K Tai, S Blain, and Tom Chau. A review of emerging access technologies for individuals with severe motor impairments. *Assistive Technology*, 20:204–219, 2008.

[2] Jonathan R Wolpaw, Niels Birbaumer, William J Heetderks, Dennis J McFarland, P Hunter Peckham, Gerwin Schalk, Emanuel Donchin, Louis A Quatrano, Charles J Robinson, and Theresa M Vaughan. Brain-Computer Interface Technology: A Review of the First International Meeting. *IEEE Transactions on Rehabilitation Engineering*, 8(2):164–173, 2000.

[3] Ranganatha Sitaram, Haihong Zhang, Cuntai Guan, Manoj Thulasidas, Yoko Hoshi, Akihiro Ishikawa, Koji Shimizu, and Niels Birbaumerb. Temporal classification of multichannel near-infrared spectroscopy signals of motor imagery for developing a brain-computer interface. *NeuroImage*, 34:1416–1427, 2007.

[4] Marcel van Gerven, Jason Farquhar, Rebecca Schaefer, Rutger Vlek, Jeroen Geuze, Anton Nijholt, Nick Ramsey, Pim Haselager, Louis Vuurpijl, Stan Gielen, and Peter Desain. The brain-computer interface cycle. *Journal of Neural Engineering*, 6(4), 2009.

[5] R Sitaram, Y Hoshi, and C Guan. Near infrared spectroscopy based brain-computer interface. *Proceedings of SPIE - The International Society for Optical Engineering*, 5852(1):434–442, 2005.

[6] M Naito, Y Michioka, K Ozawa, Y Ito, M Kiguchi, and T Kanazawa. A Communication Means for Totally Locked-in ALS Patients Based on Changes in Cerebral Blood Volume Measured with Near-Infrared Light. *IEICE Transactions on Information and Systems*, E90-D(7):1028–1037, 2007.

[7] S Coyle, T Ward, C Markham, and G McDarby. On the suitability of near-infrared (NIR) systems for next-generation brain-computer interfaces. *Physiological Measurements*, 25:815–822, 2004.

[8] S M Coyle, T E Ward, and C M Markham. Brain-computer interface using a simplified functional near-infrared spectroscopy system. *Journal of Neural Engineering*, 4:219–226, 2007.

[9] R Sitaram, A Caria, and N Birbaumer. Hemodynamic brain-computer interfaces for communication and rehabilitation. *Neural Networks*, 22(9):1320–1328, November 2009.

[10] Fiachra Matthews, Barak A Pearlmutter, Tomas E Ward, Christopher Soraghan, and Charles Markham. Hemodynamics for Brain-Computer Interfaces. *IEEE Signal Processing Magazine*, 25(1):87–94, January 2008.

[11] Arno Villringer and Britton Chance. Non-invasive optical spectroscopy and imaging of human brain function. *Trends in Neurosciences*, 20(10):431–433, October 1997.

[12] Gert Pfurtscheller, G´unther Bauernfeind, Selina Christin Wriessnegger, and Christa Neuper. Focal frontal (de)oxyhemoglobin responses during simple arithmetic. *International Journal of Psychophysiology*, 76(3):186–192, 2010.

[13] H. Ogata, T. Mukai, and T. Yagi. A study on the frontal cortex in cognitive tasks using near-infrared spectroscopy. In *Proc. IEEE Conf. of the Engineering in Medicine and Biology Society*, pages 4731–4734, 2007.

[14] H Ayaz, M Izzetoglu, S Bunce, T Heiman-Patterson, and B Onaral. Detecting cognitive activity related hemodynamic signal for brain-computer interface using functional near-infrared spectroscopy. In *Proceedings of the IEEE Conference of the Engineering in Medicine and Biology Society*, pages 342–345, 2007.

[15] MJ Herrmann, A.C. Ehlis, and AJ Fallgatter. Prefrontal activation through task requirements of emotional induction measured with NIRS. *Biological Psychology*, 64(3):255–263, 2003.

[16] J. Leon-Carrion, J. Damas, K. Izzetoglu, K. Pourrezai, J.F. Martín-Rodríguez, J.M.B. Martin, and M.R. Dominguez-Morales. Differential time course and intensity of PFC activation for men and women in response to emotional stimuli: A functional near-infrared spectroscopy (fNIRS) study. *Neuroscience Letters*, 403(1-2):90–95, 2006.

[17] S Power, T Falk, and T Chau. Classification of prefrontal activity due to mental arithmetic and music imagery using hidden markov models and frequency domain near-infrared spectroscopy. *Journal of Neural Engineering*, 7:026002, 2010.

[18] Sarah D Power, Azadeh Kushki, and Tom Chau. Automatic single-trial discrimination of mental arithmetic, mental singing and the no-control state from prefrontal activity: toward a three-state nirs-bci. *BMC Research Notes*, 5(141), March 2012.

[19] Tiago Falk, M Guirgis, S Power, and T Chau. Taking nirs-bcis outside the lab: Achieving robustness against ambient noise. *IEEE Trans Neural Syst Rehab Eng*, 19(2):136–146, 2011.

[20] Boris Kotchoubey, Anna Dubischar, Herbert Mack, Jochen Kaiser, and Niels Birbaumer. Electrocortical and behavioral effects of chronic immobility on word processing. *Cognitive Brain Research*, 17(1):188–199, June 2003.

[21] Toshiki Endo, Teiji Tominaga, and Lars Olson. Cortical Changes Following Spinal Cord Injury with Emphasis on the Nogo Signaling System. *The Neuroscientist*, 15(3):291–299, 2009.

[22] S B Frost, S Barbay, K M Friel, E J Plautz, and R J Nudo. Reorganization of Remote Cortical Regions After Ischemic Brain Injury: A Potential Substrate for Stroke Recovery. *Journal of Neurophysiology*, 89:3205–3214, 2003.

[23] E Altenmüller, K ASchürmann, V K Lim, and D Parlitz. Hits to the left, flops to the right: different emotions during listening to music are reflected in cortical lateralisation patterns. *Neuropsychologia*, 40(13):2242–2256, 2002.

[24] C L Krumhansl. An Exploratory Study of Musical Emotions and Psychophysiology. *Canadian Journal of Experimental Psychology*, 51(4):336–353, 1997.

[25] M Boso, P Politi, F Barale, and E Enzo. Neurophysiology and neurobiology of the musical experience. *Functional Neurology*, 21(4):187–191, 2006.

[26] A J Blood, R J Zatorre, P Bermudez, and A C Evans. Emotional responses to pleasant and unpleasant music correlate with activity in paralimbic brain regions. *Nature Neuroscience*, 2(4):382–387, 1999.

[27] A J Blood and R J Zatorre. Intensely pleasurable responses to music correlate with activity in brain regions implicated in reward and emotion. *Proceedings of the National Academy of Sciences U.S.A.*, 98:11818–11823, 2001.

[28] B Kleber, N Birbaumer, R Veit, T Trevorrow, and M Lotze. Overt and imagined signing of an Italian aria. *Neuroimage*, 36:889–900, 2007.

[29] Sarah D Power, A Kushki, and Tom Chau. Towards a system-paced near-infrared spectroscopy brain-computer interface: differentiating prefrontal activity due to mental arithmetic and mental singing from the no-control state. *Journal of Neural Engineering*, 8(6):066004, December 2011.

[30] C D Tsang, L Trainor, D L Santesso, S L Tasker, and L A Schmidt. Frontal EEG responses as a function of affective musical features. *Annals of the New York Academy of Sciences*, 930:439–442, 2001.

[31] S Dalla Bella, I Peretz, L Rousseau, and N Gosselin. A developmental study of the affective value of tempo and mode in music. *Cognitio*, 80:B1–10, 2001.

[32] S K Law. Thickness and Resistivity Variations over the Upper Surface of the Human Skull. *Brain Topography*, 6(2):99–109, 1993.

[33] B Obermaier, C Guger, C Neuper, and G Pfurtscheller. Hidden Markov models for online classification of single trial EEG data. *Pattern Recognition Letters*, 22:1299–1309, 2001.

[34] I Sase, H Eda, A Seiyama, H C Tanabea, A Takatsuke, and T Yanagida. Multi-channel optical mapping: Investigation of depth information. *Proceedings of SPIE*, 4250, 2001.

[35] K. Tai and T. Chau. Single-trial classification of nirs signals during emotional induction tasks: towards a corporeal machine interface. *Journal of NeuroEngineering and Rehabilitation*, 6(39), 2009.

[36] Arlene Duncan, Judith H Meek, Matthew Clemence, Clare E Elwell, Lidia Tyszczuk, Mark Cope, and David T Delpy. Optical pathlength measurements on adult head, calf and forearm and the head of the newborn infant using phase resolved optical spectroscopy. *Physics in Medicine and Biology*, 40:295–304, 1995.

[37] Mark Cope. *The development of a near infrared spectroscopy system and its application for non invasive monitoring of cerebral blood and tissue oxygenation in the newborn infant*. Ph.d., University of London, 1991.

[38] Lawrence R. Rabiner. A Tutorial on Hidden Markov Models and Selected Applications in Speech Recognition. *Proceedings of the IEEE*, 77(2):257–286, February 1989.

[39] R. Hu, X. Li, and Y. Zhao. Acoustic model training using greedy EM. In *proceedings of the IEEE International Conference on Acoustics, Speech, and Signal Processing, ICASSP'05, March 18-23 2005, Philadelphia*, volume 1, 2005.

[40] Kevin Murphy. Hidden Markov Model (HMM) Toolbox for Matlab. http://www.cs.ubc.ca/~murphyk/Software/HMM/hmm.html.

[41] S. Luu and T. Chau. Decoding subjective preference from single-trial near-infrared spectroscopy signals. *Journal of Neural Engineering*, 6(4), 2009.

[42] V. Gumenyuk, O. Korzyukov, K. Alho, C. Escera, and R. Naatanen. Effects of auditory distraction on electrophysiological brain activity and performance in children aged 8-13 years. *Psychophysiology*, 41(1):30–36, 2004.

Chapter 8

Equivalent-Current-Dipole-Source-Localization-Based BCIs with Motor Imagery

Toshimasa Yamazaki, Maiko Sakamoto,
Shino Takata, Hiromi Yamaguchi, Kazufumi Tanaka,
Takahiro Shibata, Hiroshi Takayanagi,
Ken-ichi Kamijo and Takahiro Yamanoi

Additional information is available at the end of the chapter

http://dx.doi.org/10.5772/55805

1. Introduction

This chapter will propose a new paradigm for single-trial-electroencephalogram (EEG)-based Brain-Computer Interfaces (BCIs) with motor imagery (MI) [1] tasks. Among such BCIs, the sensorimotor rhythm (SMR)-based ones, when using common spatial patterns (CSPs), require features over broad frequency bands, such as mu, beta and gamma rhythms [2]. Therefore, very high-dimensional feature vectors and continuous-valued patterns necessary for spatio-temporally checking the features [3,4] could yield an enormous amount of data and much computational time [5]. So, various data reduction such as downsampling [6,7] and optimal EEG channel configuration [8,9,10] have been investigated for the BCIs.

The present method consists of 1) the categorization of single-trial EEGs as data reduction, and 2) the classifiers for the categorical data. 1) is realized by equivalent current dipole source localization (ECDL) after independent component analysis (ICA). For 2), we have been applying both Hayashi's second method of quantification (H2MQ) and Bayesian network model (BNM) to the ECDL-based categorical data. For the former, we have obtained the good accuracy, for example, the accuracy average across all the ten subjects for left- and right-hand imageries in each 10-trial validation was more than 90 % [11].

This chapter addresses itself to the single-trial-EEG-based BCI using the BNM and to the generalization to dynamic BNM (DBNM) because of the time-varying functional networks in the brain. For the purposes, two experiments were conducted to obtain single-trial EEGs scalp-recorded during the MI tasks and movement-related potentials (MRPs) including the Bereitschaftspotential (BP) [12].

Recently, neuroscience has been attempting to take in various methodologies in network science, because the brain could be considered to be a kind of complex systems forming networks of interacting components, and the collective actions of the components, that is, individual neurons, linked by a dense web of intricate connectivity [13]. In addition to the network approach, one of the applied researches in neuroscience, the BCI, has extensively received probabilistic approaches whose aims are mainly two. One is to cope with non-stationarities in EEG signals such intertrial and intersubject variations, and the other to incorporate time-varying brain states and uncertainties into BCI design. For the former aim, adaptive classifications were executed by Kalman filtering [14,15], while the DBN achieved the latter one [16]. Micheloyannis et al. [17] analyzed multi-channel EEGs using graph theory. However, because the nodes are electrode positions, they have few functional meanings. In addition, all the above methods had been throughout applied to continuous-valued data.

A BN could be one of graphical models in neuroscience, where brain connectivity would be quantified by conditional probabilities. However, the existing graphical models require a large-scale anatomical data [18] and huge quantities of diffusion MRI data [19,20]. In this study, the brain connectivity will be calculated from the neural activity data even less than that in the above graphical models.

Figure 1 shows a typical BN, showing both the topology and the conditional probability tables (CPTs), given the joint probability distribution:

where X_i (i=1,…,5) (nodes) are random variables whose values could be 0 or 1, and B_S represents the BN topology, and Table 1 depicts 20 sample data generated from the BN model (BNM) [21]. The BN construction refers to that the topology of BNMs is estimated from such data in Table 1. In this study, BNM and DBNM consist of functionally distinct sites of the brain as nodes and directed relationships among these sites as edges, each of which is accompanied by conditional probabilities.

In order to predict the tasks which would have been executed by the subjects, in particular to discriminate between left- and right-hand imageries, the conditional probabilities at all the nodes in the BNM must be calculated for each trial. For the purpose, the probabilistic inference is made by the belief propagation [21], where the ECDL results for each trial correspond to the evidences. Hereafter, *node activities* are defined to be the summation of conditional probabilities at each node. Based on the node activities, a rule is proposed to classify into left- and right-hand imageries. This classification rule will be examined by the statistical tests.

Moreover, our method will be validated and compared with the existing one with the best performance, called common spatial pattern (CSP) [22]. In the section 3, MRPs will be modeled by the DBNM. Finally, we will mainly mention future perspectives.

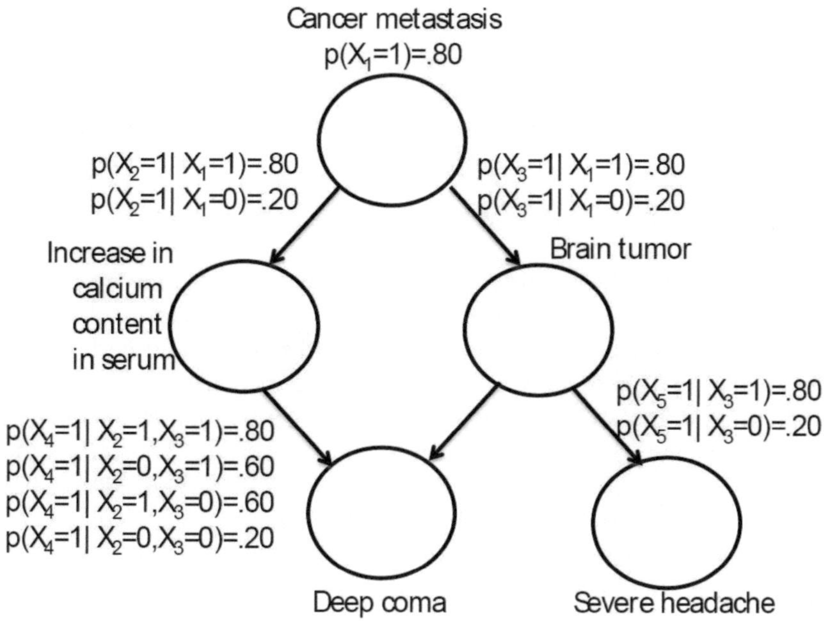

Figure 1. An example for causal model of Bayesian Network [21].

	node number				
	1	2	3	4	5
1	1	0	1	1	1
2	0	0	0	1	0
3	1	1	1	1	1
4	1	1	1	1	0
5	1	1	1	1	0
6	1	1	0	0	0
7	1	0	0	0	0
8	0	0	0	0	0
9	0	0	0	0	0
10	0	1	1	1	1
11	0	0	0	0	0
12	1	1	1	1	1
13	0	0	1	1	1
14	1	1	1	1	1
15	1	0	1	1	1
16	1	1	1	0	0
17	1	1	0	1	0
18	1	1	1	0	0
19	1	1	0	1	0
20	1	1	1	0	1
ave	.7	.6	.6	.6	.4

Table 1. Data example [21] generated by the BN shown in Figure 1.

2. Bayesian network models for single-trial-EEG-based BCI

2.1. Materials and methods

Subjects. Ten healthy subjects (two females and eight males; mean age: 28.4 ± 4.27 years) participated in this experiment. All the subjects were right-handed according to the Edinburgh Inventory [23]. Some of the subjects were paid volunteers and received 2000 Yen (about US 25$).

EEG data acquisition. The subjects were seated inside an electrically shielded room with sound attenuation, and gazed at a monochromatic monitor of an AV tachistscope (IS-701B, IWATSU ISEL) 0.9 m away from their eyes. They were requested to relax their both hands on a table and with their chins on a chinrest (Figure 2A). The present experiment used a visual oddball paradigm, and three kinds of line drawings of hands were presented on the monitor: (1) right-hand stimulus to imagine being shaken with the subject's right hand, (2) left-hand one for the subject's left hand imagery and (3) open-right-hand one as control (Fig.2B). These stimuli were sequentially and randomly presented with probabilities of 0.20, 0.20 and 0.60, respectively. That is, (1) and (2) are rare targets or rare non-targets, and (3) is frequent non-target. We tried four conditions consisting of movement imagery of right hand, left one and the actual movements, where each condition was separately carried out. Names of the conditions and the instruction to subjects were as follows: R-MIRP (right-hand-movement-imagery-related potential) condition is to imagine grasping the right-hand stimulus with her or his own right hand as soon as possible when the stimulus was displayed; L-MIRP (left-hand-MIRP) condition to image grasping the left-hand stimulus with her or his own when the stimulus was presented; R-MRP (right-hand-movement-related potential) condition to actually grasp and loosen her or his own right palm as soon as possible if right-hand stimuli as the rare targets were displayed; L-MRP (left-hand-MRP) condition to grasp and loosen her or his palm when left-hand stimuli as the rare targets were presented. Both hands were hidden under a black coverlet so that it is easier for the subjects to imagine the hand movement. There was the following training session. At first, each subject was instructed to actually reach the monitor for the line drawing, then to shake (the stimulus) by her or his hand, and to practice the task scores of times. Then, after covering both of the hands with the coverlet, the subject was requested to imagine being shaken and to practice the MI tasks scores of times. One test session includes all the four conditions with a five-minute break between the conditions, where each condition contains 130, 130 and 400 trials of rare targets, rare non-targets and frequent non-targets, respectively. Therefore, it took about 90 minutes to finish one session. Note that different subject had different order of the conditions. This study addressed itself to only the L- and R-MIRP conditions, while the L- and R-MRP ones will be used in our another research in future.

With an electro cap (ECI, Electrocap International), EEG was from 32 electrodes (FP1, FPz, FP3, F7, F3, Fz, F4, F8, FC5, FC1, FC2, FC6, T3, C3, Cz, C4, T4, CP5, CP1, CPz, CP2, CP6, T5, P3, Pz, P4, T6, PO3, POz, PO4, O1, Oz, O2) defined on the basis of the International 10-20 System [24]. All the electrodes were referred to A1, the ground electrode was attached to FPz and their impedances were kept below 5kΩ. Vertical and horizontal eye movements were monitored

http://dx.doi.org/10.5772/55805

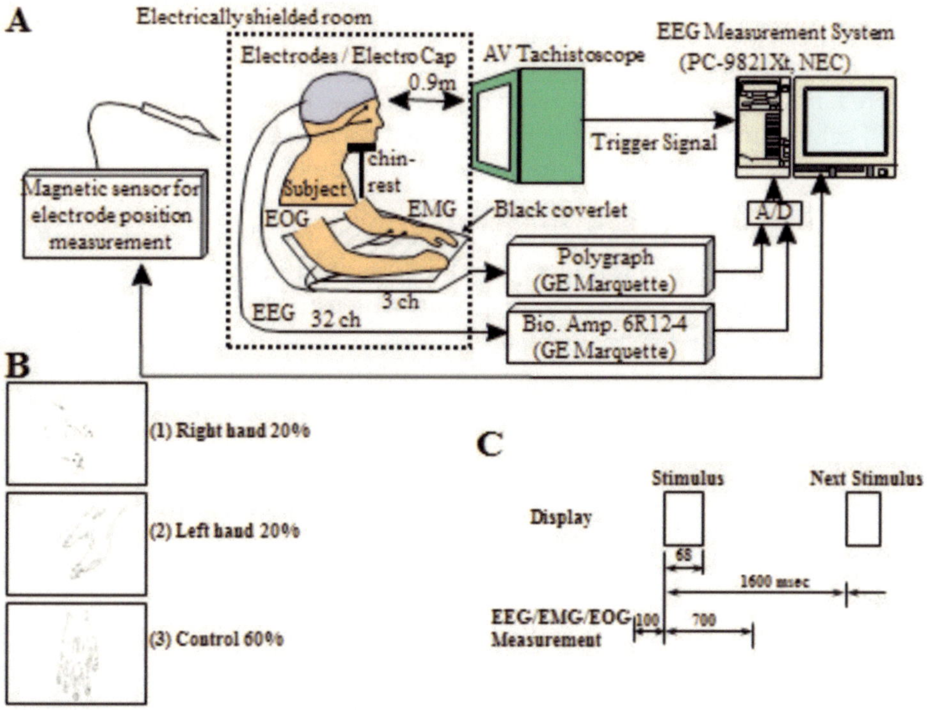

Figure 2. Experimental design: (A) EEG, EOG, EMG and electrode position measurement and stimulus presentation; (B) stimulus contents; (C) time-scheduling of the stimulation and the measurement of EEG, EOG and EMG.

with two electrodes placed directly above the nasion and the outer canthus of the right eye as electrooculogram (EOG). Another two electrodes were placed at both the medial antibrachiums to record arm electromyogram (EMG) so that EEGs could be excluded when mistakenly grasping during the movement imagery.

The 32 signals of the EEGs were amplified by a Biotop 6R12-4 amplifier (GE Marquette Medical Systems Japan, Ltd.), and filtered a frequency bandwidth of 0.01-100 Hz. The amplified signals were sampled at a rate of 1 kHz during an epoch of 100 ms preceding and 700 ms following the stimulus onset. The inter-stimulus interval (ISI) was 1600 ms (Figure 2C). The on-line A/D converted EEG signals were immediately stored on a hard disk in a PC-9821Xt personal computer (PC) (NEC Corporation). The EOG and EMG data were also amplified by a Polygraph 360 amplifier (GE Marquette Medical Systems Japan, Ltd.), and sent to the same PC.

Independent component analysis (ICA). Fast ICA [25] was applied to each single-trial EEG in the L- and R-MIRP conditions, using ICALAB [26]. After ICA for each trial, among 32 ICs, we removed those associated with eye movement and line noise, and having a broader high frequency (50-100 Hz) spectrum that might be likely to be generated by scalp muscles [27], according to the spectra of all the ICs for each trial. Consequently, the following ECDL was applied to about 20 ICs containing only neural activity.

Equivalent current dipole source localization (ECDL). Independent EEG sources obtained by ICA are dipolar [28]. ECDL was applied to the reconstructed EEGs, namely the projection of each IC on the scalp surface by the deflation procedure, using "SynaCenterPro" (PC-based commercial software for multiple ECDL) (NEC Corporation). This software estimates unconstrained dipoles [29] at any timepoint, using the three-layered concentric sphere head model by the nonlinear optimization methods [30]. An unconstrained dipole was estimated at any timepoint with maximal peak or trough in the reconstructed EEGs for each IC. Here, we searched for appropriate and reliable dipole solutions that had goodness of fit (GOF) of more than 90 % and the simplified confidence limit [31] of less than 1 mm and had stable localization to the same brain site around the peak or trough. The brain sites, where dipoles were located, were determined by inspection with reference to the textbook of neuroanatomy (e.g., [32]). The inspectors had a good knowledge of neuroanatomy. Thus, one brain site was assigned to each IC.

Bayesian network model (BNM) construction. The present BNM consists of functionally distinct sites of the brain as nodes and directed relationships among these sites as edges. Nodes of the BNM are the brain sites where ECDs were located by the ECDL method. The BNM structure was constructed by the conditional independency (CI) test [33]. The BNMs obtained for each subject had fifteen nodes corresponding to the brain sites such as the frontal, temporal, occipital and cingulate gyri, hippocampus, insula, left and right parietal cortices, left and right motor areas, left and right cerebellum, left and right somatosensory areas, and others. The BNM initialization was made so that there are edges from the mesial prefrontal areas to the premotor and primary motor cortices because the early BP begins in the pre-supplementary motor area (preSMA) and the SMA proper and then in the premotor cortex, and the late BP (NS') occurs in the primary motor and premotor cortices [12].

Probabilistic inference for classification rule. In order to discriminate between left- and right-hand imageries, the conditional probabilities at all the nodes in the BNM must be calculated for each trial. For the purpose, the probabilistic inference is made by the belief propagation using the clique tree algorithm [34], where the ECDL results for each trial correspond to the evidences. A free software, "MSBNx" (Microsoft Research) [35] enables this inference. On the basis of the *node activities*, a rule was proposed to classify into left- and right-hand imageries.

2.2. Results

Figure 3 shows an example for a series of our results for one trial by one subject: (A) 32-channel raw EEG data; (B) ICA results (showing the first 10 ICs); (C) deflation for the 10th IC; (D) ECDL result, where when to be estimated is depicted by a black arrow at the 11th reconstructed EEG in (C) and the same time is for the rest EEGs, and one localized dipole is represented by a blue arrow in (D). This figure exemplifies that the dipole was located at the left pre-central gyrus, for the single-trial EEG recorded during the right-hand movement imagery task. Table 2 illustrates a summary for these categorized ECDL results, including the same data as in Figure 3. That is, this table indicates that the 10th IC, after the deflation procedure, from the single-trial EEGs recorded during the 7th right-hand movement imagery task, was localized to the left motor area (the pre-central gyrus), where n1 to n15 correspond to the above 15 brain sites, in particular n1 the left motor area.

2.3. BN structure

Figure 4 shows a representative BNM constructed for subject 1, who satisfied the classification rule mentioned later. The BNM construction required each about 30 trials of the left-hand and right-hand-movement imageries. This number will be confirmed later. The BNM for subject 1 directs the link from the "occipital" node to the "frontal" one via the cingulate gyrus, and that from the "frontal" node to directly to the "left motor area" one and, to the "right motor area" one via the somatosensory cortex. The "frontal" node contains the superior and inferior frontal gyri. The "motor area" node includes the primary motor and premotor cortices. This BNM might reveal the neural network involving from the visual stimulus input to the movement imageries.

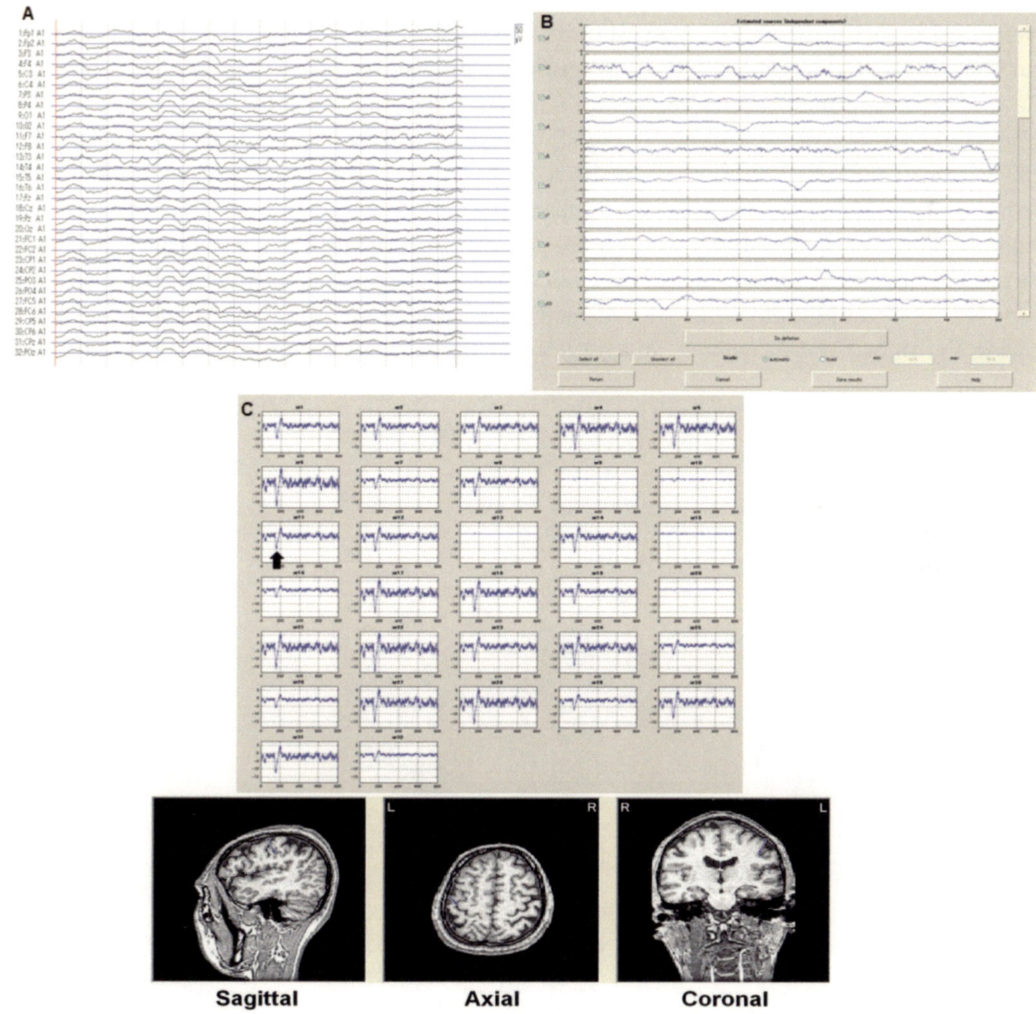

Figure 3. A series of the present results for one trial by one subject: (A) raw EEG data; (B) ICA; (C) deflation; (D) ECDL.

2.4. Node activities

A BN topology could be determined from the ECDL results on all the trials for each subject. For all the nodes, however, the connectivity between any two nodes, that is, the conditional probability cannot be estimated from even all the ECDL results for each subject. Especially, for any one trial, the ECDL results do not necessarily enrich all the nodes in the subject's BN. However, the probabilistic inference could enrich all the nodes for each trial in terms of the conditional probabilities.

Assuming that the summation of these conditional probabilities in each node reflects the neural activity of the node, the node activity was calculated for each trial. Moreover, we focused on the "left and right motor areas" nodes, because there have been many findings about the involvement of the primary and/or premotor cortices during the motor imagery [36-41]. The t-test concerning the mean of the node activities across the trials for each subject was as follows. For the right-hand imagery, there were significant differences in the node activities between the "left and right motor areas" nodes for subjects 1, 2, 3, 4, 5, 6 and 9 ($t(51)=2.41$, $p=0.0193$; $t(59)=-2.81$, $p = 0.00672$; $t(60)=-7.27$, $p=1.05E-09$; $t(54)=-2.18$, $p=0.0336$; $t(58)=-2.77$, $p=0.00754$; $t(57)=5.11$, $p=3.90E-06$; $t(50)=2.19$, $p=0.0330$, respectively). On the other hand, for the left-hand imagery, there were no differences for subjects 1, 2, 4, 5, 7, 8 and 10 ($p>0.05$). These findings might lead us to one possibility of classification rules to discriminate between left and right hand to be imagined for our single-trial-EEG-based BCI. That is, for right-handed subjects, there is a significant difference in the node activities between left and right "motor area" nodes during the right-hand-movement imagery, while no difference during the left-hand-movement one.

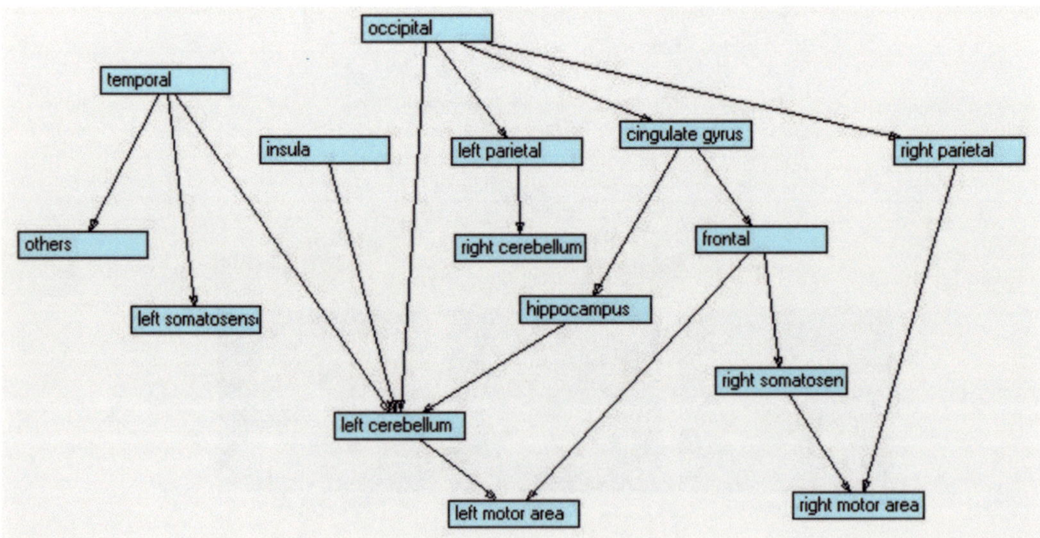

Figure 4. Bayesian network model of motor imagery for subject 1

		1st IC			2nd IC			···	10th IC			···
trials		n1	···	n15	n1	···	n15		n1	···	n15	
L	⋮											
R	⋮											
	7	···	···	···	···	···	···	···	1	···	···	···
	⋮											

Table 2. A summary for categorized ECDL results. "L" and "R" represent the left- and right-hand movement imageries, respectively. "IC"s independent components and n1 to n15 the 15 brain sites (see the text in more details).

2.5. Discussion

2.5.1. The present BNMs supported by the topological map of human cortical network

For subjects 1, 3 to 6[1], the paths to left and right "motor area" nodes were consistent with the existing topological map of human cortical network. For example, "frontal" → "right somatosensory" and "occipital" → "right parietal" are exemplified by MFG.R – PoCG.R and SOG.R – ANG.R in [20] (p.530, Fig.4), respectively.

2.5.2. Classification rule

Subjects 1, 2, 4 and 5 perfectly met the classification rule proposed above. This rule, which might show bilaterally non-symmetrical event-related desynchronization (ERD) patterns [42], contrary to that of Qin et al. [43], is strongly supported by Bai et al. [44].

2.5.3. Number of trials for BNM learning

Figure 5 shows the number of trials necessary to satisfy with the rule for subject 1, plotting the p-values in the t-test, as functions of the number of trials, for subject 1. The t-test examines difference in node activities between the "left and right motor areas" nodes for the left- and right-hand imageries. Figure 5 depicts the p-values for every 5 trials. This figure demonstrates that the above rule is effective after about 25 trials. That is, the present BNM learning for BCI requires about 25 trials.

1 The BNMs of subjects 3 to 6 are not here.

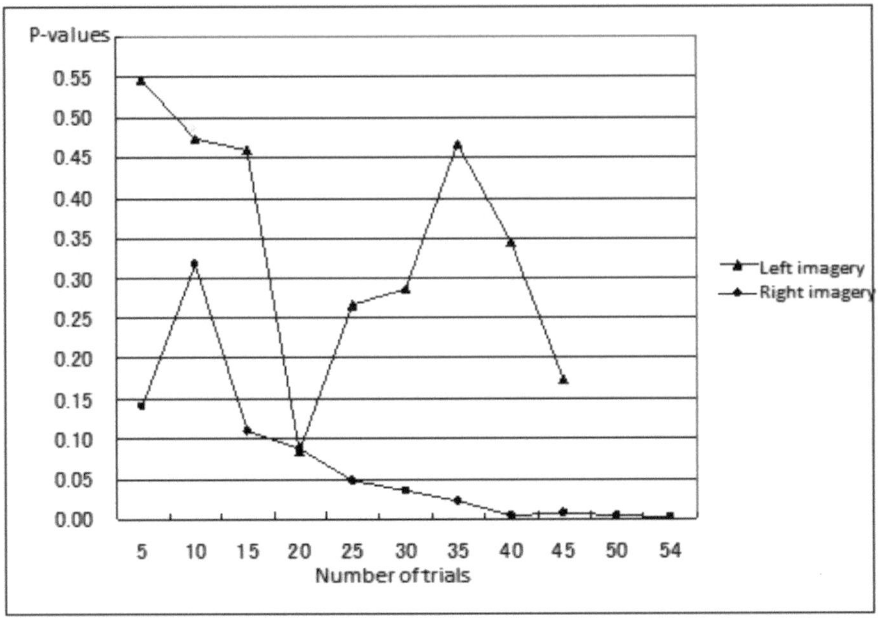

Figure 5. P-values in the t-test concerning the differences in conditional probabilities between the "left and right motor areas" nodes, as a function of number of trials.

2.5.4. Comparison with CSP

The present BCI based on the classification rule was validated and compared with the common spatial pattern (CSP) method [22]. The test data includes 20 trials with left- and right-hand movement imageries. In our BCI after the probabilistic inference for each trial, on the basis of the classification rule, if "the left motor areas" node activity are significantly different from "the right motor areas" one, the trial was judged to be a right hand imagery, while both of the node activities are not so different, the trial a left hand imagery.

The CSP is an algorithm for obtaining a spatial filter to transform multi-channel EEG data with two conditions into the surrogate space enabling the optimal discrimination of the conditions. This filtering is achieved by solving the generalized eigenvalue problem for the estimates of the covariance matrices of the band-pass filtered EEG signal. For each trial, 1-dimensional feature is calculated after operating the spatial filter on the single-trial EEG. From these features, the threshold is determined so that all the trials for the learning are optimally discriminated between the two conditions as exemplified in Figure 6. Thus, for each of α, μ, β and γ frequency bands, we conducted one CSP classifier with its threshold, using the same EEG data as in the subject 1's BNM (Figure 4) construction. Finally, for subjects 1 and 2 among ones who satisfied with the proposed classification rule, the accuracy of the present BNM and the 1-CSP classifier was 90 % and 75 %, and 85 % and 70 %, respectively.

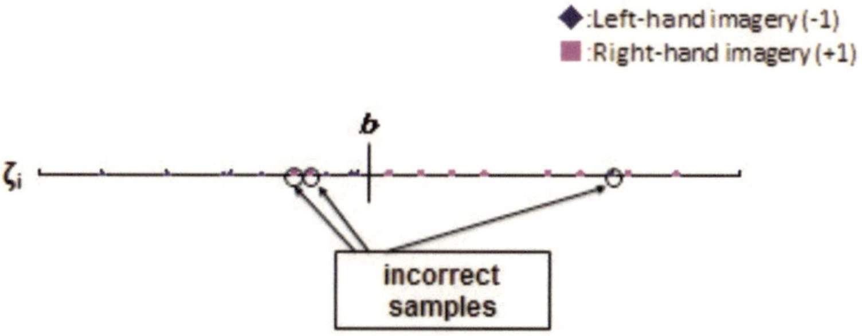

$$\textbf{Classifier:} f(\zeta_i) = \begin{cases} -1 \; (\zeta_i < b) \\ +1 \; (\zeta_i > b) \end{cases}$$

Figure 6. Principle of 1-CSP classifier. ζ_i is a feature value for the ith trial, and b is the threshold.

3. Generalization to dynamic BNM

3.1. Materials and methods

Acquisition of single-trial EEGs. This experiment was carried out to obtain MRPs with BP in term of single-trial EEGs. Subjects reclined in an EEG chair in an electrically shielded room, and gazed at a display 90 cm away from their eyes (Figure 7). For any one trial, on the display, "choice" was presented at first, "+" was presented 3.5 s after "choice" and "report" was presented 2 s after "+" in turn. The duration of "choice" was 2 s, that of "+" was 0.2 s and that of "report" was 2.5 s (Figure 8). In case of "left" or "right" selection in "choice", the subjects were requested to grasp their hand of the same side as the selection as soon as possible when "+" was presented, and then to speak aloud the selection in "report". Otherwise, there was no grasping and no speaking. During this task, 32-channel single-trial EEGs, EMG and EOG were recorded. This section reports results on only the same subject as in the section 2 (subject 1).

Division of the EEGs. According to Shibasaki and Hallett [12], the EEG data was divided into three intervals. That is, assuming that the time when the onset of the EMG is 0 ms, the interval between -1700 and -400 ms refers to early-BP (E-BP), that between -400 and 0 ms NS' (negative slope) and that between 0 and 200 ms MP (motor potential).

ICA, ECDL then BNM and DBNM construction and probabilistic inference. For each interval, ECDL was applied to single-trial EEGs after ICA. For each interval, using the categorical data concerning the ECDL results on both the "left" and "right" tasks, each including 10 trials, a BNM structure was determined by the CI test. Moreover, connecting with the frontal node on the top of each BN led to a DBNM. Then, the probabilistic inference enriched all the nodes of the DBNM for each trial, in terms of conditional probabilities.

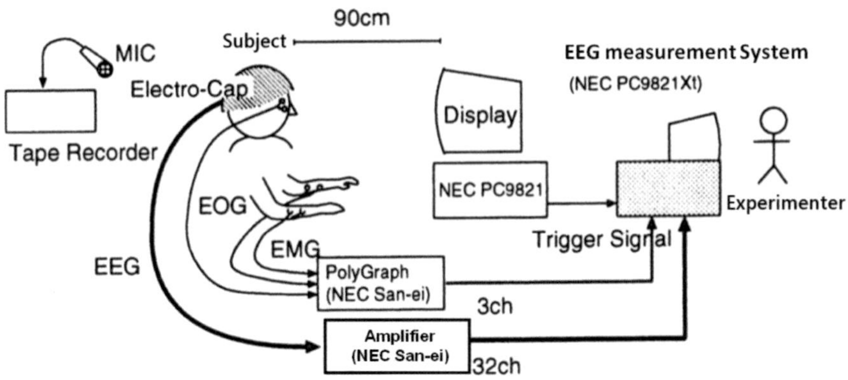

Figure 7. EEG measurement and stimulus presentation system.

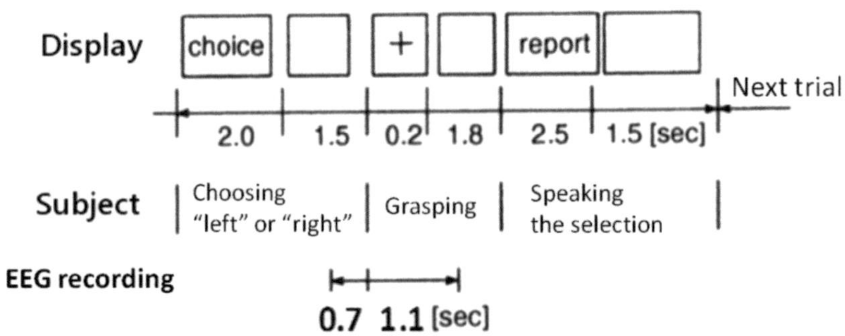

Figure 8. Time-scheduling of the stimulus presentation, the task and the EEG measurement.

http://dx.doi.org/10.5772/55805

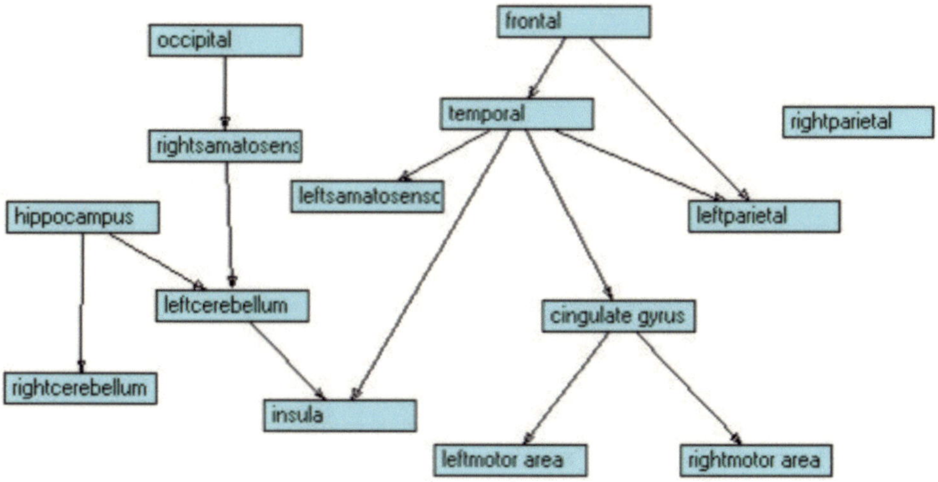

Figure 9. E-BP BNM, where open rectangles and arrows depict nodes and edges, respectively.

3.2. Results and discussion

Figure 9 shows a BNM obtained for the E-BP. This BNM is also consistent with the topological map of human cortical network (for example, "cingulate gyrus" →"left motor area" was found in ACG.L-SMA.L-PreCG.L [20]), and reflects the previous neurophysiological findings (for example, "hippocampus"→"left/right cerebellum" might be explained by that lesions of the cerebellar nuclei abolish conditioned increases in hippocampal CA1 neural activity evoked by the tone-conditioned stimulus [45]). The DBNM, shown in Figure 10, contains the neural generators for the MRPs. Namely, the neural generator of the E-BP is the pre-SMA at first, next the SMA and then the premotor cortex, that of the NS' the premotor cortex at the first and next the motor cortex and that of the MP the somatosensory cortex [8]. In the E-BP BNM, there is no difference in node activities between the "left- and right-motor area" nodes for the left- ($t(14)=-2.0018$, $p=0.06507$) and right-hand ($t(16)=-1.0849$, $p=0.294$) movement. There was also the same tendency (left-hand movement: $t(14)=-1.0832$, $p=0.297$; right-hand one: $t(16)=-0.1059$, $p=0.917$) in the NS' BNM. In the MP-BNM, however, there were significant differences between the two nodes both for the right-hand movement ($t(16)=-3.9817$, $p=0.001072$) and for the left-hand one ($t(14)=-2.2532$, $p=0.04081$). These findings suggest that there may be differences in neural network connectivity between the MP BNM and the others. On the other hand, also in the present DBNM, there were significant differences between the two nodes both for the left-hand movement ($t(46)=-2.9645$, $p=0.004791$) and for the right-hand one ($t(52)=-2.6109$, $p=0.01177$). The difference between the DBNM and the BNM obtained in the section 2 might not reflect only that in the neural connectivity but also that in the tasks, that is, the MI and the actual movement.

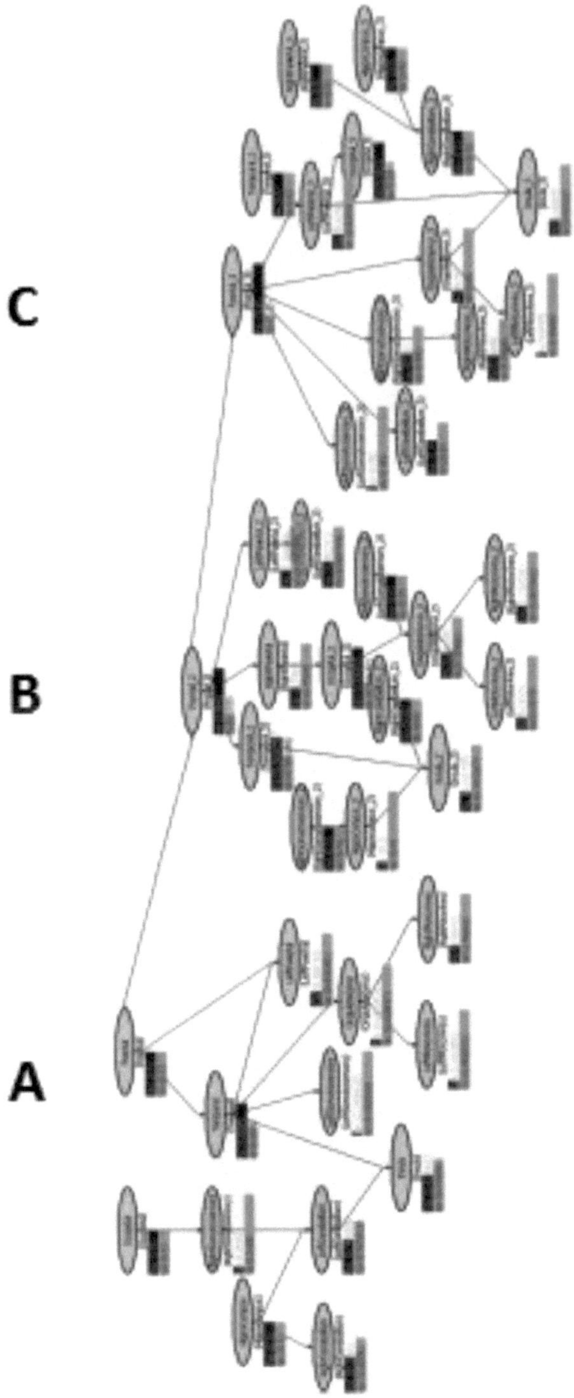

Figure 10. DBNM including (A) E-BP, (B) NS' and (C) MP.

http://dx.doi.org/10.5772/55805

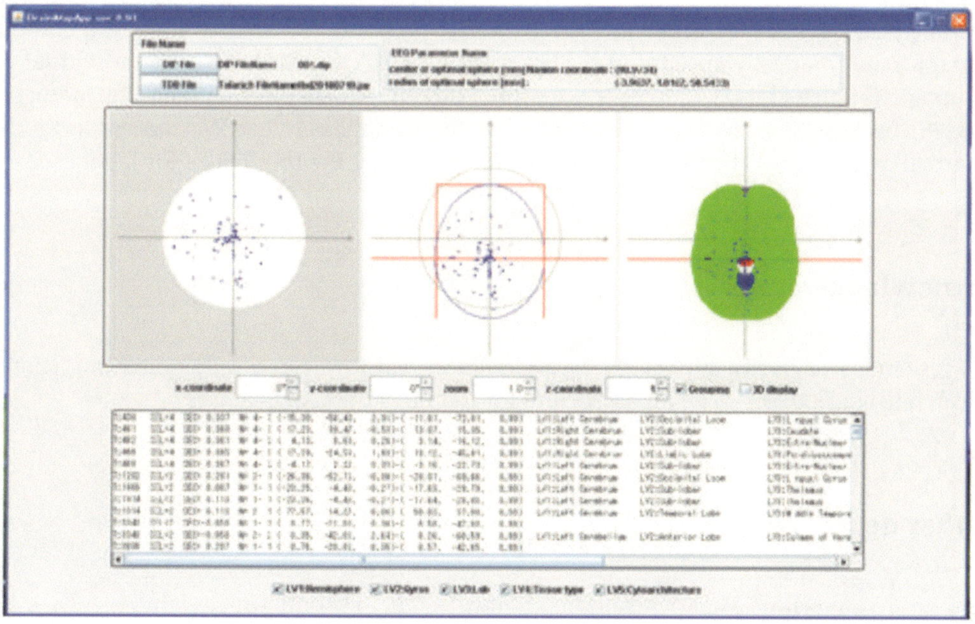

Figure 11. An example of a system for automatically specifying the brain sites where estimated ECDs are located.

4. Consideration and conclusion

In this chapter, we have proposed a new framework for single-trial-EEG-based BCIs with the MI tasks. This framework consists of the categorization of the EEGs, which could lead us to data reduction, and the classifiers for the categorical data. The ECDL after ICA enabled us the former. For the latter, the classifier using Hayashi's second method of quantification has yielded the accuracy of more than 90 % [11]. This chapter has concentrated on another classifier for the categorical data, called Bayesian networks. The present BCI learning required 25 trials at least. Although for the results on only two subjects, the accuracy in 20-trial validation was higher than that by the CSP, in addition to exceeding the existing ECDL-based BCIs [43,46]. If any subject met the classification rule, the subject would be expected to achieve the good accuracy.

To our knowledge, Shenoy and Rao [16] made the first report of the application of DBNM to BCIs. Although the DBN allowed continuous tracking and prediction of the brain states over time, it included hidden but ambiguous state variables. Our DBNM has revealed the difference among the E-BP, NS' and MP in MRPs and that between the MI and the actual movement tasks. However, the DBNMs for BCIs are still in the data-processing stage, not in the validation one.

When obtaining ECDL results on 20 ICs for each of 50 (=25x2) trials by one subject, inspection with reference to the textbook of neuroanatomy must be iterated 1000 (=20x50) times, at least.

Even if the inspector has the full knowledge of neuroanatomy, different inspectors might yield different ECDL results. In order to cope with this problem, we are developing a computer system for automatically specifying the brain sites for ECDL results on each individual with MR images (Figure 11) [47]. However, we cannot directly utilize the Talairach-Tournoux brain atlas [48], because there are big differences in the brain shape between Westerners and Asians, in particular Japanese. Therefore, we are now constructing the brain atlas for Japanese.

Acknowledgements

This research was partly supported by a Grants-in-Aid for Scientific Research on Scientific Research (B) (20300196) - The Japan Society for the Promotion of Science.

Author details

Toshimasa Yamazaki[1*], Maiko Sakamoto[2], Shino Takata[3], Hiromi Yamaguchi[1], Kazufumi Tanaka[1], Takahiro Shibata[4], Hiroshi Takayanagi[5], Ken-ichi Kamijo[6] and Takahiro Yamanoi[7]

*Address all correspondence to: t-ymzk@bio.kyutech.ac.jp

1 Department of Bioscience and Bioinformatics, Kyushu Institute of Technology, Iizuka, Fukuoka, Japan

2 Hitachi Public System Service Co. Ltd., Tokyo, Japan

3 Lincrea Corporation, Tokyo, Japan

4 Olympus Software Technology Corporation, Tokyo, Japan

5 Information Science Research Center, Tokyo, Japan

6 NEC Corporation, Tokyo, Japan

7 Hokkai Gakuen University, Sapporo, Japan

References

[1] Wolpaw J, Birbaumer N, McFarland D, Pfurtscheller G, Vaughan T. Brain-computer interfaces for communication and control. Clinical Neurophysiology 2002; 113 767-791.

[2] Pfurtscheller G, Lopes da Silva FH. Functional meaning of event-related desynchronization (ERD) and synchronization (ERS). In: Pfurtscheller G., Lopes da Silva FH. (eds) Event-Related Desynchronization. Handbook of Electroencephalography and Clinical Neurophysiology, Revised Series, Vol.6. Elsevier Science B.V.; 1999. p51-65.

[3] Zhou J, Yao J, Deng J, Dewald JPA. EEG-based classification for elbow versus shoulder torque intentions involving stroke subjects. Computer in Biology and Medicine 2009;39 443-452.

[4] Wang D, Miao D, Blohm G. Multi-class motor imagery EEG decoding for brain-computer interfaces. Frontier in Neuroscience 2012;6 1-13.

[5] Hsu W-Y. EEG-based motor imagery classification using neuro-fuzzy prediction and wavelet fractal features. Journal of Neuroscience Methods 2010;189 295-302.

[6] Krusienski DJ, Sellers EW, McFarland DJ, Vaughan TM,Wolpaw JR. Toward enhanced P300 speller performance. Journal of Neuroscience Methods 2008;167 15-21.

[7] Sakamoto Y, Aono M. Supervised adaptive downsampling for P300-based brain computer interface. In: Proceedings of the 31st Annual International Conference of the IEEE EMBS, 2009; 567-570.

[8] Kamrunnahar M, Dias NS, Schiff SJ. Optimization of electrode channels in brain computer interfaces. Conference Proceedings of the IEEE Engineering in Medicine and Biology Society, 2009; 6477-6480.

[9] Sannelli C, Dickhaus T, Halder S, Hammer E-M, Müller K-R, Blankertz B. On optimal channel configurations for SMR-based brain-computer interfaces. Brain Topography 2010; 23 186-193.

[10] Arvaneh M, Guan CT, Ang KK, Quek C. Optimizing the channel selection and classification accuracy in EEG-based BCI source. IEEE Transactions on Biomedical Engineering 2011;58 1865-1873.

[11] Shibata T. Accuracy of single-trial-EEG-based BCIs using Hayashi's second method of quantification. MS-thesis, Kyushu Institute of Technology, Fukuoka, Japan; 2012, in Japanese.

[12] Shibasaki H, Hallett M. What is the Bereitschaftspotential? Clinical Neurophysiology 2006; 117 2341-2356.

[13] Sporns O. Networks of the Brain. Cambridge, Massachusetts, London, England: MIT Press; 2011.

[14] Sykacek P, Roberts SJ, Stokes M. Adaptive BCI based on variational Bayesian Kalman filtering: an empirical evaluation. IEEE Transactions on Biomedical Engineering 2004; 51 719-727.

[15] Yoon JW, Roberts SJ, Dyson M, Gan JQ. Adaptive classification for Brain Computer Interface systems using sequential montecarlo sampling. Neural Networks 2009; 22 1286-1294.

[16] Shenoy P, Rao RPN. Dynamic Bayesian networks for brain-computer interfaces. Advances in NIPS17; 2005.

[17] Micheloyannis S, Pachou E, Stam CJ, Vourkas M, Erimaki S, Tsirka V. Using graph theoretical analysis of multi channel EEG to evaluate the neural efficiency hypothesis. Neuroscience Letters 2006;402 273-277.

[18] Honey CJ, Kötter R, Breakspear M, Sporns O. Network structure of cerebral cortex shapes functional connectivity on multiple time scales. PNAS 2007;104 10240-10245.

[19] Hagmann P, Kurant M, Gigandet X, Thiran P, Wedeen VJ, Meuli R, Thiran J-P. Mapping human whole-brain structural networks with diffusion MRI. PLoS ONE 2007;issue 7:e597.

[20] Gong G, He Y, Concha L, Lebel C, Gross DW, Evans AC, Beaulieu C. Mapping anatomical connectivity patterns of human cerebral cortex using in vivo diffusion tensor imaging tractography. Cerebral Cortex 2009;19 524-536.

[21] Shigemasu K. Ueno M, Motomura Y. Introduction to Bayesian Networks. Tokyo: BAIFUKAN CO., LTD; 2006, in Japanese.

[22] Blankertz B, Tomioka R, Lemm S, Kawanabe M, Müller K-R. Optimizing spatial filters for robust EEG single-trial analysis. IEEE Signal Processing Magazine 2008; 25 41-56.

[23] Oldfield RC. The assessment and analysis of handedness: the Edinburgh Inventory. Neuropsychologia 1971; 9 97-113.

[24] Soufflet L, Toussaint M, Luthringer R, Gressor J, Minot R, Macher JP. A statistical evaluation of the main interpolation methods applied to 3-dimensional EEG mapping. Electroencephalography and Clinical Neurophysiology 1991; 79 393-402.

[25] Hyvärinen A, Oja E. A fast fixed-point algorithm for independent component analysis. Neural Computation 1997;91483-1492.

[26] Cichocki A, Amari S, Siwek K, Tanaka T, Phan AH, Zdunek R,Cruces S, Georgiev P, Washizawa Y, Leonowicz Z, Bakardijan H, Rutkowski T, Choi S, Belouchrani A, Barros A, Thawonmas R, Hoya T, Hashimoto W, Terazono Y. ICALAB version 3 toolbox, RIKEN BSI.http://www.bsp.brain.riken.jp/ICALAB/ (accessed 2007).

[27] Makeig S, Bell AJ, Jung TP, Sejnowski TJ. Independent component analysis of electroencephalographic data. In: Touretzky D, Mozer M, Hasselmo M. (eds) Advances in Neural Information Processing Systems; 1996. p145-151.

[28] Delorme A, Palmer J, Onton J, Oostenveld R, Makeig S. Independent EEG sources are dipolar. PLoS ONE 2012;7 e30135.

[29] Mosher JC, Lewis PS, Leahy RM. Multiple dipole modeling and localization from spatio-temporal MEG data. IEEE Transactions on Biomedical Engineering 1992; 39 541-557.

[30] Kamijo K, Kiyuna T, Takaki Y, Kenmochi A, Tanigawa T, Yamazaki T. Integrated approach of an artificial neural network and numerical analysis to multiple equivalent current dipole source localization. Frontiers of Medical and Biological Engineering 2001; 10 285-301.

[31] Yamazaki T, Kamijo K, Kenmochi A, Fukuzumi S, Kiyuna T, Takaki Y,Kuroiwa Y. Multiple equivalent current dipole source localization of visual event-related potentials during oddball paradigm with motor response. Brain Topography 2000; 12 159-175.

[32] Kretschmann H-J, Weinrich W. KlinischeNeuroanatomie und kranielleBilddiagnostik, 3rd ed., Stuttgart: Georg ThiemeVerlag; 2003 (translated into Japanese).

[33] Cheng J, Greiner R, Kelly J, Bell D, Liu W. Learning Bayesian networks from data: an information-theory based approach. Artificial Intelligence 2002; 137 43-90.

[34] Tung L. A clique tree algorithm exploiting context specific independence. MS-thesis. University of British Columbia; 2002.

[35] Kadie CM, Hovel D, E.Horvitz E. MSBNx: A Component-Centric Toolkit forModeling and Inference with Bayesian Networks. Technical ReportMSR-TR-2001-67; 2001.

[36] Hallett M, Fieldman J, Cohen LG, Sadato N, Pascual-Leone A. Involvement of primary motor cortex in motor imagery and mental practice. Behavioraland Brain Sciences 1994;17 210.

[37] Porro CA, Francescato MP, Cettolo V, Diamond ME, Baraldi P, Zuiani C, Bazzocchi M, di Prampero PE. Primary motor and sensory cortex activation during motor performance and motor imagery: A functional magnetic resonance imaging study. Journal of Neuroscience 1996;16 7688-7698.

[38] Deiber MP, Ibanez V, Honda M, Sadato N, Raman R, Hallett M. Cerebral processes related to visuomotor imagery and generation of simple finger movements studied with positron emission tomography. Neuroimage 1998; 7 73-85.

[39] Gerardin E, Sirigu A, Lehéricy S, Poline J-B, Gaymard B, Marsault C, Agid Y, Le Bihan D. Partially overlapping neural networks for real and imagined hand movements. Cerebral Cortex 2000;10 1093-1104.

[40] Hanakawa T, Immisch I, Toma K, Dimyan MA, Van Gelderen, Hallett M. Functional properties of brain areas associated with motor execution and imagery. Journal of Neurophysiology 2003;89 989-1002.

[41] Ehrsson HH, Geyer S, Naito E. Imagery of voluntary movement of fingers, toes, and tongue activates corresponding body-part-specific motor representations. Journal of Neurophysiology 2003;90 3304-3316.

[42] Pfurtscheller G, NeuperCh, Flotzinger D, Pregenzer M. EEG-based discrimination between imagination of right and left hand movement. Electroencephalography and Clinical Neurophysiology 1997;103 642-651.

[43] Qin L, Ding L, He B. Motor imagery classification by means of source analysis for brain–computer interface applications. Journal of Neural Engineering 2004;1 135-141.

[44] Bai O, Maria Z, Vorbacha S, Hallett M. Asymmetric spatiotemporal patterns of event-related desynchronization preceding voluntary sequential finger movements: a high-resolution EEG study. Clinical Neurophysiology 2005;116 1213-1221.

[45] Clark GA, McCormick DA, Lavond DG, Thompson RF. Effects of lesions of cerebellar nuclei on conditional behavioral and hippocampal neuronal responses. Brain Research 1984;291 125-136.

[46] Kamousi B, Liu Z, He B. Classification of motor imagery tasks for Brain-Computer Interface applications by means of two equivalent dipoles analysis. IEEE Transactions on Neural Systems and Rehabilitation Engineering 2005;13(2) 166-171.

[47] Tanaka K, Motoi M, Sasaguri Y, Yamazaki T, Takayanagi H, Yamanoi T, Kamijo K. A new single-trial-EEG-based BCI –Validation of quantification method of type II modelling. Clinical Neurophysiology 2010;121 S161 (Abstracts of ICCN 2010), 29th International Congress of Clinical Neurophysiology, Oct 28 – Nov 1, 2010, Kobe, Japan.

[48] Talairach J, Tournoux P. Co-Planar Sterotaxic Atlas of the Human Brain. New York: Thieme; 1988.

Chapter 9

Sources of Electrical Brain Activity Most Relevant to Performance of Brain-Computer Interface Based on Motor Imagery

Alexander Frolov, Dušan Húsek, Pavel Bobrov,
Olesya Mokienko and Jaroslav Tintera

Additional information is available at the end of the chapter

http://dx.doi.org/10.5772/55166

1. Introduction

A brain-computer interface (BCI) provides a direct functional interaction between the human brain and the external device. Many kinds of signals (from electromagnetic to metabolic [23, 38, 42]) could be used in BCI. However the most widespread BCI systems are based on EEG recordings. BCI consists of a brain signal acquisition system, data processing software for feature extraction and pattern classification, and a system to transfer commands to an external device and, thus, providing feedback to an operator. The most prevalent BCI systems are based on the discrimination of EEG patterns related to execution of different mental tasks [14, 21, 24]. This approach is justified by the presence of correlation between brain signal features and tasks performed, revealed by basic research [24, 28, 30, 45]. By agreement with the BCI operator each mental task is associated with one of the commands to the external device. Then to produce the commands, the operator switches voluntary between corresponding mental tasks. If BCI is dedicated to control device movements then psychologically convenient mental tasks are motor imaginations. For example, when a patient controls by BCI the movement of a wheelchair its movement to the left can be associated with the imagination of the left arm movement and movement to the right - with right arm movement. Another advantage of these mental tasks is that their performance is accompanied by the easily recognizable EEG patterns. Moreover, motor imagination is considered now as an efficient rehabilitation procedure to restore movement after paralysis [4]. Thus, namely the analysis of BCI performance based on motor imagination is the object of the present chapter.

The most stable electrophysiological phenomenon accompanying motor performance is the decrease of EEG mu-rhythm recording from the central electrodes located over the brain areas representing the involved extremity [29]. This decrease (Event Related Desynchronization, ERD) occurs also when the subject observes the movement of another person [34] and during motor preparation and imagination [30]. In the state of motor relaxation the increase of EEG mu-rhythm is observed [29] which is called Event Related Synchronization (ERS). The exposure of ERD and ERS in specific brain areas during motor imagination of different extremities is the reason of the high efficiency of BCI based on motor imagination [32]. From the other hand, BCI training allows to stabilize and to contrast brain activity corresponding to different mental tasks and hence to facilitate the search of brain areas involved in their performance.

Until now the most widespread technique to localize brain functions is fMRI study which provides high spatial but low temporal resolution. By contrast EEG study provides high temporal but low spatial resolution. The most prospective seems to be the combination of these techniques [9] especially if to take into account the fast progress in methods of solving inverse EEG problem [13, 19] dedicated to localize sources of brain activity by distribution of electric potential over head surface. One of the approaches towards the integration of these techniques was suggested in our previous work [11]. Here we develop the approach and apply it to the analysis of more mental states used for BCI control.

2. Methods

2.1. Experimental procedure

Eight subjects (4 male, 4 female) aged from 25 to 65 participated in the study. All subjects were right-handed and had no neurological diseases. The subjects have provided written participation consent. The experimental procedure was approved by the Board of Ethics at the Institute for Higher Nervous Activity and Neurophysiology of the Russian Academy of Sciences.

The experiment with each subject was conducted for 10 experimental days, the one series per day. Each series consisted of training and testing sessions (Fig. 1 A). The first, training, session was designed to train BCI classifier. The following, testing session was designed to provide subjects with the output of the BCI classifier in real time to enhance their efforts to imagine a movement. The subjects had to perform one of the four instructions presented on a screen of a monitor: to relax and to imagine the movement of the right or left hand or feet. The movement which they were asked to imagine was a handgrip or feet pressure.

Subject was sitting in a comfortable chair, one meter from a 17″ monitor, and was instructed to fix a gaze on a motionless circle (1 cm in diameter) in the middle of the screen. Four gray markers were placed around the circle to indicate the mental task to be performed. The change of the marker color into green signaled the subject to perform the corresponding mental task. Left and right markers corresponded to left and right hand movement imagining respectively. The lower marker corresponded to feet movement imagining and the upper one corresponded to relaxation. Each command was displayed for 10 seconds. Each clue was preceded by a 4-second warning when the marker color changed into blue.

http://dx.doi.org/10.5772/55166

Four such instructions presented in random order constituted a block, one block constituted a training session and nine blocks a testing session (Fig. 1). Thus each subject received 10 blocks of instructions at each experimental day.

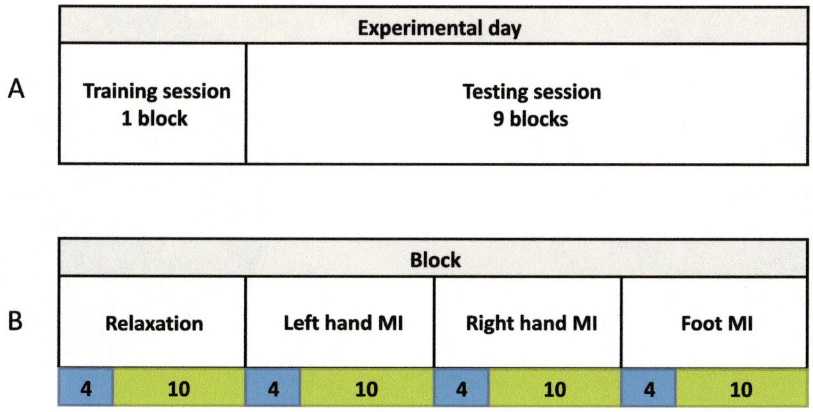

Figure 1. Schematic representation of the experimental protocol and the stages of each experimental session. A. The sequence of sessions. B. The structure of the experimental block. In each block each instruction was presented once. The sequence of their presentation in each block was random. The duration of instructions is given in seconds. Green areas - instructions for performance, blue areas - warnings

During the training session classifier was switched off and recording was used only for its learning. During the following testing sessions classifier was switched on and the result of classification was presented to a subject by color of the central circle. The circle became green if the result coincided with the instruction and its brightness increased with the increase of classifying confidence. During the instruction to relax the presentation of classifying result was switched off not to attract the subject‘s attention.

EEG was recorded by 48 active electrodes using g.USBamp and g.USBamp API for MATLAB (g-tec, Graz, Austria) with sampling frequency 256 Hz and filtered by notch filter to suppress supply noise. Electrode positions were Fz, F3, F4, Fcz, Fc3, Fc4, F7, F8, Fcz, Fc3, Fc4, Fc5, Fc6, Fc7, Fc8, Cz, C1, C2, C3, C4, C5, C6, T7, T8, Cpz, Cp1, Cp2, Cp3, Cp4, Cp5, Cp6, Tp7, Tp8, Pz, P1, P2, P3, P4, P5, P6, P7, P8, Poz, Po3, Po4, Po7, Po8, Oz, O1, O2. Afz was a reference.

The data of the last BCI session were used for solving inverse EEG problem, that is to localize the sources of EEG signals inside the brain. We solved it taking into account individual geometry of brain and its covers. To identify the source positions relative to the brain structures, electrodes positions have to be also identified relative to these structure. Since brain structures are given in MRI coordinate system electrode positions have to be also identified in MRI coordinate system. To that end not moving the cap on the subject head we removed electrodes from nodes at the cap and replaced them by small pellets visible on MRI slices (Fig. 2). Just after this procedure the subject was placed in MRI chamber. Since the position of each electrode was marked by the pellet, then identification of the pellet positions on slices allowed to obtain the electrodes coordinates in MRI reference frame.

During fMRI recording instructions to relax or to imagine hand or feet movements were presented to the subject without EEG recording. Since the efficiency of BCI control depends

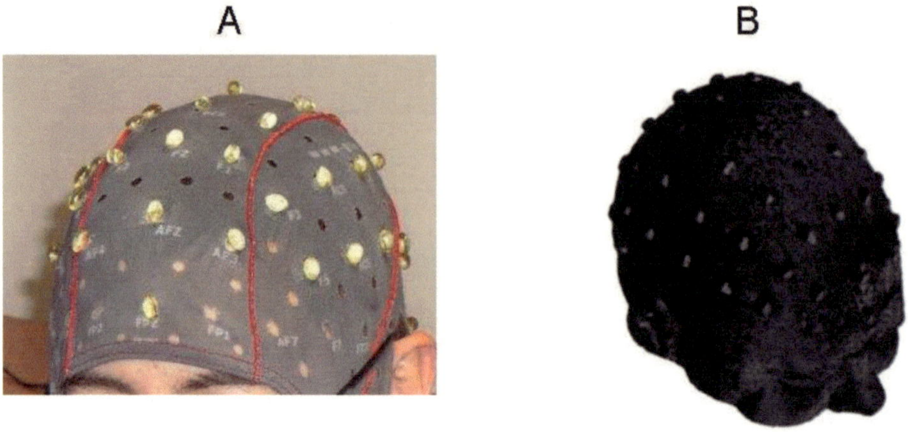

Figure 2. Pellets marking electrode positions on the head surface (A) and their images reconstructed by MRI slices (B).

on the subject's ability to stabilize and to contrast patterns of the brain activity following different instructions, then we believe that the subjects who demonstrate an efficient BCI control are able to produce stable and contrast patterns of the brain activity during both EEG and fMRI experiments. The fMRI examinations were conducted with 3T MR scanner (Siemens Trio Tim, Erlangen, Germany) using 12-channel head coil. Functional MRI data were acquired with a T2*weighted gradient echo EPI sequence (40 slices, TR=2500 ms, TE=30 ms, 64 $\times$ 64 matrix, FOV=192 $\times$ 192 mm, slice thickness 3 mm, voxel size= 3$\times$3$\times$3 mm, BW=2232 Hz/pixel, axial orientation). Total of 240 dynamic measurements were acquired during fMRI scans resulting to 10 minutes of acquisition time. A T1-weighted anatomical scan using MP-RAGE sequence (224 slices, TR=2300 ms, TE=4.64 ms, FOV=256$\times$256, slice thickness 1 mm, voxel size of 1$\times$1$\times$1 mm, PAT=2, sagittal orientation) was also acquired for each subject. The measurement lasted of 5 min.

2.2. Classifier

One crucial part of a BCI system is the EEG pattern classifier which can be designed by many methods [1]. We used in our experiments the simplest Bayesian classifier based on EEG covariance matrices. As shown in [10] it provides classification accuracy comparable with other more sophisticated classifiers.

Suppose that there are L different mental tasks to be distinguished and probabilities of each task to be performed are equal to $1/L$. Let also for each mental task the EEG signal distribution be Gaussian with zero mean. Also, let $\mathbf{C}_i$, a covariance matrix of the signal corresponding to execution of the i-th mental task ($i = 1, \ldots, L$), be non-singular. Then probability to obtain EEG signal $\mathbf{X}$ under the condition that the signal corresponds to performing the i-th mental task is $P(\mathbf{X} \mid i) \propto e^{-\frac{V_i}{2}}$, where $V_i = \mathbf{X}^{\mathrm{T}}\mathbf{C}_i^{-1}\mathbf{X} + \ln(\det(\mathbf{C}_i))$. Following the Bayesian approach, the maximum value of $P(\mathbf{X} \mid i)$ over all i determines the class to which $\mathbf{X}$ belongs. Hence, the signal $\mathbf{X}$ is considered to correspond to execution of the k-th mental task as soon as $k = \text{argmin}_i \{V_i\}$. The equality $\mathbf{X}^{\mathrm{T}}\mathbf{C}_i^{-1}\mathbf{X} = \text{trace}\left(\mathbf{C}_i^{-1}\mathbf{X}\mathbf{X}^{\mathrm{T}}\right)$ implies that

$$V_i = \text{trace}\left(\mathbf{C}_i^{-1}\mathbf{X}\mathbf{X}^{\mathrm{T}}\right) + \ln\left(\det(\mathbf{C}_i)\right) \tag{1}$$

In practice all V_i are rather variable, so it is more beneficial to split signal into epochs and compute average value $\langle V_i \rangle$ for each EEG epoch to be classified, using equation (1)

$$\langle V_i \rangle = \text{trace}\left(\mathbf{C}\mathbf{C}_i^{-1}\right) + \ln\left(\det(\mathbf{C}_i)\right) \tag{2}$$

where $\mathbf{C}$ denotes an epoch data covariance matrix estimated as $\left\langle \mathbf{X}\mathbf{X}^{\mathrm{T}} \right\rangle$. Therefore to perform the classifier training it is sufficient to compute the covariance matrices corresponding to each mental task. It makes BC computationally inexpensive.

During testing sessions covariance matrix $\mathbf{C}$ was calculated every 250 msec over 1 second sliding window. Respectively, the variable s defining the accuracy of brain state recognition was updated each 250 msec. It took 1 if the state recognized corresponded to the instruction and 0 in the opposite case. Then the variable S was updated according to the formula $S = (1 - \gamma_s)S + \gamma_s s$. At the beginning of new instruction presentation S was set to be zero. The brightness of the central circle which indicated the quality of BCI performance was proportional to S. The value of γ_s was taken to be 0.1. So the characteristic time of the biofeedback was about 2.5 sec.

The covariance matrices $\mathbf{C}_i$ were calculated during the training session and then updated during the testing session at the end of each block according to the formula $\mathbf{C}_i = (1 - \gamma_c)\mathbf{C}_i + \gamma_c \mathbf{c}_i$ where $\mathbf{c}_i$ is a covariance matrix for the i-th state calculated over block data. In our experiments we used $\gamma_c = 0.1$.

The quality of BCI performance was estimated by the results of on-line classifying during the testing session of each experimental day and offline by the data obtained during both training and testing sessions. For offline analysis the data were additionally filtered within 5-30 Hz bandpass. Then 7 blocks of 10 were randomly chosen for classifier learning, i.e. for calculation of covariance matrices for all mental states. Recordings of the remaining 3 blocks were split into epochs of 1 second length. These epochs were used for classifier testing. 50 such classification trials were made. Averaging over all classification trials resulted in $L \times L$ confusion matrix $\mathbf{P} = \left(p_{ij}\right)$. Here p_{ij} is an estimate of probability to recognize the i-th mental task in case the instruction is to perform the j-th mental task.

We chose the mean probability of correct classification p, mutual information g between states recognized and instructions presented, and Cohen's κ as indices of classification efficacy.

Given the confusion matrix **P** these indices can be calculated as follows:

$$p = \frac{1}{L}\sum_{i=1}^{L} p_{ii},$$
$$g = -\sum_{i,j=1,1}^{L,L} p_{ij} p_{0j} \log_2 \left(p_{ij}/p_{i0}\right), \quad (3)$$
$$\kappa = \frac{\sum_{i=1}^{L} p_{ii} p_{0i} - \sum_{i=1}^{L} p_{0i} p_{i0}}{1 - \sum_{i=1}^{L} p_{0i} p_{i0}}$$

where $p_{0j} = 1/L$ is probability of the j-th instruction to be presented and $p_{i0} = \sum_{j=1}^{L} p_{ij} p_{0j}$ is probability of the i-th mental state to be recognized.

The better classifier performs the more confusion matrix is close to identity matrix. In case L states are classified perfectly $p = 1$, $g = \log_2 L$, and $\kappa = 1$. If classification is random, i.e. $p_{ij} = p_{i0}$ for all j, then $p = 1/L$, $g = 0$, and $\kappa = 0$.

Index p has an advantage of being evidently interpreted as the percentage of correct classification while its disadvantages are, first, that it does not account for distribution of errors since it does not depend on nondiagonal elements of confusion matrix, second, its lower value depends on the number of states classified. For example the value $p = 0.5$ corresponds to a random recognition when $L = 2$ and twice exceeds the random level when $L = 4$. Thus it is difficult to compare the qualities of BCIs with different states classified. Both indices g and κ have the advantage of considering the error distribution over nondiagonal elements of confusion matrix and of being normalized to the case of random classifying independently of L. In this case both indices are equal to zero. Moreover, κ is also normalized to the case of perfect classifying. It takes one in this case, while g depends on L. Thus, on one hand κ is more convenient for comparing qualities of BCI with different L, but on another hand g gives the estimate of BCI quality directly in the rate of information transfer. Since g is calculated every second then it can be measured in bits per second. Thus all three indices are reasonable.

When all probabilities of correct classification are equal, i.e. $p_{ii} = p$ for all i, and all probabilities of incorrect classification are equal, i.e. $p_{ij} = (1-p)/(L-1)$ for all $i \neq j$, the mutual information between instructions presented and the states classified can be obtained as:

$$g = \log_2 L + p \log_2 p + (1-p) \log_2 \left(\frac{1-p}{L-1}\right) \quad (4)$$

Based on [43], (4) is often used to estimate BCI efficacy ([3], [5] [44]). But if the corresponding assumptions do not hold true, the value of g, calculated according to (4), is lower than the actual mutual information. In this study we used the general formula (3).

To estimate the on-line BCI quality we used confusion matrix obtained over the data of testing session based on EEG signal classification every 250 msec as described above.

2.3. ICA

To identify the sources of brain activity the most relevant to BCI performance we used Independent Component Analysis (ICA). Last years ICA becomes widely used in EEG processing, particularly in BCI studies [16]. ICA provides representation of a multidimensional EEG signal $\mathbf{X}(t)$ (where components of $\mathbf{X}(t)$ represent electric potentials recording from N individual electrodes at the head surface) as a superposition of activities of independent components ξ:

$$\mathbf{X}(t) = \mathbf{W}\xi(t) = \mathbf{W}_1\xi_1 + \mathbf{W}_2\xi_2 + \cdots + \mathbf{W}_N\xi_N \quad (5)$$

Columns $\mathbf{W}_i$ of matrix $\mathbf{W}$ specify the contribution of the corresponding independent component (or source) into each of the electrodes and the components ξ_i of the vector $\xi(t)$ specify sources intensity in each time point. The combination of active sources is supposed to be specific and individual for each mental task. Thus their activities in many tasks can be treated as independent.

There exist a lot of methods to represent the signal $\mathbf{X}$ in the form (5). We used algorithm RUNICA (MATLAB toolbox EEGLab,[7]). RUNICA provides the identification of the independent components maximizing distinction of their distributions from normal one in terms of kurtosis [15]. The using of this method is reasonable because it corresponds to the suggestion that activities of sources are different in different mental states: in some states they expose ERD, in others - ERS. Thus in one state the distribution of EEG amplitude should be narrow, in others - wide. So the common distribution would be maximally different from the normal one.

To reveal the sources of brain activity the most significant for BCI performance the quality index κ was calculated in dependence on the number N_{cmp} of ICA components used for mental state classifying. For each N_{cmp} we found the optimal combination of components providing the highest κ. Since the total number 2^N (where $N = 48$) of possible component combinations is extremely large we used exhaustive search to find the optimal combination of components only for $N_{cmp} = 3$. To find the optimal combination of components for $N_{cmp} > 3$ we used a "greedy" algorithm which added components one by one starting from the optimal combination of 3 components. At each step a component was added to the optimal component combination found at the previous step, so that extended combination provided the highest κ.

When all ICA components are used for mental states classifying, i.e. $N_{cmp} = N$, then $\xi = \mathbf{W}^{-1}\mathbf{X}$ where $\mathbf{W}^{-1}$ is non-singular. In this case $\mathbf{C}_i^{\xi} = \mathbf{W}^{-1}\mathbf{C}_i(\mathbf{W}^{-1})^T$ and

$$\begin{aligned} V_i^{\xi} &= \text{trace}((\mathbf{C}_i^{\xi})^{-1}\xi\xi^T) + \ln(\det(\mathbf{C}_i^{\xi})) = \text{trace}((\mathbf{C}_i)^{-1}\mathbf{X}\mathbf{X}^T) \\ &+ \ln(\det(\mathbf{C}_i)) - 2\ln(\det(\mathbf{W})) = V_i - 2\ln(\det(\mathbf{W})) \end{aligned}$$

Since $\ln(\det(\mathbf{W}))$ does not depend of the mental state, then V_i^{ξ} and V_i reach minima for the same mental state and the mental state classified by Bayesian classifier in terms of ξ coincides with that classified in terms of $\mathbf{X}$. Thus, the case $N_{cmp} = N$ directly corresponds to BCI performance based on classifying the original signal X.

2.4. Sources localization

With respect to the EEG analysis, it is reasonable to assume that independent sources of electrical brain activity recorded at the head surface are current dipoles distributed over the neocortex. As shown below our experiments confirm this assumption and at least for the sources the most relevant for BCI performance the distribution of electrical potential over the head produced by each of these sources could be actually interpreted in terms of electrical field produced by single current dipole. Thus, for each of such sources its localization was searched in a single dipole approximation. In other words, position and orientation of a single current dipole were searched which provided maximal matching between patterns of EEG distribution on the head surface given by ICA and by a dipole. The pattern of EEG distribution for dipole with given position and orientation was calculated by solving the direct EEG problem.

It was solved by the finite element method (FEM) which allows to take into account individual geometry of the brain and its covers. In FEM, one critical requirement for the mesh generation is to represent the geometric and electrical properties of the head volume conductors. To generate the FEM meshes from the MRI data, MR images were segmented into five sub-regions: white matter, gray matter, cerebrospinal fluid (CSF), skull and scalp. The segmentation of the different tissues within the head was made by means of SPM8 New Segmentation Tool. To construct the FE models of the whole head the FEM mesh generation was performed using tetrahedral elements with inner-node spacing of 2 mm. Thus, the total number of nodes amounted to about 1.5 millions. Electrical conductivities were assigned to the tissues segmented in accordance with each tissue type: 0.14 S/m for white matter, 0.33 S/m for gray matter, 1.79 S/m for CSF, 0.0132 S/m for skull, and 0.35 S/m for scalp [17, 46]. To solve the EEG forward problems, the FEM mesh along with electrical conductivities were imported into the commercial software ANSYS (ANSYS, Inc., PA, USA).

3. Results

3.1. The ICA components most relevant for BCI control

For all subjects three indices averaged over all experimental days are shown in Fig. 3. The subjects are ranged according to mean κ computed for on-line classification. Note that subjects ranking according to p completely preserves their order and according to g changes it only slightly (S5 must be shifted before S3). Thus all indices give good relative estimation of subject ability to control BCI. Mean on-line and offline estimates of BCI performance by all indices are shown to be very close. However on-line estimations are more variable. This is reasonable because on-line estimation is based on one classification trial obtained directly during experiment performance, while offline estimation is based on 50 classification trials as described above. Therefore, confusion matrix computed offline is more confident than that computed on-line.

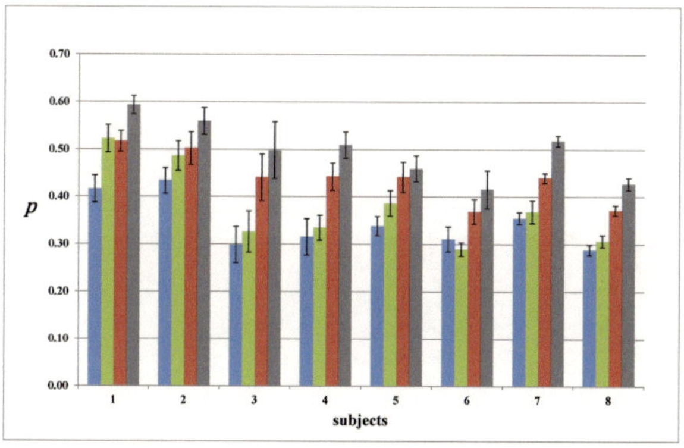

(a)

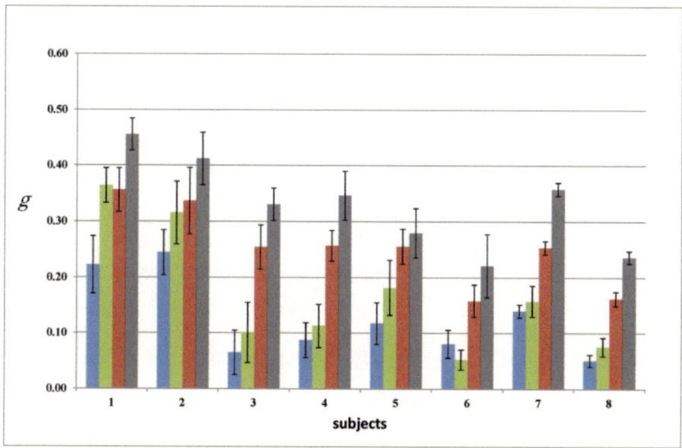

(b)

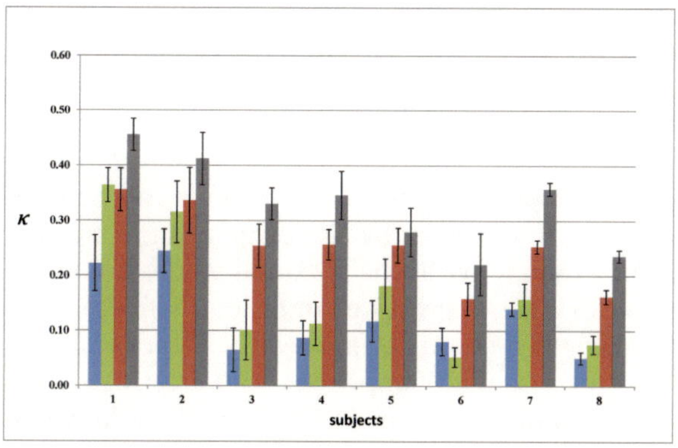

(c)

Figure 3. Indices p, g and κ of BCI control accuracy for all subjects averaged over all experimental days (means and standard errors). Blue bars - on-line, green bars - offline, red - three the most relevant components, grey - optimal components. The subjects are ranged according to κ computed on-line. The most relevant components and optimal components were calculated to maximize κ. Then these components were used to compute p and g.

Fig. 4 demonstrates the dependency of κ on the number N_{cmp} of ICA components for all subjects on the last experimental day. For each N_{cmp} index κ is shown for individual optimal component combination.

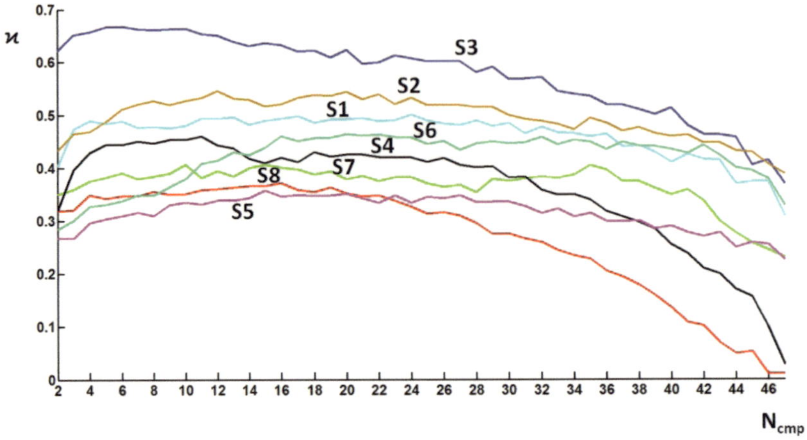

Figure 4. Index κ of BCI control accuracy in dependence on the number N_{cmp} of ICA components used for mental states classifying. The optimal combination of three components ($N_{cmp} = 3$) was obtained by the exhausted search. The other optimal combinations were obtained by the "greedy" algorithm. Each curve represents the data for each individual subject obtained for the last day of BCI training.

As shown in Fig. 4 κ depends on N_{cmp} not monotonically and reaches maximum when some ICA components are discarded. However the classifying accuracy for $N_{cmp} = 3$ is very close to that obtained for optimal combination of components providing maximal κ. Thus the obtained combinations of 3 components can be considered as good representations of the components which are the most relevant for BCI performance. Indices p, g and κ for three the most relevant components and for optimal components averaged over all experimental days are shown in Fig. 3 for all subjects. As shown, elimination of not relevant (noisy) components improves BCI performance several times. Basing on the most relevant and optimal components BCI classifier provides the accuracy of mental state recognition significantly exceeding the random level for all subjects and all indices (t-test, $P < 0.001$). For Subject 1 index g computed for optimal components reached 0.83 that is twice more than g computed on-line for this subject by the original EEG signal. This maximal value can be also compared, for example, with the maximal value of $g = 0.58$ obtained for Berlin BCI [5] in experiments with a large group of untrained subjects. Thus, filtering of noisy ICA components is an efficient method to improve BCI performance. Note that although filtering of noisy components essentially improves BCI performance for all subjects it almost preserves the order of their ability to control BCI. Thus the relative subjects skill is mainly determined by their inherent properties but not by the properties of BCI classifier. Note also that the quality of BCI performance is rather variable over experimental days for each subject. Due to this variability the order of subjects ability to control BCI was not the same every day. For example, as shown in Fig. 4 on the last experimental day the quality of BCI control for S3 was higher than for subjects S1 and S2, although on average it was lower.

http://dx.doi.org/10.5772/55166

For each experimental day three the most relevant components and optimal components were chosen to maximize κ for the data of namely this day. The components happened to be not identical for all experimental days and all subjects but some of them appeared very repeatedly. Four such components which appeared most often among the most relevant ones over all subjects and all experimental days are shown in Fig. 5. The features of these components are shown in terms of their contribution into EEG electrodes (topoplots) and their spectrograms for four considered mental states: relaxation, right or left hand movement imagination and feet movement imagination. The data relates to the last experimental day of Subject 1 who showed the best BCI control on average.

Three of these components ($\mu1$, $\mu2$ and $\mu3$) demonstrate very well exposed Event Related Desynchronization (ERD) of mu-rhythm. For the component denoted $\mu1$ mu-rhythm is suppressed during the left hand motor imagery. Its focus is in the right hemisphere presumably above the primary sensorimotor areas presenting the left hand. Respectively, for the components $\mu2$ and $\mu3$ mu-rhythm is suppressed during the right hand and feet motor imagery and their foci are presumably above the areas presenting right hand and feet. The fourth component denoted β we ascribed to the activity of supplementary motor areas (SMA). First, they are located on the midline surface of the hemispheres and hence their activity can produce the focus corresponding to the topoplot of this component. Second, as shown in [27] by electrocorticographic recordings, during the motor act SMA demonstrates ERD in the spectral band 10 - 40 Hz. Just the same is shown for the component β. Remind that for our offline analysis EEG signal was filtered in the band 5 - 30 Hz, so ERD for this component is shown in Fig. 4 up to 30 Hz.

Three of four ICA components discussed here ($\mu1$, $\mu2$ and β) are completely identical to those obtained in [11] (Compare Fig. 5 with the first and last rows in Fig. 3 of [11]). Component β was identified but not discussed in [11]. Component $\mu3$ is new because only three mental tasks (relaxation and left or right hand motor imagery but not feet motor imagery) were used for BCI control in [11].

As in [11] components $\mu1$ and $\mu2$ demonstrate also well exposed Event Related Synchronization (ERS) during the motor imagery of the opponent extremities. Especially it is seen for $\mu1$. Mu-rhythm of this component essentially increased during the motor imagery of both right hand and feet. It is worth to note that the topoplots of four described components were very stable for all experimental days but the manifestation of ERD and ERS was rather variable. Namely the variability of their manifestation determined the variability of BCI control quality. However in any case ERD and ERS are much better exposed in terms of ICA components than in direct EEG recording. The level of ERD can be estimated as $r = S_{im}/S_{rel}$ where S_{im} and S_{rel} are the maximal spectral densities in the alpha band during the motor imagination and relaxation, respectively. For Subject 1 on average over all experimental days and imagination of both hands r amounted to 0.2 in terms of ICA components and to 0.69 for two central electrodes C3 and C4 where ERD was maximally exposed. Thus ICA allowed to rectify ERD and ERS due to excluding the components not exposing these changes of the brain activity.

3.2. Sources localization

Although the shown ICA components happened to be rather stable and repeatable over all subjects and all experimental days one could expect that they are only the formal

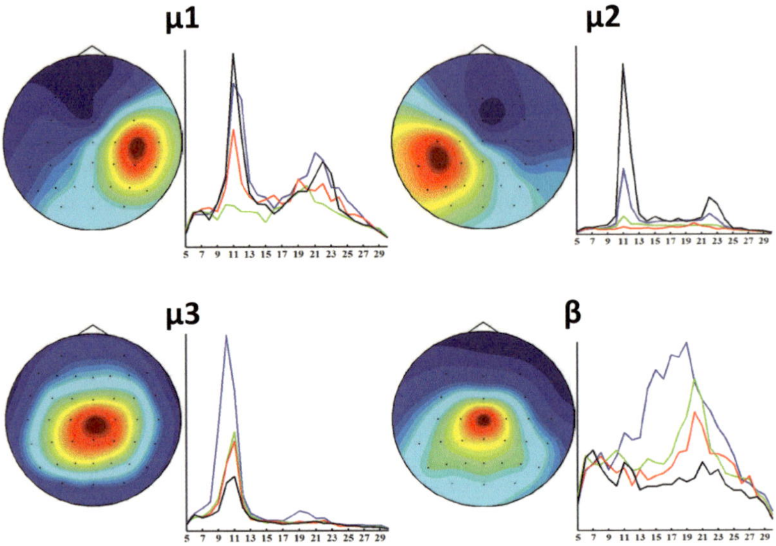

Figure 5. Topoplots and spectrograms for four sources of electrical brain activity the most relevant to BCI performance. $\mu1$, $\mu2$ and $\mu3$ demonstrate ERD of mu-rhythm during imagination of left hand, right hand and feet movement. β demonstrates ERD in the band 10 - 30 Hz. Spectral frequency is given in Hz, blue curves - relaxation, red lines - right hand motor imagery, green lines - left hand motor imagery, black lines - feet motor imagery.

results of some mathematical transformations of the actual experimental data and have no physiological sense. To clarify their sense we show, first, that their contribution to EEG recordings can be explained by the current dipole sources of brain activity located in the sensorimotor cortical areas, and, second, that locations of these sources coincide with locations of brain activity identified in fMRI study.

As an example, topoplot of $\mu1$ is compared in Fig. 6 with that produced by a current dipole model found by solving inverse EEG problem. To solve it we found the location and orientation of the dipole provided the best fit between its contribution to EEG electrodes obtained by solving the direct EEG problem and the contribution obtained for $\mu1$. As shown in Fig. 6 the found dipole provides a good coincidence between both types of contribution. On average over all subject and all components the residual variance of the single dipole approximation amounted only 1%.

Examples of dipole localization along with results of fMRI analysis are shown in Fig. 7. Figure demonstrates voxels for which BOLD level was significantly higher left hand (a), right hand (b), and feet (c) motor imagery compared to relaxation.

Dipole positions obtained for components $\mu1$ and $\mu2$ happened to be very close to the sensorimotor "hand areas" marked in Fig. 7a,b. Dipole position obtained for component $\mu3$ is close to the sensorimotor "feet areas" in the superior regions of post- and precentral gyri (Fig.7c) and for component β slightly more anterior, i.e. close to SMA. However, the positions of dipoles corresponding to $\mu1$, $\mu2$ and $\mu3$ happened to be a little deeper than foci of fMRI activity near "hand" and "feet" areas. Small discrepancy (in the limit of 25

http://dx.doi.org/10.5772/55166

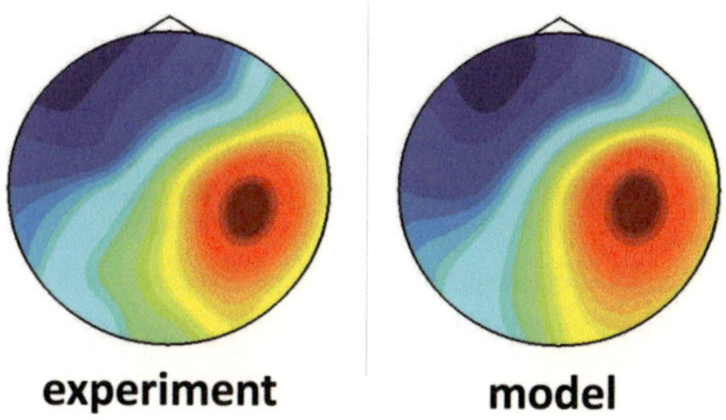

Figure 6. Topoplot of component $\mu 1$ (experiment) compared with topoplot produced by a single dipole model (subject S1)

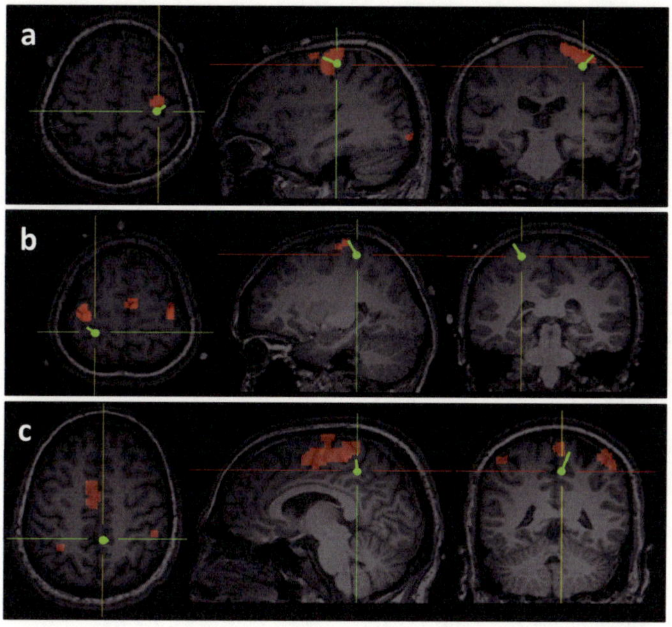

Figure 7. Examples of dipole localization for $\mu 1$ (a), $\mu 2$ (b) and $\mu 3$ (c) components along with the results of fMRI analysis.

mm) between current dipole positions and areas of maximal fMRI activity was also obtained in the most studies with measurements of somatosensory activity as a response to hand electrical stimulation (see, for example, [6, 12, 41]). This may be explained by the fact that different processes are responsible for EEG and fMRI outcomes. EEG is the result of neuronal electric activity while fMRI relates to blood flow activity associated with the energetically dominant processes. If, for example, neuronal electric activity in the depth of central sulcus is less energy-expensive than in the crown of pre- and postcentral gyrus than fMRI activity removes up comparing with EEG activity. Moreover, in our experiments a motor imagination results in the increase of fMRI activity but decrease of EEG activity. Since relation between fMRI activity and neuronal electric activity is rather complex [25], then the brain areas where these two kinds of brain activity are maximally exposed could be slightly different. Hence the small discrepancy of their positions does not evidence against the precision of dipole location. In our experiments the distance between dipole location and the COM of fMRI activity near central sulcus averaged over subjects and components amounted to 9 ± 1.5 mm. The dipoles corresponding to components $\mu1$, $\mu2$ and $\mu3$ were located at the bottom of the central sulcus (Fig. 7), i.e. at the area 3a responsible for proprioceptive sensation. According to reports of the subjects this corresponds to their internal feeling of the imagined movement.

4. Discussion

Generally, the difficulties in interpreting the original EEG signals are due to the overlapping of activities coming from different brain sources, due to the distortion of the current flows caused by the inhomogeneity in the conductivity of the brain and its covers and due to uncertainty not only in dipole source locations but also in the dipole orientation which determines the relation between its position and the EEG amplitude maxima which it produces at the head surface. These difficulties result in common notion that EEG data provide high temporal but very low spatial resolution comparing to fMRI data. Last years there were many efforts to match these techniques to enhance both resolutions [25]. One of the approaches is presented here in the chapter. It contains the following steps:

1. Subjects training in BCI control to stabilize and to contrast the patterns of EEG activities related to the mental tasks under consideration.
2. When subjects are sufficiently trained, finding the ICA components which are the most relevant for the BCI control. This allows to suppress the influence of not relevant sources of brain activity and to refine the most relevant ones.
3. Obtaining of individual geometries of the brain and its covers (e.g. by MRI data) - as result inverse problem can be solved taking geometries into account
4. The inverse EEG problem solving for each individual relevant component. This allows to perform the solution in the single dipole approximation.
5. Verifying the found dipole locations by fMRI data to be sure that the found ICA components are not only the formal results of some mathematical transformations.

This approach allowed us to find the location of the sources of the brain activity which are the most relevant for motor imagination. Three of them denoted as $\mu1$, $\mu2$ and $\mu3$ happened to be localized at the bottom of central sulcus close to the Brodmann area 3a responsible for proprioceptive sensation. This location corresponds to the internal feeling of the imagined hand or feet movement according to the reports of subjects. Thus, the experience of imagery (at least for motor imagery) involves perceptual structures despite the absence of perceptual stimulation.

There is a long story of the debates concerning the brain areas involved into the motor imagination, especially the involvement of the primary sensorimotor cortex. Activated areas in or around primary motor area have been described in PET studies [40] during imagination of arm movement, but not of the grasping movement [8]. Primary sensorimotor cortex fMRI activation during the motor imagination was denied in [35, 37], but was claimed in [9, 20, 36].

There were also many efforts to reveal whether SM1 is active during motor imagery basing on EEG data [2, 26, 30]. Particularly, in [26, 30] the conclusion that it activates was based on the observation that ERD is maximally exposed at the electrodes related to SM1 activity.

http://dx.doi.org/10.5772/55166

However as mentioned above it is difficult to prescribe electrical activity to some particular brain area on the base of original EEG data. We believe that our approach allows to do this more substantiated. The reasonable and well interpreted results were obtained here due to solving the inverse EEG problem with the data refined by ICA. The components which are the most relevant to the performance of BCI based on the hand motor imagination were also obtained in [22]. They are very close or may be even identical to the components obtained in the present paper. But in [22] they were not interpreted in terms of dipole sources and consequently the inverse EEG problem was not solved. We tried to solve it with the most realistic head model as a volume conductor taking into account the individual geometry of brain and its covers and the difference in conductivity of white and grey matters, CSF, skull and scalp. The only thing that we ignored is the anisotropy of the white matter (WM). Although as shown in [19] the head model incorporating realistic anisotropic WM conductivity distributions do not substantially improve the accuracy of EEG dipole localization, our next step is to take into account also the anisotropy.

Besides the foci of fMRI activity which were associated with three sources of EEG activity the most relevant for BCI performance (foci in primary sensorimotor areas 3 and 4 shown in Fig. 7) we observed many other foci. Among them are foci in cerebellum, superior temporal area 22, ventral anterior cingulate area 24 and insula. Thus motor imagery involves rather wide brain networks. According to the literature it can involve also superior and inferior parietal lobule, pre-frontal areas, inferior frontal gyrus, secondary somatosensory area and basal ganglia (see, for example [9, 39]). We also obtained many other ICA components which were relevant to motor imagination except four main components $\mu 1$, $\mu 2$, $\mu 3$ and β. Since we obtained good relation between these components and fMRI data the natural goal of our future research is to reveal the relations between other fMRI foci and other ICA components.

Acknowledgments

This research has been partly funded by project GACR P202/10/0262, by the IT4Innovations Centre of Excellence project, reg. no. CZ.1.05/1.1.00/02.0070 supported by Operational Programme "Research and Development for Innovations" funded by Structural Funds of the European Union and state budget of the Czech Republic and by long-term strategic development financing of the Institute of Computer Science (RVO:67985807).

Author details

Alexander Frolov[1,2,*], Dušan Húsek[3], Pavel Bobrov[1,2],
Olesya Mokienko[1] and Jaroslav Tintera[4]

* Address all correspondence to: aafrolov@mail.ru

1 Institute of Higher Nervous Activity and Neurophysiology, RAS, Moscow, Russia
2 Faculty of Electronics and Informatics, VŠB-Technical University of Ostrava, Ostrava – Poruba, Czech Republic
3 Institute of Computer Science, Academy of Sciences of the Czech Republic, Prague, Czech Republic
4 Institute for Clinical and Experimental Medicine, Prague, Czech Republic

References

[1] Bashashati A, Fatourechi M, Ward R, Birch G (2007) A survey of signal processing algorithms in brain-computer interfaces based on electrical brain signals. Journal of Neural engineering 4: R32.

[2] Beisteiner R, Hollinger P, Lindinger G, Lang W, Berthoz A (1995) Mental representations of movements. Brain potentials associated with imagination of hand movements. Electroecephalogr. Clin. Neurophysiol. 96:183-193.

[3] Besserve M, Jerbi K, Laurent F, Baillet S, Martinerie J, et al. (2007) Classification methods for ongoing EEG and MEG signals. Biological research 40: 415-437.

[4] Birbaumer N., Cohen L.G. (2007). Brain-computer interfaces: communication and restoration of movement in paralysis, J Physiol., 579, pp. 621-636.

[5] Blankertz B., Dornhege G., Krauledat M., Muller K.R, Curio G. The non-invasive Berlin Brain Computer Interface: Fast acquisition of effective performance in untrained subjects. Neuroimage. 2007. 37(2): 539Ű550.

[6] Christmann C, Ruf M, Braus D F, Flor H (2002) Simultaneous electroencephalography and functional magnetic resonance imaging of primary and secondary somatosensory cortex in humans after electric stimulation. Neuroscience Letters 333: 69-73.

[7] Delorme A., Makeig S., 2004, EEGLAB: an open source toolbox for analysis of single-trial EEG dynamics. Journal of Neuroscience Methods 134:9-21

[8] Decety J, Perani D, Jeannerod M, Bettinardi V, Tadary B, Woods R, Mazziotta JC, Fazio F (1994) Mapping motor representations with positron emission tomography. Nature 371: 600-602

[9] Formaggio E, Storti SF, Cerini R, Fiaschi A, Manganotti P (2010) Brain oscillatory activity during motor imagery in EEG-fMRI coregistration. Magnetic Resonance Imaging 28(10):1403-12

[10] Frolov A, Husek D., Bobrov P. (2011) Comparison of four classification methods for brain computer interface. Neural Network World, 21(2) 101-115

[11] Frolov A, Husek D, Bobrov P, Korshakov A, Chernikova L, Konovalov R, Mokienko O (2012) Sources of EEG activity most relevant to performance of brain-computer interface based on motor imagery. NNW 1/12: 21-37.

[12] Del Gratta C, Della Penna S, Ferretti A, Franciotti R, Pizzella V, Tartaro A, Torquati K, Bonomo L, Romani G L, Rossini PM (2002). Topographic organization of the human primary and secondary somatosensory cortices: comparison of fMRI and MEG findings. Neuroimage, 17(3):1373-83.

[13] Grech R, Cassar T, Muscat J, Camilleri KP, Fabri SG, Zervakis M, Xanthopoulos P, Sakkalis V, Vanrumste B (2008) Review on solving the inverse problem in EEG source analysis. Journal of NeuroEngineering and Rehabilitation 5(25): 1-33.

[14] Haynes J, Rees G (2006) Decoding mental states from brain activity in humans. Nature Reviews Neuroscience 7: 523-534.

[15] Hyvarinen A., Karhunen J., Oje E. (2001) Independent component analysis. Willey, New-York. 480 pp.

[16] Kachenoura A., Albera L., Senhadji L., Comon P. (2008) ICA: a potential tool for BCI systems. IEEE Signal Processing Magazine 25(1) 57-68

[17] Kim TS, Zhou Y, Kim S, Singh M (2002). EEG distributed source imaging with a realistic finite-element head model. IEEE Trans Nucl Sci; 49:745-52.

[18] Kohavi R, Provost F (1998): Glossary of terms. Machine Learning - Special Issue on Applications of Machine Learning and the Knowledge Discovery Process. 30, 271-274.

[19] Lee WH, Liu Z, Mueller BA, Limb K, He B (2009). Influence of white matter anisotropic conductivity on EEG source localization: Comparison to fMRI in human primary visual cortex. Clin Neurophysiol 120(12): 2071-2081

[20] Leonardo M, Fieldman J, Sadato N, Campbell G, Ibanez V, Cohen L, Deiber M-P Jezzard P, Pons T, Turner R, Le Bihan D, Hallett M (1995) A functional magnetic resonance imaging study of cortical regions associated with motor task execution and motor ideation in humans. Hum. Brain. Mapp. 3: 135-141.

[21] Leuthardt E, Schalk G, Roland J, Rouse A, Moran D (2009) Evolution of brain-computer interfaces: going beyond classic motor physiology. Neurosurgical focus 27: E4.

[22] Lou B., Hong B., Task-irrelevant alpha component analysis in motor imagery based brain computer interface. 30th Annual International IEEE EMBS Conference, Vancuver, Canada, 2008, 1021-1024.

[23] Mellinger J, Schalk G, Braun C, Preissl H, Rosenstiel W, Birbaumer N, Kubler A (2007) An MEG-based brain-computer interface (BCI). Neuroimage. 36: 581-593.

[24] Millan J, Mourino J, Marciani M, Babiloni F, Topani F, et al. Adaptive brain interfaces for physically-disabled people; 1998. Citeseer. pp. 2008-2011.

[25] Mulert C, Lemieux L (Eds) (2010) EEG-fMRI. Physiological basis, techniques and application. Springer

[26] Neuper C, Scherer R, Reiner M, Pfurtscheller G (2005) Imagery of motor actions: Differential effects of kinesthetic and visual-motor mode of imagery in single-trial EEG. Cognitive Brain Reserch 25: 668-677.

[27] Ohara S, Ikeda A, Kunieda T, Yazawa S, Baba K, Nagamine T, Taki W, Hashimoto N, Mihara T, Shibasaki H (2000) Movement-related changes of electrocorticographic activity in human supplementary motor are proper. Brain 123: 1203-1215.

[28] Pfurtscheller G, Flotzinger D, Kalcher J (1993) Brain-computer Interface–a new communication device for handicapped persons. Journal of Microcomputer Applications 16: 293-299.

[29] Pfurtscheller, G., Neuper, C. (1994). Event-related synchronization of mu rhythm in the EEG over the cortical hand area in man. Neurosci. Lett. 174, 93-96.

[30] Pfurtscheller G, Neuper C, Flotzinger D, Pregenzer M (1997) EEG-based discrimination between imagination of right and left hand movement. Electroencephalography and clinical Neurophysiology 103: 642-651.

[31] Pfurtscheller G, Neuper C (1997) Motor imagery activates primary sensorimotor area in humans. Neuroscience Letters. 239: 65-68.

[32] Pfurtscheller G., Neuper C. (2001) Motor imagery and direct brain-computer communication. Proceedings of the IEEE, 82 (7), 1123-1134.

[33] Pfurtscheller G., Brunner C., Schlogl A., Lopes da Silva F. (2006) Mu rhythm (de) synchronization and EEG single-trial classification of different motor imagery tasks. NeuroImage 31: 153-159.

[34] Pineda J.A. (2005) The functional significance of mu rhythm: Translating "seeing" and "hearing" into "doing". Brain Research Reviews 50: 57- 68.

[35] Rao SM, Binder JR, Bandettini PA, Hammeke TA, Yetkin FZ, Jesmanowicz A, Lisk LM, Morris GL, Mueller WM, Estkowski LD, Wong EC, Haughton VM, Hyde JS (1993) Functional magnetic resonance imaging of complex human movements. Neurology 43: 2311-2318.

[36] Sabbah P, Simond G, Levrier O, Habib M, Trabaud V, Murayama N, Mazoyer BM, Briant JF, Raybaud C, Salamon G (1995) Functional magnetic resonance imaging at 1.5 T during sensory motor and cognitive tasks. Eur. Neurol. 35: 131-136/

[37] Sanes JN, Stern CE, Baker JR, Kwong KK, Donoghue JP, Rosen BR (1993) Human frontal motor cortical areas related to motor performance and mental imagery. Soc. Neurosci. Abstr. 18: 1208

[38] Sitaram R, Zhang H, Guan C, Thulasidas M, Hoshi Y, Ishikawa A, Shimizu K, Birbaumer N (2007) Temporal classification of multichannel near-infrared spectroscopy signals of motor imagery for developing a brain-computer interface. NeuroImage 34.4, 1416-1427

[39] Solodkin A, Hlustik P, Chen EE, Small SL (2004) Fine modulation in network activation during motor execution and motor imagery. Cerebral Cortex 14.11, 1246-1255

[40] Stephan K M., Fink GR, Passingham RE., Silbersweig D., Ceballos-Baumann AO., Frith CD., Frackowiak RSJ (1995) Functional anatomy of the mental representation of upper extremity movements in healthy subjects. Journal of Neurophysiology, 73 (1): 373-386

[41] Thees S, Blabkenburg F, Taskin B, Curio G, Villringer A (2003) Dipole source localization and fMRI of simultaneously recorded data applied to somatosensory categorization. NeuroImage 18: 707-719

[42] Weiskopf N, Veit R, Erb M, et al. Mathiak K, Grodd W, Goebel R, Birbaumer N. (2003) Physiological self-regulation of regional brain activity using real-time functional magnetic resonance imaging (fMRI): methodology and exemplary data. Neuroimage. 19: 577-586

[43] Wolpaw J, Birbaumer N, Heetderks W, McFarland D, Peckham P, et al. (2000) Brain-computer interface technology: a review of the first international meeting. IEEE Transactions on Rehabilitation Engineering 8: 164-173.

[44] Wolpaw J, Birbaumer N, McFarland D, Pfurtscheller G, Vaughan T (2002) Brain-computer interfaces for communication and control. Clinical neurophysiology 113: 767-791.

[45] Wolpaw J., McFarland D.: Control of a two-dimensional movement signal by a noninvasive brain-computer interface in humans. Proceedings of the National Academy of Sciences of the United States of America 101: 17849, 2004

[46] Wolters CH, Anwander A, Tricoche X, Weinstein D, Koch MA, MacLeod RS. Influence of tissue conductivity anisotropy on EEG/MEG field and return current computation in a realistic head model: a simulation and visualization study using high-resolution finite element modeling. NeuroImage 2006;30:813-26.

Chapter 10

A Review of P300, SSVEP, and Hybrid P300/SSVEP Brain-Computer Interface Systems

Setare Amiri, Ahmed Rabbi, Leila Azinfar and
Reza Fazel-Rezai

Additional information is available at the end of the chapter

http://dx.doi.org/10.5772/56135

1. Introduction

There are several techniques for measuring brain activities such as magnetoencephalogram (MEG), near infrared spectroscopy (NIRS), electrocorticogram (ECoG), functional magnetic resonance imaging (fMRI), and electroencephalography (EEG). Each technique has some advantages and disadvantages compared to other techniques. For example, in EEG the temporal resolution is high but the special resolution is low compared to fMRI. Because of low cost and portability, EEG has been largely used in both clinical and research applications [1][2] [3][4].

One of the EEG research applications is in a brain computer interface (BCI) system. A BCI can provide a new way of communications for special users who cannot communicate via normal pathways. A BCI system can send commands, controlled by brain activity and distinguished by EEG signal processing. There are many features which can be extracted from EEG, for example, six brain rhythms can be distinguished in EEG based on the differences in frequency ranges; delta (1- 4 Hz), theta (4-7 Hz), alpha (8-12 Hz), mu (8-13 Hz), beta (12-30 Hz), and gamma (25-100 Hz). The delta and theta rhythms occur in high emotional conditions or in a sleep stage. The alpha rhythm happens in awake and eyes closed relax condition. The oscillation in alpha rhythm has smooth pattern. The beta rhythm pattern is desynchronized and the condition is the normal awake open eyes. The gamma rhythm can be acquired from somatosensory cortex and mu rhythm from sensorimotor cortex.

BCIs are categorized based on the EEG brain activity patterns into four different types: event–related desynchronization/synchronization (ERD/ERS) [5], steady state visual evoke potentials (SSVEP) [6][7][8], P300 component of event related potentials (ERPs) [9], and slow cortical potentials (SCPs) [6][10]. The focus of this chapter is on P300, SSVEP and hybrid P300-SSVEP BCI systems.

Compared to other modalities for BCI approaches, such as the P300-based and the SCP BCIs, SSVEP-based BCI system has the advantage of having higher accuracy and higher information transfer rate (ITR). In addition, short/no training time and fewer EEG channels are required. However, similar to other BCI modalities, most current SSVEP-based BCI techniques also face some challenges that prevent them from being accepted by the majority of the population. Two important features of each BCI system are information transfer rate and required training time. A general comparison of different BCI approaches is shown in Figure 1.

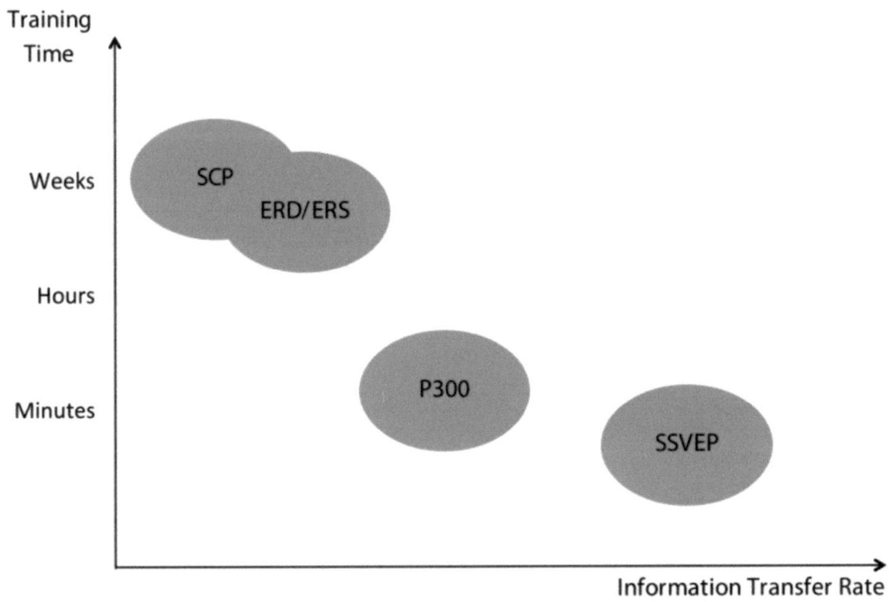

Figure 1. A general comparison of SCP, ERD/ERS, P300, and SSVEP with respect to their training time and information transfer rate.

The process of detecting patterns from EEG is divided into three steps [11]: signal pre-processing, feature extraction and classification. The first step is to remove noise such as artifacts or power line noise which is added to EEG. So filtering is the first step in EEG signal pre-processing. Band pass and notch filters are the most common filters utilized in EEG signal filtering.

In the next step, features that are selected in feature extraction step and the type of classifier should be chosen based on the type of BCI. For example, for P300, time domain or time-frequency domain features such as wavelets are appropriate and for SSVEP BCIs frequency domain features are more appropriate. Classifiers such as Fischer's linear discriminant analysis (FLDA), Bayesian linear discriminant analysis (BLDA), stepwise linear discriminant analysis (SWLDA), and support vector machine (SVM) are utilized [12][13] for P300 classifications. For SSVEP feature extraction and classification, different methods such as the Fast Fourier transform (FFT), the canonical correlation analysis (CCA), stimulus-locked inter-trace correlation (SLIC), and the common special patterns (CSPs) have been used [14][15] [16].

In recent years, the BCI research projects and the number of publications in this area have been increased rapidly [17]. Different areas of research such as new feature extraction methods, new classification techniques, new BCI paradigms, or new approaches for combining different BCI types have been investigated for improving accuracy, reliability, information transfer rate, and user acceptability. Combining different BCI types called a hybrid BCI is a new trend in BCI research which is the main focus of this chapter. In the next sections, the P300 and SSVEP BCI are explained and then different approaches for building a P300-SSVEP hybrid BCI are discussed.

2. P300-based BCI

2.1. The P300 component

Event related potentials (ERPs) are the measurement of brain responses to specific cognitive, sensory or motor events. One of the main approaches towards BCI is based on ERPs. P300 is a major peak and one of the most used components of an ERP. The presentation of stimulus in an oddball paradigm can produce a positive peak in the EEG, 300 msec after onset of the stimulus. The stimulus can either be visual, auditory or somatosensory. This evoked response in EEG is called P300 component of ERP.

2.2. Properties of P300

The spatial amplitude distribution is strongest in the occipital region of brain and is symmetric around central location Cz recorded based on the 10-20 international system [18]. The spatial amplitude distribution of 10-20 international system and the electrodes that P300 is typically recorded from are shown in the following Figure 2. In terms of temporal pattern, P300 wave amplitude is typically in the range of 2 to 5 μV with duration of 150 to 200 msec as shown in Figure 3. Considering the P300 low amplitude relative to background activities of the brain (in the rage of 50 μV), it is clear that P300 detection requires special signal processing. One of the simplest approaches is ensemble averaging EEG over multiple responses to enhance P300 amplitude to identify it while suppressing background EEG activities.

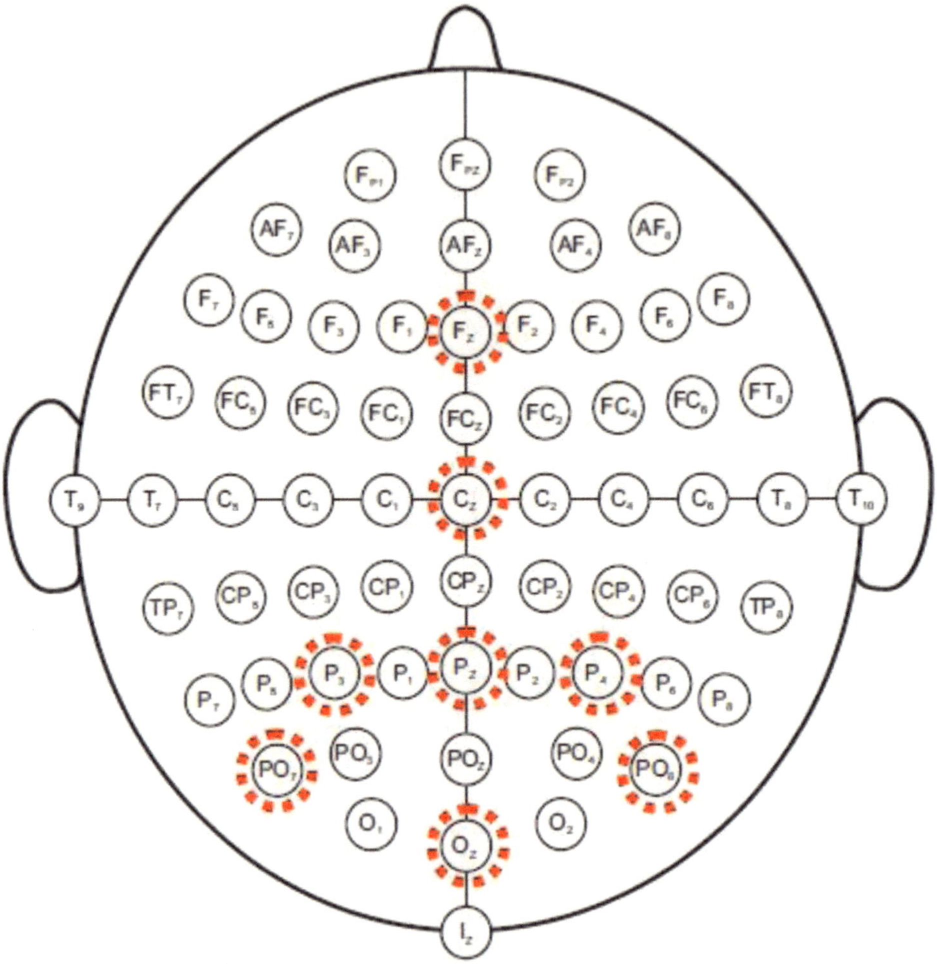

Figure 2. Recoding of EEG based on 10-20 system and location of the electrodes typically used for P300 detection [18].

P300-based BCI has been used as one of the most widely used BCI systems since 1988 [1]. New advancements in inexpensive and portable hardware made it possible to have real-life application outside of laboratory environment [17][1][20][21][22]. P300-based BCI has been used from controlling a wheelchair for helping disable people to a virtual keyboard for spelling word and interacting with computers. This type of BCI systems possesses the potential to improve the quality of life.

P300-based visual speller paradigms are attracting much attention as they could provide means to communicate letters, words, and simple commands to computer directly from the

http://dx.doi.org/10.5772/56135

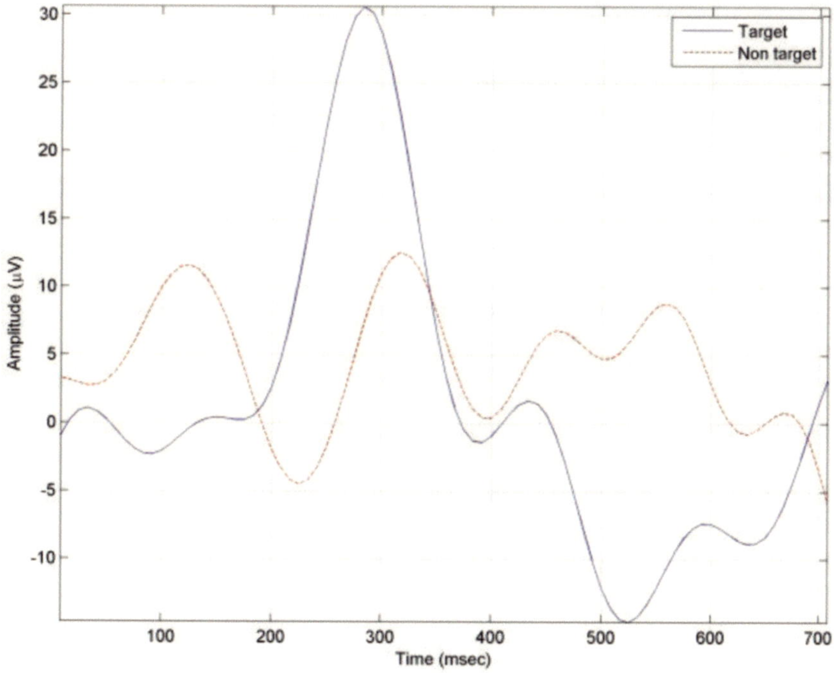

Figure 3. Temporal pattern of P300 component.

brain. In the following sections, we will review the classical speller paradigm and discuss current and future trends in this area.

Processing and successful use of P300 wave in a BCI application requires several processing steps. First of all, the recorded EEG data have to be processed to reduce the effect of noise. A feedback mechanism is required where a visible signal is presented in the monitor correlated with the recorded signal. A pattern recognition or classification algorithm has to be developed to identify the P300 wave in the recorded ERP epochs. The algorithm parameters should be adjustable to adapt according to the change of user characteristics [11][17].

Figure 4 shows a typical BCI setting for speller application. Stimulus is presented by random flashing of the characters on the screen. This eventually evokes P300 wave in the recorded EEG. A signal processing technique performs the processing of P300 related information and the classifier contains the pattern recognition algorithm as described earlier [17].

The classical paradigm for P300-based BCI speller was originally introduced by Farwell and Donchin in 1988 [1]. This Row-Column (RC) paradigm is the most popular speller format. It consists of 6 × 6 matrix of characters as shown in Figure 5. This matrix is presented on computer screen and the row and columns are flashed in a random order. The user is instructed to select a character by focusing on it. The flashing row or column evokes P300 response in EEG. The

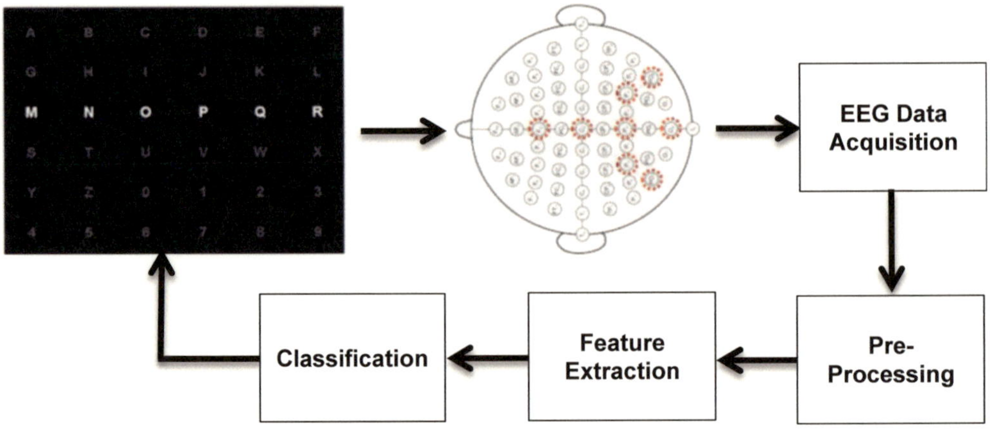

Figure 4. A typical P300 BCI setup with visual feedback.

non-flashing rows and columns do not contribute in generating P300 [1]. Therefore, the computer can determine the desired row and column after averaging several responses. Finally, the desired character is selected.

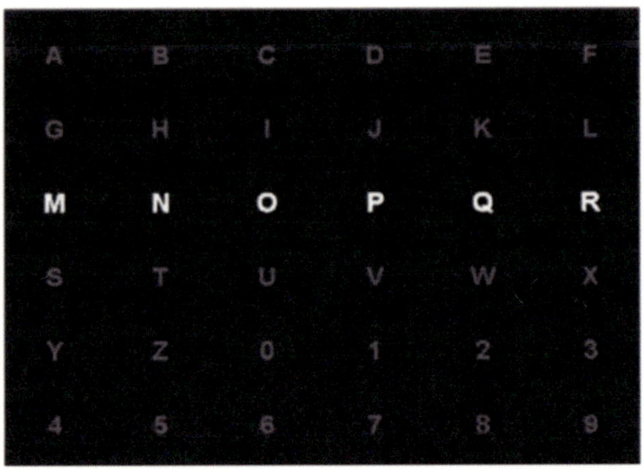

Figure 5. A typical row/column paradigm [1].

It is interesting to note that P300-based BCI did not receive much attention when it was first proposed. However, recent trend is quite different where P300 BCI has emerged as one of the main BCI approaches. The researchers have focused on identifying the scopes of improvement of the traditional paradigm by introducing new ways of flashing, introducing colors, or investigating other ways to enhance the ERPs. Much focus has put on applying advanced digital signal processing techniques and classification methods in order to improve the classification results. Also, there have been several attempts to introduce new paradigms to evoke P300 potentials. Figure 6 shows such a different approach which is called single character

(SC) paradigm that only single character is flashed instead of a row or column. The SC paradigm randomly flashes one character at a time with a delay between flashes [17]. The delay in SC speller is longer than the delay in RC speller. Though SC speller is slower than RC speller, SC speller can produce larger P300 amplitude [17].

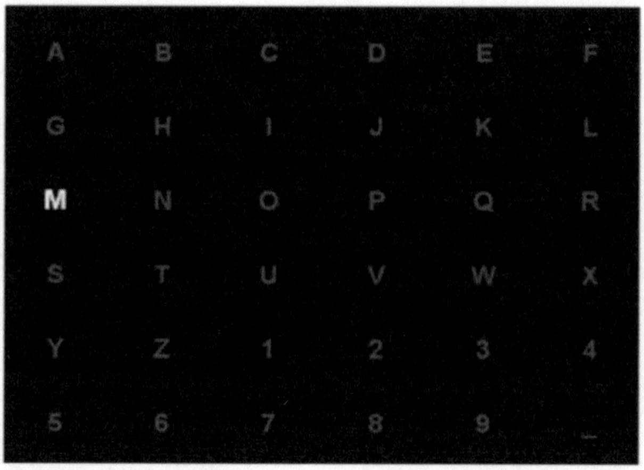

Figure 6. Single character paradigm where each character is flashed [14][1].

Checkerboard (CB) speller is another paradigm proposed to overcome a problem associated with RC speller [17]. This drawback is arising from the distraction or inherent noise due to row/column association [17]. CB speller effectively reduces these two limitations as the characters are arranged in a checkerboard style as shown in Figure 7. CB speller also increases ITR [20].

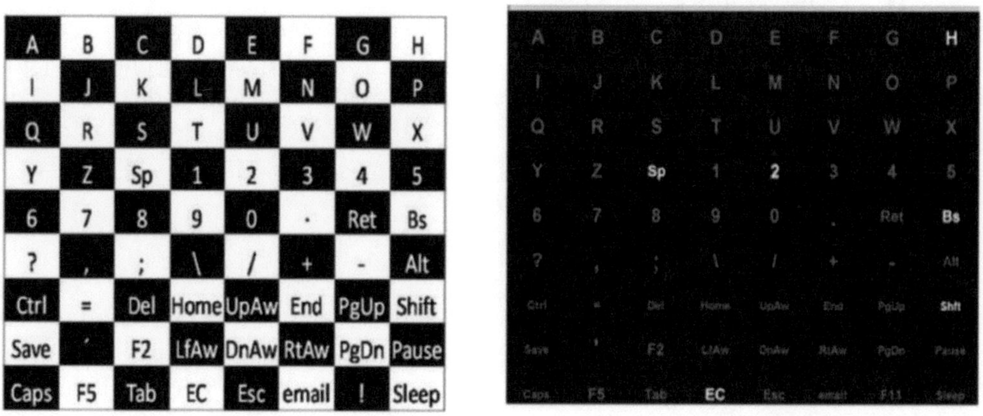

Figure 7. Checkerboard paradigm [20].

The region-based (RB) paradigm was proposed by Fazel-Rezai et. al. in 2009 [21]. It is a two-level speller where the regions have to flash instead of rows and columns. In the first level, characters are placed in several regions (seven groups) as shown in Figure 8 [17][1][20][21]. The users are instructed to focus attention on a specific character in one of the seven regions. After several flashes the desired region is selected. In the second level, characters are distributed following the same rule used in the first level and each character flashes in similar order. After several flashes, the desired character is identified [21].

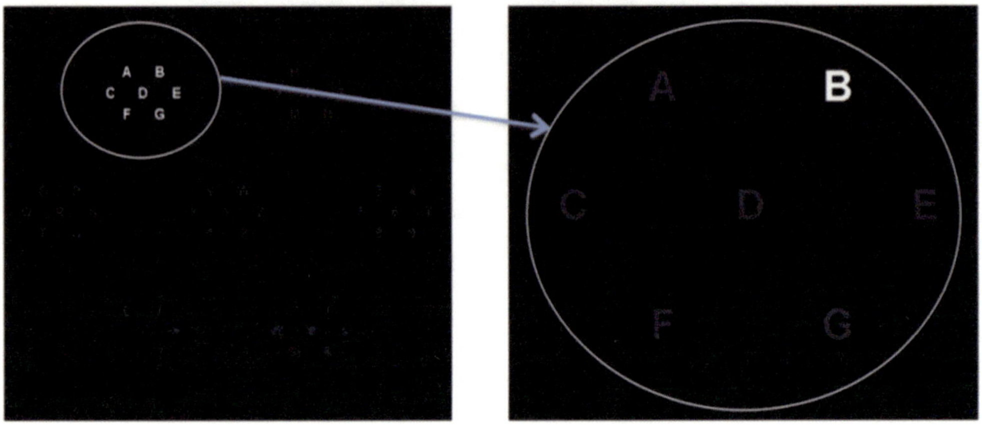

Figure 8. Region based paradigm where a set of characters in level 1 (E) are expanded in level 2 for spelling character "B" (F).

It is reported that RB speller has decreased the adjacency problem significantly [17][1][20][21]. The RB and CB paradigms show new directions in BCI speller paradigms apart from RC speller.

There has been much progress in bringing BCI technology out of lab environment to real-life applications. BCI has widely been studied in helping disable people, for example, enabling controlling a wheel chair using brain signals [22]. The other promising applications are in managing smart home environment, controlling a virtual reality environment, and next generation gaming [12].

3. SSVEP BCI

Electrophysiological and neurophysiological studies have demonstrated increases in neural activity elicited by gazing at a stimulus [23]. Visual evoked potentials are elicited by sudden visual stimuli and the repetitive visual stimuli would lead to stable voltage oscillations pattern in EEG that is called SSVEP.

SSVEP is considered as a concept with two different definitions. Ragan [24] proposed that SSVEP is a direct response in the primary visual cortex. On the other hand, Silberstein *et al.* [25]

http://dx.doi.org/10.5772/56135

assumed that the SSVEP includes indirect cortical responses via cortical-loops, from the peripheral retina, while a cognitive task is performed. SSVEP in this model has a complex amplitude and phase topography across the posterior scalp with considerable inter-subject variability. Although the main mechanism of SSVEP still is unknown, generally SSVEP is considered as a continuous visual cortical response evoked by repetitive stimuli with a constant frequency on the central retina. As a nearly sinusoidal oscillatory waveform, the SSVEP usually contains the same fundamental frequency as the stimulus and some harmonics of the fundamental frequency. For example, when the retina is excited by a visual stimulus at presentation rates ranging from 3.5 Hz to 75 Hz, the brain generates an electrical activity at the same and different frequency of the visual stimulus. The flickering stimulus of different frequency with a constant intensity can evoke the SSVEP in verity of amplitudes, ranging from (5-12Hz) as low frequencies, (12-25 Hz) as medium ones and (25-50 Hz) as high frequency bands [26]. This type of stimulus is a powerful indicator in the diagnosis of visual pathway function, visual imperceptions in patients with cerebral lesions, loss of multifocal sensitivity in patients with multiple sclerosis, and neurological abnormalities in patients with schizophrenia and other clinical diagnoses [26].

In addition to the usual clinical purpose of diagnosing visual pathway and brain mapping impairments, the SSVEP can serve as a basis for BCI. Recently, SSVEP BCI systems have gained a special place in the BCI paradigms continuum because of having a variety of different possibilities. SSVEP BCIs are useful in different applications, especially the ones that need some major requirements as follows [27]:

- Large number of BCI commands is necessary (in SSVEP BCI limitations are mostly defined only by the design).
- High reliability of recognition is necessary (in SSVEP BCI, patterns are clearly distinguishable by frequency).
- No training (or just a short time training for classifier training) is allowed.
- Self-paced performance is required.

A typical SSVEP-based BCI system uses a light-emitting diode (LED) for flickering. SSVEP responses can be measured within narrow frequency bands (e.g. around the visual stimulation frequency. Several numbers of stimuli can be implemented by using not necessarily a wide range of flickering frequencies, as the minimum detectable difference between frequencies is 0.2 Hz [27]. The occipital region is the area where this feature is generated more prominently [6]. The most wide-spread signal processing technique to extract the SSVEP responses of the brain from the raw EEG data is based on power spectral density (PSD) using FFT of a sliding data window with a fixed length. Template matching and recursive outlier rejection have also been used to show the feasibility of SSVEP BCI systems. Other methods which attempt to improve on robustness upon the FFT-based methods are autoregressive spectral analysis, and the frequency stability coefficient (SC) which has been shown to be better than power spectrum for short data windows; although training is necessary for building the SC model. Furthermore, CCA is also an efficient method for online SSVEP-BCI, as the required data window lengths are shorter than those necessary for power spectrum estimation.

Pastor et al.[28] studied the relationship between visual stimulation and SSVEP-evoked amplitudes, showing that the amplitude of SSVEPs peaks at 15 Hz, forms a lower plateau at 27 Hz, and declines further at higher frequencies (>30 Hz) as shown in Figure 9.

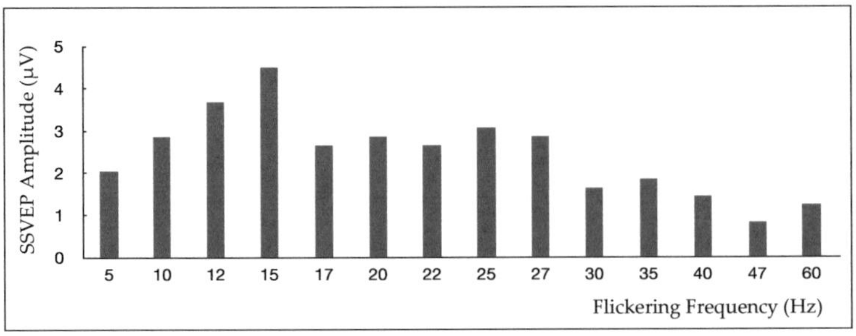

Figure 9. SSVEP amplitude with different flickering frequency [28].

In low-frequency stimulation, SSVEP detection is more accurate. In spite of its favorable detection properties, this band presents two major inconveniences [28],

- According to visual perception studies, stimulation frequencies in this band are rather annoying and tiring for the subject
- The risk for inducing photo epileptic seizures is higher for stimulation frequencies in the 15 – 25 Hz.

A simple solution could be in using higher stimulation frequencies. From empirical and subjective evidence, the threshold could be set to 40 Hz for low stimulation [28].

Ding *et al.* [23] demonstrated that a person's attention level modulates his/her SSVEP. Since the SSVEP depends directly on the stimulation frequency of visual flickering, user's attended target can be identified by analyzing the frequency contents in the induced SSVEP. By tagging different flickers with distinct flickering frequencies, subjects can shift their gaze to their desired flickers. These gaze targets can then be identified using the Fourier spectrum of the measured SSVEP signals. Middendorf *et al.* [29] designed a flight simulator controlled by two flickering lights that controlled leftwards or rightwards movement with a classification accuracy of 92%. Cheng *et al.* [30] implemented a SSVEP-based virtual keypad that achieved a mean ITR of 27.15 bits/min using twelve frequency-tagged flickering lights. Using two EEG electrodes positioned at the primary visual cortex, Kelly *et al.* [31] developed a method allowing participants to interact with a computer game.

Moreover, some visual BCIs have been developed as independent from users' eye gaze. Allison *et al.* [6] investigated selective attention using overlapping stimulus to induce SSVEPs difference in an online control study. Zhang *et al.* [32] also modulated the SSVEP amplitude and phase response by means of shifting covert attention on two sets of random dots with distinct colors, motion direction and flickering frequencies in the same visual field. Trader *et al.* [33] compared the performance of the Hex-o-Spell and matrix design using covert attention. Their results demonstrated that the Hex-o-Spell is more than 50% better than those with matrix design with covert attention. This SSVEP-based BCI identifies user's intended targets on calculated Fourier spectra. Nevertheless, the Fourier spectrum requires a time window (e.g., 1 or 2 sec) for computation to achieve sufficient frequency resolution in identifying two distinct gaze targets. Data segment with insufficient length in Fourier spectrum computation usually results in reduction of frequency resolution, which can limit the number of available targets in SSVEP-based BCI. Since BCI performance depends on accuracy and speed, a reliable method for extracting SSVEPs and recognizing gaze targets in an appropriate data segments is crucial.

It has been shown that the refreshing frequency, of a cathode ray tube (CRT) monitor can evoke a clear SSVEP. For SSVEP-based BCI development, the decoding accuracy is the most important factor, and a suitable stimulator is very crucial in this regard [34]. In previous studies, CRT flicker has been the most widely adopted stimulator, the LED flicker has only been reported in a small number of studies, and liquid crystal display (LCD) flicker has not appeared in the literature [23]. Since each of the three kinds of flicker can successfully evoke SSVEP, it is important to investigate the SSVEP differences that result from these different stimulators, and ascertain the type of flicker is most helpful in improving the accuracy of SSVEP-based BCI application. In the selection of the stimulating frequencies in a BCI application, one must ensure that the responses are as unique as possible. Thus, the stimulating frequencies are neither harmonics nor sub–harmonics from each other. From a practical point of view, the advantages of SSVEP BCI systems can be summarized as follows [34]:

- User is allowed to have small eye movements.
- User is capable of mild but sustained attention effort.
- User's visual system is not engaged in other activities.
- Visual stimulation can be performed by usual equipment like computer display or LED panel.
- Command delays of 1-3 s are allowed.

4. Hybrid BCIs SSVEP-P300 hybrid BCIs

There are some obstacles for BCIs to be more applicable, such as reliability, BCI illiteracy [35], low ITR, and no satisfactory accuracy for all different subjects. In recent years, an extensive amount of work in BCI has been invested based on utilizing the combination of different types of BCI systems, or BCI and non-BCI, called hybrid BCI systems. Overcoming the limitations and disadvantages of the conventional BCI systems is the main goal of hybrid BCI. The focus and attraction toward hybrid BCI field has been extended in recent years. This is shown in Figure 10, based on the Scopus search engine [36], and the keyword (("hybrid" AND ("BCI" OR "brain computer interface"))) and ("SSVEP" AND "P300") and limited to "Engineering", "Neuroscience" and "Computer Science" subject areas.

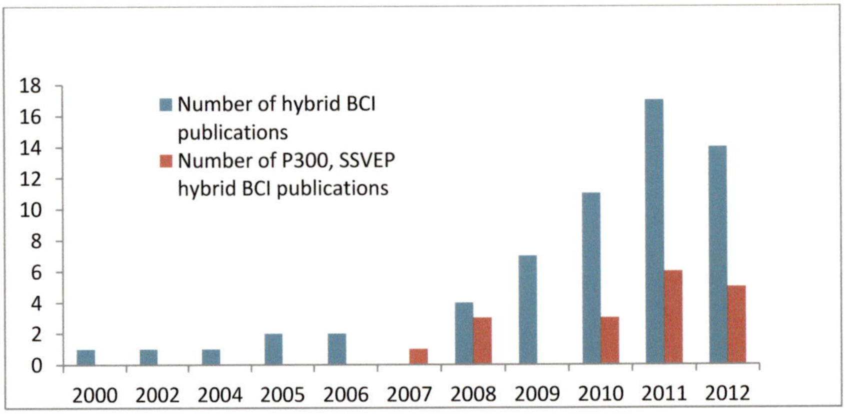

Figure 10. The increasing research trend in hybrid BCI area.

In general, the BCI systems can be combined in the way that, each system has separate input signal or the output of one system would be the input of the second system. The systems are called sequentially and simultaneously hybrid BCI, respectively [37]. Figure 11 shows a general block diagram of a sequential and a simultaneous hybrid BCI system. In sequential hybrid BCI, the first system mostly acts as a switch [37]. For this task, one of the appropriate options is SSVEP. SSVEP has high classification accuracy; high information transfer rate does not need training.

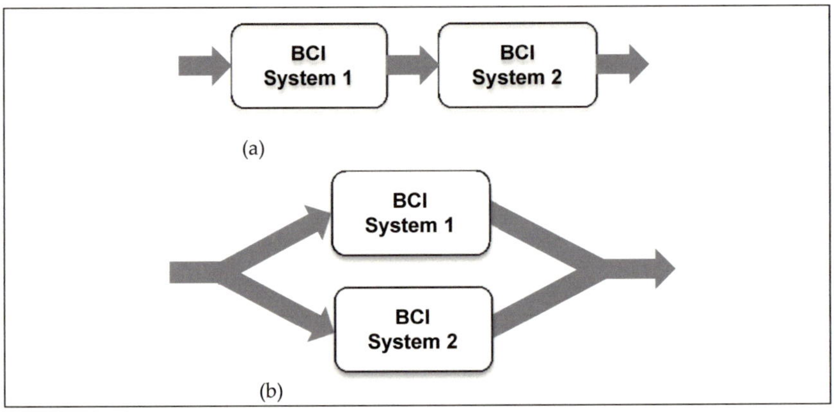

Figure 11. a) Sequential and (b) simultaneous hybrid BCI systems.

One of the main issues in this area is the optimum combination and selection of conventional BCIs. Several combinations of hybrid BCI systems have been introduced [37]. Conventional BCI systems are combined together based on the features of each system and the application of the hybrid BCI. If there are different tasks to be performed by the hybrid BCI, for each task, the more appropriate BCI can be chosen and, depending on the how the tasks are related to each other, the overall system can be combined. Some of the combinations for hybrid BCI that have been studied in recent years are shown in Table 1. Most of the studies in this area are focused on the combinations of BCI systems and few studies are on BCI and other physiological systems or devices.

Papers Numbers	Brain								Non-Brain (Non-Invasive)		
	Non-Invasive							Invasive			
	EEG			Non-EEG							
	P300	SSVEP	ERD	SCP	fMRI	NIRS	MEG	ECoG	EOG	EMG	ECG
[40]		■	■								
[39]		■	■								
[38]		■	■								
[41]		■	■								
[42]			■						■		
[43]			■			■					
[44]			■							■	
[13]	■	■									
[12]	■	■									
[45]	■		■								
[46]	■		■								
[47]	■		■								

Table 1. The covered cells in each row have been introduced as hybrid BCI systems

In control applications, the BCI systems should be capable to cover multi-tasks. Hybrid BCIs has opened new opportunities for BCI systems to have more intense application in different areas. One of the areas in which hybrid BCI could play an important role is smart home control. There have been several studies done in this field [12][46]. The smart home or virtual environment systems are consisting of several stages and several control command types in each stage. In motor control systems, hybrid BCI shows improvement in accuracy and facilitates control tasks. Control commands, have different characteristics, and are divided to different types. Based on the characteristics, for each type, special types of BCI would be appropriate and for combination of control commands, two or more BCI types would fit. In discrete control commands, the task is the selection of one option from several options. P300 and Mu-Beta are more appropriate for this type of control commands. For series of the commands, continuous commands, ERD and SSVEP are more suitable. Also other features of the conventional BCIs should be considered, e.g., P300 is a slow responded system, but reliable. Mu-beta is fast responded, but not as efficient as P300.

The main enhancement that has been made by hybrid BCI is improvement in the applicability of BCI systems. As presenting two or more BCI type to the user, in the simultaneously combination, the user has the chance to get more efficient respond through utilizing the BCI type that is more appropriate for him or her. It also can decrease the fatigue, as the user can shift to another BCI option. It is shown that the accuracy is improved in the hybrid condition [42][43].

In [39], the hybrid BCI is introduced for Functional Electrical Stimulation (FES) control. Two tasks were considered to be implemented by the BCI systems; selecting one object among three objects and movement imagination to trigger FES. The high true positive rate (TPR) for SSVEP and ERD shows the capability of hybrid BCI for implementing several tasks that can be used in various control fields. SSVEP switch was introduced for smart home control [12]. The selection of control options, displayed on the screen is based on P300 BCI and SSVEP is operated as toggle switch. SSVEP was introduced as a switch for P300-based system [13]

Another BCI that can be introduced as a brain switch is ERS. In [41], post-imagery beta ERS-based brain switch was introduced for activating and deactivating the process of opening and closing the orthosis hand which was operated using SSVEP BCI.

More studies have focused on the simultaneous combinations of the conventional BCIs. As for one task, two or more BCI type are presented at the same time, the difficulty and complexity of performing the task is increased but, on the other hand, the accuracy in most of the cases increases for majority of the users. In addition, the fatigue may decrease, as users can switch between the BCI types that may be more comfortable for them. Another parameter is BCI illiteracy that can be decrease as users have the opportunity of accessing multi approaches [35]. The task of tracking the hint arrow was presented by SSVEP and ERD, and the accuracy was improved in the hybrid condition [38].

In another type of hybrid, more than one source of measurement is presented for one BCI type, for example, EEG and NIRS were acquired simultaneously for the ERD-based BCI [43] EEG and ECG were fused for motor imagery (MI) based BCI system[48]. EEG and EMG were utilized as hybrid in [44]. In this hybrid BCI, improvement in accuracy was shown. In some application areas, the tasks may be divided to two or more parts and each part is implemented by one BCI or non-BCI system. In this way, based on the features of the task, the system is selected. For example, in [42] control commands were divided to two parts and were implemented by EEG and electrooculography (EOG).

One of the issues in hybrid BCIs is that the system may be feasible but not optimum in all features. The hybrid BCI may improve the performance or accuracy but not compared to each of conventional BCI systems. For example, in the simultaneous combination of SSVEP and ERD, as in the conventional SSVEP, the accuracy is enhanced compared to ERD-based BCI system but not a lot changes compared to SSVEP.

P300 and SSVEP BCI were introduced as hybrid in an asynchronous BCI system in [13]. It seems that P300 and SSVEP combination works well as the stimuli for evoking both patterns can be shown on one screen simultaneously. The P300 paradigm considered in this study is a 6x6 speller matrix based on the original P300 row/column paradigm introduced by Farwell and Donchin [19]. Only one frequency is allocated for SSVEP paradigm. Background color was flashed with the frequency slightly less than 18 Hz. This facilitates the SSVEP detection. During the classification, P300 and SSVEP signals are separated by a band pass filter. The SSVEP is utilized as a control state (CS) detection, in the way that, when the user is gazing at the screen, the SSVEP is detected and it is assumed that the user intends to send a command. The system detects P300 target selection and CS simultaneously.

For SSVEP detection, the mean power spectral density (PSD) in the narrow band near the desired frequency and the PSD in the wider range near the desired frequency were utilized in an objective function (these values were subtracted from each other and divided over the PSD value from the wide band) and the function value was compared to a specified threshold. During the data acquisition, the channels for acquiring EEG signal were not fixed for all subjects. For P300 classification, FLDA or BLDA was utilized [14][15]. The experiment was presented as offline and online test. Ten subjects participated in the experiment. Subjects had training runs. In offline test, forty characters were presented for detection, divided to four groups. For better evaluation of SSVEP effect, two groups with and two groups without SSVEP were presented. In control state, subjects were instructed to count the number of time they distinguish the highlighted character. In non-control state (NCS), subjects were instructed to do a mental task like multiplication of two numbers and relax with closed eyes. For four out of five subjects, the accuracy was improved inconsiderably during the presence of SSVEP and P300 detection was not determinate. Between ten characters detection, there was a break and the time of the break depends on the time subjects pressed a keyboard button, and an auditory cue alerted about the finish of NCS time. The average classification accuracy of 96.5% and control state detection accuracy of 88% with the ITR of 20 bits/min were achieved during the offline test. The online test was presented under the semi synchronous condition. The experiment was consisted of blocks with 5 rounds, for detecting each character. SSVEP detection for at least three out of five runs showed the control state detection by the subject and P300 was detected during the control state. If the control state was not detected, the '=' character was shown on the screen. The break time and the auditory alert was the same as offline test. The average control state detection accuracy of 88.15%, the classification accuracy of 94.44% and the ITR of 19.05 bits/min were achieved during the online test. P300 and SSVEP combination was also introduced to control smart home environment in [12]. P300-based BCI was used for controlling the virtual smart home environment and SSVEP was implemented as a switch for the P300 BCI operation. Results from this experiment show that P300 is suitable for discrete control commands and SSVEP is suitable for continuous control signals. The hybrid BCI achieved high accuracy and reliability in all subjects. In this chapter, P300, SSVEP and the hybrid P300 and SSVEP BCI systems were reviewed. The new trend and direction in BCI systems is to use new approaches in stimulating brain patterns such as hybrid BCIs while keeping the system complexity low and user acceptability high.

Author details

Setare Amiri, Ahmed Rabbi, Leila Azinfar and Reza Fazel-Rezai

Biomedical Image and Signal Processing Laboratory, Department of Electrical Engineering, University of North Dakota, Grand Forks, USA

References

[1] Wolpaw, J, Birbaumer, N, Mcfarland, D, Pfurtscheller, G, & Vaughan, T. Brain-computer interfaces for communication and control. Clinical neurophysiology (2002). , 113-767.

[2] Weiskopf, N, Veit, R, Erb, M, Mathiak, K, Grodd, W, Goebel, R, & Birbaumer, N. Physiological self-regulation of regional brain activity using real-time functional magnetic resonance imaging (fMRI): methodology and exemplary data. Neuroimage (2003). , 19-577.

[3] Waldert, S, Preissl, H, Demandt, E, Braun, C, Birbaumer, N, Aertsen, A, & Mehring, C. Hand movement direction decoded from MEG and EEG. The Journal of neuroscience (2008). , 28-1000.

[4] Coyle, S, Ward, T, Markham, C, & Mcdarby, G. On the suitability of near-infrared (NIR) systems for next-generation brain-computer interfaces. Physiological Measurement (2004).

[5] Pfurtscheller, G. and Lopes Da Silva FH. Event-related EEG/MEG synchronization and desynchronization: basic principles. Clinical Neurophysiology (1999). , 110(11), 1842-1857.

[6] Allison, B, Faller, J, & Neuper, C. H. BCIs that use steady state visual evoked potentials or slow cortical potentials. Brain-Computer Interfaces: Principles and Practice. Wolpaw and E. W. Wolpaw, Eds. Oxford University Press; (2012).

[7] Vidal, J. J. Toward direct brain-computer communication. Annual Review of Biophysics and Bioengineering (1973). , 2-157.

[8] Vidal, J. J. Real-time detection of brain events in EEG. Proceedings of the IEEE (1977). , 65(5), 633-64.

[9] Sellers, E, Arbel, Y, & Donchin, E. BCIs that uses event related potentials. Brain-Computer Interfaces: Principles and Practice. J. Wolpaw and E.W. Wolpaw, Eds. Oxford University Press; (2012). , 300.

[10] Birbaumer, N, Ghanayim, N, & Hinterberger, T. A spelling device for the paralysed. Nature (1999). , 398(6725), 297-298.

[11] Sanei, S, & Chambers, J. A. EEG Signal Processing. West Sussex: Wiley; (2007).

[12] Edlinger, G, Holzner, C, & Guger, C. A hybrid brain-computer interface for smart home control Human-Computer Interaction. Interaction Techniques and Environments (2011). , 417-426.

[13] Panicker, R, Puthusserypady, S, & Sun, Y. An Asynchronous BCI with SSVEP-Based Control State Detection. IEEE Transactions on Biomedical Engineering (2011). , 300.

[14] Hoffmann, U, Vesin, J. M, Ebrahimi, T, & Diseren, K. An efficient brain-computer interface for disabled subjects. Journal of neuroscience methods (2008). , 300.

[15] Krusienski, D J, Sellers, E. W, Cabestaing, F, Bayoudh, S, Mcfarland, D. J, Vaughan, T. M, & Wolpaw, J. R. A comparison of classification techniques for the speller. J. Neural ENG (2006). , 300.

[16] Anderson, T. W. An Intoduction to Multivariate Statistical Analysis. 2nd ed. New York: Wiley; (1984).

[17] Fazel-rezai, R, Allison, B. Z, Guger, C, Sellers, E. W, Kleih, S, & Kubler, A. P. brain computer interface: current challenges and emerging trends. Frontiers in Neuroengineering (2012). doi:fneng.2012.00014.

[18] Homan, R. W, Herman, J, & Purdy, P. Cerebral location of international 10-20 system electrode placement. Electroencephalogr Clin Neurophysiol (1987). , 66(4), 376-382.

[19] Farwell, L, & Donchin, E. Talking off the top of your head: toward a mental prosthesis utilizing event-related brain potentials. Electroencephalogr. Clin. Neurophysiol. (1988).

[20] Ryan, D, Frye, G, Townsend, G, Berry, D, Messa-g, S, Gates, N, & Sellers, E. Predictive spelling with a brain computer interface: increasing the rate of communication. Int. J. Hum. Comput. Interact. (2011). , 300.

[21] Fazel-rezai, R, Abhari, K, & Region-based, A. speller for brain-computer interface. Can J. Electr. Comput. Eng. (2009). , 300.

[22] Iturrate, I, Antelis, J. M, Kubler, A, & Minguez, J. A noninvasive brain-actuated wheelchair based on a neurophysiological protocol and automated navigation. IEEE Trans. Rob (2009). , 300.

[23] Ding, J, Sperling, G, & Srinivasan, R. Attentional modulation of SSVEP power depends on the network tagged by the flicker frequency. Cerebral Cortex (2006). , 16(7), 1016-1029.

[24] Regan, D. Steady-state evoked potentials. J Opt Soc Am (1977).

[25] Silberstein, R. B. Steady state visually evoked potential (SSVEP) topography in a graded working memory task. International journal of psychophysiology (2001).

[26] Wu, Z. Stimulator selection in SSVEP-based BCI. Medical engineering physics (2008).

[27] Gao, X, Xu, D, Cheng, M, & Gao, S. A BCI-based environmental controller for the motion-disabled. IEEE Trans. Neural Syst. Rehabil.Eng Jun. (2003). , 11(2), 137-140.

[28] Pastor, M. A. Human cerebral activation during steady-state visual-evoked responses. The Journal of neuroscience (2003).

[29] Middendorf, M. Brain-computer interfaces based on the steady-state visual-evoked response. IEEE Transactions on Rehabilitation Engineering (2000).

[30] Cheng, M. Ming Cheng. Design and implementation of a brain-computer interface with high transfer rates. IEEE Transactions on Biomedical Engineering (2002).

[31] Kelly, S. P, Lalor, E. C, Reilly, R. B, & Foxe, J. J. Visual spatial attention tracking using high-density SSVEP data for independent brain-computer communication. Neural Systems and Rehabilitation Engineering, IEEE Transactions on (2005). , 13(2), 172-178.

[32] Zhang, D, Gao, X, Gao, S, Engel, A. K, & Maye, A. An independent brain-computer interface based on covert shifts of non-spatial visual attention. Engineering in Medicine and Biology Society, 2009. EMBC (2009). Annual International Conference of the IEEE: IEEE; 2009.

[33] Treder, M. S, & Blankertz, B. Research (C) overt attention and visual speller design in an ERP-based brain-computer interface (2010).

[34] Bakardjian, H. Optimization of SSVEP brain responses with application to eight-command Brain-Computer Interface. Neurosci Lett (2010).

[35] Kubler, A, & Muller, K. R. An introduction to brain-computer interfacing Toward Brain-Computer Interfacing, Ed. Dornhedge G, Millan JR, Hinterberger T, McFarland DJ, and Muller KR (Cambridge, MA: MIT Press) ; , 2007-1.

[36] wwwscopus.com/scopus/home.url

[37] Pfurtscheller, G, Allison, B, Brunner, C, Bauernfeind, G, Solis-escalante, T, Scherer, T. O, Zander, R, Mueller-putz, G, Neuper, C, & Birbaumer, N. The hybrid BCI Frontiers in Neuroscience (2010).

[38] Allison, B, Brunner, C, Kaiser, V, Mueller-putz, G, Neuper, C, & Pfurtscheller, G. Toward a hybrid brain-computer interface based on imagined movement and visual attention Journal of Neural Engineering (2010).

[39] Savic, A, Kisic, U, & Popovic, M. Toward a Hybrid BCI for Grasp Rehabilitation in Proceedings of the 5th European Conference of the International Federation for Medical and Biological Engineering Proceedings (2012). , 806-809.

[40] Brunner, C, Allison, B, Altstätter, C, & Neuper, C. A comparison of three brain-computer interfaces based on event-related desynchronization, steady state visual evoked potentials, or a hybrid approach using both signals. Journal of neural engineering (2011).

[41] Pfurtscheller, G, Solis-escalante, T, Ortner, R, Linortner, P, & Muller-putz, G. Self-paced operation of an SSVEP-Based orthosis with and without an imagery-based ,brain switch: a feasibility study towards a hybrid BCI IEEE Transactions on Neural Systems and Rehabilitation Engineering (2010). , 18-409.

http://dx.doi.org/10.5772/56135

[42] Punsawad, Y, Wongsawat, Y, & Parnichkun, M. Hybrid EEG-EOG brain-computer interface system for practical machine control. IEEE Engineering in Medicine and Biology (2010). , 1360-1363.

[43] Fazli, S, Mehnert, J, Steinbrink, J, Curio, G, Villringer, A, Muller, K. R, & Blankertz, B. Enhanced performance by a hybrid NIRS-EEG brain computer interface Neuroimage (2011). , 59-519.

[44] Leeb, R. Sagha Chavarriaga R, and Millan JR. A hybrid brain-computer interface based on the fusion of electroencephalographic and electromyographic activities. Journal of Neural Engineering (2011).

[45] Redsamen B, Burdet E. Hybrid P300 and Mu-Beta brain computer interface to operate a brain controlled wheelchair. Proceedings of the 2nd International Convention on Rehabilitation Engineering & Assistive Technology: Singapore Therapeutic, Assistive & Rehabilitative Technologies (START) Centre; 2008.

[46] Su, Y, Qi, Y, Luo, J, Wu, B, Yang, F, Li, Y, et al. A hybrid brain-computer interface control strategy in a virtual environment. Journal of Zhejiang University-Science C (2011). , 12(5), 351-361.

[47] Riechmann, H, Hachmeister, N, Ritter, H, & Finke, A. Asynchronous, parallel on-line classification of and ERD for an efficient hybrid BCI. In IEEE Engineering in Medicine and Biology (2011). , 300.

[48] Shahid, S, Prasad, G, & Kumar, R. On fusion of heart and brain signals for hybrid BCI. Neural Engineering (NER), 2011 5th International IEEE/EMBS Conference on: IEEE; (2011).

Chapter 11

Review of Wireless Brain-Computer Interface Systems

Seungchan Lee, Younghak Shin, Soogil Woo,
Kiseon Kim and Heung-No Lee

Additional information is available at the end of the chapter

http://dx.doi.org/10.5772/56436

1. Introduction

Over the past two decades, the study of the Brain Computer Interfaces (BCI) has grown dramatically. According to Scopus search engine, a search result with the keyword "Brain Computer Interface" returns only two papers for year 1991. But, the same query returns 897 journals and conference papers for year 2011 (date of search: March 14, 2013). BCI systems provide a new communication channel to humans who use it. They measure neurophysiological signals of the human, electroencephalogram (EEG) in particular. EEG based BCI systems are designed to decode the intension of the human user and generate commands to control external devices or computer applications. The human can produce these commands by generating the neurophysiological signals intentionally. This process can become more successful – fast and accurate – through training and practice. This technology allows the users with new experiences which enable a direct communication between the human and the computers or external devices such as home appliances, and prosthetic devices.

The BCI systems consist of two parts, signal acquisition and translation (see page 7 Figure 2). The signal acquisition part contains electrodes, analog circuit and digital system for neurophysiological signal recording and transmission. The translation part is normally computing devices which are equipped with high performance processor such as laptops, PDAs, and smart phones. With an application program, this part performs algorithmic processes such as feature extraction and classification to convert the raw neurophysiological signals into computer readable messages. Depending on the type of connection between the two parts, we can divide BCI systems into two kinds, wired versus wireless BCI systems.

Many conventional BCI systems are wired. With just three electrodes positioned at the occipital lobe, the acquisition part of wired BCI systems generally comes with bulky and heavy amplifiers and preprocessing units. Connection wiring is usually complicated with a large number of cables between the electrodes and the acquisition part. For these reasons, preparation time for measuring EEG signals is typically very long. In addition, user's movement is limited due to cable constraints. Therefore, the application of BCI systems is difficult to escape from laboratory scale experiments. These restrictions make the types of applications for which BCI systems can be made useful be severely limited. Wireless BCI systems are to eliminate the wire connection, between the signal acquisition and the translation part, with the use of a wireless transmission unit such as Bluetooth and Zigbee modules. Removing wire connections, portability of BCI systems is greatly improved. Postures and movements of users wearing the acquisition part of wireless BCI systems are also unimpeded. These desirable aspects of wireless BCI systems promote to go beyond a laboratory scale experiments and to develop everyday-life applications.

With portable wireless BCI systems, various real-life applications are under development now. In the early days of BCI researches, cursor control and speller applications were developed mainly targeted for helping the disabled people. Recently, with growing interest, wireless BCI systems have been applied in entertainments as well. For example, Emotiv and Neurosky companies have recently released their wireless BCI headsets for entertainment uses such as brain gaming and mind monitoring. Moreover, international research groups have applied wireless BCI systems for interesting new applications such as home automation system based on monitoring human physiological states [29], cellular phone dialing [28], and drowsiness detection for drivers [19][20][32].

In this book chapter, we will review recent research trends in wireless BCI systems. In Section 2, we summarize several research topics in wireless BCI systems such as electrodes, embedded systems, user-friendly designs, and novel applications. We then take a closer look into emerging wireless BCI systems designed by BCI researchers, and discuss general BCI systems recently introduced into the market in Section 3. In Section 4, we discuss current challenges and possible future research directions on wireless BCI systems. Finally, we provide concluding remarks in Section 5.

2. Research trends of wireless BCI systems

Wireless brain computer interface (BCI) systems are neurophysiological signal acquisition and processing systems where acquired physiological signals are wirelessly transmitted to the translation unit. Wireless systems, unlike their traditional wired counterparts, are designed to provide convenience in monitoring the neurophysiological signals of users.

Compared to conventional wired BCI systems, wireless BCI systems provide enhanced portability and wearability, facilitated by elimination of the wire connections between the wearable acquisition unit and the translation unit. The translation unit is usually housed in a portable device such as laptops and smart phones. This improvement provides an easy installation process and freedom of postures for users. Furthermore, owing to advanced integrated circuit designs, the components of the wireless BCI systems are small in sizes and efficient in power consumption. Employing these components, the acquisition part of wireless BCI systems can be miniaturized. These advantages allow wireless BCI systems to be shaped in user friendly styles such as baseball caps [14][19][21][29], headsets [16][17][23][25][27], and headbands [18][20][22][28][30][32]; thus, applying them in various applications such as entertainments and health care becomes easier than ever before.

Even though wireless BCI systems may provide a number of advantages, there are still many issues that need to be resolved including improving signal quality, more compact and stylish system designs, and excavation of useful applications. First, the quality of the measured EEG signals has to be improved for more precise classification of user's intensions. The measured EEG signals are easily contaminated by various noise sources such as the presence of other physiological signals and the power line noise. Moreover, various impediments exist in electrodes-scalp interfaces such as hairs, sweat, and stratum corneum of skin [6]. These obstacles cause deleterious effects in signal measurements with high leakage currents and high contact impedances. Due to these difficulties, EEG signals get easily corrupted and the quality of measured signals is often undesirable. Consequentially, these factors lead to drop of application accuracy. Second, stylish, miniaturized and light weight wireless BCI systems are necessary for daily life application and long-term wearing. Conventional wired BCI systems are bulky, not user-friendly in system appearances because of their complicated connection between electrodes and signal acquisition part. Multi-channel electrode installation is also inconvenient and time-consuming, usually taking more than 30 minutes. Thus, the users are easily irritated and long-term monitoring becomes difficult. Third, killer applications are needed. Many researchers and developers introduced various applications related to entertainments and health care. But such contributions are still not enough to make any fundamental change in our life.

To help these issues, research groups are paying attention to the following aspects:

1. Advanced electrodes for measuring clean EEG signals

2. Low-power, miniaturized, portable and wearable BCI systems

3. A *killer* application, an application of such a great value and popularity that it assures the success of the BCI technology.

In this section, we aim to analyze the current status of research and development efforts in these directions.

2.1. New electrodes for EEG signal acquisition

Among the above research topics, the development of advanced EEG electrodes which measure brain signals precisely with low noise is the most important challenge. Practically, the signal acquisition part of general wireless BCI systems only contains a signal acquisition circuit and a micro-processor based embedded system for transmission of the measured EEG signals. For example, a well-known Emotiv EPOC neuro-headset is composed of 14 channel electrodes and a small integrated embedded system powered by an onboard battery for signal conditioning and transmission. In the translation part of wireless BCI systems, analysis of acquired signals is performed either online or offline on a computer or a mobile device which is equipped with high-performance processors. For this segregated structure to work well, signal acquisition part of a wireless BCI system should be devoted to high fidelity signal recording. To provide clear EEG signal acquisition at the electrode-skin interface, development of outstanding electrodes becomes a critical issue. For this reason, many research groups have recently been interested in developing advanced electrodes which can provide low-noise recording, convenience in installation, and comfort even in long-term wearing.

In conventional wired BCI systems, passive electrodes are widely used to measure EEG signals. Generally, these electrodes are disc or ring shaped and are made of Ag/AgCl alloy [10]. Due to their simple structure, it is easy to make them small. However, they have many disadvantages as well. Extra treatments are essential for recording reliable EEG signals because the scalp potentials are only on the order of several micro-volts and thus very noise-sensitive. Treatments are needed, including a hair preparation step and the use of conductive gels or glues for better attachment and higher conductivity. These preparations induce discomfort and require long preparation time. Furthermore, the conductive gels easily desiccate and lose their adhesion. These problems bring about worse contact impedances at electrode-scalp interfaces, causing a large reduction of signal-to-noise ratio. In addition, the quality of recorded signals is sensitive to cable vibrations [17]. For these reasons, the long-term monitoring of EEG signals using passive electrodes is not feasible.

Recently, to overcome the weaknesses of passive electrodes, many researchers have studied advanced electrodes. For examples, research of dry electrodes is active recently. Generally, dry electrodes are defined as those that do not require the use of conductive gels or glues for installation process. Thus, a user can conveniently attach the electrodes to the user's scalp without any hair arrangement. To make dry contact at the electrode-skin interface, researchers employ special materials or shapes in the design of dry electrodes. Extensive research has produced a huge variety of electrode materials and structures, including conductive rubber [8][9], conductive carbon nanotubes [7], micro-tip structures [6], micro-machined structures [14][15][20], non-contact types [4][5], spring-loaded fingers [2][13], bristle structures [3], and conductive foams [27]. The most widely used dry electrode design is a set of contact posts which look like fingers [13][16]. This design has an advantage in contact ability because it is easy to penetrate into the scalp through the hair without an extended hair arrangement. Recently, some research groups have altered this finger design to produce advanced mechanical designs, such as spring-loaded fingers [2] or bristle structures [3]. These designs seem to provide flexibility and geometric adaptation between the sensor and the irregular scalp surface to obtain low interface impedance. To achieve low contact impedance and provide a robust and stable electrical interface, some research groups have employed multi-walled carbon nanotube arrays [7] and micro-tip structures [6], which are able to penetrate the outer skin layer (which is 5 to10 um thick and called the *stratum corneum*).

While we can reduce the installation time significantly using dry electrodes, the contact impedance between the scalp and the electrodes is higher than that with gel-based passive electrodes due to the absence of conductive gels. Thus, signal quality of dry electrodes would be not better than that of the gel-based passive electrodes. To overcome this draw-

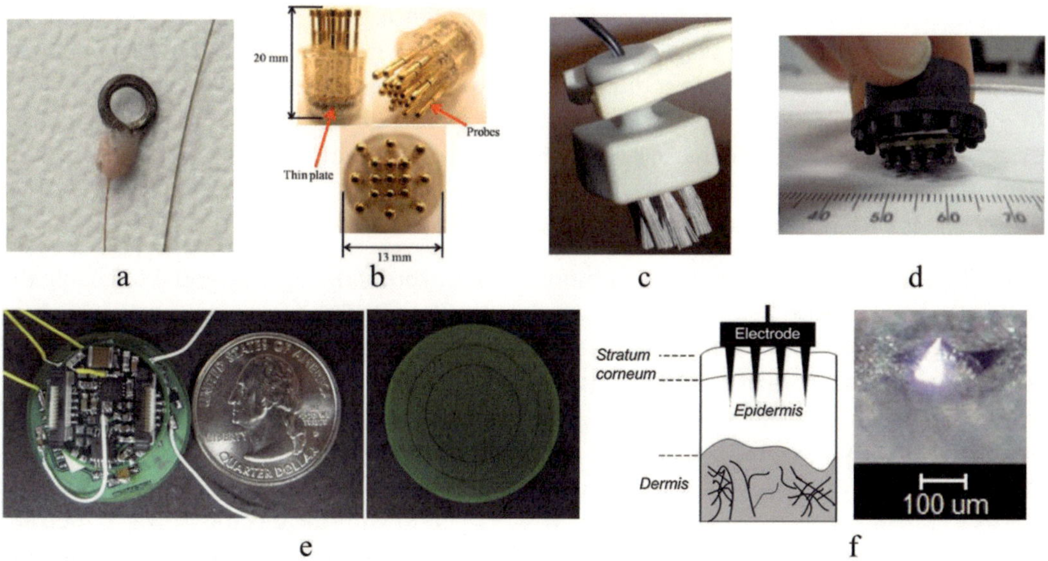

Figure 1. Various EEG electrode types. (a) a miniature passive ring electrode [10] (b) a spring-loaded dry electrode [2] (c) a bristle-type dry electrode [3] (d) the Quasar hybrid EEG biosensor [11] (e) a non-contact-type active dry EEG sensor [4] (f) Diagram of a micro-tip electrode and the pyramidal shape of a micro-tip [6].

back, many research groups have been interested in active electrodes. Active electrodes contain amplifier or buffer circuits integrated to the electrodes themselves [1][4][5][7][11][12][13]. This amplifier or buffer circuits are located between the electrodes and the signal acquisition frontend. They are aimed at impedance conversion. Providing high input impedance on the electrode-amplifier interface, active circuits reduce the distortion of the measured signals. This is desired for dry electrodes which do not use conductive fluids. Also, the low output impedance of the amplifier eliminates artifacts caused by posture changes in mobile environments. Therefore, the quality of measured physiological signals can be remained in a desirable state by the use of active electrodes.

Recent wireless BCI systems are equipped with active dry electrodes to combine the advantages of active and dry electrodes such as convenient installation and high fidelity signals. Because these electrodes provide more robust and stable signal quality in mobile environments, they are suitable for wireless BCI systems. Researchers working on the development of advanced electrodes have produced a variety of active dry electrodes. Valchinov *et al.* designed body surface electrodes equipped with a biopotential amplifier using two op-amps [1]. Matthews *et al.* designed an ambulatory wireless EEG system using Quasar hybrid biosensors [11][12][13]. In this type of sensors, they employ a special circuit which uses the common mode follower (CMF) technology. This technology provides an ultra-high input impedance to ensure low distortion of the biopotential signals. Chi *et al.* designed and built dry and non-contact electrodes [5]. In their dry electrodes, a unity gain buffer is used to reduce the effects of cable artifacts and external interference. Their non-contact electrodes also integrate discrete circuits to achieve high input impedance. To further optimize the size and power consumption of such electrodes, some researchers have employed customized ASIC designs for amplifiers. Xu *et al.* produce a low-power 8-channel active electrode system [17]. In this system, to reduce the power consumption of voltage buffers in dry electrodes, they designed active electrodes including ASICs based on chopper instrumentation amplifiers.

2.2. Wireless BCI system design and structure

In EEG-based wireless BCI systems, additional signal conditioning is essential to enable the transmission of precise neurophysiological signals. Many noise sources are present such as physiological interferences and power line noise. Physiological interferences are the other biopotential signals such as electromyogram (EMG), electrocardiogram (ECG), and electrooculogram (EOG). They have relatively lager amplitudes around 50uV and up to 20-30mV while the amplitude of EEG signals is much smaller on the scale of roughly 10~100uV. Thus, the EEG signals are easily buried by these physiological signals unavoidably. In the case that the BCI system is connected to a desktop which operate with the electric power outlet, we also have to consider the power line noise as well. The power line noise contaminates the desired EEG signals in the range of 50 or 60Hz. Furthermore, the users of portable wireless BCI systems are usually in an active state making free motions and postures, whereas the users of wired BCI system are asked to stay in a motionless state, while their EEG signals are monitored. Therefore, the measured EEG signals of wireless BCI systems are also subject to heavy motion and vibration artifacts.

To avoid interference from the various noise components and recognize the user's intention correctly, the system must be designed carefully. Figure 2 is the general block diagram of a typical wireless BCI system. In EEG acquisition block of the system, there are two main parts, namely, the analog front end circuit and the digital system.

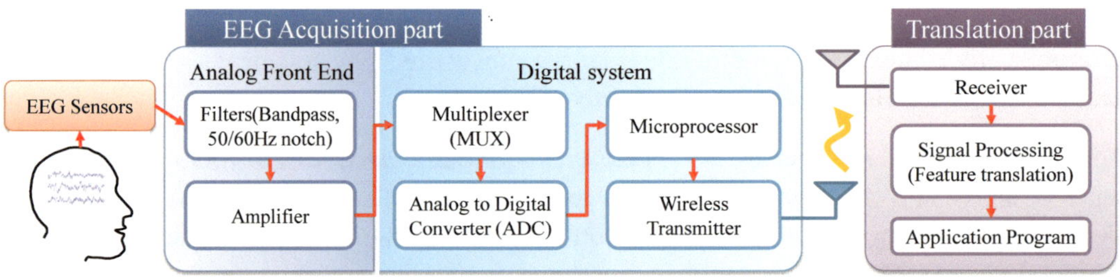

Figure 2. Block diagram of a typical wireless BCI system

In the analog front-end stage, the amplifier and bandwidth limiter circuits are included to make more robust and reliable EEG signals from the sensitive raw signals. Because the amplitude of EEG signals is quiet small, the pre-amplification of the measured EEG signals at the analog front end is extremely important. In this amplification process, many developed wireless BCI systems use operational amplifiers or instrumentation amplifiers. Those amplifiers normally provide a gain ranging from thousands to hundreds of thousands. Amplification with high gain provides greater robustness against a variety of noise sources. However, we need to determine a suitable amplification gain to maximize the signal resolution in the analog digital converter (ADC) because the ADC has a restricted input dynamic range. Therefore, the amplification gain of the analog front end varies depending on the components of the digital system.

We also need a frequency filtering procedure to remove various noise components. The EEG signals occupy a narrow bandwidth: normally from 0.1Hz to less than 50 Hz. Thus, filtering is helpful for extracting useful signals from the desired frequency bands. To filter out signals from useless frequency bands, the analog front-end of the system takes both a low-pass filter and a high-pass filter. Especially to filter out the power line noise, a notch filter which eliminates the specific frequency components of signals is also applied in this stage. Those filtering processes are performed using passive or active filtering circuits [24][26].

In the digital system stage, four integrated circuits are included: a multiplexer, an ADC, a microprocessor, and a wireless transmission unit. Generally, most EEG-based wireless BCI systems support multi-channel recording. To measure multi-channel signals simultaneously, a multiplexer is needed to access all of the channels. Because the measured EEG signals are analog signals, an ADC has to be included to process the recorded EEG data on the digital circuits. This integrated circuit transforms the EEG analog signals into discrete digitized data with a specific sampling frequency. The sampling frequency is determined by the speed of the microprocessor, wireless transmission, and translated frequencies of EEG features. Formally, researchers and system developers choose the sampling frequency between about 100 Hz and 1000 Hz. The microprocessor makes data packets from the corrected EEG data and hands them over to the wireless transmission unit. The microprocessor also manages the components of the entire system. Some wireless BCI systems load the feature extraction algorithm on the microprocessor to process the EEG signals internally [19][20][21][29][30]. Because the recorded multichannel EEG data is transmitted from the portable EEG acquisition device to the host system, the wireless transmission unit is essential. Regarding the protocol of wireless transmissions, various communication modules are employed for transmission of the measured signals from the signal acquisition unit to the translation unit, such as Bluetooth and IEEE 802.15.4 Zigbee. Bluetooth has many advantages such as sufficient transmission rates and wide accessibility. Thus, many wireless BCI systems employ this transmission module. Including analog front-end and digital system stage, the acquisition unit of wireless BCI systems generally operates onboard power sources such as Li-ion, Li-polymer, and NiMH batteries.

Because the analog front-end and digital system parts have to be loaded in portable and wearable acquisition part of wireless BCI systems, longer operation time and small size are necessary in system specifications. Thus, system developers should choose low-power components with smaller packages. Recently, many semiconductor manufacturers have released low-power microprocessors and integrated analog front end circuits for bio-potential measurements. For example, Texas Instruments released the ADS129x series integrated circuit solutions [34] for the analog front end of ECG/EEG applications. This series provides up to 8-channel high-resolution ADCs and a built-in programmable gain amplifier (PGA) with low noise and low power consumption features. In the microprocessor area, various ultra-low power processors have been released on the market for portable devices. The most widely used microprocessors are the PIC24 microcontroller series [35], the dsPIC digital signal controller series [36] (manufactured by Microchip Technology) and the MSP430 microcontroller series [37] (manufactured by Texas Instruments). In particular, the dsPIC processor series is applied as the processing unit of the Emotiv EPOC system [38].

Regarding the design approach of system appearance, a variety of designs have been adopted depending on the application purpose and target users. Widely used styles of the acquisition part of wireless BCI systems include headsets [16][17][23][25][27], head bands [18][20][22][28][30][32], baseball caps [14][19][21][29], and military helmets [13]. In designing the appearance of wireless BCI systems, we need to consider several factors, such as wearability, stability, and convenience of installation. To provide long-term monitoring capability, wearable part of wireless BCI systems has to be light with comfort fitting. Also, convenient installation is necessary to save time in the set up process. Appropriate pressures are also needed to maintain stable electrode positions and low impedance characteristics at the sensor-skin interfaces. Additionally, to allow for the diversity of users' head sizes, the materials used in wireless BCI systems should be flexible, or size adjusters must be added. Various designs of wireless BCI systems are shown in Figure 3.

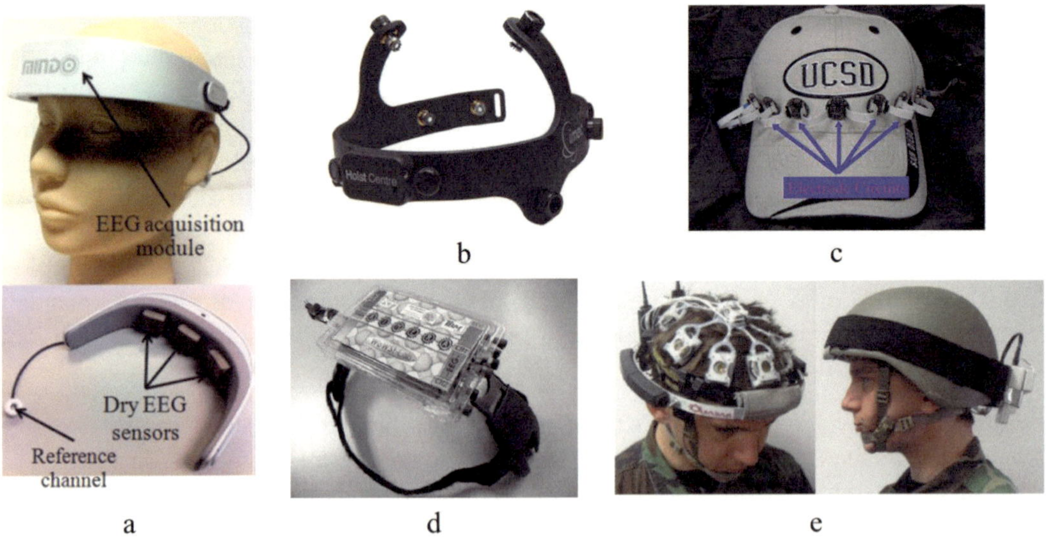

Figure 3. Various designs of wireless BCI systems: (a) wearable EEG acquisition headset [27], (b) 8-channel EEG monitoring headset [16], (c) baseball cap-based EEG acquisition device [14], (d) wireless EEG system for SSVEP application [25], and (e) soldier's Kevlar helmet-based ambulatory wireless EEG system for real-time workload classification [13].

2.3. Signal features and applications

In EEG-based BCI systems, they translate the specific signal features that reflect the user's intentions or cognitive states into commands or feedback signals for controlling of the target applications. For these operations, BCI systems analyze and capture the user's intensions based on detection of ERPs [33] or power spectra changes in specific brain rhythms.

Most research groups have focused on sensorimotor rhythms (SMRs) [39] and event related potentials (ERPs) [40], including visual evoked potentials (VEPs) such as P300 [41] and steady-state visual evoked potentials (SSVEP) [42]. The SMRs are spontaneous responses which can be actively generated by motor imageries, such as the left hand, the right hand, or the foot movements measured by electrodes placed on the scalp over the sensorimotor cortex area. These rhythms appear as suppression or enhancement of the power spectra, called event-related desynchronization (ERD) and event-related synchronization (ERS). The VEPs are behavioral responses which are passively synchronized by the frequency of flickering visual stimulus from the occipital lobe. Because the SMRs and VEPs reflect the user's intensions, we can utilize them as a means to control commands in applications. Moreover, various cognitive states are also studied, such as drowsiness, alertness, and mental focusing [27][29][30][32]. These cognitive states are related to the power changes of specific rhythms, called alpha, beta, theta rhythms and so on. Several studies have shown that the power of the alpha rhythm has a negative relationship with mental concentration [27][29][30]. Also, researchers have found that when subjects feel sleepy or fall into a deep sleep, the power spectra of alpha and theta bands change depending on these drowsiness conditions [29][30][32]. Using these relationships, the BCI systems detect the user's cognitive states and provide feedbacks such as focusing indicator [27] and sleep warning [32].

Among the signal features mentioned above, many researchers have chosen VEPs or users' cognitive states as a means for BCI based controls. The reason is that these features are easy to generate and provide good accuracy in the application of BCI systems. Also, the features of VEPs and cognitive state make it easy to classify users' intentions with a relatively simple feature extraction method, and a small number of electrodes and training session are needed to achieve higher accuracy. Compared with ERPs like VEPs, the SMRs can be generated by voluntary imagination, such as motor imagery, generally require long-term training to achieve higher accuracy in BCI applications. Furthermore, approximately 30% of normal people cannot generate SMRs due to the phenomenon of BCI illiteracy [43].

In the application parts of BCI systems a variety of promising rehabilitation-related applications have already been developed with EEG-based wired BCI systems. Because BCI systems measure and analyze neurophysiological signals, these systems provide practical assistance for patient diagnosis, treatment, and rehabilitation. For example, using BCI systems, long-term monitoring of EEG signals assists the diagnosis of epilepsy and the prediction of epileptic seizures [44]. For people with severe motor disabilities, the P300 speller [41] and wheelchair control [45] applications provide practical assistance in everyday life by providing non-muscular motor functions.

In spite of these useful applications, the dissemination of BCI systems is limited because of the drawbacks of wired BCI systems. Wired BCI systems are generally bulky, complicated, and expensive. Also, the users of wired BCI systems are confined to a limited space without freedom of postures and movements. To overcome these limitations, wired BCI systems are gradually being replaced with the wireless BCI systems.

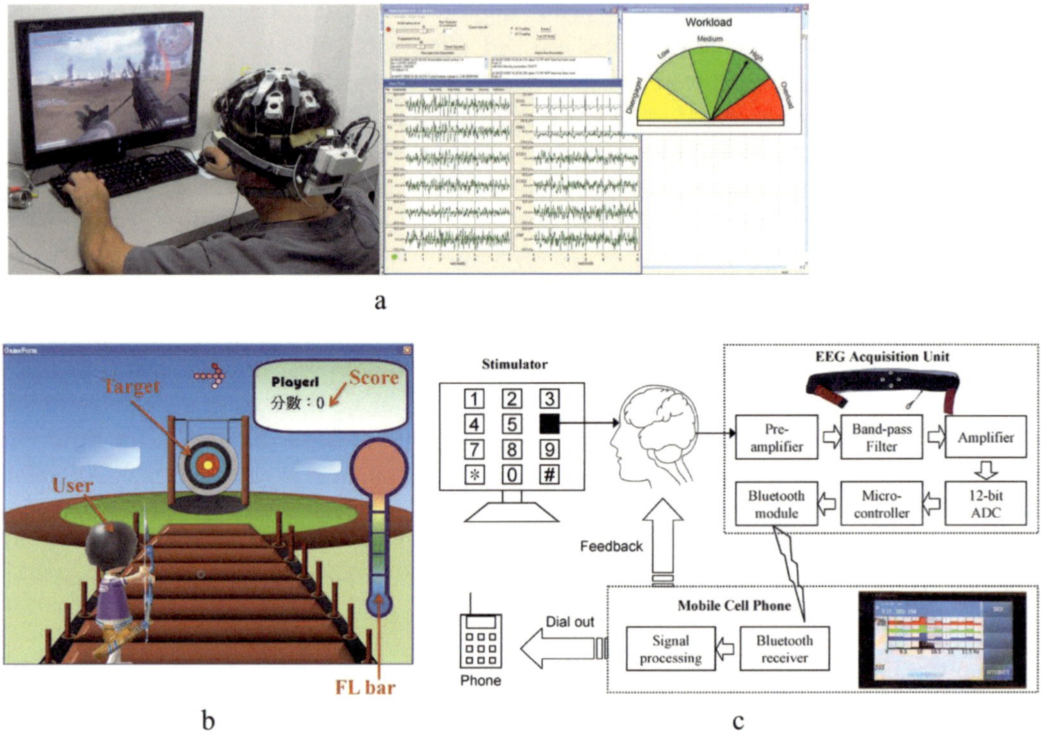

Figure 4. Applications of wireless BCI systems: (a) workload classification application screenshot (data collection and engagement classifier running on the gaming subject) [13], (b) EEG-based BCI archery game screenshot [27], and (c) SSVEP-based dialing application using smart phone [28].

Recently, with the development of wireless BCI systems, researchers have shifted their focus from applications for disabled people to applications of interest to the general public in the entertainment, smart living environment, and cognitive neuroscience areas. In the entertainment area, Liao *et al.* developed an EEG-based gaming interface based on a real-time focusing detection algorithm with a wireless EEG acquisition device [27]. For smart living environment, Lin *et al.* developed an environmental auto-control system based on human physiological states, such as drowsiness and alertness [29][30]. Similarly, Guge *et al.* developed a smart home control system based on P300 EEG response [31]. For mobile applications, Wang *et al.* developed a cellular phone dialing application [28]. In cognitive state monitoring, D'Arcy *et al.* developed a diagnostic device which provides an evaluation of an individual's conscious awareness based on various ERP components [33]. In this research, they found that sensation, perception, attention, memory, and language are properly related with the P1, mismatch negativity (MMN), P300 (tones), P300 (speech), and N400 responses. Also, Matthews *et al.* developed a real-time workload classification system during subject motion with a compact ambulatory wireless EEG system [13]. Figure 4 shows application examples of wireless BCI systems.

3. Review of wireless BCI systems

Over the past 20 years, many research achievements associated with BCI and the neurosciences have been made and they have helped stimulate the interest of the general public. Owing to the advances in wireless BCI systems, bulky wired biopotential acquisition systems have been replaced with portable and wearable devices. Following this trend, the number of published papers with the topic of wireless BCI systems and (their) applications is being continuously increased. A few commercial companies have developed and released portable wireless EEG acquisition systems with interesting new entertainment applications. Now, measuring brain activity is no longer limited to hospital-based medical diagnostics, but includes more courageous applications aiming at changing the lifestyle of users. In this section, we aim to first review several wireless BCI systems which have appeared in recent research articles. Second, we will introduce several examples of wireless BCI systems which have been lately released into the market for consumer and research usages.

3.1. Wireless BCI systems in scientific papers

In the research field, many research articles have been published in the last decade with the topic of wireless BCI systems. There are some distinct features in them such as the use of dry electrodes and novel applications which we are interested in reviewing in this subsection. For example, see the wireless BCI systems listed in Table 1. This table shows system specifications such as the number of channels and operation hours. They are all wireless and wearable systems, some aiming for applications that average people can find useful, including drowsiness detection and workload monitoring. Specifications for each system are optimized for its own target application.

In what follows, we will briefly review each of the system listed in Table 1

3.1.1. Wireless BCI system for archery game control

Recently, utilizing wireless BCI systems, the number of game applications has been increased. For example, Liao *et al.* [27] have developed an EEG based BCI device for an archery game control. This device is designed as a user friendly headset (see Figure 3 (a)) and equipped with three channels, each channel with a dry EEG sensor. For the control of archery game, the sensors measure the power of alpha rhythm collected off of user's forehead when a user concentrates on a target. This power value is converted to a measure of focusing intensity in real time. Any user can test out the level of one's concentration effort using

Reference	Liao et al., 2012 [27]	Yu Mike Chi et al., 2012 [5]	Nuno Sérgio Diasa et al., 2012 [6]	Chin-Teng Lin et al., 2010 [20]	R. Matthews et al., 2008 [13]	Lindsay Brown et al., 2010 [16]
Signal features	Mental focusing feature	SSVEP	Not mentioned	Alpha and Theta rhythms	Cognitive state (workload)	Not mentioned
Application	Archery game control	Neuro-feedback	Not mentioned	Drowsiness detection	Workload monitoring	Not mentioned
Sensor type	Dry foam-based EEG sensor	Dry and noncontact electrodes	Micro tip dry electrodes	Not mentioned	Finger type hybrid biosensor	Dry electrode with contact post
# of channels	3 channels	Not mentioned	5 channels	3 channels	7 channels EEG, ECG, EMG, EOG 2 channels	8 channels
Frontend processing unit	TI MSP430	Microchip PIC24F	Atmel Atmega128	TI MSP430	Not mentioned	TI MSP430 and ASIC
Backend processing unit	PC	Nokia N97 cellular phone	PC	ADSP-BF533 embedded processor	Laptop	Not mentioned
Transmission protocol	Bluetooth v2.0 +EDR	Bluetooth	Bluetooth	Bluetooth v. 2.0+EDR	Bluetooth	2.4GHz
Signal resolution and sampling rate	12bit, 256Hz	24 bit	16bit, 1kHz	12bit, 512Hz	16bit, 240Hz for EEG	11bit, 256 ~ 1024Hz
Power source and operation time	23 hours with a 3.7v 750mAh Li-ion battery	10 hours with 2 AAA batteries	25 hours using 2 AA batteries	33 hours with a 3.7v 1.1Ah Li-Ion battery	80 hours with 2 AAA batteries	30 hours with a 3.7v 140mAh Li-Ion battery
Design	Headset with elastic band	Not mentioned	Brain cap	Headband	Soldier helmet	Headset

Table 1. Comparison of wireless BCI systems in scientific articles

this game (see Figure 4 (b)). If a user maintains for a certain period a high level of concentration state, for example, the arrow will hit the center of target.

3.1.2. Mobile BCI using dry and noncontact EEG sensors

These days, smart phones come with high performance processors. They can be useful for wireless EEG monitoring. In [5], Yu Mike Chi *et al.* have developed a wireless BCI device based on smart phones. They have developed an smartphone application with a GUI interface for signal monitoring and analysis. They have tested two types of electrodes, dry and noncontact EEG sensors. Dry sensors consist of several spring-loaded electrodes, each comes with a finger post and a unity gain buffer. Noncontact electrodes employ CMOS amplifiers to improve their impedance performance. Both electrodes offer easy installation and good signal quality.

3.1.3. Wireless BCI system based on dry electrodes with a needle-shape structure

As mentioned in Section 2, novel electrode design is important part in wireless BCI systems. In [6], Nuno Sérgio Dias *et al.* have developed a wireless EEG acquisition system with novel dry electrodes. For the electrode design, they have employed 16 micro tip structures each looks like a needle (see Figure 1 (f)). They are designed to make direct contacts with electrolyte fluids of the inner skin layers of the scalp. Therefore, signal quality is satisfactory without the use of conductive gels. The proposed system consists of an EEG brain cap with five dry electrodes, an acquisition device which is attached to the brain cap, and a wireless base station connected with a computer. The acquisition device can operate for 25 hours with two AA batteries.

3.1.4. Design of wireless BCI system for drowsiness detection

Wireless BCI systems can be utilized in practical applications such as house control system [29][30][31] and drowsiness detection system [20] for drivers. In [20], Chin-Teng Lin *et al.* have proposed a real-time wireless EEG-based BCI system for drowsiness detection and shown usefulness in providing sleep alerts to a driver in car driving simulation. They have designed a wireless signal acquisition module and a signal processing module. The acquisition module is small enough to be embedded into a wearable headband. These modules are linked with each other via a Bluetooth connection. Therefore, it provides the advantages of mobility and long-term monitoring (more than 33 hours with a 1100-mA Li-Ion battery). Also, they have developed a real-time drowsiness detection algorithm. The algorithm detects the user's drowsiness by analyzing the theta rhythm and the alpha rhythm of the EEG signals.

3.1.5. Ambulatory wireless BCI system for real time workload classification

A compact, lightweight, and ultra-low power ambulatory wireless BCI system has been developed in [13]. This system consists of soldier's helmet with biosensors and a data acquisition unit (see Figure 3 (e)). They use Quasar hybrid biosensors which are equipped with dry electrodes shaped like a set of fingers (see Figure 1 (d)). This system provides high freedom of motions with data quality as good as that of wet electrodes. They have also developed a real time classifier for determination of the cognitive workload of a user.

3.1.6. Design of wireless EEG monitoring headset

In [16], Lindsay Brown *et al.* have introduced a design of wireless EEG monitoring headset. This headset is equipped with the 8-channel dry electrodes as shown in Figure 3 (b). Each electrode is designed with contact posts which are coated with Ag/AgCl for easy penetration into the user's hairs. Each electrode is connected to its electrode housing via a magnetic ball and a socket for tilting and vertical movement of electrodes. They have employed an 8-channel EEG acquisition application-specific integrated circuit (ASIC) into which preamplifiers are embedded for low power consumption. This system can operate for long time over 30 hours using a 140 mAh Li-Ion battery.

3.2. Wireless BCI systems for consumer use

In the market of consumer-grade wireless BCI systems, there are many commercial companies such as Emotiv, Neurosky, MyndPlay, PLX devices, and OCZ technology. These companies have competitively released their own wireless BCI systems along with various applications related to gaming, utilities, and mental-state monitoring. In this section, we review these wireless BCI devices for consumer use shown in Figure 5.

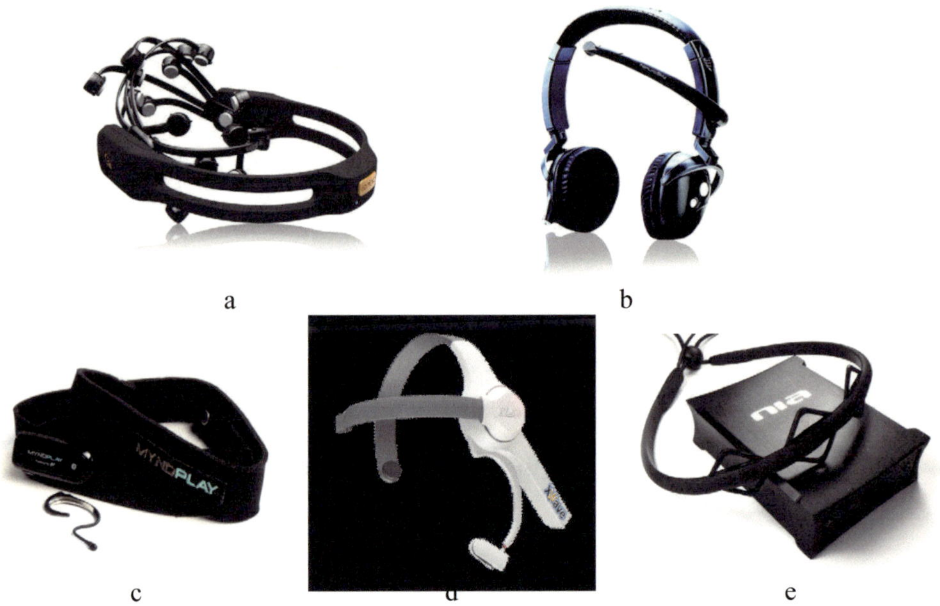

Figure 5. Pictures of Wireless BCI systems for consumer use: (a) Emotive EPOC headset [38], (b) NeuroSky Mind Set [46], (c) MyndPlay Brainband [50], (d) PLX devices XWave headset [49], (e) OCZ Neural Impulse Actuator [51].

The device released by Emotiv is the EPOC headset. The EPOC headset [38] is a multi-channel wireless BCI system. This headset is equipped with 14 saline-based wet-contact resistive electrodes for measuring EEG, Electrooculogram (EOG), and facial Electromyogram (EMG). Additionally, the EPOC headset also has a 2-axis gyroscope for measuring the head rotation. Employing 2.4GHz wireless connectivity, this system provides wide accessibility for devices such as PCs, laptops, and smart phones. The package of the EPOC headset provides a bundle software which contains a suite of built-in signal processing algorithms for interpretation of EEG signals. The built-in algorithms discern the user's conscious intentions, emotional states, and facial expressions based on measured EEG, Electromyogram (EMG) and Electrooculogram (EOG) signals. Through this software, the users can interact with various applications related to virtual reality, game controlling, and brain state monitoring. These applications can be downloaded by accessing their web site.

The Neurosky Mind Set [46] is a wireless headset added with an EEG signal acquisition unit. This headset is equipped with earphones and a microphone, and a single dry-contact electrode for measuring the user's EEG signals on the user's forehead. Along with the capability of raw EEG recording, the Mind Set has the patented algorithm, named as eSense [47]. This algorithm interprets the user's mental states such as attention and meditation. These translations are estimated by monitoring the power levels in specific frequency bands such as alpha, beta and theta rhythms. The monitoring values of the brain state are utilized for making a control commands in applications.

The MyndPlay and the PLX devices are released with their own model of wireless BCI systems. MyndPlay Brainband [50] and PLX devices XWave [49] headset utilizes the ThinkGear Application-Specific Integrated Circuit (ASIC) module [48]. This module, designed by Neurosky, is a system-on-chip integrated circuit equipped with signal acquisition components. These devices come in a headset or a harness style. They have supported the control of various applications such as media player, cognitive state visualization, and arcade games for PC and mobile devices.

OCZ technology, a PC component manufacturer such as solid-state drives (SSD) and power supplies, has released a game controller by utilizing an wireless BCI technology. The name of this controller is Neural Impulse Actuator (NIA) [51]. Using NIA, the users can control a PC game by translating facial expressions, eye movements, and concentrated brainwave activity, instead of using traditional input devices such as a keyboard and a mouse. This device now supports various PC games including shooting, role playing, virtual worlds, and racing.

3.3. Wireless BCI systems for research uses

Wireless BCI systems have many advantages, such as freedom of user's postures and convenient installation. Therefore, wireless BCI systems are useful in the research field as well. Some companies have been involved in research with universities and research institutes to develop wireless BCI systems for research uses. They include, but not limited to, Advanced Brain Monitoring, Quasar, Starlab and Guger technologies (G.tec). In this subsection, we review their wireless BCI systems, as shown in Figure 6.

Advanced Brain Monitoring has recently released the B-Alert X series wireless EEG systems [52] for mobile neurophysiological data acquisition and analysis. These systems include three models that have different numbers of channels, i.e., 4, 10, and 24. Among these models, the B-Alert X24 system is equipped with 24 channel electrodes for biopotential measurements, such as EEG, Electrocardiogram (ECG), Electromyogram (EMG), and Electrooculogram (EOG). This system measures and delivers real-time EEG signals via a Bluetooth connection. The system provides more than 8 hours of operation time and less than 10 minutes of installation time. Also, this system supports a variety of applications such as drowsiness, cognitive workload, and neuro-dynamics monitoring.

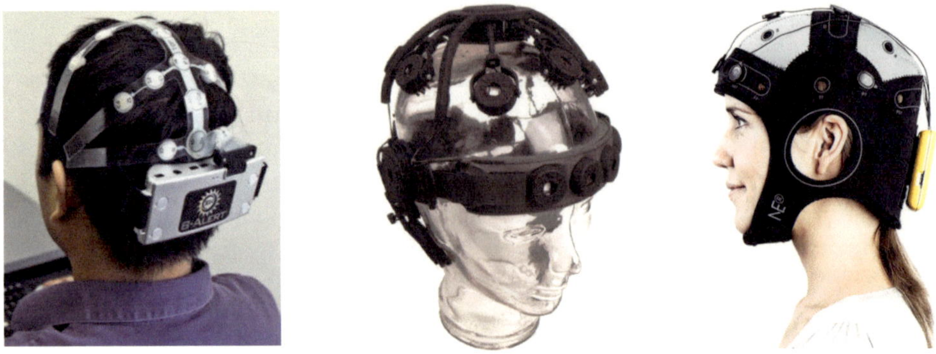

a b c

Figure 6. Pictures of Wireless BCI systems for research use: (a) Advanced Brain Monitoring B-Alert X24 system [52], (b) Quasar DSI 10/20 system [53], (c) Starlab Enobio system [54].

Quasar [53] has developed and released a wireless BCI solution. This solution includes Dry Sensor Interface (DSI) 10/20, wireless Data Acquisition (DAQ), and a suite of software of its own. DSI 10/20 is a wireless BCI headset which is equipped with up to 21 EEG sensors. The EEG sensors are dry electrodes and provide high input impedance good for measuring the high fidelity EEG signals. Wireless DAQ is a peripheral device for signal transmission and onboard recording using a flash memory. QStreamer is a suite of software which contains data acquisition algorithms as well as different cognitive state classification algorithms. The classification algorithms estimate user's mental states in terms of workload, engagement, and fatigue.

Enobio [54] is a wireless EEG acquisition device developed by Starlab. This device is a cap style with light weight feature (only 65g). It has multiple channels, supporting an option of 8 or 20 channels in particular; each is equipped with a dry electrode. It can operate up to 16 hours long using a rechargeable Lithium Polymer battery. It is connected with a computer via a Bluetooth connection. A bundle software provides real time visualization of EEG signals such as power spectrum and raw signal monitoring. This system has been applied to various applications associated with medical, neurofeedback, and cognitive state monitoring.

Guger technologies (G.tec) is a medical engineering company which provides comprehensive BCI solutions. This company has released a mobile biopotential acquisition system named as g.MOBIlab+ [55]. This system is available in two different modes: the 8 channel EEG acquisition mode and the multi-modal acquisition mode. In the multi-modal acquisition mode, this system can measure the EEG signals with other physiological signals such as Electrocardiogram (ECG), Electromyogram (EMG), and Electrooculogram (EOG). With a Bluetooth connection, it operates up to 100 hours using four AA batteries.

4. Challenges and future research directions for wireless BCI systems

Many wireless BCI systems have already been developed for consumers or research uses, and they are attracting public attention. However, only limited areas of applications, such as medical and entertainment applications, have taken advantages of these systems so far. Wireless BCI systems have not yet fully made their way into our life. In this section, we aim to analyze the current challenges the wireless BCI systems research must face, and discuss a few possible future research directions to enable wireless BCI systems to be practically utilized in a much wider scale.

4.1. Challenges in wireless BCI systems research

Wireless BCI systems currently face the following problems: 1) insufficiency in features controllable by EEG signals, 2) deficiency in accuracy in EEG signal interpretation, and 3) lack of killer applications.

First, the available features of EEG signals are limited to be utilized for increasing the speed and accuracy of brain computer communications. The EEG signals are not easy for a user to freely generate in user's own intension. It means that the controllable dimension of EEG signals is not large. In the EEG-based BCI systems, sensorimotor rhythms (SMRs), visual evoked potentials (VEPs) and brain rhythms which generated by particular cognitive states are used as controllable features. Among these features, SMRs usually require long-term training to be adopted in control of BCI applications. Without enough training, the accuracy of SMR-based BCI is usually very low. Also, VEPs cannot be generated without visual stimulations. Therefore, among the wireless BCI systems on scientific articles and commercial products, many BCI systems have utilized the specific brain rhythms generated under the specific cognitive states of users [27][46][49][50][51], such as attention and relaxation, as controllable features of EEG signals. The users can control an application by intentionally changing their own cognitive state. For example, in [27], the users can control the direction of arrows in an archery game, using a wireless BCI system. The direction of arrows is determined from the quantification of the focusing intensity of the users. As can be seen here, the intensity level is only single dimensional; the degree of control the users can issue cannot but be limited. This limitation in the control dimension comes with easiness in adapting to a program within a short learning time, but it plays a limiting role as well. Consequently, the applications BCI systems can be applied are limited as well. To remedy this limitation, some research groups have focused on discovering other controllable EEG features. One example is to use detection of various cognitive states, such as drowsiness and alertness [20][29][30][32]. With all these efforts, however, the number of features that can be obtained is still considered very limited. Namely, wireless BCI systems today can interpret only simple massages from user's intensions.

Second, current BCI systems are not reliable enough to be used in accuracy-critical applications, such as vehicle controls and data telecommunications. To utilize them in a wide range of applications, improving the accuracy of brain computer communication is one of most important issues. In wireless BCI systems, many features of the EEG signals, such as cognitive states, event related potentials (ERPs) in P300, and steady-state visual evoked potentials (SSVEP), are used for BCI based controls. These features are easily affected by various noise and inference sources. For example, in ambulatory applications, such as the workload monitoring [13], a user may need to wear a wireless EEG acquisition device for a long period of time and may need to be able to move around. In such a situation, the accuracy of applications can easily decline due to vibrations and noises. Furthermore, because every person has somewhat different characteristics in EEG features, training to find the best feature set should be carried out in the individual basis for achieving higher accuracy. For these reasons, most commercial wireless BCI systems are developed for less accuracy-critical applications such as computer games and home appliances.

Third, killer applications for wireless BCI systems are needed. In wireless BCI systems, a killer application can be said to be a useful application which influenced on the life of an average person. What BCI system provides ultimately is a human computer interface. But it is not the only form that human can interact with the computer. Speech recognition and hand-motion recognition are, for example, other easier means perhaps with faster and more accurate performance than a BCI can provide. In commercial wireless BCI systems, applications for game and utility control have been mostly developed for entertainment uses. In these applications, it is possible to choose an alternative control interface, such as speech recognition and hand motion, instead of the EEG signals for application controls. Thus, these applications are not a killer application. In the research field, valuable applications related to smart living environment [29][30][32], drowsiness detection [15][19][20][32], and communications [28] have been developed for wireless BCI systems, but they are still not suitable due to lack of sufficient field verifications. Therefore, identification of a killer application still remains to be an urgently needed research topic for wireless BCI systems to thrive.

4.2. Future research directions for wireless BCI systems

Future research on wireless BCI systems should take the following directions: 1) hybrid signal acquisition and 2) development of adaptive classification algorithms.

First, hybrid signal acquisition is needed for higher accuracy and fast brain computer interaction. Hybrid signal acquisition through simultaneous recording of multiple brain signals has been shown to ensure higher accuracy thanks to complementary analysis of user's motivations. There are two different ways to do a hybrid signal acquisition we wish to discuss here. The first is utilizing other biopotential measurements, such as Electrocardiogram (ECG), Electromyogram (EMG), and Electrooculogram (EOG). This approach is already employed in commercial wireless BCI systems such as Emotiv's EPOC system, OCZ technology's Neural Impulse Actuator, and Advanced Brain Monitoring's B-Alert X series. With these additional physiological signal measurements, the users can use not only brain waves but also facial expressions and eye movements. The second is utilizing the multiple features among the available EEG features, such as sensorimotor rhythms (SMRs), P300, and steady-state visual evoked potentials (SSVEP) simultaneously. Most commercial wireless BCI systems use only the cognitive states as the controllable feature of wireless BCI systems. If wireless BCI systems employ additional features of EEG signals which are not generated by

http://dx.doi.org/10.5772/56436

the same motivation, the accuracy of the applications will be improved by adoption of the complementary classification. Recently, Brunner *et al.* [56] have published a paper on a hybrid BCI. In that paper, a hybrid approach using both the event-related desynchronization (ERD) and the SSVEP was experimentally found to provide better accuracy with little or no training.

Second, adaptive algorithms are needed to reduce training time and achieve higher accuracy. Because every person has a unique set of their own EEG characteristics, most applications require training procedures for learning the user's EEG patterns. However, the EEG patterns typically change continuously affected by many factors such as the mental state of the users and the circumstance surrounding the users. Furthermore, long-term training can make the users tired and induce degradation in accuracy. For these reasons, the reduction of training in applications is an important issue in BCI researches. To reduce trainings, additional signal processing schemes likes adaptive classification algorithms can be added to BCI systems. Because these schemes can discern changes in EEG features, the accuracy of applications can be improved. In the BCI research field, some researchers have already studied adaptive classification. Vidaurre *et al.* have published papers about adaptive discriminant analysis [57][58]. This algorithm is based on quadratic discriminant analysis (QDA) and linear discriminant analysis (LDA). Using this algorithm, they have shown that accuracy can be improved greatly in their own BCI experiments built on imagery motor movements.

5. Conclusion

BCI is a useful technology for people with disabilities as it can offer them an additional means of communication, and reinstate a damaged motor control function. Recently, BCI has started its way to grab the attention of the general public as well because this technology has shown the possibility of a new type of user experience. For example, drowsiness detection can be applied to car drivers for preventing traffic accidents. And, real time monitoring of bio-potential signals is useful for diagnosis of patients who have brain diseases such as epilepsy and Alzheimer's disease. To use BCI systems in real-life applications on a daily basis, portable, wearable wireless BCI systems are critical, instead of bulky and cumbersome wired BCI systems. Recently, several wireless BCI systems have been introduced by leading research groups and commercial companies.

In this book chapter, we have reviewed the recent research trends in the development of wireless BCI systems. Various research groups have focused on biosensors, user friendly system designs, and more influential applications. Also, there are a few companies which have developed and released wireless BCI systems into that market, with some commercial successes. Nevertheless, research challenges, such as the insufficiency in controllable features, the deficiency in BCI's control accuracy, and the lack of killer applications are still the issues remained to be resolved. The first two challenges are technical issues which will be resolved in time with continuous research efforts. When good wireless BCI systems which provide high-fidelity data acquisition and fast onboard signal processing are available at low cost, they will surely promote the creation of very useful real-life applications.

Acknowledgements

This work was supported by the National Research Foundation of Korea (NRF) grant funded by the Korean government (MEST) (Do-Yak Research Program, No. 2012-0005656)

Author details

Seungchan Lee, Younghak Shin, Soogil Woo, Kiseon Kim and Heung-No Lee*

*Address all correspondence to: heungno@gist.ac.kr, seungchan@gist.ac.kr

Gwangju Institute of Science and Technology(GIST), Cheomdan-gwagiro, Buk-gu, Gwangju, Republic of Korea

References

[1] Emil S Valchinov and Nicolas E Pallikarakis, "An active electrode for biopotential recording from small localized bio-sources," BioMedical Engineering Online, Vol. 3, Iss. 1, 2004.

[2] Lun-De Liao, I-Jan Wang, Sheng-Fu Chen, Jyh-Yeong Chang and Chin-Teng Lin, "Design, Fabrication and Experimental Validation of a Novel Dry-Contact Sensor for Measuring Electroencephalography Signals without Skin Preparation," Sensors, Vol. 11, Iss. 6, pp. 5819-5834, 2011.

[3] Cristian Grozea1, Catalin D. Voinescu, and Siamac Fazli, "Bristle-sensors - Low-cost Flexible Passive Dry EEG Electrodes for Neurofeedback and BCI Applications," Journal of Neural Engineering, Vol. 8, Iss. 2, 2011.

[4] Thomas J. Sullivan, Stephen R. Deiss, and Gert Cauwenberghs, "A Low-Noise, Non-Contact EEG/ECG Sensor," Biomedical Circuits and Systems Conference, pp. 154 – 157, 2007.

[5] Yu Mike Chi, Yu-Te Wang, Yijun Wang, Christoph Maier, Tzyy-Ping Jung, and Gert Cauwenberghs, "Dry and Noncontact EEG Sensors for Mobile Brain–Computer Interfaces," IEEE Trans. on Neural Systems and Rehabilitation Engineering, Vol. 20, No. 2, 2012.

[6] Nuno Sérgio Diasa, João Paulo Carmo, Paulo Mateus Mendes, José Higino Correiac, "Wireless instrumentation system based on dry electrodes for acquiring EEG signals," Medical Engineering & Physics, Vol. 34, pp. 972-981,

[7] Giulio Ruffini, Stephen Dunne, Esteve Farrés, Ívan Cester, Paul C. P. Watts, S. Ravi P. Silva, Carles Grau, Lluís Fuentemilla, Josep Marco-Pallarés and Bjorn Vandecasteele,

"ENOBIO dry electrophysiology electrode; first human trial plus wireless electrode system," 29th IEEE EMBS, pp. 6689 – 6693, 2007.

[8] Gaetano Gargiulo, Rafael A. Calvo, Paolo Bifulco, Mario Cesarelli, Craig Jin, Armin Mohamed, André van Schaik, "A new EEG recording system for passive dry electrodes," Clinical Neurophysiology, Vol. 121, pp. 686–693, 2010.

[9] Gaetano Gargiulo, Paolo Bifulco, Rafael A. Calvo, Mario Cesarelli, Craig Jin and André van Schaik, "A mobile EEG system with dry electrodes," BioCAS, pp. 273 – 276, 2008.

[10] Vadim V. Nikulin, Jewgeni Kegeles, Gabriel Curio, "Miniaturized electroencephalographic scalp electrode for optimal wearing comfort," Clinical Neurophysiology, Vol. 121, Iss. 7, 2010.

[11] Robert Matthews, Neil J. McDonald, Paul Hervieux, Peter J. Turner, and Martin A. Steindorf, "A Wearable Physiological Sensor Suite for Unobtrusive Monitoring of Physiological and Cognitive State," 29th IEEE EMBS, pp. 5276 – 5281, 2007.

[12] Robert Matthews, Neil J. McDonald, Harini Anumula, Jamison Woodward, Peter J. Turner, Martin A. Steindorf, Kaichun Chang, and Joseph M. Pendleton, "Novel Hybrid Bioelectrodes for Ambulatory Zero-Prep EEG Measurements Using Multi-channel Wireless EEG System," Foundations of Augmented Cognition Lecture Notes in Computer Science, Vol. 4565, pp. 137-146, 2007.

[13] R. Matthews, P.J. Turner, N. J. McDonald, K. Ermolaev, T. Mc Manus, R.A. Shelby, and M. Steindorf, "Real Time Workload Classification from an Ambulatory Wireless EEG System Using Hybrid EEG Electrodes," 30th IEEE EMBS, pp. 5871-587, 2008.

[14] Thomas J. Sullivan, Stephen R. Deiss, Tzyy-Ping Jung, Gert Cauwenberghs, "A Brain-Machine Interface Using Dry-Contact, Low-Noise EEG Sensors," IEEE ISCAS, pp. 1986-1989, 2008.

[15] Jin-Chern Chiou, Li-Wei Ko, Chin-Teng Lin, Chao-Ting Hong, Tzyy-Ping Jung, Sheng-Fu Liang and Jong-Liang Jeng, "Using Novel MEMS EEG Sensors in Detecting Drowsiness Application," IEEE BioCAS, pp. 33-36, 2006.

[16] Lindsay Brown, Jef van de Molengraft, Refet Firat Yazicioglu, Tom Torfs, Julien Penders and Chris Van Hoof, "A low-power, wireless, 8-channel EEG monitoring headset," 32nd IEEE EMBS, pp. 4197-4200, 2010.

[17] Jiawei Xu, Refet Firat Yazicioglu, Bernard Grundlehner, Pieter Harpe, Kofi A. A. Makinwa, and Chris Van Hoof, "A 160uW 8-Channel Active Electrode System for EEG Monitoring," IEEE Trans. on Biomedical Circuit and system, Vol. 5, No. 6, 2011.

[18] Lun-De Liao, I-Jan Wang, Che-Jui Chang, Bor-Shyh Lin, Chin-Teng Lin, and Kevin C. Tseng, "Human Cognitive Application by Using Wearable Mobile Brain Computer Interface," TENCON, pp. 346-351, 2010.

[19] Chin-Teng Lin, Yu-Chieh Chen, Teng-Yi Huang, Tien-Ting Chiu, Li-Wei Ko, Sheng-Fu Liang, Hung-Yi Hsieh, Shang-Hwa Hsu, and Jeng-Ren Duann, "Development of Wireless Brain Computer Interface with Embedded Multitask Scheduling and its Application on Real-Time Driver's Drowsiness Detection and Warning," IEEE Trans. on Biomedical Engineering, Vol. 55, No. 5, 2008.

[20] Chin-Teng Lin, Che-Jui Chang, Bor-Shyh Lin, Shao-Hang Hung, Chih-Feng Chao, and I-Jan Wang, "A Real-Time Wireless Brain–Computer Interface System for Drowsiness Detection," IEEE Trans. on Biomedical Circuit and system, pp. 214 – 222, 2010.

[21] Chin-Teng Lin, Li-Wei Ko, Jin-Chern Chiou, Jeng-Ren Duann, Ruey-Song Huang, Sheng-Fu Liang, Tzai-Wen Chiu, and Tzyy-Ping Jung, "Noninvasive Neural Prostheses Using Mobile and Wireless EEG," Proceedings of the IEEE, Vol. 96, No. 7, July 2008.

[22] Chin-Teng Lin, Li-Wei Ko, Che-Jui Chang, Yu-Te Wang, Chia-Hsin Chung, Fu-Shu Yang, Jeng-Ren Duann, Tzyy-Ping Jung, and Jin-Chern Chiou, "Wearable and Wireless Brain-Computer Interface and Its Applications," HCII 2009, pp. 741–748, 2009.

[23] Thorsten Oliver Zander, Moritz Lehne, Klas Ihme, Sabine Jatzev, Joao Correia, Christian Kothe, Bernd Picht and Femke Nijboer, "A dry EEG-system for scientific research and brain-computer interfaces," Frontiers in Neuroscience, Vol. 5, 2011.

[24] Robert Lin, Ren-Guey Lee, Chwan-Lu Tseng, Yan-Fa Wu, Joe-Air Jiang, "Design and Implementation of Wireless Multi-Channel EEG Recording System and Study Of EEG Clustering Method," Biomedical Engineering applications Basis & Communications, Vol. 18 No. 6, 2006.

[25] Luca Piccini, Sergio Parini, Luca Maggi and Giuseppe Andreoni, "A Wearable Home BCI system: preliminary results with SSVEP protocol," 27th IEEE EMBS, pp. 5384 – 5387, 2005.

[26] Alexandre Ribeiro, António Sirgado, João Aperta, Ana Lopes, Jorge Guilherme, Pedro Correia, Gabriel Pires and Urbano Nunes, "A Low-Cost EEG Stand-Alone Device For Brain Computer Interface," BIODEVICES, pp. 430-433, 2009.

[27] Lun-De Liao, Chi-Yu Chen, I-Jan Wang, Sheng-Fu Chen, Shih-Yu Li, Bo-Wei Chen, Jyh-Yeong Chang and Chin-Teng Lin, "Gaming control using a wearable and wireless EEG-based brain-computer interface device with novel dry foam-based sensors," Journal of Neuro Engineering and Rehabilitation, Vol.9 No.5, 2012.

[28] Yu-Te Wang, Yijun Wang and Tzyy-Ping Jung, "A cell-phone-based brain–computer interface for communication in daily life," Journal of Neural Engineering, Vol.8, 2011.

[29] Chin-Teng Lin, Fu-Chang Lin, Shi-An Chen, Shao-Wei Lu, Te-Chi Chen, Li-Wei Ko, "EEG-based Brain-computer Interface for Smart Living Environmental Auto-adjust-

ment," Journal of Medical and Biological Engineering, Vol. 30, Iss. 4, pp. 237-245, 2010.

[30] Chin-Teng Lin, Bor-Shyh Lin, Fu-Chang Lin, and Che-Jui Chang, "Brain Computer Interface-Based Smart Living Environmental Auto-Adjustment Control System in UPnP Home Networking," IEEE Systems Journal, 2012.

[31] Guger C, Holzner C, Grönegress C, Edlinger G, Slater M, "Control of a Smart Home with a Brain-Computer Interface," 4th International Brain-Computer Interface Workshop and Training Course, 2008.

[32] Shao-Hang Hung, Che-Jui Chang, Chih-Feng Chao, I-Jan Wang, Chin-Teng Lin, Borshyh Lin, "Development of Real-time Wireless Brain Computer Interface for Drowsiness Detection," ISCAS 2010, pp. 1380-1383, 2010.

[33] Ryan C. N. D'Arcy, Sujoy Ghosh Hajra, Careesa Liu, Lauren D. Sculthorpe, and Donald F. Weaver, "Towards Brain First-Aid: A Diagnostic Device for Conscious Awareness," IEEE Transactions on Biomedical Engineering, Vol. 58, No. 3, March 2011.

[34] http://www.ti.com/product/ads1298

[35] http://www.microchip.com/pagehandler/en-us/family/16bit/architecture/pic24f.html

[36] http://www.microchip.com/pagehandler/en-us/family/16bit/architecture/dspic33f.html

[37] http://www.ti.com/lsds/ti/microcontroller/16-bit_msp430/overview.page

[38] http://emotiv.com/store/hardware/epoc-bci/epoc-neuroheadset/

[39] Gert Pfurtschellera, Christa Neuper, "Motor imagery activates primary sensorimotor areas," Neuroscience Letters, Vol. 239, pp. 65-68, 1997.

[40] Simon P. Levine, Jane E. Huggins, Spencer L. BeMent, Ramesh K. Kushwaha, Lori A. Schuh, Mitchell M. Rohde, Erasmo A. Passaro, Donald A. Ross, Kost V. Elisevich, and Brien J. Smith, "A direct brain interface based on event-related potentials," IEEE Trans. on Rehabilitation Engineering, Vol. 8, Iss. 2, pp. 180-185, 2000.

[41] Emanuel Donchin, Kevin M. Spencer, and Ranjith Wijesinghe, "The mental prosthesis: assessing the speed of a P300-based brain-computer interface," IEEE Trans. on Rehabilitation Engineering, Vol. 8, Iss. 2, pp. 174-179, 2000.

[42] Ming Cheng, Xiaorong Gao, Shangkai Gao, and Dingfeng Xu, "Design and implementation of a brain-computer interface with high transfer rates," IEEE Trans. on Biomedical Engineering, Vol. 49, Iss. 10, pp. 1181-1186, 2002.

[43] Carmen Vidaurre, Benjamin Blankertz, "Towards a Cure for BCI Illiteracy," Brain Topography, Vol. 23, Iss. 2, pp. 194-198, 2010.

[44] Ling Guo, Daniel Rivero, Alejandro Pazos, "Epileptic seizure detection using multiwavelet transform based approximate entropy and artificial neural networks," Journal of Neuroscience Methods, Vol. 193, pp.156-163, 2010.

[45] F. Galán, M. Nuttinc, E. Lewa, P.W. Ferreza, G. Vanackerc, J. Philipsc, J. del R. Millán, "A brain-actuated wheelchair: Asynchronous and non-invasive Brain–computer interfaces for continuous control of robots," IEEE Trans. on Rehabilitation Engineering, Vol. 8, Iss. 4, pp. 441-446, 2000.

[46] http://www.neurosky.com/Products/MindSet.aspx

[47] http://developer.neurosky.com/docs/doku.php?id=esenses_tm

[48] http://www.neurosky.com/Products/ThinkGearAM.aspx

[49] http://www.plxdevices.com/product_info.php?id=XWAVESONIC

[50] http://myndplay.com/products.php?cat=1

[51] http://www.ocztechnology.com/nia-game-controller.html

[52] http://advancedbrainmonitoring.com/neurotechnology/systems/

[53] http://www.quasarusa.com/

[54] http://neuroelectrics.com/enobio

[55] http://www.gtec.at/Products/Hardware-and-Accessories/g.MOBIlab-Specs-Features

[56] C Brunner, B Z Allison, C Altstätter and C Neuper, "A comparison of three brain–computer interfaces based on event-related desynchronization, steady state visual evoked potentials, or a hybrid approach using both signals," Journal of Neural Engineering, Vol. 8, 2011.

[57] C. Vidaurre, A. Schlögl, R. Cabeza, R. Scherer, and G. Pfurtscheller, "A Fully On-Line Adaptive BCI," IEEE Transactions on Biomedical Engineering, Vol. 53, No. 6, 2006.

[58] C. Vidaurre, A. Schlögl, R. Cabeza, R. Scherer, and G. Pfurtscheller, "Study of On-Line Adaptive Discriminant Analysis for EEG-Based Brain Computer Interfaces," IEEE Transactions on Biomedical Engineering, Vol. 54, No. 3, 2007.

Chapter 12

Brain Computer Interface for Epilepsy Treatment

L. Huang and G. van Luijtelaar

Additional information is available at the end of the chapter

http://dx.doi.org/10.5772/55800

1. Introduction

A brain computer interface (BCI) is a communication system converting neural activities into signals that can control computer cursors or external devices (Fetz, 2007). BCI was initially and mainly employed for patients with severe motor disorders such as amyotrophic lateral sclerosis (ALS) by providing non-muscular bidirectional communication and control. However, the application of BCI has been extended to control various EEG signals for therapeutic purposes, such as seizure control in epilepsy patients. Although such BCIs did not demonstrate rapid control as in non-muscular communication, it still assumes that EEG based bidirectional control is possible (Wolpaw et al., 2002). More specifically, a BCI in epilepsy research, as in the current chapter, refers to a communication system capable to acquire signal and to implement real-time seizure detection/prediction and contingent delivery of warning stimuli or therapies such as electrical stimulation to control seizures (see the diagram). Such systems became feasible with technological development, and have been implemented in animal and human to control seizures. In the current chapter we will first give an overview of application of BCI, especially with deep brain stimulation in epilepsy research. Then we will discuss different components of a BCI system: input (signal acquisition), algorithm (seizure detection/prediction) and output (application and users), in particular stressing some important issues on BCI performance.

2. BCI application in epilepsy research

2.1. Introduction of epilepsy treatment

Epilepsy is a common chronic neurological disorder that afflicts 0.5-1% of the world's population (Hauser et al., 1993). More than one third patients do not respond to the antiepileptic

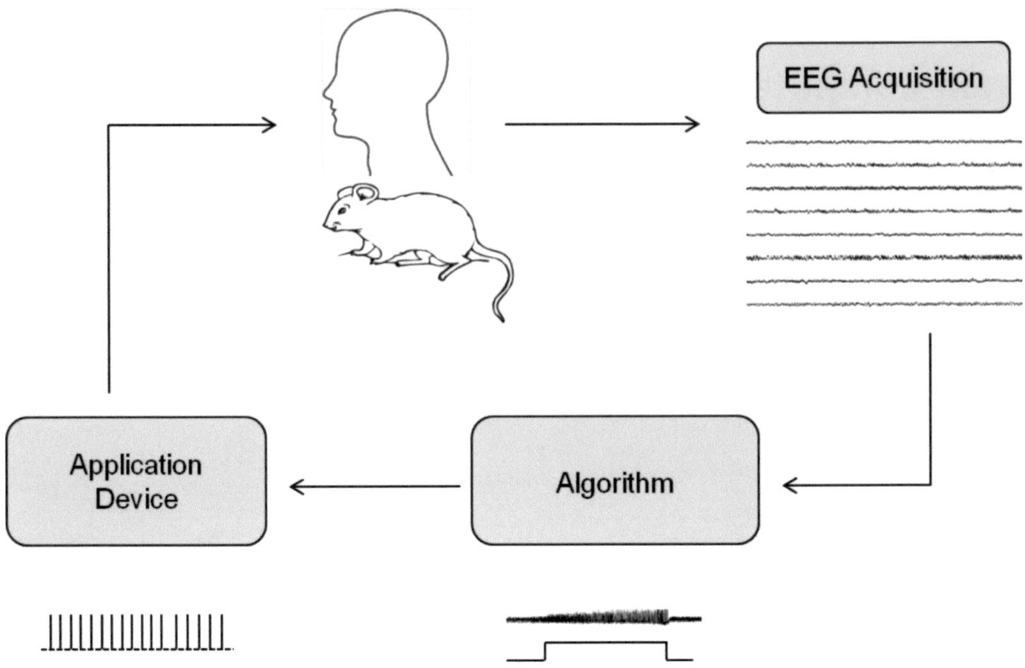

Diagram 1. A brain-computer interface (BCI) in epilepsy research. A BCI system here has three components: input to acquire EEG signal (obtained by implanted electrodes or scalp electrodes, amplified, band-pass and notch filtered, and at the end was digitized), an algorithm to distinguish a seizure event from non-seizure state (seizure detection or prediction algorithm), and output of application device to deliver warning or therapies such as electrical stimulation to subjects in order to disrupt or modulate seizures.

drugs (AEDs) (Kwan and Brodie, 2000). Resective surgery, the main treatment for drug resistant patients, is not proper for certain patients such as those who have multiple foci or have generalized seizures without a clear local origin. In addition, it might be accompanied with some post-operation complications such as memory, language, sensory or motor deficits (Engel et al., 2003). Alternative treatments such as neurostimulation have been developed for the treatment of these patients. Deep brain stimulation (DBS), one type of neurostimulation, delivers electrical current to neural tissue to achieve therapeutic effects. Compared to surgery, DBS is less invasive, reversible and has the potential to customize treatment to individual patients. Following its success in the treatment of movement disorders (Nguyen et al., 2000; Pollak et al., 2002; Volkmann, 2004), DBS has received increasing attention as a viable treatment option for patients with refractory epilepsy.

While stimulation is conventionally delivered at the predefined protocol (scheduled stimulation), stimulation integrated in a BCI system is delivered depending on the neurophysiologic state of the brain (responsive stimulation). Such responsive stimulation as output application of BCI has the potential of advantages such as targeting seizure dynamics with higher temporal specificity, minimization of its side effects, reduction of neural tissue damage and of course a longer battery life. The following section will review research of responsive stimulation by BCI in animals and human respectively.

2.2. Responsive stimulation by BCI in animals

Within the framework of a BCI concept, early neurophysiologic studies mainly adopted detection algorithm and feedback control to examine the effect of responsive stimulation on interictal spikes or seizure-like activities in slices. Psatta and colleagues (1983) delivered low frequency stimulation (5 Hz) to the caudate nucleus by feedback control in the epileptic foci in adult cats. Durand and his group (Kayyali and Durand, 1991; Nakagawa and Durand, 1991; Warren and Durand, 1998) applied current with feedback control in the focal area in hippocampal slices of rats. Meanwhile, Gluckman and colleagues (2001) applied a direct current (DC) electric field to hippocampal slices by using a computer controlled feedback algorithm. The outcomes of all these studies suggested antiepileptic effects of responsive stimulation by BCI.

Further, BCI with stimulation output was tested in vivo. Stimulation was applied to the motor cortex, the focus in the penicillin induced seizure model in rats by using proportional feedback control (Colpan et al., 2007). The results showed a significant reduction of mean amplitudes of seizures, suggesting positive effects of stimulation. Studies in a genetic absence epilepsy model (GAERS rats) were aimed at the search for optimal stimulation parameters of stimulation of the substantia nigra reticularis. Bilateral, bipolar and monophasic stimulation at 60 Hz and with 60-μs pulse width was optimal in the interruption of typical spike-wave discharges for absence epilepsy. However, when used for repeated stimulations, long-term suppression did not occur and even the number of spike-wave discharges increased (Feddersen et al., 2007). Stimulation by BCI was also tested with an automated detection program in the same model (Nelson et al., 2011a). Three types of stimulation frequency were investigated (130, 500, 1000 Hz) and the two high frequencies were more effective to reduce the duration of spike-wave discharges.

BCI with a prediction algorithm was also applied in experimental epilepsy animal models. Stimulation was delivered in the hippocampus during the preictal period in the status epilepticus (SE) model in rats (Nair et al., 2006). The preliminary results showed a reduction in seizure frequency and longer seizure free periods, indicating antiepileptic effects of responsive hippocampal stimulation. Recently, BCI with a seizure prediction algorithm was also implemented in the SE model of TLE in six rats by delivering stimulation in the centromedial thalamus (Good et al., 2009). Apart from responsive stimulation, the study also tested scheduled stimulation. BCI with a seizure prediction algorithm was implemented in a penicillin induced seizure model in rats with low frequency stimulation (1 Hz) in the cortex (Wang et al., 2012), comparing with the scheduled stimulation and non-stimulation group. The outcomes of the last two studies favored responsive stimulation over scheduled stimulation, supporting BCI with stimulation output in seizure control.

Apart from conventional deep brain stimulation, application of BCI was recently extended to low frequency transcranial electrical stimulation (TES) in another rat model of generalized absence epilepsy (Berenyi et al., 2012). The results proved positive outcomes of responsive TES by BCI in terms of reducing the duration of spike-wave discharges without a subsequent rebound.

2.3. Responsive stimulation by BCI in human

In clinic, some early patient studies have used afterdischarges (ADs) - elicited during routinely functional mapping - as model of seizures to investigate the effects of responsive stimulation as ADs are epileptiformic activities and can evolve into seizures. The promising results from some early studies (Lesser et al., 1999; Motamedi et al., 2002) justify the application of BCI in patients.

Osorio and his group (1998) developed a generic seizure detection algorithm by using wavelet analysis for early detection of seizure events. Based on that, Peters and colleagues (2001) described a BCI system- the first bedside prototype - integrated with such a real-time seizure detection algorithm and contingent delivery of stimulation at or near seizure onset. The performance and safety of this BCI system was further evaluated in eight patients (Osorio et al., 2005). The study demonstrated that BCI with stimulation output near seizure onset was practicable in real time and could be applied in a reliable and safe manner.

Following the success of BCI with stimulation application in seizure control, there is recognition of the need of implantable circuitry for clinical use. Recently, the first implantable BCI system – responsive neurostimulator (RNS) system (Fig 1) has been developed (NeuroPace, Mountain View, CA) in order to automatically detect early seizure events and deliver contingent stimulation. As proof of principle, Kossof and his group (2004) first evaluated the safety of BCI with output of an external stimulator in four epilepsy patients. While two patients had brief transient side effects, stimulation in general was well tolerated and safe. Although the efficacy of stimulation was not the aim of that study, electrographic seizures were altered and suppressed in these patients. Consistent with this study, Fountas and colleagues (2005) using an implantable BCI device, delivered responsive stimulation in eight patients. Seven out of eight patients displayed more than a 45% decrease in seizure frequency. Using the same BCI system, Smith and colleagues (2010) delivered responsive insular stimulation in one patient with refractory focal epilepsy after the resection of focal insular area. The patient showed a 50% reduction in seizure frequency after responsive stimulation. In another case report (Enatsu et al., 2012), a TLE patient received responsive stimulation (200 Hz) with RNS system in bilateral mesial temporal areas. An up to 50% decrease in seizure frequency was reported after delivery of stimulation.

Morrell and colleagues (2011) evaluated the efficacy and safety of the RNS device in a multicenter, double-blind, randomized controlled trial in 191 patients. These patients had improved quality of life and tolerated the treatment without obvious mood or cognitive adverse effects. In addition, seizures were significantly reduced for a 12-week blind period in the treatment group. Thus, the implantable BCI can be a promising therapeutic avenue for epilepsy treatment.

3. The components of a BCI

Like any other BCI systems, the BCI system discussed here consists of an input to obtain signal, algorithm to detect or predict seizures and output to apply warning or therapies to users.

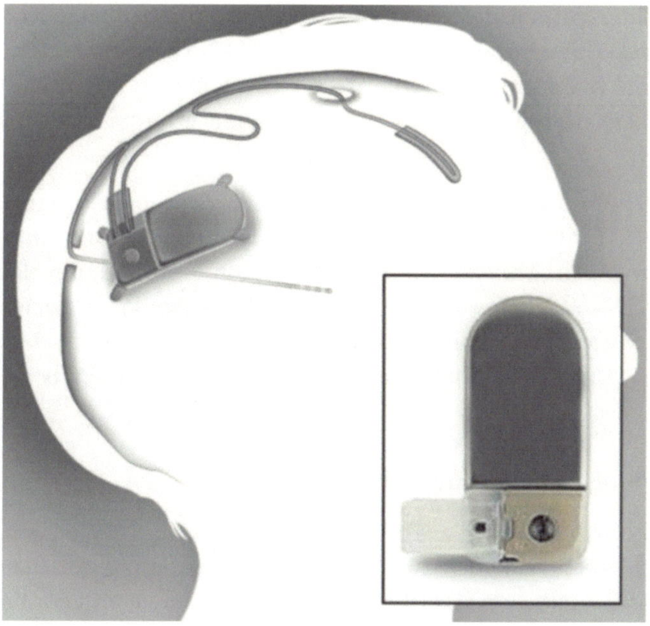

Figure 1. schematic graph of an implanted RNS stimulator, depth lead and cortical strip lead (NeuroPace, Mountain View, CA). The RNS neurostimulator (inset) has up to two leads. Either depth lead or cortical (subdural) strip lead is used in the system. Each has four electrode contacts that can be used for sensing and delivering stimulation. To obtain early seizure detection and delivery of focal electrical stimulation, leads are placed close to the seizure focus (Morrell et al, 2011).

3.1. Signal acquisition

The purpose of input in the BCI system discussed here is to acquire signal relevant for seizure detection and subsequent delivery of warning and therapy. The input is normally EEG recorded from the scalp or within the brain. The chosen input is acquired by electrode, then amplified and digitized in the BCI system. Recently, extracerebral signals such as cardiac (heart rate) or motor signals (speed, direction and joint movement) have emerged as a promising direction for seizure detection (Osorio and Schachter, 2011). Signals can be categorized as non-invasive (scalp EEG, extracerebral) or invasive (intracranial EEG). Scalp electrodes are the common sources of signals in clinic. In most cases, intracranial electrode allow better for early detection than scalp electrode, especially for partial seizures (Jouny et al., 2011).

One important factor that could affect BCI in signal acquisition operation is localization of ictal onset zone. Ictal onset zone is the area that generates the epileptic seizures. The ictal zone can be regional or broad, differing from one subject to another. A seizure event is more likely to be detected early after an ictal onset zone has been identified. One way to improve the localization of the ictal zone is to develop high-density scalp EEG recordings. These high density recordings provide higher spatial resolution with possibilities for dipole source localization compared to the more classical macroelectrode EEG recording systems. Intracranial recordings with microelectrode arrays on suspected candidate brain regions allow for a next improvement in localization. Information obtained with intracranial EEG recordings are considered the golden standard as far as spatial resolution of the source of epileptiformic activity is concerned. These intracranial recordings are also used for better understanding the interaction of local networks in the course of a seizure event (Jouny et al., 2011). With help of these new electrode recording systems, an ictal onset zone is much more likely to be identified correctly.

Another fundamental issue in BCI in this stage involves which signal to look at besides seizures, particularly for the purpose of the efficacy of therapy. For example, some interictal spikes are similar to seizures but last for only a few seconds without developing into a seizure (Jouny et al., 2011). Despite their short duration, they share similar characteristics components with a seizure. Highly localized activity such as microseizures might be correlated with partial seizure (Stead et al., 2010). If that holds true, these microseizures might be potential candidates for stimulation therapy.

3.2. Seizure detection/prediction algorithm

In the BCI system discussed here, algorithms should be able to detect a seizure event from non-seizure state (detection algorithm) or predict an upcoming seizure event (prediction algorithm). Quite some detection algorithms using various linear and nonlinear methods have been reported and obtained with various degrees of success. The validity and reliability of prediction algorithms remain questionable, despite some promising results (Mormann et al., 2007) as most of them were based on selective or limited EEG recordings or without statistical validation on sensitivity and specificity of each method (Carney et al., 2011).

Early detection is one issue that is less challenging but currently still far from being optimal for application in BCI research; it determines the time window in which warning or therapeutic devices are triggered. For warning purpose, the ideal condition is to detect seizure event before subjects lose awareness or consciousness. For therapy purpose, it requires to detect seizure as early as possible. As mentioned earlier, the use of high density arrays or microelectrodes are involved in signal acquisition and detection process; they favorably influence the ability to detect seizures early. The capability of an algorithm per se can directly determine how early a seizure event is detected. On the other hand, early detection always comes at the cost of specificity of an algorithm. Some improvements can be made to enhance the quality of early detection, such as using combination of linear and nonlinear features, multi-channel approach and decision making procedure (Jouny et al., 2011).

Another difficulty for BCI in algorithm operation is to include interaction of different states such as circadian fluctuations or vigilance state and seizures. Seizure probability can be affected by sleep stage, sleep debt and diurnal and other physiological rhythms (Haut et al., 2007; Malow, 2005). Circadian phases (Quigg et al., 2000; Smyk et al., 2012; Van Luijtelaar and Coenen, 1988) and sleep stage (Shouse et al., 2004; van Luijtelaar and Bikbaev, 2007) have been reported to have effects on seizures in rat models of epilepsy. Moreover, false positives by prediction algorithms were also found to favor some states of vigilance, in particular deep sleep (Navarro et al., 2005; Schelter et al., 2006). More efforts such as computational modeling need to be taken to probe states of vigilance and circadian phase to improve prediction of seizures.

3.3. Application and users

The output of BCI here is the device that can trigger warning or therapies to users. Given its therapeutic purpose, therapy efficacy is the standard tool to evaluate BCI performance. In addition to electrical stimulation, other therapies have also been used such as anti-seizure compounds (Stein et al., 2000), thermal energy (cooling) (Hill et al., 2000), and operant conditioning (Osterhagen et al., 2010; Sterman, 2000). Compared to current, the main limitation of pharmacological and thermal energy therapy is their slow tissue diffusivity, which means that therapies will be delivered or arrive late to fully control the target area, even when delivered locally (Osorio and Frei, 2009). On the other side, electrical stimulation is the most common application of BCI and is also our focus in this section.

3.3.1. Therapy parameters for users

One challenge for BCI in application is how to stimulate, that is, selection of proper stimulation parameters. Stimulation parameters in human are often determined by trial and error with adjustment to avoid side effects while respecting safety limits for charge density (Sun et al., 2008). A number of studies especially in animals explored which stimulation parameters - stimulation frequency, waveform, amplitude, duration- can result in better seizure control.

Stimulation frequency seems to be a key factor. High frequency stimulation (HFS) (> 100 Hz) is typically used in clinic for treatment of movement disorders such as Parkinson's disease (Pollak et al., 2002; Volkmann, 2004) and also used for treatment of patients with refractory epilepsy. HFS has been delivered in various brain areas such as the anterior nucleus of the thalamus, hippocampus and thalamus (Andrade et al., 2006; Fisher et al., 2010; Velasco et al., 2000a; Velasco et al., 2000b) and has achieved various degree of success in seizure control.

In contrast, low frequency stimulation has limited and mixed effects. Stimulation at low frequency (0.5-3 Hz) in kindled animal models were found to raise the threshold of ADs (Carrington et al., 2007; Gaito et al., 1980; Ghorbani et al., 2007; Goodman et al., 2005). Yamamoto and colleagues (2002) demonstrated that LFS in the cortex had antiepileptic effects in the focus in patients with TLE. However, no other studies have further reported such effects of LFS in animal models and human of TLE. Even some clinical study reported contradictory evidence – aggravation of seizures by LFS on the centromedian thalamic nucleus in 12 patients (Velasco et al., 1997).

Furthermore, a few studies compared HFS and LFS under the same experimental condition. Albensi and colleagues (2004) compared the effects of HFS (100 Hz) and LFS (1 Hz) on epileptiform activities in hippocampal slices. Both types of stimulation suppressed epileptiform activities but with one difference: the onset of suppression by LFS was gradual but persistent while that of suppression by HFS was rapid but transient. The effects of LFS (5 Hz) and HFS (130 Hz) were compared on ADs in kindled rats (Wyckhuys et al., 2010b). HFS was more effective with higher ADs threshold and longer latency. Boex and colleagues (2007) compared both types of stimulation on three patients and found that HFS was more effective in reducing seizure rate. Rajdev and colleagues (2011) examined stimulation frequency (high, medium and low), pulse width (high and low) and amplitude (high and low) in seizures in kainite treated rats. The results showed that low (5Hz) and high frequency (130 Hz) were effective to suppress epileptic activities compared to medium frequency (60 Hz). Taken together, these studies suggested that HFS is most effective in seizure suppression while LFS has rather complicated effects depending on which animal model and epilepsy type is chosen for LFS application.

Other factors such as pulse width and waveform could also affect the effects of stimulation. In the aforementioned study, Rajdev and colleagues (2011) investigated the influences of different pulse widths (60, 120, 240 us) on ADs. With increase of pulse width (120, 240 us), less stimulation amplitude was needed to evoke ADs, indicating higher threshold of AD interruptions for shorter pulse width (60 us). The power of the pulse (intensity times duration) determines its efficacy in this model. In addition, the waveform of stimulation can also act on the effects of stimulation. The threshold for suppression of both somatic and axonal activity was lower with sinusoidal HFS than pulse train HFS (Jensen and Durand, 2007).

Recently, a new method of stimulation has been proposed: 'temporal coding'. Cota and colleagues (2009) reported that stimulation with a 'pseudo-randomized inter stimulus interval' significantly increased the threshold to tonic-clonic seizures in the pentylenetetrazole (PTZ) model. Similarly, Poisson distributed stimulation was found to reduce spontaneous seizures in the SE model of TLE (Wyckhuys et al., 2010a) and in the GEARs model of absence epilepsy (Nelson et al., 2011a). Further, cortical stimulation at multiple stimulation sites was investigated in different combinations of periodic/aperiodic (periodic – with fixed inter stimulus interval) and synchronous/ asynchronous stimulation manner (synchronous – stimulation at the same time) in rats (Nelson et al., 2011b). The results showed that asynchronous stimulation was more effective in suppression of seizure severity and duration.

Although it remains unclear which parameters are the best for which seizure model, these studies give us more insights on how to improve efficacy of therapy.

3.3.2. Selection of target area

Another basic question regarding BCI in application is where to stimulate. So far a variety of areas have been investigated for the effects of stimulation. These areas are either areas where seizures are generated or areas which are involved in progression of seizures. The intrinsic and extrinsic characteristics of these areas determine their different responses to stimulation. In each target area, for example, the constitutions of various neuron types and their biophysical properties are different, affecting responses of individual neuron and neuronal ensemble to stimulation. Besides, the anatomical connections among these target areas vary from each other, which can influence the dynamics of neuronal populations and sensitivity to stimulation (Sunderam et al., 2010).

3.3.3. Patient-specific therapy

It is also true that patient-specific therapy is the new direction for BCI in application operation. In clinic, stimulation parameters are usually adjusted in individual patients to avoid adverse effects while maintaining therapeutic effects. Osorio and his group (Osorio et al., 2010) used linear regression to examine in a retrospective study the results of a trial in which responsive stimulation was applied in eight patients with refractory epilepsy. Regression models tested the contributions of multiple potentially relevant factors such as parameter configurations (that is, different combinations of stimulation frequency, current intensity, duration, pulse width and location) to changes of seizure severity. The results showed that certain parameter configurations were more effective in reduction of seizure severity in some patients but not in others, indicating individual difference in parameters setting for stimulation. Thus adaptive, patients-specific stimulation settings might be a necessary new step for BCI in application in order to achieve optimal efficacy.

4. Conclusion

Unlike conventional BCIs, a BCI system in epilepsy emphasizes EEG-based communication for therapeutic purposes. The need of BCI rises from delivery of contingent therapies such as stimulation to control seizures. Although a large body of work has been done to explore contingent stimulation with help of BCI for epilepsy research in animal and human, it is still in an experimental stage. With development of technique in engineering and computer science, BCI is at the stage of becoming feasible for application of therapy in the treatment of patients in some forms of refractory epilepsy.

Future progress depends on the following crucial factors: development of electrode arrays or microelectrode, improvement of early detection, algorithms embedding variables such as vigilant states and circadian phases, exploration of patient-specific optimization of parameters, selection of proper target areas to maximize BCI performance. The development of BCI is an interdisciplinary challenge requiring vigorous and continuous efforts on relevant fields such as neuroscience, computer science, mathematics, and engineering. Although BCI in epilepsy research is still developing, it provides a promising therapeutic option to those who do not respond to conventional treatment.

Author details

L. Huang and G. van Luijtelaar

Dept Biological Psychology, Donders Center for Cognition, Donders Institute for Brain Cognition and Behaviour, Radboud University Nijmegen, Nijmegen, the Netherlands

References

[1] Albensi, B. C, Ata, G, Schmidt, E, Waterman, J. D, & Janigro, D. (2004). Activation of long-term synaptic plasticity causes suppression of epileptiform activity in rat hippocampal slices. Brain Res. , 998, 56-64.

[2] Andrade, D. M, Zumsteg, D, Hamani, C, Hodaie, M, Sarkissian, S, Lozano, A. M, & Wennberg, R. A. (2006). Long-term follow-up of patients with thalamic deep brain stimulation for epilepsy. Neurology. , 66, 1571-3.

[3] Berenyi, A, Belluscio, M, Mao, D, & Buzsaki, G. (2012). Closed-loop control of epilepsy by transcranial electrical stimulation. Science. , 337, 735-7.

[4] Boex, C, Vulliemoz, S, Spinelli, L, Pollo, C, & Seeck, M. (2007). High and low frequency electrical stimulation in non-lesional temporal lobe epilepsy. Seizure. , 16, 664-9.

[5] Carney, P. R, Myers, S, & Geyer, J. D. (2011). Seizure prediction: methods. Epilepsy Behav. 22 Suppl 1, S, 94-101.

[6] Carrington, C. A, Gilby, K. L, & Mcintyre, D. C. (2007). Effect of focal low-frequency stimulation on amygdala-kindled afterdischarge thresholds and seizure profiles in fast- and slow-kindling rat strains. Epilepsia. , 48, 1604-13.

[7] Colpan, M. E, Li, Y, Dwyer, J, & Mogul, D. J. (2007). Proportional feedback stimulation for seizure control in rats. Epilepsia. , 48, 1594-603.

[8] Cota, V. R. Medeiros Dde, C., Vilela, M.R., Doretto, M.C., Moraes, M.F., (2009). Distinct patterns of electrical stimulation of the basolateral amygdala influence pentylenetetrazole seizure outcome. Epilepsy Behav. 14 Suppl , 1, 26-31.

[9] Enatsu, R, Alexopoulos, A, Bingaman, W, & Nair, D. (2012). Complementary effect of surgical resection and responsive brain stimulation in the treatment of bitemporal lobe epilepsy: a case report. Epilepsy Behav. , 24, 513-6.

[10] Engel, J. Jr., Wiebe, S., French, J., Sperling, M., Williamson, P., Spencer, D., Gumnit, R., Zahn, C., Westbrook, E., Enos, B., (2003). Practice parameter: temporal lobe and localized neocortical resections for epilepsy. Epilepsia. , 44, 741-51.

[11] Feddersen, B, Vercueil, L, Noachtar, S, David, O, Depaulis, A, & Deransart, C. (2007). Controlling seizures is not controlling epilepsy: a parametric study of deep brain stimulation for epilepsy. Neurobiol Dis. , 27, 292-300.

[12] Fetz, E. E. (2007). Volitional control of neural activity: implications for brain-computer interfaces. J Physiol. , 579, 571-9.

[13] Fisher, R, Salanova, V, Witt, T, Worth, R, Henry, T, Gross, R, Oommen, K, Osorio, I, Nazzaro, J, Labar, D, Kaplitt, M, Sperling, M, Sandok, E, Neal, J, Handforth, A, Stern, J, Desalles, A, Chung, S, Shetter, A, Bergen, D, Bakay, R, Henderson, J, French, J, Baltuch, G, Rosenfeld, W, Youkilis, A, Marks, W, Garcia, P, Barbaro, N, Fountain, N, Bazil, C, Goodman, R, & Mckhann, G. Babu Krishnamurthy, K., Papavassiliou, S., Epstein, C., Pollard, J., Tonder, L., Grebin, J., Coffey, R., Graves, N., (2010). Electrical stimulation of the anterior nucleus of thalamus for treatment of refractory epilepsy. Epilepsia. , 51, 899-908.

[14] Fountas, K. N, Smith, J. R, Murro, A. M, Politsky, J, Park, Y. D, & Jenkins, P. D. (2005). Implantation of a closed-loop stimulation in the management of medically refractory focal epilepsy: a technical note. Stereotact Funct Neurosurg. , 83, 153-8.

[15] Gaito, J, Nobrega, J. N, & Gaito, S. T. (1980). Interference effect of 3 Hz brain stimulation on kindling behavior induced by 60 Hz stimulation. Epilepsia. , 21, 73-84.

[16] Ghorbani, P, Mohammad-zadeh, M, Mirnajafi-zadeh, J, & Fathollahi, Y. (2007). Effect of different patterns of low-frequency stimulation on piriform cortex kindled seizures. Neurosci Lett. , 425, 162-6.

[17] Gluckman, B. J, Nguyen, H, Weinstein, S. L, & Schiff, S. J. (2001). Adaptive electric field control of epileptic seizures. J Neurosci. , 21, 590-600.

[18] Good, L. B, Sabesan, S, Marsh, S. T, Tsakalis, K, Treiman, D, & Iasemidis, L. (2009). Control of synchronization of brain dynamics leads to control of epileptic seizures in rodents. Int J Neural Syst. , 19, 173-96.

[19] Goodman, J. H, Berger, R. E, & Tcheng, T. K. (2005). Preemptive low-frequency stimulation decreases the incidence of amygdala-kindled seizures. Epilepsia. , 46, 1-7.

[20] Hauser, W. A, Annegers, J. F, & Kurland, L. T. (1993). Incidence of epilepsy and unprovoked seizures in Rochester, Minnesota: 1935-1984. Epilepsia. , 34, 453-68.

[21] Haut, S. R, Hall, C. B, Masur, J, & Lipton, R. B. (2007). Seizure occurrence: precipitants and prediction. Neurology. , 69, 1905-10.

[22] Hill, M. W, Wong, M, Amarakone, A, & Rothman, S. M. (2000). Rapid cooling aborts seizure-like activity in rodent hippocampal-entorhinal slices. Epilepsia. , 41, 1241-8.

[23] Jensen, A. L, & Durand, D. M. (2007). Suppression of axonal conduction by sinusoidal stimulation in rat hippocampus in vitro. J Neural Eng. , 4, 1-16.

[24] Jouny, C. C, Franaszczuk, P. J, & Bergey, G. K. (2011). Improving early seizure detection. Epilepsy Behav. 22 Suppl 1, S, 44-8.

[25] Kayyali, H, & Durand, D. (1991). Effects of applied currents on epileptiform bursts in vitro. Exp Neurol. , 113, 249-54.

[26] Kossoff, E. H, Ritzl, E. K, Politsky, J. M, Murro, A. M, Smith, J. R, Duckrow, R. B, Spencer, D. D, & Bergey, G. K. (2004). Effect of an external responsive neurostimulator on seizures and electrographic discharges during subdural electrode monitoring. Epilepsia. , 45, 1560-7.

[27] Kwan, P, & Brodie, M. J. (2000). Early identification of refractory epilepsy. N Engl J Med. , 342, 314-9.

[28] Lesser, R. P, Kim, S. H, Beyderman, L, Miglioretti, D. L, Webber, W. R, Bare, M, Cysyk, B, Krauss, G, & Gordon, B. (1999). Brief bursts of pulse stimulation terminate afterdischarges caused by cortical stimulation. Neurology. , 53, 2073-81.

[29] Malow, B. A. (2005). Sleep and epilepsy. Neurol Clin. , 23, 1127-47.

[30] Mormann, F, Andrzejak, R. G, Elger, C. E, & Lehnertz, K. (2007). Seizure prediction: the long and winding road. Brain. , 130, 314-33.

[31] Morrell, M. J. (2011). Responsive cortical stimulation for the treatment of medically intractable partial epilepsy. Neurology. , 77, 1295-1304.

[32] Motamedi, G. K, Lesser, R. P, Miglioretti, D. L, Mizuno-matsumoto, Y, Gordon, B, Webber, W. R, Jackson, D. C, Sepkuty, J. P, & Crone, N. E. (2002). Optimizing parameters for terminating cortical afterdischarges with pulse stimulation. Epilepsia. , 43, 836-46.

[33] Nair, S. P, Sackellares, J. C, Shiau, D. S, Norman, W. M, Dance, L. K, Pardalos, P. M, Principe, J. C, & Carney, P. R. (2006). Effects of acute hippocampal stimulation on EEG dynamics. Conf Proc IEEE Eng Med Biol Soc. , 1, 4382-6.

[34] Nakagawa, M, & Durand, D. (1991). Suppression of spontaneous epileptiform activity with applied currents. Brain Res. , 567, 241-7.

[35] Navarro, V, & Martinerie, J. Le Van Quyen, M., Baulac, M., Dubeau, F., Gotman, J., (2005). Seizure anticipation: do mathematical measures correlate with video-EEG evaluation? Epilepsia. , 46, 385-96.

[36] Nelson, T. S, Suhr, C. L, Freestone, D. R, Lai, A, Halliday, A. J, Mclean, K. J, Burkitt, A. N, & Cook, M. J. seizure control with very high frequency electrical stimulation at seizure onset in the GAERS model of absence epilepsy. Int J Neural Syst. , 21, 163-73.

[37] Nelson, T. S, Suhr, C. L, Lai, A, Halliday, A. J, Freestone, D. R, Mclean, K. J, Burkitt, A. N, & Cook, M. J. (2011b). Exploring the tolerability of spatiotemporally complex electrical stimulation paradigms. Epilepsy Res. , 96, 267-75.

[38] Nguyen, J. P, & Lefaucher, J. P. Le Guerinel, C., Eizenbaum, J.F., Nakano, N., Carpentier, A., Brugieres, P., Pollin, B., Rostaing, S., Keravel, Y., (2000). Motor cortex stimulation in the treatment of central and neuropathic pain. Arch Med Res. , 31, 263-5.

[39] Osorio, I, Frei, M. G, & Wilkinson, S. B. (1998). Real-time automated detection and quantitative analysis of seizures and short-term prediction of clinical onset. Epilepsia. , 39, 615-27.

[40] Osorio, I, Frei, M. G, Sunderam, S, Giftakis, J, Bhavaraju, N. C, Schaffner, S. F, & Wilkinson, S. B. (2005). Automated seizure abatement in humans using electrical stimulation. Ann Neurol. , 57, 258-68.

[41] Osorio, I, & Frei, M. G. (2009). Real-time detection, quantification, warning, and control of epileptic seizures: the foundations for a scientific epileptology. Epilepsy Behav. , 16, 391-6.

[42] Osorio, I, Manly, B, & Sunderam, S. (2010). Toward a quantitative multivariate analysis of the efficacy of antiseizure therapies. Epilepsy Behav. , 18, 335-43.

[43] Osorio, I, & Schachter, S. (2011). Extracerebral detection of seizures: a new era in epileptology? Epilepsy Behav. 22 Suppl 1, S, 82-7.

[44] Osterhagen, L, Breteler, M, & Van Luijtelaar, G. (2010). Does arousal interfere with operant conditioning of spike-wave discharges in genetic epileptic rats? Epilepsy Res., 90, 75-82.

[45] Peters, T. E, Bhavaraju, N. C, Frei, M. G, & Osorio, I. (2001). Network system for automated seizure detection and contingent delivery of therapy. J Clin Neurophysiol., 18, 545-9.

[46] Pollak, P, Fraix, V, Krack, P, Moro, E, Mendes, A, Chabardes, S, Koudsie, A, & Benabid, A. L. (2002). Treatment results: Parkinson's disease. Mov Disord. 17 Suppl 3, S, 75-83.

[47] Psatta, D. M. (1983). Control of chronic experimental focal epilepsy by feedback caudatum stimulations. Epilepsia., 24, 444-54.

[48] Quigg, M, Clayburn, H, Straume, M, Menaker, M, & Bertram, E. H. rd, (2000). Effects of circadian regulation and rest-activity state on spontaneous seizures in a rat model of limbic epilepsy. Epilepsia., 41, 502-9.

[49] Rajdev, P, Ward, M, & Irazoqui, P. (2011). Effect of stimulus parameters in the treatment of seizures by electrical stimulation in the kainate animal model. Int J Neural Syst., 21, 151-62.

[50] Schelter, B, Winterhalder, M, Maiwald, T, Brandt, A, Schad, A, Timmer, J, & Schulze-bonhage, A. (2006). Do false predictions of seizures depend on the state of vigilance? A report from two seizure-prediction methods and proposed remedies. Epilepsia., 47, 2058-70.

[51] Shouse, M. N, Scordato, J. C, & Farber, P. R. (2004). Sleep and arousal mechanisms in experimental epilepsy: epileptic components of NREM and antiepileptic components of REM sleep. Ment Retard Dev Disabil Res Rev., 10, 117-21.

[52] Smith, J. R, Fountas, K. N, Murro, A. M, Park, Y. D, Jenkins, P. D, Morrell, M, Esteller, R, & Greene, D. (2010). Closed-loop stimulation in the control of focal epilepsy of insular origin. Stereotact Funct Neurosurg., 88, 281-7.

[53] Smyk, M. K, Coenen, A, Lewandowski, M. H, & Van Luijtelaar, G. (2012). Internal desynchronization facilitates seizures. Epilepsia., 53, 1511-8.

[54] Stead, M, Bower, M, Brinkmann, B. H, Lee, K, Marsh, W. R, Meyer, F. B, Litt, B, Van Gompel, J, & Worrell, G. A. (2010). Microseizures and the spatiotemporal scales of human partial epilepsy. Brain., 133, 2789-97.

[55] Stein, A. G, Eder, H. G, Blum, D. E, Drachev, A, & Fisher, R. S. (2000). An automated drug delivery system for focal epilepsy. Epilepsy Res., 39, 103-14.

[56] Sterman, M. B. (2000). Basic concepts and clinical findings in the treatment of seizure disorders with EEG operant conditioning. Clin Electroencephalogr., 31, 45-55.

[57] Sun, F. T, Morrell, M. J, & Wharen, R. E. Jr., (2008). Responsive cortical stimulation for the treatment of epilepsy. Neurotherapeutics., 5, 68-74.

[58] Sunderam, S, Gluckman, B, Reato, D, & Bikson, M. (2010). Toward rational design of electrical stimulation strategies for epilepsy control. Epilepsy Behav. , 17, 6-22.

[59] Van Luijtelaar, E. L, & Coenen, A. M. (1988). Circadian rhythmicity in absence epilepsy in rats. Epilepsy Res. , 2, 331-6.

[60] Van Luijtelaar, G, & Bikbaev, A. (2007). Midfrequency cortico-thalamic oscillations and the sleep cycle: genetic, time of day and age effects. Epilepsy Res. , 73, 259-65.

[61] Velasco, A. L, Velasco, M, Velasco, F, Menes, D, Gordon, F, Rocha, L, Briones, M, & Marquez, I. and chronic electrical stimulation of the hippocampus on intractable temporal lobe seizures: preliminary report. Arch Med Res. , 31, 316-28.

[62] Velasco, M, Velasco, F, Velasco, A. L, Brito, F, Jimenez, F, Marquez, I, & Rojas, B. (1997). Electrocortical and behavioral responses produced by acute electrical stimulation of the human centromedian thalamic nucleus. Electroencephalogr Clin Neurophysiol. , 102, 461-71.

[63] Velasco, M, Velasco, F, Velasco, A. L, Boleaga, B, Jimenez, F, Brito, F, & Marquez, I. (2000b). Subacute electrical stimulation of the hippocampus blocks intractable temporal lobe seizures and paroxysmal EEG activities. Epilepsia. , 41, 158-69.

[64] Volkmann, J. (2004). Deep brain stimulation for the treatment of Parkinson's disease. J Clin Neurophysiol. , 21, 6-17.

[65] Wang, L, Guo, H, Yu, X, Wang, S, Xu, C, Fu, F, Jing, X, Zhang, H, & Dong, X. (2012). Responsive electrical stimulation suppresses epileptic seizures in rats. PLoS One. 7, e38141.

[66] Warren, R. J, & Durand, D. M. (1998). Effects of applied currents on spontaneous epileptiform activity induced by low calcium in the rat hippocampus. Brain Res. , 806, 186-95.

[67] Wolpaw, J. R, Birbaumer, N, Mcfarland, D. J, Pfurtscheller, G, & Vaughan, T. M. (2002). Brain-computer interfaces for communication and control. Clin Neurophysiol. , 113, 767-91.

[68] Wyckhuys, T, Boon, P, Raedt, R, Van Nieuwenhuyse, B, Vonck, K, & Wadman, W. (2010a). Suppression of hippocampal epileptic seizures in the kainate rat by Poisson distributed stimulation. Epilepsia. , 51, 2297-304.

[69] Wyckhuys, T, Raedt, R, Vonck, K, Wadman, W, & Boon, P. (2010b). Comparison of hippocampal Deep Brain Stimulation with high (130Hz) and low frequency (5Hz) on afterdischarges in kindled rats. Epilepsy Res. , 88, 239-46.

[70] Yamamoto, J, Ikeda, A, Satow, T, Takeshita, K, Takayama, M, Matsuhashi, M, Matsumoto, R, Ohara, S, Mikuni, N, Takahashi, J, Miyamoto, S, Taki, W, Hashimoto, N, Rothwell, J. C, & Shibasaki, H. (2002). Low-frequency electric cortical stimulation has an inhibitory effect on epileptic focus in mesial temporal lobe epilepsy. Epilepsia. , 43, 491-5.

Chapter 13

Emotion Recognition Based on Brain-Computer Interface Systems

Taciana Saad Rached and Angelo Perkusich

Additional information is available at the end of the chapter

http://dx.doi.org/10.5772/56227

1. Introduction

Emotions are intrinsically related to the way that individuals interact with each other as well as machines [1]. A human being can understand the emotional state of another human being and behave in the best manner to improve the communication in a certain situation. This is because emotions can be recognized through words, voice intonation, facial expressions and body language. In contrast, machines cannot understand the feelings of an individual.

In this context, affective computing aims to improve the communication among individuals and machines by recognizing human emotions and thus making that interaction easier, usable and effective. There are several studies using different approaches in human emotion detection [2]. For instance, McDaniel et. al. in [3] investigated facial expressions to detect emotions in a learning activity by the interaction among university students and a computer. The students were asked to show their emotions while interacting with a software called AutoTutor. Facial expressions were recorded by video cameras to recognize six kinds of emotions, namely: confusion, surprise, boredom, frustration, pleasure and acceptance. The authors observed that all emotions were able to be detected, except the boredom which it was indistinguishable from a neutral facial expression.

Lee et. al. in [4] explored the use of information concerning the dialogues and speeches along with voice intonation to recognize emotions from speech signals. The focus of the study was to detect negative and non-negative emotions using the information obtained from the spoken language of a call center. The main problems in emotion recognition systems based on facial expressions or spoken language is that these two sources of information are susceptible to ambiguity and false simulations. Bernhardt in [5] developed a emotion recognition system based on body language in daily activities such as walking, picking up an object, among others.

Beyond the detection systems based on affective facial expressions, spoken language and body language, there are several applications in affective computing that focus in detecting emotions through learning techniques to identify patterns in physiological activity that match the expression of different emotions. Liu et. al. in [6] investigated the use of cardiovascular signals, electrodermal activity, electromyography and peripheral temperature for affective detection. The aim of this study was to recognize the emotions of children affected by autism to develop a system that works as a therapist. Systems based on electroencephalogram (EEG) signals have also been used to detect emotions. For instance, in Schaaff and Schultz [7] implemented a system based on brain signals to enable a robot to recognize human emotions. Emotions were elicited by images and classified in three categories, namely: pleasant, unpleasant and neutral. Brain signals are a reliable information source due to the fact that the process of emotion interpretation starts in the central nervous system. Furthermore, an individual cannot control his brain signals to simulate a fake emotional state.

This chapter presents an emotion recognition system based on brain signals. We used a brain computer interface (BCI) as a technique to acquire and classify the brain signals into emotions. This BCI system is based on EEG signals. We used the discrete wavelet transform to select EEG features and a neural network to map these features to emotions.

The rest of this chapter is divided in six sections. In Section 2 the main concepts related to BCI and the key problem are presented. Section 3 shows some application areas of emotion recognition systems based on brain computer interface. Section 4 discusses the research course. Section 5 illustrates the methods used to acquire and process the brain signals into human emotions. Section 5 presents the results achieved using our approach. Finally, in conclusion Section 6 are presented.

2. Problem statement

BCIs are systems that enable any user to exchange information with the environment and control devices by using brain activity, i.e., without using the neuromuscular output pathways of the brain [8]. Brain signals can be acquired by means of invasive or non-invasive methods. In the former, electrodes are implanted directly in the brain. In the latter, the signal is acquired from the scalp of the user. Despite the existence of several methods to acquire brain signals, the most used method is the electroencephalogram (EEG) because it is non-invasive, portable, inexpensive, and can be used in almost all environments [9]. Moreover, low cost and increasingly portable EEG equipment have been developed in the last years.

As discussed by Wang et al. In [10], BCIs systems have been used in rehabilitation, e.g., speller systems, neuroscience, e.g., monitoring attention systems and cognitive psychology, e.g., treatment of attention-deficit hyperactivity disorder. BCIs systems have been investigated recently in recognizing emotions and are seen as a promising technique in this area because the emotions are generated in the brain.

There are several challenges in using BCIs systems for detecting emotions, such as the choice of the method and the channels of acquisition of brain signals that best provide information regarding the emotional state of an individual as well as processing techniques in order to reach a good accuracy in the recognition of emotions.

3. Application area

The emotion recognition systems based on BCI can be applied to many areas, such as:

- Entertainment
- Education
- Medicine
- Gaming
- Intelligent tutoring systems

An example of application in the field of entertainment is EEG-based music player [11]. In this application, the current emotional state of the user is identified, and a music related to this state is played. The songs are classified into six emotion types: fear, sad, frustrated, happy, satisfied and pleasant.

4. Research course

The way which a person acts with other people, objects and situations in their day-to-day is fully connected with their emotions. In this context, the recognition of human emotions has been target of several studies recently.

The recognition of emotions can be performed from the facial and body expressions, voice and physiological signals, among others. Since the focus of this work is the definition of processing techniques of EEG signals to provide better results in the classification of the brain signals into emotions, this section presents works based on EEG signals for recognition of emotions.

In [12], the authors used the EEG signals and facial expressions together for the recognition of emotions. The authors aim was to investigate which emotion (positive or negative) is generated from the execution of a particular song. EEG signals were acquired by electrodes placed in the temporal region of the brain and facial expressions were acquired from video images. As a result of this work, the authors determined that it was not possible to distinguish the type of emotion from the signals used together.

Liu et al in [11] presented an algorithm for classification of brain electrical signals in human emotions. This algorithm was based on the model of fractal dimension. The authors used some songs in the first experiment and sounds of the international affective digitized sounds in a second experiment to induce certain emotions in the participants of this study, The brain signals were acquired from three channels, FC6, F4 and AF3. Through the channel FC6 was possible to classify emotions regarding the level of excitement. The channels AF3 and F4 were used in the classification of emotions with respect to valence. According to the authors, in the forebrain of an individual can be identified greater activation in one hemisphere during the feeling of positive emotion and greater activation in the other hemisphere during feeling a negative emotion. But what hemisphere corresponds to that kind of emotion depends on each individual. Therefore, for this approach to be used, a training phase was included in the work. Using the fractal dimension model for recognition of emotions, the authors identified six basic emotions in the bi-dimensional valence-arousal graph, as shown in Figure 1.

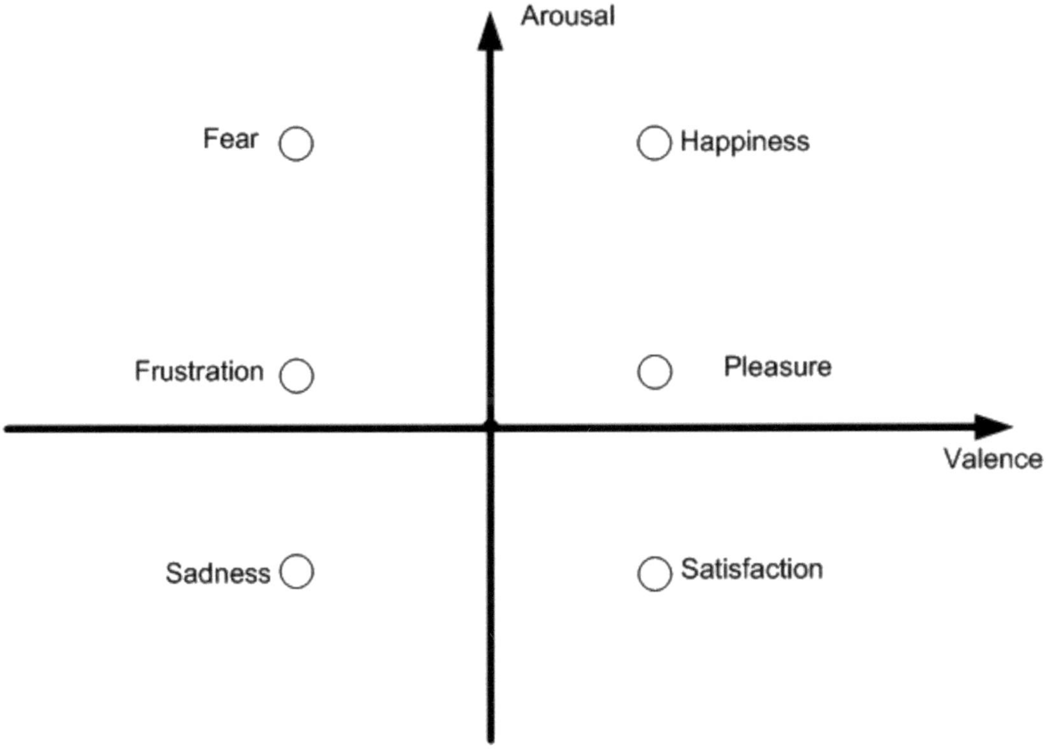

Figure 1. Bi-dimensional valence-arousal approach

Bos in [13] investigated the use of EEG signals for recognition of human emotions. The author used auditory and visual stimuli extracted from such international affective digitized sounds and affective figures, respectively, to induce the feeling of a certain emotion in the participants of the experiment. The brain electrical signals were acquired through three channels, F3, F4 and FPZ, according to the international 10-20 system [14]. The signal characteristics of EEG, alpha (8-12 Hz) and beta (12-30 Hz), were selected to be used in the recognition of emotions. According to the authors of this paper, the noise signals due to the electrooculogram (EOG) are dominant below the frequency of 4 Hz, the noise related to the electrocardiogram (ECG) signals is around 1.2 Hz and above 30 Hz we can find the noise related to electromyogram

(EMG). Therefore extracting features only alpha and beta reduced the noises. Bos used a band pass filter to extract only the features in the frequency range 8-30 Hz.

The algorithm frequency Fourier analysis divided the original signal into frequency bands. The principal components analysis reduced the number of features. And finally, Bos classified the EEG signals into emotions with the binary Fisher linear classifier. The classification of emotions was based in the bi-dimensional valence-arousal approach. As a result, Bos obtained a rate of 82.1% accuracy in classification of emotions in brain signals.

In [7], the authors investigated the use of EEG for the recognition of human emotions by humanoid robots. The goal was to provide the ability for robots to detect emotion and react to it in the same way as occurs in a human-human interaction. Also, an EEG device developed by the authors was used to obtain the brain signals. The EEG device consists of only four channels for data acquisition, located in the forebrain according to 10-20 International system in the positions Fp1, Fp2, F7 and F8.

Images of the international affective pictures induced the emotional states pleasant, neutral and unpleasant in participants of the experiments. The classification of emotions was performed using the support vector machine method. It was verified an accuracy of 47.11 % in the recognition of three emotional states mentioned above. According to the authors, to improve the accuracy of the system would require the development of a more complex system, considering multiple data sources, such as cameras and microphones.

Savran et al. [15] studied the use of brain signals and facial expressions for the recognition of human emotions. According to the authors, due to the sensitivity of the signals of EEG to electrical signals generated by the facial muscles while emotions are expressed, the EEG signals and facial expressions cannot coexist. For this reason, the authors used the near infrared spectroscopy as a technique for acquiring brain signals together with facial expressions. Although the spectroscopic technique is non-invasive and low cost, its main problem is the low temporal resolution, which limits the use of this technique in real time applications. The authors used the international affective pictures to induce emotions in participants of the experiment for the recognition of emotions and built a database with the information regarding the facial expressions and brain signals acquired through video and spectroscopy, respectively. Despite the development of the database, the authors performed the data analysis separately, not reporting results on fusion of brain signals and facial expressions for recognizing emotions.

The authors also constructed a second database with the EEG, near infrared spectroscopy and physiological signals, such as skin conductance and heart rate. These signals were acquired during an experiment of induction of emotions taking pictures of the international affective pictures as stimuli. They used a EEG device with 64 channels, but 10 channels were eliminated due to obstruction of the near infrared spectroscopy equipment. The authors did not discuss the results obtained in the classification of brain signals, only presented the protocol used in the construction of databases.

Murugappan et al. [16] showed a brain-computer interface system (ICC) for the recognition of human emotions. The acquisition of brain signals was performed by an EEG device with 64 channels. A Laplace filter was applied in pre-processing of EEG signals. The authors used the wavelets transform algorithm analysis in selecting the characteristics of brain signals and two methods for features classification, the k nearest neighbors and linear discriminant. The authors of this study chose the classification using the discrete emotions approach (happiness, surprise, fear, disgust and neutral).

Twenty subjects aged between 21 and 39 years participated in this experiment. Audio-visual induced emotions in participants of the aforementioned experiment. EEG signals were acquired at a rate of 256 Hz and have been preprocessed using the Laplace filter, as previously mentioned. The wavelet decomposed the EEG signals into five frequency bands (delta, theta, alpha, beta and gamma). The authors calculated the statistical data of alpha band (entropy, energy, standard deviation and variance) and applied this information as input for the classifiers k nearest neighbors and linear discriminant analysis. Table 1 presents the results obtained by the authors of this study.

Results	62 channels	24 channels	8 channels
k nearest neighbors	78,04 %	77,61 %	71,3 %
linear discriminant analysis	77,83 %	70,65 %	56,09 %

Table 1. Results obtained in [16]

5. Methods

This section presents the system developed for the recognition of human emotions based on a BCI system. We use only information from brain signals to detect the emotional state of an individual in this work. Furthermore, due to the lack of an apparatus for reading brain signals, we use one database of EEG signals [17]. Figure 2 shows the architecture of the emotion recognition system proposed in this chapter.

The architecture presented in Figure 2 includes a normal BCI system composed by the brain signal acquisition, signal pre-processing, features selection and classification. The output of the BCI system can be one between four different kind of emotions: positive/excited, positive/calm, negative/excited, and negative/calm. The next subsections discuss about each step of our emotion recognition system based on BCI interface.

5.1. Database

We use an EEG database as the source of brain signals [17]. This database was recorded by using music videos to induce emotions in the participants of the experiment. Initially, the authors selected 120 stimuli. Half of these stimuli was selected by a semi-automatically method [18] and the another half was selected manually. After the stimuli selection, one minute of each video was extracted to be used in the research, as stimuli. Finally, the authors of the database chose 40 stimuli [18]. Those stimuli were selected to elicit four different emotions in the

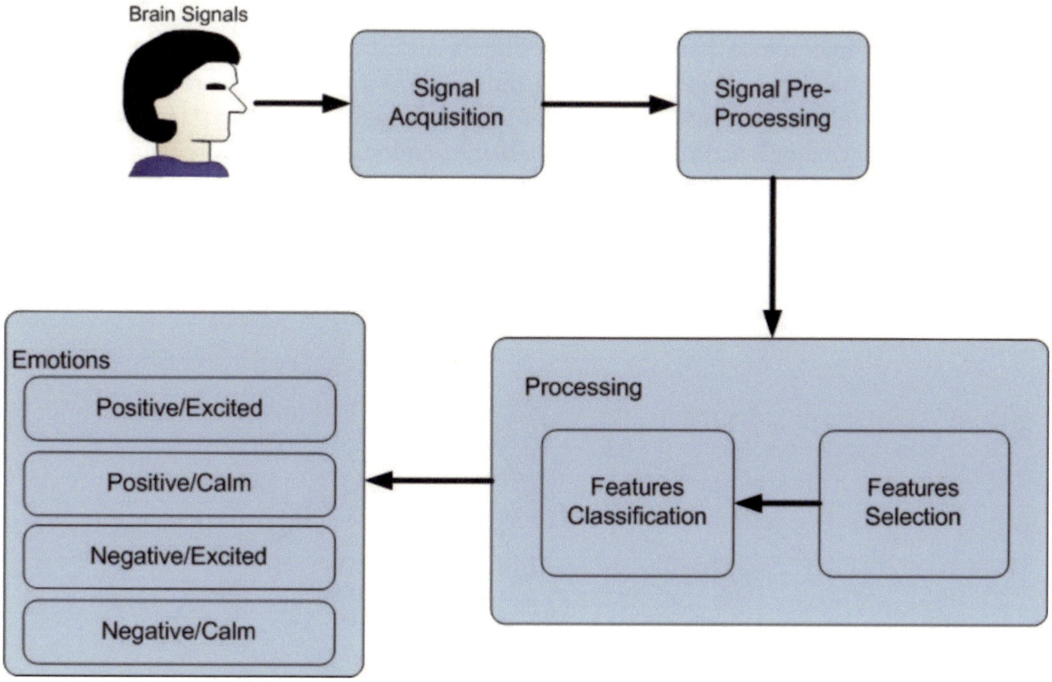

Figure 2. Emotion recognition system architecture

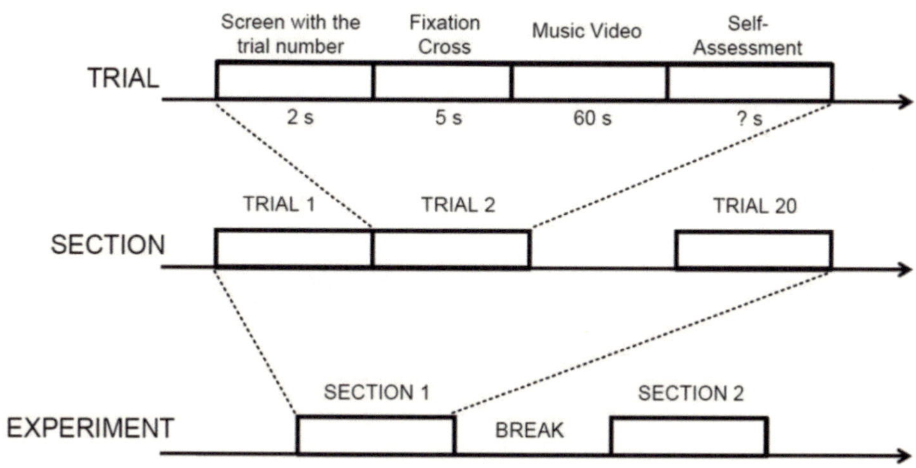

Figure 3. Experiment protocol

individuals: calm/positive, calm/negative, excited/positive and excited/negative. Figure 3 presents the protocol used to conduct the experiment.

The experiments were conducted in two laboratory environments with controlled lighting. Thirty-two participants took part in the experiment, and their EEG signals and peripheral physiological signals (eye movements, facial muscles movements, temperature and blood pressure, among others) were acquired with the system Biosemi Active Two. The signals were recorded from 32 channels according to the 10-10 international system. Moreover, these EEG signals in the database were filtered and the electrooculogram (EOG) artifacts were removed. It was used a camera to capture the images of 22 among the 32 participants in the frontal position. Figure 4 presents the 10-10 international system.

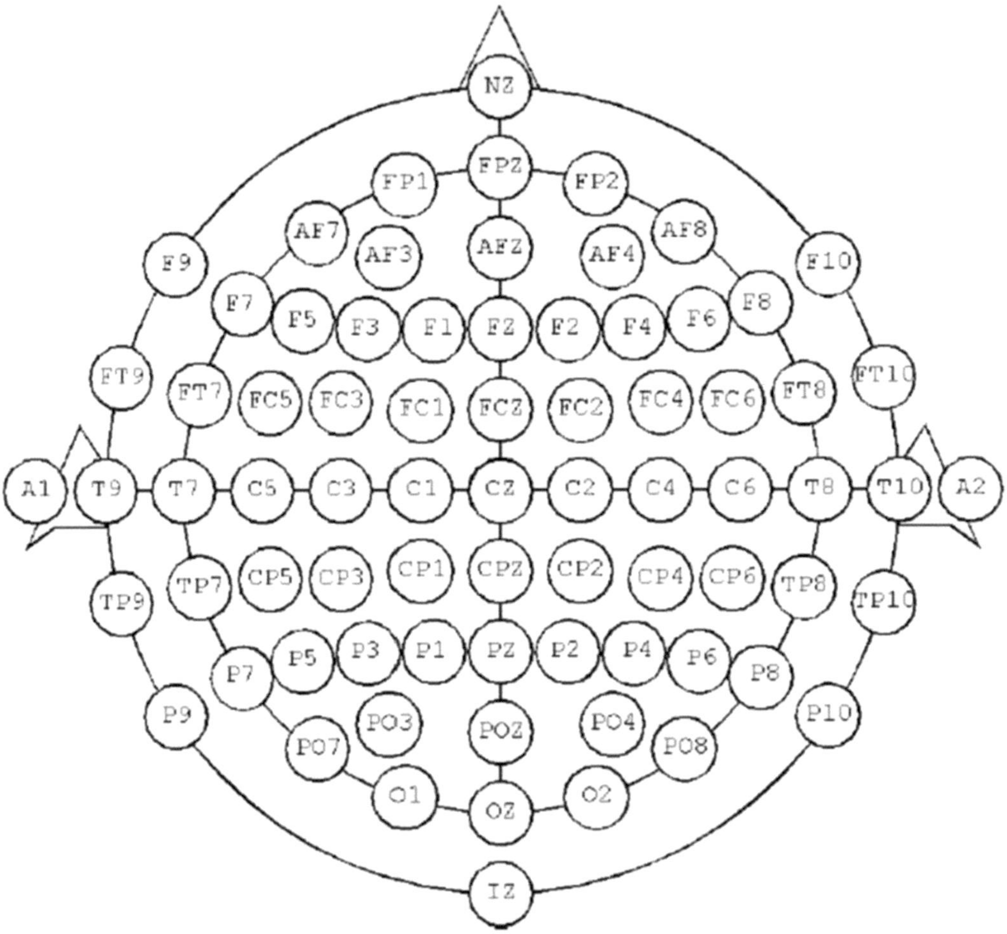

Figure 4. Illustration of the 10-10 international system

Two computers were used in this experiment, one for storing data and another for presentation of stimuli. To keep two computers synchronized bookmarks were sent from one computer to another [18].

The EEG data was stored

There are some areas of the brain that are related with the human emotional behavior: brainstem, hypothalamus, thalamus, prefrontal area and limbic system. We chose to use the EEG signals acquired from the channel FP1 in this work. The channel FP1 is located on the prefrontal area of the brain. The prefrontal area is involved in the following functions:

- The choice of options and behavioral strategies most appropriate to the physical and social conditions of an individual, as well as the ability to change them when such situations are modified.
- Sustained attention and the ability to follow sequences of thoughts sorted.
- Control of emotional behavior.

5.2. Signals pre-processing

In the pre-processing of data from database used in this study, first the data had their sample rate reduced from 512Hz to 128 Hz. The authors of the database removed the artifacts due to eye movements from EEG signals using the technique discussed in [18]. These signals were filtered with a band pass filter with minima cutoff frequency of 4 Hz and maxima of 45 Hz. A common reference was used for all EEG channels. The data was segmented into 60 second samples being the 3 first seconds eliminated. The preprocessing of data in the database was not done in the context of this work.

The authors of the database [17] stored the EEG data pre-processed in 32.mat (matlab) files, one per participant. Each participant file contains two arrays, as illustrated in Table 2.

Array name	Array shape	Array contents
data	40 x 40 x 8064	Video/trial x channel x data
labels	40 x 4	Video/trial x label (valence, arousal, dominance, liking)

Table 2. Contents of each participant file

5.3. Signals processing

The processing of EEG signals in a BCI system is divided into two parts: the selection of the signal characteristics and classification of these characteristics. The choice of the method to be used in the first step depends if the signal characteristics are time or frequency domain. In the second stage, the choice of method is independent of the signal domain.

5.3.1. Signal characteristics selection

Wavelets [16] has been widely used to select the characteristics of the EEG signals in emotion recognition systems and are defined as small waves that have limited duration and average values as zeros. They are mathematical functions, in which a function or data set are located on both time and frequency.

Wavelet analysis consists in the decomposition of a signal into different shifted versions in different scales from the original wavelet. The wavelet analysis is divided into continuous and discrete.

We used the Daubechies 4 discrete wavelet (db4) in this work. We chose the Daubechies 4 based on [16]. The authors performed several experiments with several families of wavelets. In those experiments, the authors found that the wavelet db4 best represents the EEG signals. Figure 5 illustrates an example of the wavelet db4.

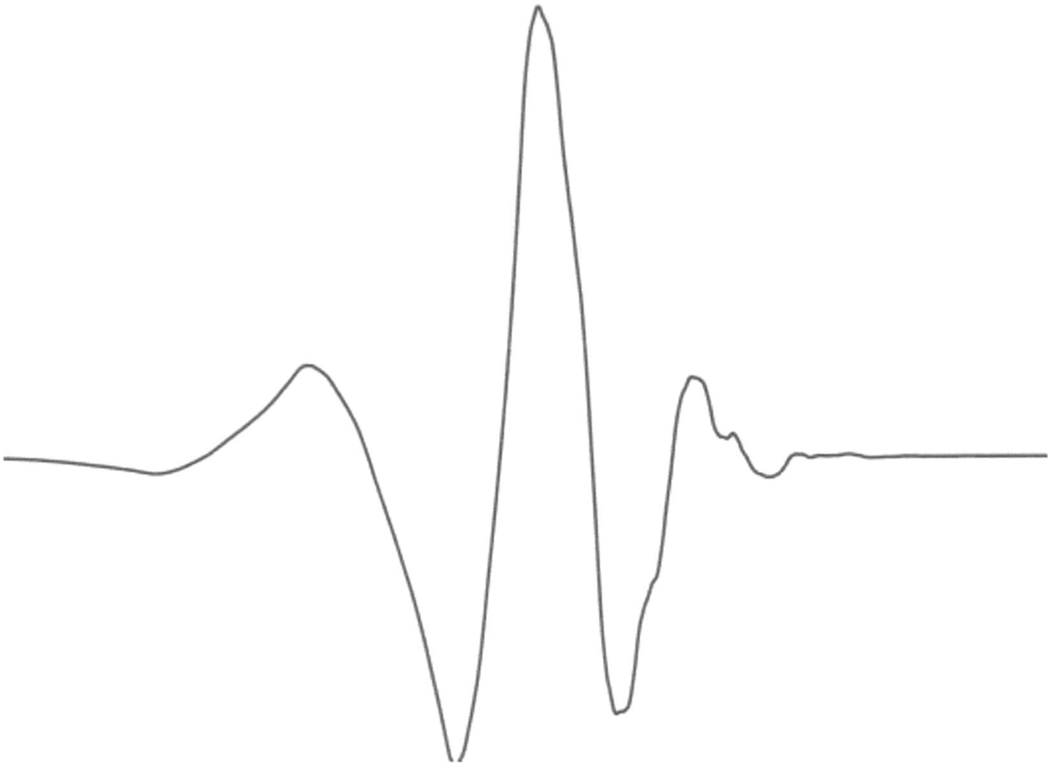

Figure 5. An example of the wavelet db4

The family of Daubechies wavelets was invented by Ingrid Daubechies, one of the most important people in wavelets research. These wavelets are orthonormal compact, making discrete wavelet transform practice.

We developed a routine in Matlab for reading the EEG signals from the database used in this work. Beyond that, the routine selects the features delta, theta, alpha and beta from the EEG signals. Table 3 presents the rhythmic characteristics of the EEG signals along with their frequency bands.

Characteristics	Frequency
Delta	1 – 4 Hz
Theta	4 - 7 Hz
Alpha	8 – 12 Hz
Beta	12 – 30 Hz

Table 3. Rhythmic characteristics of the EEG signal

The EEG signals from the database presented in Section 5.1 were charged using the aforementioned routine. We extracted the EEG data of the FP1 channel from each participant file, discussed in Section 5.2 The EEG data extracted was stored in an new file per participant. Table 4 shows the content of each participant file.

Array name	Array shape	Array contents
data	40 x 8064	label (valence, arousal, dominance, liking) x data

Table 4. Content of the new participant file

The EEG signals were sampled at a sampling rate of 512 Hz, but as discussed in Section 5.2, in the pre-processing of the signal that rate was reduced to 128 Hz. Therefore, we used a db4 wavelet of order 4 for selecting the characteristics of the signal.

First, we calculated the wavelets coefficients using two matlab functions: detcoef (it returns the details coefficients of a wavelet) and appcoef(it returns the approximation coefficients of a wavelet). Then, we calculated the details and approximations of the wavelet using the upcoef matlab function. These steps were applied for each row of the data array

The human emotions are related with the theta and alpha characteristics. For that reason, we chose to select theta and alpha features to classify them into emotions. We calculated the values of entropy and energy components of the alpha and theta to evaluate which parameter can provide better results when classified into emotions.

We calculated the entropy and energy using the wentropy and wenergy matlab functions, respectively. That functions receive as parameter an array. In this work, we used arrays with theta and alpha features to estimate the entropy and energy.

5.3.2. Signal characteristics classification

The second stage in EEG signals processing is the classification of the signals into signals of interest for a given application using translation algorithms. Examples of translation algorithms include linear discriminant analysis, k-nearest neighbor, support vector machine, and artificial neural network [19], among others.

Artificial neural network has been widely used as algorithm to classify different kind of human information into human emotions. We chose use this technique based on the literature where we can find good results with the use of the artificial neural network.

Artificial neural networks are computational learning models inspired in the biology of the human brain. These models consist of neurons interconnected by synapses. From a functional point of view, neural networks copy the ability of the brain to learn and ideally can be trained to recognize any information, given a set of input data, by adjusting the synaptic weights. A properly trained network, in principle, should be empowered to apply their knowledge and respond appropriately to completely new entries. The most common application of neural networks is the supervised classification and therefore it requires a set of training and test data. Since learning is performed by the training data, the mathematical formalization is based on these data.

The classification of the characteristic of the brain signals in emotions was performed by neural networks algorithm in this work. A neural network consists of input layer, hidden layer and output layer. The input layer is composed of neurons that receive input stimuli. The output layer is composed by neurons which have as their output the network output. The hidden layer or intermediate layer is composed of neurons which perform any data processing network. This layer may be composed of only one layer or several layers of neurons depending on the complexity of the network. In Figure 6, is shown a neural network with two layers.

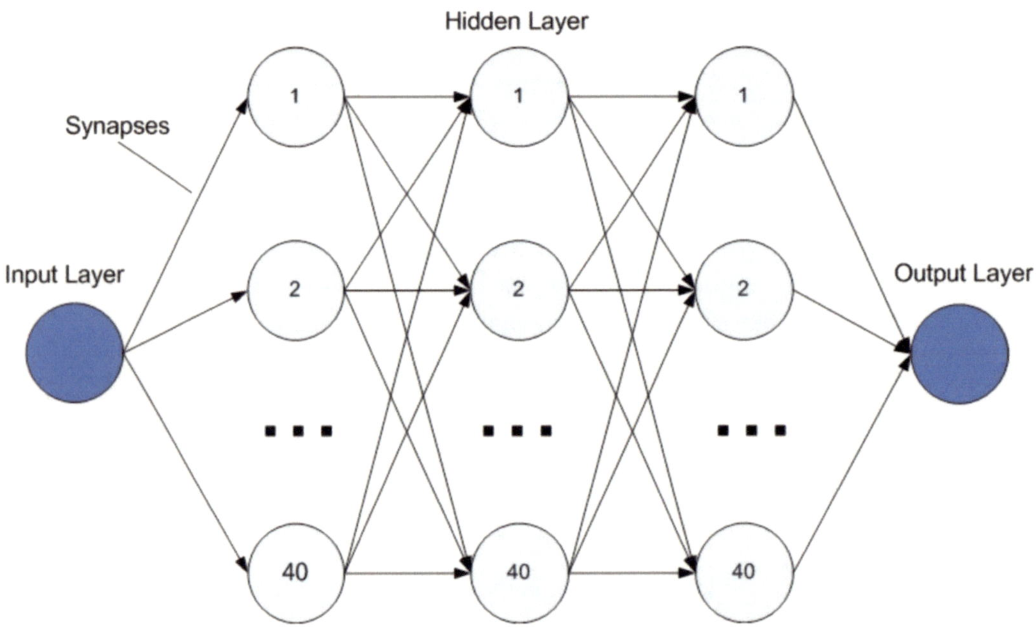

Figure 6. Representation of a neural network

In a neural network there are several parameters to be defined as the number of hidden layers, the number of neurons in each layer of the network and training method. The choice of these parameters in this study was performed based on the literature and in some experiments with the data from the database discussed Section 5.1.

There are several methods to train a neural network. In this work, experiments were performed with three of these methods: Levenberg-Marquardt, Bayesian regularization and resilient propagation algorithms. With the Levenberg-Marquardt algorithm, despite being the fastest, it were not obtained good results, since this method is suitable for solving problems of nonlinear regression and not to problems of pattern recognition. The worst results were obtained with the Bayesian regularization algorithm. As expected, the best results were obtained with the resilient propagation technique that according to the literature is more suitable for pattern recognition.

After the experiments, it was defined that the most appropriate neural network to classify the characteristics of alpha and theta EEG signals on emotions has the following parameters:

- An input layer with one input signal. The neural network was trained and evaluated with the energy and entropy from the characteristics theta and alpha as input data. However, all four data types were used one at a time
- Three hidden layers with 40 neurons in each hidden layer.
- An output layer with the one network output. The neural network output can be one of the EEG signals classified into emotions: positive/excited, positive/calm, negative/excited, and negative/calm.
- The technique used for training the network was resilient propagation.

The neural network described above was used to classify the data of the database on human emotions. The results of this experiment are discussed in Section 6.

6. Results

We chose to use the EEG signals acquired by channel FP1 due to its location. As discussed previously, the prefrontal lobe of the brain is intrinsically related to human emotions.

We processed a total of 1280 trials of EEG signals among all thirty two participants of our experiment. We selected theta and alpha rhythms from the EEG signals and calculated the energy and entropy from both features. We applied energy and entropy as inputs for the neural network used to classify brain signals into four emotional human states. As discussed in Section 5.3.2, the neural network used in classifying EEG signals into emotions in this work has just one input, therefore, we applied those parameters as input for the neural network one at a time.

First, we trained, validate, and tested the neural network with the energy calculated based on the theta feature. Then, we used the entropy obtained from the theta rhythm as the input of the neural network. The same steps were done with the energy and entropy calculated based on the alpha feature. Finally, we estimate for each classified emotion the mean and standard deviation of the results achieved for the thirty two participants of the experiment.

The Table 5 illustrates the mean and standard deviation of the results of our experiments for the emotion positive/excited.

	Emotion Positive/Excited	
Feature	**Mean**	**Standard Deviation**
Theta (Energy)	78.125 %	19.572 %
Theta (Entropy)	90.625 %	7.7771 %
Alpha (Energy)	64.8438 %	27.7586 %
Alpha (Entropy)	95.5781 %	7.6855 %

Table 5. Mean and standard deviation of the results related to the emotion positive/excited

One can observe in Table 5 that the best results in classifying EEG signals into the emotion positive/excited was achieved when we used the entropy calculated based on the alpha features as the input for the neural network. When we applied the entropy based on the theta features as the input for the neural network, a good result was obtained.

The Table 6 illustrates the mean and standard deviation of the results of our experiments for the emotion positive/calm.

	Emotion Positive/Calm	
Feature	**Mean**	**Standard Deviation**
Theta (Energy)	65 %	27.0006 %
Theta (Entropy)	90.625 %	11.8967 %
Alpha (Energy)	71.875 %	20.8586 %
Alpha (Entropy)	86.875 %	12.2967 %

Table 6. Mean and standard deviation of the results related to the emotion positive/calm

One can observe in Table 6 that the best results in classifying EEG signals into the emotion positive/calm was achieved when we used the entropy calculated based on the theta features as the input for the neural network. When we applied the entropy based on the alpha features as the input for the neural network, a good result was obtained.

The Table 7 illustrates the mean and standard deviation of the results of our experiments for the emotion negative/calm.

Emotion Negative/Calm		
Feature	**Mean**	**Standard Deviation**
Theta (Energy)	76.6667 %	19.5348 %
Theta (Entropy)	90 %	10.16 %
Alpha (Energy)	72,1875 %	26.7285 %
Alpha (Entropy)	87.125 %	8.7009 %

Table 7. Mean and standard deviation of the results related to the emotion negative/calm

One can observe in Table 7 that the best results in classifying EEG signals into the emotion positive/excited was achieved when we used the entropy calculated based on the theta features as the input for the neural network. When we applied the entropy based on the alpha features as the input for the neural network, a good result was obtained.

The Table 8 illustrates the mean and standard deviation of the results of our experiments for the emotion negative/excited.

Emotion Negative/ Excited		
Feature	**Mean**	**Standard Deviation**
Theta (Energy)	74.9719%	16.9485 %
Theta (Entropy)	91.4031%	7.188 %
Alpha (Energy)	81.2469%	12.5276 %
Alpha (Entropy)	93.7562 %	6.3564 %

Table 8. Mean and standard deviation of the results related to the emotion negative/excited

One can observe in Table 8 that the best results in classifying EEG signals into the emotion negative/excited was achieved when we used the entropy calculated based on the alpha features as the input for the neural network. When we applied the entropy based on the theta features as the input for the neural network, a good result was obtained.

Finally, we observed that using FP1 channel for EEG acquisition, wavelets as the algorithm to select characteristics from EEG signals, and the neural network in classifying those features into emotions, we can recognize at least four human emotions with a good accuracy. Furthermore, we achieved the best results achieved when we used the entropy calculated based on theta or alpha features as the input for the neural network.

7. Conclusions

The emotional state of a person defines their interaction with other people or objects. Therefore, the recognition of human emotions is becoming a concern in the development of systems that require human-machine interaction. The goal in recognizing human emotions is easier and more enjoyable computer use, for example.

There are several sources of information to assist in the recognition of emotions, such as facial expressions, voice and physiological signals, among others. In this study we implemented an emotion recognition system based on the BCI interface. We used a database of EEG signals acquired during experiments to induce emotions in the participants.

The database includes brain signals from thirty-two subjects. Those signals were recorded from thirty-two channels according the 10-10 international system. The database signals were pre-processed and the artifacts due to eye movements were removed. We chose use just the signals from the channel FP1 because your location and to avoid wasting time processing unnecessary information.

We selected the characteristics theta and alpha with the algorithm wavelets. We used in this work a discrete wavelet transform Daubechies db4. We calculated the parameters energy and entropy based on theta and alpha rhythms. The classification of these parameters into emotional states was accomplished with the method neural networks.

We could observe that we achieve good results in recognizing emotions with our approach. When we considered our system based on theta features with the entropy as input for the neural network, we had 90.625 %, 90.625 %, 90 % and 91.4031 % of accuracy for the emotions positive/excited, positive/calm, negative/calm, and negative/excited, respectively.

When we considered our system based on alpha features with the entropy as input for the neural network, we had 95.5781 %, 86.875 %, 87.125 % and 93.7562 % of accuracy for the emotions positive/excited, positive/calm, negative/calm, and negative/excited, respectively.

We recognized four different kinds of emotions based on the bi-dimensional approach: positive/excited, positive/calm, negative/excited, and negative/calm. The best result that we achieved was 95.5781 % when we classified EEG signals into the emotion positive/excited using the entropy calculated based on the alpha characteristics.

Therefore, we could conclude that the combination of wavelets and neural network algorithms is a good choice for classifying emotions by emotion recognition systems based on BCI interface. Furthemore, the FP1 as the signal acquisiton was a good choise based on the results achieved in this work.

According to [20], some individuals have their theta features more active than alpha features during the feeling of emotions. In other cases, the opposite happens, i. e., the subjects have the alpha rhythms more active than the theta rhythms.

As future work, we plan improve our results analyzing what EEG feature is more active during the feeling of emotion by each participant of our experiment. According to this evaluation, we will insert a step to identify the feature that is more active during the experiments in each user and adapt our emotion recognition system to receive the more significant rhythm for each participant.

http://dx.doi.org/10.5772/56227

Author details

Taciana Saad Rached and Angelo Perkusich

Campina Grande Federal University, Brazil

References

[1] Scherer, K. What are emotions? And how can they be measured? Social Information, January (2005).

[2] Calvo, R. A, & Mello, D. S. Affect detection: An interdisciplinary review of models, methods, and their applications. IEEE Transactions on Affective Computing, January (2010)., 1(1), 18-37.

[3] Mcdaniel, B, Mello, D, King, S, Chipman, B, Tapp, P, & Graesses, K. A. Facial features for attractive state detection in learning environments. Proc. 29th Ann. Meeting of the Cognitive Science Soc., (2007).

[4] Lee, C. M, & Narayanan, S. S. Toward detecting emotions in spoken dialogs. Speech and Audio Processing, IEEE Transactions on, (2005)., 13(2), 293-303.

[5] Bernhardt, D. Emotion inference from human body motion. Technical Report 787, Computer Laboratory- University of Cambridge, October (2012).

[6] Liu, C, Conn, K, Sarkar, N, & Stone, W. Physiology-based affect recognition for computer- assisted intervention of children with autism spectrum disorder. Int. J. Hum.-Comput. Stud., September (2008)., 66, 662-677.

[7] Schaaff, K, & Schultz, T. Towards an EEG-based emotion recognizer for humanoid robots. In RO-MAN 2009- The 18th IEEE International Symposium on Robot and Human Interactive Communication, IEEE, September (2009)., 792-796.

[8] Wolpaw, J. R, Birbaumer, N, Mcfarland, D. J, Pfurtscheller, G, & Vaughan, T. M. Brain-computer interfaces for communication and control. Clinical Neurophysiology, March (2002)., 1, 767-791.

[9] Schölgl, A, & Brunner, C. Biosig: A free and open source software library for BCI research. Computer, (2008)., 41(10), 44-50.

[10] Wang, J, Yan, N, Liu, H, Liu, M, & Tai, C. Brain-computer interfaces based on attention and complex mental tasks. In Proceedings of the 1 st International Conference on Digital Human Modeling, ICDHM'07, Berlin, Heidelberg, (2007). Springer-Verlag., 467-473.

[11] Liu, Y, Sourina, O, & Nguyen, M. K. Real-time EEG-based emotion recognition and its applications. In Transactions on computational science XII, Berlin, Heidelberg, (2011). Marina L. Gavrilova and C. J. Kenneth Tan (Eds.). Springer-Verlag., 256-277.

[12] SuprijantoSari L., Nadhira V., Merthayasa IGN., Farida I. M. Development system for emotion detection based on brain signals and facial images. World Academy of Science, Engineering and Technology 50, (2009).

[13] Bos, D. O. EEG-based emotion recognition the influence of visual and auditory stimuli. Emotion, (2006)., 57(7), 1798-806.

[14] Kubler, A, & Muller, K. R. Toward brain-computer interfacing, chapter An introduction to Brain-computer interfacing, The MIT Press, (2007)., 1-25.

[15] Savran, A, Ciftci, K, Chanel, G, Mota, J. C, Viet, L. H, Sankur, B, Akarun, L, Caplier, A, & Rombaut, M. Emotion detection in the loop brain signals and facial images. In Proceedings of the eNTERFACE 2006 Workshop, Dubrovnik, July (2006).

[16] Murugappan, M, Nagarajan, R, & Yaacob, S. Appraising human emotions using time frequency analysis based EEG alpha band features. In Innovative Technologies in Intelligent Systems and Industrial Applications, (2009). CITISIA 2009, July 2009., 70-75.

[17] DEAPdataset: a dataset for emotion analysis using eegphysiological and video signals. http://www.eecs.qmul.ac.uk/mmv/datasets/deap/accessed 23 February (2012).

[18] Koelstra, S, Muhi, C, Soleymani, M, Lee, J-S, Yazdani, A, Ebrahimi, T, Pun, T, Nijholt, A, & Patras, I. DEAP: A database for emotion analysis using physiological signals. Affective Computing IEE Transactions on, Jan.-March (2012)., 3(1), 18-31.

[19] JananKhani PKodogiannis V., Revelt K. EEG signal classification using wavelet feature extraction and neural networks. In Procedings of the IEEE John Vincent Atanasoff 2006 International Symposium on Modern Computing, Washington, DC, USA, (2006). IEEE Computer Society., 120-124.

[20] Benbadis, S, Husain, A, Kaplan, P, & Tatum, W. Handbook of EEG interpretation. Demos Medical Publishing. Springer Demos Medic Series, (2007).